I AM NOT A PhD

I AM NOT A Ph.D.

By R. E. Chapman

Published by R. E. Chapman

Scripture passages taken from the RSV Second Catholic Edition

Library of Congress Cataloguing-Publication Data

ISBN: 978-0-578-70709-9 (Trade Paperback)

R. E. Chapman
I Am Not a PhD
Version 3
Published by R. E. Chapman through Create Space by Amazon Books.
iamnotaphd@gmail.com
Book cover art and arrangement by R. E. Chapman

Table of Contents

INTRODUCTION

We the people of these United States of America are an idea set forth in blood, honor and courage. Designed to prevent the very fabric of our morality from being trampled upon by cunning, deceit and the sheer absurdity of the human mind. So, that civility can propagate in such a way as to attain a threshold of human existence that has never been achieved by any previous generation.

We the people of these United States of America are a nation of dreamers, artists, philosophers, conceptualizers, and inventors designed to progress, without breaking tradition. To overcome the stalemate of repeating history, and encourage a systematic growth of the whole for the whole. To make an accounting of all historical events, and to never allow them to be dissolved, manipulated or dissected in such a way as to benefit any personal agenda. Our Judeo-Christian values are key to a clear and prosperous social structure. All aspects of who we are must involve our religious values in their entirety or they become polluted, and ultimately; meaningless. Resulting in we the people becoming nothing.

We the people of these United States of America are the centerpiece of all countries, cultures and beliefs, regulated by the words of the Christ. No other religion has ever conceptualized the idea of resolving critical issues, violent issues through a peaceable means. Even at the cost of one's own life. Doing, so, is an alien concept in regards to our natural instinct towards survival and the subduing of earth. From man's stubborn point of view in his meaning of subdue, would include even himself.

We the people of these *fifty* United States of America are in desperate need of a Christian Renaissance, for the benefit of the coming generation, whom will inherit the mistakes of we; whom came before them. For the coming generation will be in search of answers to certain questions that we; the prior generation cannot, could not or did not want to answer; because we broke with tradition.

Broke the harmony that was leading us on the path to salvation. Of course, it was our parents, whom set the stage for the breaking of that harmony. The misguided fathers of the war years, whom planted the seeds for the military industrial complex. Broke up the old Ma Bell, which led to the disruption of a fluid and sound means of connecting the country. Laid the foundation for the disarray of our education system, and set the framework for immorality to be openly accepted as a normal part of life. Yes, it is their actions that made it impossible for our modern society to live a reasonable, comfortable existence. Flooded crack cocaine into the black experience, creating a generation of fatherless lost souls. Drove our children into a sexual upheaval of which marriage would have no meaning. This was the fall of an American empire, and it happened right under our very noses. Everyone jumped on the Devil's bandwagon. Even the media did everything in its power to make the Church look as though corruption was interwoven into the very fabric of its nature. Bias journalism was coming into question because, while journalists claim to be the watchdogs of what is proper and improper, no one bothered to ask the most basic question of all. Who watches the watchdog?

The irony of it all is that the one institution that journalistic media wants, so, desperately to bring down, has all of the answers we are searching for. An institution that survived the brutality of Pagan Rome; the movers and shakers of the early Christian movement; the rise of Islam, the Black Death of Europe, the Protestant Reformation, the modern movers and shakers, and all of the wars that were ever declared upon it. Yes, it has also survived its own internal strifes and conflicts because when the Christ established that institution known as His bride, he did not say it would be made up of people whom are without flaw. He knew there would be flaws; for nothing on earth is flawless; however, the Church has always been the one beacon of hope that has kept civilization from falling into complete despair. When you are down on your luck, and ready to cash it all in, look towards the horizon. Take a stroll down the block, and you will see the sign of salvation. Blow the dust off the good ol' days. That, which your parents we're, so, quick to cast aside in order to live a reprehensible lifestyle is waiting. Yes; your parents are afraid to admit that they are the cause of why we are upside down in today's United States of America. No generation wants to take the blame for its failures. Notice the period during the Flower Power Movement. Perhaps the one time a person could actually get someone to follow the Church's mandate of love your neighbor. They had forgotten where their peaceful thinking had come from. Who it was that implanted that peaceful state of mind into their consciousness in the first place. Overconfidence is the killer of all cultures, kingdoms and common sense.

The billion-dollar question: Where does all of the negativity that is plaguing us, come from? Who are these people sitting behind closed doors that keep the hate alive? We have it in our heads that great corporate moguls are in charge of our collective destiny, and that they are pulling the strings on what we do and say; however, this author is here to tell you; *not necessarily, so.* Where the problems come from, is us. Yes; you are reading correctly. The problem is us, and no one else. Bend to reality. When someone admits to wrong doing, it is not enough that they did something wrong. People want the juicy tidbits to make a more applied consensus, which in most cases manifests into an unhealthy attitude of negativity that worsens, due to our interactive sensory network. In other words, they want to feel better about the poor choices that they have made. Now, if a person is geared to a more positive state of mind, then seeking tidbits on someone else's bad behavior would have no practical value. A person, who is geared to a more negative state of being requires lots of detail to feed that need for; not hate, but conflict. For there are always two sides to everything in this world; benevolence and malevolence. Those whom struggle to understand, wanting others to experience their struggle, and those whom are content with their lives, regardless of their social standing. Do not confuse struggle and content with good and evil. They are two different ideologies all together.

Consequently, when all of that negativity comes together, what happens? It builds, and it grows, and sometimes it takes on a life of its own, and that is the mysterious person whom controls the whole process. Sometimes it can be a disease, and when no one is willing to oppose the negativity, it grows out of control, resulting in greed, selfishness, violence, and yes; eventually war. We think we can control the violence, but that is not always the case. Where does the hostility come from? Confusion. Plain and simple. Confusion over our very existence. We approach a situation that would seem relatively easy to rationalize, and yet, we become obsessed with making that, which is simple, complex. Look at life. We could simply enjoy the very act of living, and yet, someone always comes along and says or does something that interferes with the harmony of just living life. Notice the book of Genesis. All is going well in the Garden of Eden until someone comes along and says something that results in a conundrum of thoughts. In this case, disobeying instructions that were actually designed to protect man from unforeseeable harm. Once disobeyed, excuses manifest themselves resulting in eventual death. Influence is a very real force in our existence. It can be anyone or anything, even nature, the universe itself. The interesting thing of all is who, or perhaps what is the initial instigator of the overall process of hostility? There can only be one answer.

It will be up to you; the new generation to bring us back to the path of salvation as a whole before the return of the King. To sum it up; you have the greatest burden of any previous generation, and this author says to you; *I am sorry that this burden has been placed upon you, for your fathers and mothers were fools.*

Therefore, we must ask the question. Where did it all go wrong? No one dared asked that question until now. Words applied to a single person in the blink of an eye or the entire world in a thousand years. We bump into it in the darkness, and see it plainly in the light, and yet, we deny its very existence. Dreams are unrealized and hopes are unmeasured without it. Destiny cannot be balanced until it is identified. Accomplishments go unseen until it is acknowledged. Therefore, we choose to ignore it, and hope for the best. So, where did it all go wrong?

Thomas Jefferson once said in a letter to Henry Lee…

When forced, therefore, to resort to arms to redress, an appeal to the tribunal of the world was deemed proper for our justification. This was the object of the Declaration of Independence. Not to find out new principles, or new arguments, never before thought of, not merely to say things which had never been said before; but to place before mankind the common sense of the subject, in terms so plain and firm as to command their assent, and to justify ourselves in the independent stand we are compelled to take. Neither aiming at originality of principle or sentiment, nor yet copied from any particular and previous writing, it was intended to be an expression of the American mind, and to give to that expression the proper tone and spirit called for by the occasion.

What this author will address in this book is what the world has evolved into; *in terms, so, plain and firm as to command their assent;* because somewhere in our recent history a rumor got started that referred to something needing to be fixed; however, what was never considered is if anything was ever broken to begin with. Though a periodic fine tuning was never in question. As time went on, that tuning became fewer and fewer to the point that it was no longer applied. That is the arrogance of man. Therefore, this book is scribed for men, so, that they will resume their duties as the fine tuners of social ambivalence.

So, before you; the reader continues; consider that this book is not designed to have all of the answers, but only to reach those of you; whom may be the last generation capable of reasoning out the dilemmas; in order to begin rebuilding the moral consciousness of what it means to be civilized, without the need for human slaughter on a grand scale. This book is designed to make suggestion, not policy in order to reinvigorate imagination, generate ideas; frames of thought that would allow us to see beyond the material things of this world. Furthermore, let it be known that this author is not perfect.

5

Not a nice guy, but simply a Christian Realist whom has made many mistakes along the path of life. Done many cruel things to people, and in some cases even animals. He is not the wisest, nor the sanest; but is perhaps the greatest fool, who has ever existed. Most importantly, he is not a Ph.D.; however, it takes someone who is perhaps just a little mad to address what is painfully obvious. To encourage discussion amid the common populous in order to bring to light the fact that we are living in a world dissolving right before our very eyes; playing amid the compounding rubble of all our mistakes without consideration to the inheritance we will be passing on to our legacy.

Most of you probably have your own ideas as to why everything is falling apart, and yet, we inherently listen to those, whom, for whatever reason, have determined that they are not only qualified, but have exclusivity to explain in their own words the causes and effects of our current social dilemmas. They effectively shut out all comers without a higher degree in learning because they feel we have no choice, but to listen to them. That is why we will examine these problems not from a scientific point of view, but from a street level point of view. We will not let statistics, theories or arrogance get in the way of our perceptions and beliefs. We will examine it raw and uncut. To see if what we are doing is in fact the reason everything is coming apart, or if what we did is the cause of all our current social dilemmas.

The most important aspect of this book is that it is not going to play nice. Sometimes the truth can hurt very much, but if the truth does not come to light then everything becomes a lie, and a lie has absolutely no substance, meaning or compassion. Simply put; it is nothing, and in most respects, a fate worse than death.

GUARDIAN OF THE GARDEN

CHAPTER 1

Opening this work with the title of; "Guardian of The Garden" redresses the issue of man's responsibility to the world as a whole; from plants to animals, the very air we breathe, to the water we drink, to our children, other men, and yes, women also. Perhaps, most importantly our women. That responsibility placed upon us; the man, has not changed from the establishment of the human race. That responsibility did not go away when Adam was cast out of the garden with his wife. It was engrained into the very fiber of his being, and essentially our being as well. The idea of protector gives us; the man, purpose, and an idea for which to build a productive meaningful lifestyle, and essentially a society. That is why God charged the man with protecting the garden of Eden. Now, before this author continues, there are some of you whom are sensing the religious overtones, and are debating whether or not you should continue reading. Consider this; what this book will be addressing is the uneasiness you feel whenever the topic of religion is brought to bear on a conversation. *Why do I shun religious discussions?* Consider that it was religion that gave us foundation and purpose. It was religion that told us that we were not animals, but something more; and without religion, we as a people would probably be second-class citizens in and on our world. It was religion that gave us civilization. So, in order to keep ourselves from going too far afield, let us keep it simple. Somewhere in our distant past, the modern human began with a man and a woman.

Man, or Adam if you prefer, already sensed a purpose, but like all creatures of the flesh, he required clarification. Without this clarification, guesswork comes into play. That is why our children need a father, not all of the time, but periodically, in order to clarify purpose. Specifically, in regards to the man-child. Remember the Book of Genesis; God was not always around. He would drop in occasionally to check up on things. You can look at it as perhaps encouragement or even presence; knocking the child; Adam, back on track whenever necessary. Without clarification of purpose, the man-child falls astray; searching for answers on his own. Going through a life of supposition and hearsay, which can eventually lead to hostility and out-an-out violence. The young mind does not comprehend the need for order, thus forcing the issue of why the square peg does not fit into the round hole. He or she will either give up or give in or simply break the puzzle board, and in that case, may or may not get caught when doing, so. Those whom are caught, but are from affluent families, usually beat the odds. Those from a struggling background are usually incarcerated. In any case, whether there is a father in the home or not; unless there is fatherly, interaction with the son, it is the same as a fatherless child, and the child becomes lost in the noise. Now, this is important for you; the father to know, and that is, as-long-as you are alive, and in control of your faculties, you continue to knock your child back on track until you die. Just because your children are adults with families of their own, with careers, homes of their own, does not preclude the fact; whatsoever, that you stop being dad. This author has a secret for you the reader. We never grow up in this realm, we simply grow older. On the basis that we have no true relative perspective on what it means to grow up; to be mature in our nature. Though the Christ has shown us how we can truly mature, we choose, instead, to ignore His advice. Of course, your children will be somewhat obstinate, a bit impetuous, and even a little patronizing; constantly expressing their usual precociousness in your face. Sound familiar? For those of us, whom follow Judeo-Christian teachings; you do the same to God.

Another point to consider is that we assume that the Garden of Eden is a place in history, or perhaps some form of morality or cautionary tale. That what has happened has happened, and that we are the result of that happening. Thus, an unrecoverable event, and does not apply to us in this modern age; however, this author says to you; the reader, that the Garden of Eden is also our living existence. It is not gone, but still with us, all of it. Our actions as men in this modern age or lack thereof, epitomizes man's lack of action in the Garden of Eden. An interesting point missed by many in regards to Genesis, is that the problems of mankind occurred not when Eve ate of the tree of the knowledge of good and evil, but the man's inaction that resulted in their expulsion from the garden. Man did absolutely nothing to stop woman from being tempted by the fallen one. Which brings up an interesting point in regards to human behavior. Perhaps he was using her to express his own temptations. The best way to keep from breaking a rule is to compel another to break the rule: The lowest despicable act conceivable. Of course, there is no way of knowing Adam's reasoning; however, what the narrative does reveal is that we; the male, are wholly responsible for the female's actions, even her behavior. It also clarifies the choices available to us. The direction we choose in life. Choose poorly, and life becomes full of misery. Follow the rules, and content is assured. Ever notice how people start on a specific path, and never diverge from it no matter the consequences? Our lives follow along the same pattern as those of Adam. With careful planning, a person can choose to live in the garden; however, the planning requires a lot of thought. What we consume. What, and how we gather knowledge. How we treat others; and if you have doubts, ask yourself, have you ever had days when you feel alive, and days when you don't feel, so, animated?

Who was *man;* really? The first man was the breath of life, which means that you; today's man, are also the breath of life. A piece of God Himself simply contained within earthly material. From you came woman and essentially all of humanity comes from you. Lineage is traced through your bloodline; the male's bloodline. An interesting prospect when determining the offspring of parents with different racial backgrounds. As a Christian culture, it is easy to adopt certain Aryan ways of thinking in regards to that matter.

CHAPTER 2

Let us touch bases with our better half. A woman's purpose is to be a helper, supportive, caring, loving and generous, so, that a male does not know what it means to be lonely. Not even an animal can provide such a need. We; the man, were never meant to be alone. Loneliness is a distraction, loneliness is a killer of hopes and dreams, loneliness brings down society. Loneliness destroys the heart and the soul. Prevents the mind from functioning properly. Prevents the man from seeing his objectivity; and his objectivity should be towards the Lord. When we; the man, are lonely, we tend to seek the company of other men; however, what we do not realize is that the kind of company we are seeking cannot be provided by another man. This is a job best suited for a woman. When we come from any form of activity or event, we are high strung, full of go, go, go, and what she does is ease us down, so, that we can relax and begin our slow recovery to a domestic reality. Providing compassionate help is what a woman was created for; her overall purpose in life. Simply hold a man in her arms to let him know that misery will not torment him through the night. Let us be clear that compassion is not the same as eroticism. Providing you with illicit displays of herself or other sexual activity is not what you need; however, she may display herself accordingly as a medicinal need. Nevertheless, her help or companionship does not infer seduction. Though some psychiatrist may say otherwise. Stimulating the male does absolutely nothing to help him when he is lonely. She is being the prostitute; giving him; you; the male of the species what you want, and that is a quick fix; destroying the whole principle of helper. Instead of something that you need; which is meaning, purpose; a sense of wanting to live life. Woman should do very little, but the little that she does is a whole lot, and very important to the survival of man. That very little is far greater than any accomplishment of a man. Doubt this author? Consider that the human race has survived every war, and human brutality thrown at it. The Black Death of the Fourteenth. The industrial revolution, slaughter of the Native Americans, the indifference of the Gilded Age in the Nineteenth. The Armenian Genocide, Cristero War, Influenza Pandemic and the Jewish holocaust of the Twentieth. Every natural disaster, nuclear/biological and chemical hazard, even HIV/AIDS. Without a woman's perseverance, the human race would have perished long ago. Without a woman to protect, life would be a pointless jest of unimaginative rituals imitating a waking dream, having no basis in reality. She; the woman, bears the burden of all the annoying imperceptibles that we; the man, try to get away from. Freeing us, to pursue the more mundane things of life; such as fixing roads, erecting towns, farming fields, law enforcement, soldiering, and yes, taking care of the natural environment. Seems like we; the man, deal with all of the burdens of life. Do all of the hard work; however, going through pregnancy, childbirth, and the rearing of a child is perhaps the second hardest task of being human. The first is; of course, keeping one's faith in God. When considering her burdens then we should appreciate all that she has to offer, and what she represents: *Civilization.* What else does she go through? Besides the menstruating cycles, keeping her beauty, staying healthy and perhaps maintaining her fine figure. Applying compassion and passion when none is shown in return. Not to mention putting up with male ego. She is the true beast of burden in our civilization. Therefore, why does she feel compelled to add to her burdens? The answer is simple. The putdowns, lack of appreciation not even, so, much as a *thank you*; more or less an, *I love you* from her spouse. There is only, so, much that a person can handle. It took generations of putdowns and the brutal dictatorship-like behavior from us; the male, for the female to mass exodus from her responsibilities in the home.

Women, whom go it on their own are rebellious to the idea of male dominance, and would view this notion with great distain, but the reality is, when a woman is absent from her primary duty, she pays a devastating price, and, so, does the world around her. Do not take this author's word for it. What do you; the reader see happening today, in this modern world of the early Twenty-first?

She; whom would be a helper, must have the ability to attract that which is to be helped. If he, whom she is meant to help, does not even notice her, then how can the act of a union take effect? One must have the ability to attract the other. Without attraction, male and female would never come together to propagate the species. Therefore, with a woman's power of attraction, she holds the overall power in the greater social scheme, and essentially, what direction to take a relationship. She possesses the power to accept or reject helping a male. That one quality gives her power over us; the male of the species, for she likes to be pleased. Alas, improper upbringing and birth-control inoculants invented by us; the male, has stripped her of this power, giving us; the male, the power over her; the female, making the whole male/female interactive process unnatural, even pointless, for she is currently trying to please herself; killing the spontaneity of life.

Examine our culture of the early Twenty-first in regards to the proper implementation and understanding of helper. Considering that females have such a strong emotional influence over males; should they be in positions that would give them dominion over a male? A female policeman apprehending that for whom she is to be a helper? A female justice presiding over that for whom she is to be a helper? A female soldier killing that for whom she is to be a helper? Mayors? Governors? Presidents? A female monarch? She; whom would be a helper, ought not have dominion over that, for whom she is to be a helper to. Yes; we have forgotten that women are not the helpers of men, but that a woman is a helper to a man, and yet, she is both guardian of a man and mother to man. She is not meant to be a leader of men, but a guidance to life. She is the storehouse of knowledge. The place that man goes to when in need of help. This does not preclude the idea of females being good leaders. In fact, quite the opposite; however, for society to run smoothly there must be an order to things.

Take for instance a politician whom comes across a dilemma. Who can he discuss it with? When all else fails, he goes to his wife because she has those crucial tidbits that he needs or perhaps more compassionately speaking; she completes him in his role as a political leader. That is why it is crucial for a man to marry a woman, who is willing to *adapt* to his needs, and not the other way around. That includes the man of great wealth whom purchases a trophy. Should she be headstrong, she is not bending to his needs, but bending him to her will; however, if she is frail, she is bending to his will, and not to his needs. She is a good woman when she takes his side against others, including his family, and even her own family. As a man; you leave your mother and your father to cleave to a woman; and though she will maintain ties with her family, being a part of you is her greatest desire. Pay close attention to her when she speaks to you, either in public or in private. Realize her abilities to communicate with you on all levels, not just her voice, but her overall body-language. These are the true attributes of sexy, not the wardrobe. A shapely figure draws a lustful eye, blinding reason and logic of what is proper and what is improper gender relations. Too young and you are embarrassed. Well-educated, and you are embarrassed. Her ability to attentively communicate is the quality that sets her apart from all others. As a man; however, part of your duties are to figure out her tells, and quickly. Trust this author, all women have tells because stupidity and boy can go hand-n-hand in regards to social gatherings. Not to mention that some feminine tells are just a bit less expressive than others, and as a hint; tells are incorporated into you; the man, on a subconscious level. Sometimes through sexual interaction and accessed via your common sense on a conscious level. In other words, you feel when things are not right or whenever you are hurting her. Go with your feelings unless you are a heartless bastard whom thrives off torturing females for a living.

Now, how does the relationship between the both of you work? You interact with her. Share your life's experiences with her, so, that she can adjust herself accordingly in order to integrate herself into your lifestyle. That way she can apply assistance when you need it. Do not ignore her under any circumstances. She may be seeing something that she is unable to put into proper words; and though she may seem to be off-base, be aware that she may be hitting on something that you have failed to notice. That either one of you are capable of comprehending, that just may have a profound lifelong effect if gone unchallenged. If that is not the case, then guide her thoughts on a more useful course with patience and compassion because like you, she also likes to be challenged. She wants to feel as though she is performing her primary role in your daily life; and that is; *helper.* That is where our skill as men comes into play. Oh; and let us be clear on one certain point: Those of you whom would view her suggestion as senseless dribble, or that her very presence is a complete annoyance to you; consider that no woman is stupid when trying to help you with something; anything for that matter. She is merely following her preprogrammed directive of being a helper, and when you ignore her, or boot her away, it makes her feel useless; a failure. The one thing you do not want is a woman in your life who is not confident and competent. She's a winner. You know it. Which is why you are with her, or perhaps more accurately; copulating with her. So, treat her as such.

On the other hand; when the genders do go into a competitive lifestyle, it is only natural for the rules of being a helper to become unstable on the basis that males are defending what is perceived to be an encroachment on their very existence. What does a person do when they feel violated? They retaliate. When being violated, what is a person's stance? How do they react? In the case of sexual harassment, what is truly going on? Does a man have a right to behave as a man? A woman is competing with him in every aspect of our social existence, and he feels a certain violation of his position in life. A woman enters his sphere of influence, and he feels a need to be a man or even a childish little boy. How he does it, is not, so, much the focus, as to the addressing of the natural instincts of male/female interaction in a world that is being stripped of Godly principles, but more of, that he does it.

CHAPTER 3

What have we done in the world of man? With a woman's ability to attract, we have also given her additional powers; allowing her to reject the one aspect that makes her a helper; that makes her woman. Yes; the ability to adapt herself to that, which she is meant to be a helper to. By rejecting her adaptive ability allows her to carry-on with multiple relationships, which of course is not difficult when considering that prostitutes have been doing, so, for a very long time, and the worst aspect of all, is the strengthening apathy she is revealing to the community. This apathy has forced our entire social system to adjust to her destabilizing mind. A mind that is going crazy, for she is trying to behave in a state for which, she was not meant to behave. She is trying to live alone, and unlike men, whom are best suited for such an endeavor, women simply lose it, and we have spent the past forty years or more inventing psychological terms to explain the emotional dilemmas she is going through. We see it all of the time; women just blow apart when things do not go

14

their way. One day they want it one way, and on a different day they want it another way. They use that little cliché that we have become accustomed to; *that's different,* and we buy into it, thinking that all will return to normal somehow, but it never does. She invents some absurd explanation of why it is different, and the legal system allows it to be, and thus the contradiction and confusion sets in faster than a winter storm in upstate New York. What we have done, is turned our entire legal system into a harlot's terms of agreement manifesto. Laws geared towards pleasing an emotional state of mind instead of regulating the emotional state of being. The housewife-mentality in a public setting, and every housewife is different. Resulting in her retaining that, which makes her woman, and then given that, which makes a man attractive in a woman's eyes; wealth, position and power. She has the power to attract a male; bend his will to her needs, and no matter what he does, she is never satisfied, for her emotional state of mind is falling apart. It is she, who is supposed to be the helper; adapting to that, which she is to be helper to. What happens when something that is supposed to adapt, forces another to adapt to it? The adapter forcing that, which is supposed to be adapting to, to adapt to it. Just scribing this portion reveals the craziness of what is the Feminist Movement. The reality is, you are not adapting to her, but to the ideas of her prior relationship(s). She is molding you into the prior relationship that she fell in love with. The previous relationship whom dumped her for another prospect. What she is unaware of is that her previous relationship's ideas; his lifestyle, have become her reality, and she is either unable, or unwilling to shed that reality on the basis that she is addicted to that certain kind of lifestyle. This mostly occurs in situations where a daughter has no interactive parents, and she is perhaps living a generic lifestyle and simply wants more. Now, imagine a woman, who has been involved with a dozen or, so, men, all of whom with different ideas and lifestyles. What is she conforming you to? Nothing, but a mess; and what of your children, whom she would give birth to?

CHAPTER 4

A helper never oversteps her bounds or attempts to take charge. A helper does not take the lead, but is present when you; the man stumbles, and motivates you to take the lead again in order to get a better grip on who you are as a human being. If she is taking the lead then she is a competitor; and as a competitor she cannot perform her duties of keeping loneliness at bay. Think of loneliness as a wild, veracious animal. When it bites, the pain reaches the bone. When a woman is competing with you, then you are alone, and it hurts because she is not keeping the wild animal at bay, and you can believe this author when he says, it is a very difficult task to perform, for she can be present in your life, and allow loneliness to sneak in when you least expect it.

From a Christian standpoint, understand that Catholic priests are a continuation of the Apostles, chosen by the Christ to be the leaders of the faith. In the presence of the Christ and His Apostles, the women were helpers, not competitors to handle the logistics of the growing Christian movement. Those, whom were helpers of man were supportive, caring, loving and generous, and made great sacrifices for those men, whom would be fishers of men.

Besides being a helper, she also has another responsibility that is crucial to our existence, and that is; of course, motherhood. She is the receptacle of the breath of life by means of you; the man, seeding her womb. She is of earth, separated by God from man after his formation from the earth, and having a share of the breath of life through him from God; therefore, she is not unlike soil for which the wheat grows, and you; the man, are of heaven, seeding the soil. Except that she carries the life within her, and gives birth to that life. She is the transition from heaven to earth. Her entire being is geared for that very purpose. Pretty amazing when you think about it. A being capable of transitioning life from one state of existence to another. Accomplishing this through means of a metamorphosis; from woman to mother. Growing a person within herself, and then giving birth to that person. Providing sustenance, and then uplifting that person through varying stages of mental

16

development. This is why she is, so, different from us; the man, both physically and mentally, of which means she; who is woman, must focus on the specifics of being a mother. The stronger aspects of intuition, compassion, and book-sense to ensure that a newborn will transition effortlessly from toddlerhood to adolescence, and eventually into the world of adults.

Now, without that feminine quality to elevate a child, they would not grow into adults, but revert to mere animals, and chaos would surely ensue. Truth be told, we actually remain children for the rest of our lives. It is the single most important attribute to a civilized society. Children are simply a different kind of person, just as females are a different kind of man. Everything about children is different. Their thinking, mannerisms, social behavior; all of it requires guidance. How is that guidance attained? By a woman's unique ability to transition between what is adulthood and what is childhood. Becoming childish or being childish. Reverting to a child-like state in order to communicate on their level, to ease; even stimulate the process of mental, and social growth. Uplifting the child to adulthood. In fact, she must retain a little Peter Pan to better interact with the child to ensure a smooth transition from one state of being to another. This is not a bad thing, but a requirement of our species, to keep man atop the food chain. It is the other commodity she has outside of virginity that makes her extremely valuable to our existence. The one thing of value we need as a civilization in order to survive. In a way, God administered a similar routine when interacting with man in scripture. Without that ability, man would remain stuck in the same social routine. Unfortunately, women often use this gift in a perverse way; e.g. attempting to elevate animals to human status. Men are required by God's law to stop this kind of behavior, no matter the cost. Regardless of what the entertainment industry may have you believe, animals are simply not meant to be human.

She; who is woman is not a baby making machine. The male actually makes the baby. No; she is a nurturing modular construct, and her prime years for doing this begins early in life. Therefore, to ensure healthy offspring, motherhood must begin in her youth.

Consider youth; eyes, ears, even when you urinate, everything just works great. Then as you age, things don't work, so well, and that includes the reproductive organs. So, why do women wait until their later years to begin the reproductive process? Also consider that youth plays a big factor in her ability to reduce herself to a childish mental state. Not to mention being less polluted by opposing ideas, and life's experiences. Think about it. As we age, we start to forget what it's like to be a child, and thus are unable to truly relate with a child from a child's point of view. Waiting until her later years, places great risk to the child, unless she has a strong connection with the Lord. For it is not science that creates new life, but God's will that makes life possible.

As a side note: Consider allowing her a period of recuperation between pregnancies, depending upon her virility. Ideally, a man should be done making children in about her mid to late twenties. Just a suggestion, not a mandate because eventually a woman would like to enjoy the world, while she has her youth.

CHAPTER 5

Naturally, there are those of you, whom will deem the idea of a woman reverting to a childish state as preposterous. Those are the absolute serious-minded people whom would refuse a child a childhood, with the belief that behaving childishly is a demeaning state of being. Their kind should not be interacting with children, for it is necessary for a human to go through social stages to steady out the intricacies of social interaction. Without childishness, a person can become inflexible, lacking awareness and empathy. Unable to identify crucial markers that make us human. Such as discerning between a brazen act and an honest mistake. Likewise, our childhood is the source of honest emotions; happy-laughter. Should a child be obliged to always behave maturely, then a state of overburdening the conscious mind could result in needless social stress factors. Not, so, much to the child, but to those around the child. Being, too serious can lead to moments of tension, and the possibility of hostility. If you guide your child along advanced mature lines, then remember that others do not follow those lines, and prefer a more relaxed state of being. This is what prevents the creation of a behavioral utopia because a totally serious culture leads to social decay. *Why?* You ask. You cannot identify what it means to be serious without the existence of humor. If all sides are serious, then one side will say that the other is not serious enough, to better identify with themselves. A fact with all aspects of existence. When inflexibility becomes a force of will, fear settles in and it becomes the hub of social activity. Childishness is a behavior in need of cultivation not a psychological aptitude that is aborted. Without child you cannot identify adult.

A man's part in the functioning of the relationship is to bring the woman back to adulthood accordingly. Without us; the man, she would degrade into a state of permanent childishness; existing in a confused state of mind. That is why we men are capable of being mothers, as well as fathers. Thus, we are geared for the extremes. Woman is a creature who is already evolved into a mature state of mind; however, a child is learning what it means to be an adult, and they will either be psychologically abandoned or pushed too quickly and even harshly. Evolving in an unintended direction that would not be reasonable or even beneficial to the community.

On the other hand, a wife, who has an opportunity to bring his child out of a state of immaturity, but chooses instead to pursue ambitions outside of motherhood, forfeits God. A child needs their mother 24/7. Not when she gets home from work. Not when she is in the mood. A child requires a sense of security; a safety-net for the unforeseen. Children have questions that require immediate answers from their primary instructor at first opportunity in order to properly advance in life. These questions are crucial at varying stages of development, and if not promptly answered, the outcome is the child losing objectivity; forgetting the question. A question with crucial elements that may prevent them from critical errors later in life, and many of those questions arise in our public education method. Children go through, so, much more than education at school. They experience dilemmas that are invisible to educators on the grounds that it would require moral views to expunge the distaste and dissatisfaction of erroneous behavior. Views that are heavily based on religious values. Public schools are not Catholic schools, and thus, are regulated differently in regards to a social collaborative effort. Emphasis on the politics of social interaction instead of basic education. Politics is an alien concept to a burgeoning mind on the threshold of understanding the complexities of the psychological tempest of public living. Resulting in our schools being nothing more than secular torture chambers designed to cut out the hearts of children, so, that they can become creatures of indifference. Learning nothing more than what it means to be indiscriminate in their social choices.

The oddest point of all, is that our children are trying to tell us something. Usually by means of their actions, but their cry for help falls upon deaf ears, for the faculty have their favorites, and you; the parent, reveals little concern; for your child's problems are trivial. We listen to those who say that there is simply no room for religious values in our public schools, and hope for the best. Realistically, though; parents know what our public schools are, but are overly concerned with personal indulgences to demand restoration of our religious values, based on the understanding that our children will simply get over it; *as I did when I was the student.* Leaving us with drug addicted automatons of lust and greed with no perceptions of honor, dignity or patriotism. The curse of empire.

Does this mean a woman cannot pursue a career? No. What it means is that she must understand her overall purpose in the grand scheme of things. Bearer of something new and wonderful in the overall social construct. Responsible for the continuation of life. Society is based on feminine perception. Therefore, for those who say there are few successful women, then perhaps they should look a little closer at human existence. For nothing is possible in this plain of existence without a woman, whether it be peace, war, happiness, sadness, art or garbage.

Perhaps we should not look at men and women as individuals, but at each of the genders as a whole. Once we approach the genders from this point of view, then we can be more appreciative of the proper behavior between men and women. The most crucial aspect of this approach is that man can see how he has; again, failed the woman as he did in the Book of Genesis. Allowing the serpent to manipulate woman; feed her false advice, and provide her with a sense of false hope. It is woman who goes against the Church. It is woman who pursues the arcane arts. It is woman who questions an effective algorithm. It is woman who questions the very sanctity of life itself.

CHAPTER 6

Let us step back and ask the question of what is a man? That is something a female needs to consider before crossing the line of what is virginity, and what is sexual deviance. A man denotes great experience, useful knowledge. Key word; *useful*. Not the life and times of an athlete or hip-hopper. That is what a child brings to the relationship, and since he is still a child himself, then how can he bring the female back to adulthood when she reverts to a state of childishness? Back to a state of what it means to be a mature responsible female? The answer is; *he can't!* From his child-want-to-be-adult point of view, she needs to grow up, or become subject to his immature wrath.

When she; the woman, permits premarital sexual intercourse, clarity of mind comes into question; thus, her free-will ceases to exist. What females do not understand is that sexual intercourse creates an actual physical connection. Both sides are stirring together the human essence. In the end; two beings; male and female, form a single being that we call man, and the result of that unity is a new being that will eventually become independent. Two beings becoming one, resulting in two or more. When you look at it from that perspective then giving birth to just one child makes no sense. You would simply have two separate beings again. As a species we should be expanding, not trying to find a balance on the basis that the world is only, so, big. We exist in an ever-expanding universe of random unforeseen dangers. Of course, if the mind does not fathom the process, then the result is chaos. Which is why the male and the female need to be properly prepared for what is surely a confusing state of mind. Do not take this author's word for it. During copulation, think about what is going through your mind. Even those whom get married first, have absolutely no clue as to what is going on with them, either psychologically, and/or even physically. The act of sexual intercourse; though we think we know what it is or what it is all about, is in fact, a mystery. As-far-as anyone is concerned, it is an activity of pleasure and nothing else. No scientist, philosopher, or even this author knows what it truly comprises. We are not speaking of the dynamics, mechanics or purpose, but its overall nature in general. What is it? A beautiful aspect of the human condition that is neglected; taken for granted; used and corrupted beyond all reason and logic. Not just by the adult film industry or prostitution, but by everyone. Thoughts are in a euphoric; even a chaotic state of mind, not unlike coming under the effects of drugs. For a man: A moment of feel good, but then the aftereffects... let's just say, you go in as a bull, and you come out as a babe.

A huge downside to premarital sexual intercourse is a woman's submissiveness. An exploit of delight that is not meant for some wayward one-night stand or brief social interest. Being in such a vulnerable state, makes her susceptible to untold perversions of the flesh. Helpless to the socially unstable, which can result in dubious outcomes. Doubt this author? Then follow your history of Charles Manson. Unrealizing that she has reached a maximum level of submissiveness, while retaining the innocence of a little girl trying to bond with someone willing to acknowledge her. She wants the kind of male who can bring out that certain feel-good of being submissive. Yes; we men suffer from the same affliction for we too can be compliant, and contrary to what many people may think, sadomasochism is not a healthy activity on either a psychological or physical level. The body, her body; specifically, the vagina and anal regions are not designed for the rigors of what the socially sick are capable of applying, and those sicknesses often come from multiple sources. Her body is designed to be attended to, by a single source, namely her one and only man.

CHAPTER 7

In the meantime, let us take a look at the Church's primitive, preconceived notion of premarital sexual intercourse. In fact, let us examine their position from a different perspective. If you are copulating before marriage, it is not just morally wrong, but it is rape! *Period!* Whether consensual or not, rape is rape. All of us understand that word, do we not? The Church says, that premarital sexual intercourse is a violation of doctrine, but we do not seem to get that; so, let us modify their position, and take it from a more enlightened approach, and simply call it rape, *that's different.* We get that. Oh, yes, we do. Therefore, this author will explain to you; the reader in plain language what the Church already knows. Sexual intercourse outside of *authentic* marriage is rape at any age because honestly; how do you place a number on an understanding of what is appropriate in regards to consensual sexual intercourse? What is appropriate consensual sexual intercourse? Each one of us is different, physically and mentally. The anatomical parts of some people develop sooner than others. Some people develop faster intellectually. So, again; this author asks you; the reader, how do you place a number on consensual sexual intercourse? It is a fact of life that there are some females who are just not ready to mingle with men when they reach the prescribed age based under law. If that is the case, would there not be females who are not at the proper age who are ready? We have met adult females who exhibit childish behavior for no apparent reason, and females who are considered minors who behave maturely; who are precocious. In fact, a lot of under aged females have better insight towards sly guys, and yet we retard their social evolution until; *when?* Look, people require instructions on how to interact. If that information is not provided or not properly received, and yet allowed to be instituted, then age should not matter. No one simply goes out, and builds a skyscraper. They need to be educated on how to build a skyscraper. Does a child figure out what one-plus-one is without guidance? Some people may think it possible, but if a child does not seek a perception of mathematics to begin with, then how would they understand the basic mechanics of arithmetic? The same should be said for social interaction. Some parents teach it, and some do not; and, so, we have geared our laws to safeguard those whom are not taught? No. We have geared our laws around irresponsible parenting. People, who refuse to accept the fact that they lack the ability to apply the obvious in the world of what is proper and what is improper. Allowing psychologists, journalists and celebrities to confuse the issue in regards to child rearing. You; the parent, are aware of the difference between what is proper and what is improper conduct. They are your children, so, teach them accordingly. It's not rocket science, though some would like you to think, so, in order to hijack your wallet.

Another point to consider is that rape does not necessarily imply a physical act, but can be a psychological interaction as well. There are people who can use words to illicit a sexual reaction, and of course, with cause, there is eventual effect. When a woman adorns alluring apparel in public, she is in fact raping us; the male, our senses, our very being for existence; however, we do not look at it as such, do we? Why not? A woman's body is design to attract and to stimulate. Once our juices get going, we can simply turn them off, *right? Really?* In many situations, a woman can be, so, thorough in her rape; that we; the man, have to quite literally play out the stimulating effects of her attractiveness because it is not the woman's clothes that make her attractive, but how she wears them. It is not her skin that is stimulating, but what she wears over her skin that makes it sexy, for we men base life off what is risqué. The nearness of nudity. Perhaps being raped from a male point of view is more problematic than damaging for us.

Another aspect of our culture that requires clarity is that a female is not sexually assaulted, when another person forcibly penetrates her body. She is raped. We must separate the two ideas on the basis that rape is the conclusion to a physical act. Assault is the commencement to what can be, but not necessarily the result of a final act; though in any case, both are an action that disrupts the natural flow of normal human behavior. Think of it along these terms: Soldiers attack a castle. They are *assaulting* the barricades, but should they fail to get in, it is deemed as being repulsed; or denied entry. Should they penetrate the castle's defenses then it is *rape* and pillage. Interesting how most women who claim rape today, look as though they have just thrown open the gates to let the enemy in, unlike their contemporaries, who looked like a fallen castle. Perhaps in the past, females understood the importance of keeping their virginity intact, which explains why males had to brutalize them first to break their resolve. Since women today view their beauty as a commodity, they simply give in to the sexual intercourse, and deal with the consequences later on the basis that they are copulating with different men on a regular basis anyhow, but on their terms. Can this act of preservation be truly viewed as rape? Yes; on the basis that, again, premarital sexual intercourse is, in fact, rape, regardless of a female's age.

By forcing someone to act contradictory to human nature is a denial of their freewill. God grants freewill to all people, and any person who denies another person their freewill challenges God directly, which is interesting when it is freewill that allows a person to rob another of their freewill. Now, a girl can still be raped when she interacts with an illicit subject of any kind or as mentioned, she can be a rapist when displaying herself as with promiscuous overtures. In our modern culture, we are trying, so, hard to be appealing to women that we; the man, have forgotten why we restricted them in the first place. Consider that as a man rapes a man-child making it possible for that child to become homosexual, and even prey on adolescent and/or preteen boys later in life, so, too does a raped woman-child become a rapist in her later years with form-fitting or risqué attire. Due to this concept of what was once deemed as peculiar behavior during normal hours of the day; we never consider how much she can truly hurt a man. We always focus on spousal abuse; when a man either physically or mentally assaults a woman, or when a man or men express opinionated demeaning remarks about women or at a woman.

Yes; women hurt men more, then men hurt women, but on more of a psychological level. Specifically, when meeting for the first time. Most women do not understand how to kindly turn away a man's advances; going easy on his pride. Now, this author is not speaking of the occasional man-eater. No, we are speaking of the woman who is not cruel by nature, but lacks the patience or are simply frustrated by the constant petitioning and/or are angry with the occasional guy who does not accept; *no,* for an answer. She may even reach a point when she will laugh, make jokes; those things that hurt a man deeply; shakes his confidence, and we as a society completely ignore this aspect of human behavior. Why is that? Naturally, the things a woman goes through in life gives her the right to reject a man's advances. When she became a competitor, the insults became a part of her self-preservation. Furthermore, we; as a culture, are, so, poor on our ability to communicate that it has rotted the very foundation of our idiom. Does anyone even take the time to practice the basic fundamentals of proper use of language? Interesting how some women show regret, reverting to their kindly motherly instincts when victorious at arresting the top job away from the male competitor. That's the feminine contradiction at work. The sense of success and regret, conflicting upon the conscious mind. Now, consider this; as it is the woman who is to heal a man's pain, what of the case of when she is the cause of the pain? Ideally a man who hurts a woman will want to make it up to her in some way. Usually, he would have an affinity for her due to their similarities of interests, and would even pursue courtship; usually, however, men are known to be treacherous too, and even resentful. Unfortunately, chauvinism is still a very real thing in our modern culture of the early Twenty-first.

CHAPTER 8

The reality is, that we; the male of the species, do not have an appreciation of women when we are young, and that is a fact based on the current culture of sexual innuendo. Teenaged boys have little, if any respect for a woman, and her true purpose in society, so, why do we continue to follow the present system? There are those whom would condition the general public into believing that sex should not be restricted, and yet say that a woman can do what a man can do; and the interesting thing is there are some men out there, who agree with them. What do we call people like that? How about witches, and warlocks. For a better sense of the language

26

what would be a more appropriate description? In day's past, these kinds of people would have been regarded as perhaps witches and even warlocks, but those applications would be out of character in today's society. Therefore, let us simply say that they are feral. That their kind are behaviorally inconvenient to the health of our community; socially unacceptable, and their ideas are socially inappropriate towards the needs of the progress of our culture. As-long-as they thrive our children will die. In second thought, the idea of the witch, is a woman who has power, and does not want a man in control. What are the signs of the witch? We have men. We have women. We have men, who think they are women, and women who think they are men, of which both groups want all of the rights afforded them as women. If there is not a better definition for social confusion, this author does not know of one.

A witch will sacrifice a child. Sacrifice does not necessarily imply a stone pedestal and knife. Sacrifice can also come to mean giving the child to another person for the benefit of completing a selfish goal. Seeking fun and pleasure. Perhaps a liaison with another man, who is not the child's father or her man. Leaving the child to fend for themselves in times of need. Then there is, of course abortion, the worst offense that can be committed against a human being. A witch's involvement in the termination of a child in the womb would be convincing a young mind who has been manipulated by a warlock that aborting a child is perfectly okay. They say; *it is your body. You are not aborting a child, but simply ending a pregnancy.* The witch's number one target is, of course, the virgin. To corrupt a virgin is her greatest venture, and where do you find a great majority of witches and warlocks? In our public education system and higher institutions of learning. That is why legislators have fought, so, hard to keep religion out of our schools. They create a safe haven to perpetuate chaos, confusion, and a total disregard for a young woman's virginity, and a man-child's sense of manhood. She; the witch, and he; the warlock, thrive in this environment. Raping our children of their innocence. Realize this when your child goes off to school, for they, and even yourselves are up against insurmountable odds.

What is a warlock? More than likely a man-child, raised by a witch or seduced by one who has been conditioned to be accepting of feminist ideas. A man who deliberately wastes his seed on carnal pleasure, for it has no meaning or purpose to him other than being a catalyst for his need for delight. He works with his mistress; the witch, to bring about disruption and confusion in the ranks of those whom would strive to be something more than what they are. They use many tricks to achieve their goals. Especially in regards to those whom are young, naïve and virtuous.

Oh, and should you; the reader, think these words as crazy, then consider the following; witches and warlocks use incantations and potions to seduce the mind. From a woman's point of view, a guy is saying all of the right words, and she mysteriously finds herself in the bed next to him the following day. Consider the previous, when you see the woman wearing a slinky outfit and moving in a very sultry manner whenever there are men around. She adorns heavy cosmetics, and uses subtle physical gestures to seduce you; her brother or any of her male relatives. You are the handsome bachelor of power, and she can break you with sexual accusation, even pass on a nuisance or two to make your life miserable.

Remember; that as a man, the witch always enters your life right before the dream girl; so, be mindful of who you involve yourself with. Nothing worse than when you let the girl that fate made you for, slip right through your fingers over a technicality. That is the spell or perhaps, curse of the witch. It is not about sex with her, but power. Sure, you can call this author crazy for reverting back to a primitive, superstitious notion for identifying some kind of social imbalance; however, let's be realistic about what is going on.

When creating an orderly proficient environment, restrictions are necessary. Implementing those restrictions is an act of imposing rules. Traditionally, what do witches and warlocks do? They live outside of the rules with the understanding that they have a right to live life as they, so, choose. They believe that we should live our lives strictly under force of will only. We white-wash this idea with the modern term of secularism to avoid confronting the truth. Doubt

28

this author? We men have to accept a woman's behavior, her choice of attire, her wants and needs. She is an illusionist. Her goal is to provide you; the man, with something that is not the truth. The witch's words are lies, to get it her way. She expects the male to control his physical and psychological state of mind. Again; so, that she can have things her way. She seduces a man, copulates with him under questionable circumstances, and gets caught, and its suddenly rape? We look at women, whom are raped as a crime, but in reality, we should be looking at the ordeal as a situation instead of a crime. Yes; a crime was committed; however, we live in a culture of the independent woman, and with independence comes risk. The understanding of risk is not finite, and the one thing males realize is that you can never account for every situation. Now, examine what we are trying to do in our modern culture of the early Twenty-first. Yes; we are trying to do just that, because the female is the very epitome of vulnerability. How do you protect vulnerability against the unexpected when she wants to exist independently from protection? In a nutshell; a woman will speak an untruth just as easily as taking a breath, and will have absolutely no qualms over her victim's outcome. Should she be caught in her lie, the emotions suddenly materialize, and she will place blame on everything, but her own convictions. As-far-as she is concerned, everyone is wrong, but her.

Why does this author claim that the female is the epitome of vulnerability? As children, we would run to an authority figure when a problem arises, but as a child, we never give the complete details. We only say what we want the authority to hear, but when the authority seeks clarification, then guess what? The authority points out that we could have avoided the whole situation, and that we may have been at fault, and that we as a child should learn from that situation. Women retain this aspect of childhood into their adult years, and learn to hone the skill to such a degree as to express the details in such a way as to avoid the crucial questions from being asked. Now, imagine a situation where the authority is a woman. Then what do you get? Empowerment!

Warlocks have also destabilized the economy and driven our children to kill. How did they destabilize the economy you ask? By supporting women, whom wanted mainstream jobs that were traditionally male orientated. From that point on, the communal finances started to flow in a less socially beneficial direction. A woman's paycheck benefits only herself. The cosmetics, the hair, and of course fashion all goes towards her personal needs. Not to mention, the Japanese auto-market. Wait. What does a car have to do with beauty? Domestic automobiles were designed around a male orientated infrastructure. Men are tinkerers, and, so, if a car had a problem, he simply rolled it into the garage with a six-pack of beer and worked on it. In a crazy sort of way, it helped him to remain faithful to his wife. Women on the other hand do not like to tinker, of course there is always the exception, but as a majority, females simply do not like to tinker unless it involves their hair. Therefore, a woman will take her car to a mechanic, usually the dealer mechanic for repairs costing her the new purse, shoes or some form of other apparel. To make sure we are clear on this matter; if a woman is spending money on car repairs…; and there you have it; everything a woman needed to perpetuate the sexualizing of society. Oh, and to make sure we are especially clear on the matter of monthly expenditures, a woman will neglect the bills necessary for a comfortable home to maintain her beauty habit. Not to preclude the fact that men are great at balancing the checkbook, but that successful women find street life deplorable. When people are single, they take risks; however, when a man finds that special woman, he thinks twice about what direction his money will go. Not, so, with a woman.

CHAPTER 9

The natural processes of life, is what we strive for because we are just a little tired, and just a bit sick of the modifications in our food and drink. Even the time change for the summer months is an unnatural process that disrupts our circadian rhythm. Male-on-male copulation is also a modification of the natural process of the human body. Man is meant to be with a woman; *period.* Does not matter what he feels inside. The feelings within us are a result of our social dilemmas due to our interaction with modified behavior.

Our sensory I/O is perhaps the most sophisticated system of its kind in the known universe. We feed off each other's behaviors; emotions, feelings, and actions, and we store that data like any computing machine. We must be careful of our social interaction on all levels of existence; all of our senses collect data, and just like a computer, our minds can be fouled up. Think about all of the sensory data you pick up living in a city for example. The traffic noise, people noise, lights, smells, even the footfalls we make when we walk or run, and of course there is the pollution. The food, drugs, alcohol, marijuana, cigarettes, and of course the fossil fuels. All of the touching, banging around, and we have not even touched bases with our personal dilemmas; thoughts of anger; rage, the contemplation, paranoia, uncertainty, anticipation and even the delights. There are just, so, many things that we take for granted in regards to our sensory input that we fail to notice the subtleties of social manipulation.

When you do not keep constant thought of the Lord or make prayers for protection, you become vulnerable to the whims of the fallen one. Making you do things that you normally would not do in a conscious civil state of mind, without the effects of inebriating substances. Has your body ever done a sudden peculiar act? Do something unusual that you were not expecting; that may have caused, a car accident. Slipping on the stairs or taking a spill on a skateboard or snowboard unexpectedly? Consider that the fallen one has connected himself to you wirelessly, and has affected you. No different than a computer. We did not consider these things in the past because we did not understand what could truly affect a computer, but now, we do, and it does not take much to throw a computer out of whack. You can say the same about all of us. Certain words; music, sounds, smells, touching, visuals, even tastes can deal an exuberant amount of damage to us. Therefore, be patient as you move through life because if you're not, you will misstep, and you will blame others instead of blaming yourself and the fallen one, and that is how wars are begun.

This author proposes an idea of a known phenomenon within ourselves that we do not fully understand in regards to the general population, and that is, we have an additional sense beyond our five obvious senses of sight, sound, touch, smell, and taste. Yes; the idea of a sixth sense is not a new thing, and naturally, there are those, whom speculate on what our additional sense is, and yes, we do have one. Let us simply cut to the chase and call that sixth sense, empathy. No, there is nothing special about it. Like the first five, it has always been there, except that unlike the first five; which are linked directly to the environment, the sixth is linked directly to us. Designed to work between human beings. Do not take this author's word for it. Things that impact the body; light-waves, sound-waves, electrical fields. We know they exists. Science has proven it. We play off each other's emotions. Somehow, we feel or sense the emotions of others. Even impart our emotions on the surrounding environment. Not just other people and animals, but all matter. We both give and receive emotions. Ever ask yourself that when you are in the presence of some people, you suddenly feel good, but around others, you get a strange feeling of hostility or even reluctance? Ever see two people ready to fight? The rage increases exponentially, and unchecked until it reaches a point when even blows are exchanged, feeding off the emotions of the crowd. While at the same time, violent emotions seem to bleed off from those whom are engaged in violence, on to those whom are spectating. Feeding off each other's emotions. That is not an enigma or a mutation, but a part of who we are. When a cluster of people engage in violence or happiness, what happens? They feed off the growing emotion of the moment; however, when an angry person enters the happiness fray, their counter emotion spreads like a disease. Why does anger spread, so, easily? More easily than happiness because we become angry when someone takes away or interferes with happiness, thus compounding the anger and hatred. Christianity was designed to teach a person how to always remain happy, even in the face of despair. It takes a whole group of people to make the crowd happy, but only one bitter person to bring down the happiness of the ignorant. Now, how do you know that your empathic ability is working? That tingling sensation you get when someone is looking at you. What is truly happening is that they are focusing their emotions on you, and you are receiving those emotions, whether hatred or affection. That urging sensation you feel when violence is being applied. That sense of trepidation when you are about to commit to a forbidden activity. Realistically, do you; the reader, truly believe that a person's words alone have an effect on the people around them; on you in particular? We have all heard it before. His or her very persona charms the audience, and that is the empathic connection that we all possess, at work.

Naturally there are skeptics whom say, they do not sense the emotions of others. That is actually incorrect. If you grew up in a room without light do your eyes still work? Can a person hear in the vacuum of space? Develop touch? What is taste? What do you smell in a swimming pool? People must attune their empathic sense, just as we attune our sense of touch, smell, sight, hearing and taste. Naturally, as we grow and develop, our first five senses attune themselves to our surroundings. We are given ice cream. Told we are hearing a violin. That smell is fried onions. Pet a puppy, and play with a blue ball. We all have strengths and weaknesses in every one of our senses. To master each and every one of them takes great discipline. What we do not teach are the feelings of happiness, anger and distress from others, and that is because we allow the first five senses to dominate. We can hear and see the laughter, so, that person must be happy. We can hear and see the sorrow, so, that person must be sad. We can hear, and see the displeasure, so, that person must be angry. Now, consider, have you ever sensed a person who is laughing to be actually sad? Or to say the least, sense something was wrong with them? Interesting how the Christ teaches us to give up food and drink, and even material possessions. Could He be saying this because these things distract us from the fine tuning of our ability to sense another person's emotions? All these things interfere with the discipline of understanding our greater purpose. What is that purpose? To serve those around us, even at the cost of one's own life. This concept cannot be stressed enough, for death is a state that is greatly misunderstood. Only when a person comes to understand the Christ can they focus on living a good life, and not worry about death in order to achieve a natural death. Suicide is a cheat, and the Christ does not like a cheat. What is a cheat? A cheat is an abuse of free will and no one abuses free will more than the fallen one. The biggest cheater of all.

There is absolutely no way to avoid being programmed, but we do have a choice on what direction we want that programming to take us, and *direction* is the whole point of life. Oh, and by the way, let this author make one other crucial point about the natural processes of life, and that is, we must protect our wilderness to prevent ourselves from going insane. There are just times when we need to return to nature; our natural environment in order to preserve, and recharge our sanity. Ever feel exhausted, low on energy? That's part of it. Look at our modern culture. A person never gets a moment to simply let the mind rest. Those same forces destroy the medicine you need to get back on your feet, and that is the wilderness. A state of no civilization is what a person needs. No, television. No, urban noise. No, rap, hip-hop, rock or harsh music of any kind, and most importantly, no electronic devices. All of it, is chaos, noise; a disruption to the natural physical function of the body and mind. Instead of our politicians being in charge, perhaps a person of orchestrated music can be the leader. Music is a latent form of communication that lodges itself into the subconscious mind and the very loins of our body in such a way as to dictate the direction of physical and mental development.

Naturally, if most of our wilderness is lost, then we will be a doomed species. Oh, and just in case you are wondering, even our oceans are not safe from our destructive power. All animal life serves a symbiotic relationship with man. That is why they were created. As the male of the species of man; you; we, must tend the garden; protect the garden, and everything within it; including, most importantly, woman because right now, she is scared beyond all imagination due to our lack of concern. We must reinstate our religious values to get a clear perception of how to regain her confidence. To better manage the environment; and just, so, we are clear; population has nothing to do with the environment. This world; Earth, is capable of handling hundreds of billions. We simply need to access the full potential of human intellect when incorporating ourselves into the world. Something we are not doing, so, well. Working with nature, not against it, to avoid the environmental turmoil we are going through today.

CHAPTER 10

This author would have to say that she; the woman, is quite an amazing creature. Therefore, any man who behaves as a woman; assumes the role of the woman in a physically sexual dynamic; in fact, insults a woman's very integrity. Insults woman-hood as a whole. She is special to those of us who understand her purpose, and her importance to man. Without that specialty, we are nothing. Man and woman are the fundamental components of the overall human mechanism. A man is, what he is, and a woman is, what she is, and to allow her to be a man, and he to be a woman is by all means the greatest malfeasance imaginable. A disruption in the order of man. To acknowledge those cross behaviors as normal is equivalent to the shattering of the fundamental principles of human nature. For male and female are two parts that make up the human organism. Each being unique in their own right, and yet requiring certain behavioral methods to make the whole, operate. Any variance from this basic behavioral model affects the whole in such a way as to cause deterioration in the very fabric of humanity. That is why crossing those lines are repugnant to those who clearly see, and understand the whole. If those transgressions are not dealt with swiftly, then the result can only lead to the death of the whole. That is why females who cross that line should be put down hard and heavy by a man because it is in the man's nature to be the keeper of order. Women cannot do it, for she is compassion, and compassion will overlook order to benefit disorder; however, without compassion to sooth the savage beast, our social network falls out of alignment, and our rationality suffers. Without order to restrict compassion there can be no civilization for it is the beast that keeps the woman bound to her side of civilization. That is why boys must be allowed to be boys, but taught restraint by their mothers; and girls should be allowed to be girls, but be restricted by their fathers. More on that subject later.

In the end, there are just two understandings of man. There is the overall identity of the organism, and then there is the component of the organism. The two work hand-n-hand; however, a corrupt component affects the overall organism, which in turn interferes with the proper evolutionary process of the organism. In today's terms of the living process, we call this interference; cancer or virus. Unfortunately, corrupted components should be treated in much the same way as cancer cells or they will result in the failure of the overall organism. This is a rudimentary explanation as to the existence and need for Levitical Laws, and why they are a necessity in regards to the handling of certain defects in human behavior and culture; however, in today's society, we allow corrupted components to remain, and even allow them to evolve, and the result is a mentally polluted culture that is being accepted as the norm. We even allow the corruption to dictate social policies. Why? We as a species refuse to accept the idea of a child being flawed psychologically, and in certain cases becoming a serious burden in our culture. A physical defect can be managed; respectfully. A behavioral defect is a whole other process all together. A Ph.D. may say, that some behavioral defects are acceptable, even manageable. They even go as-far-as saying some behavioral defects are perhaps not defects at all. Strange how their conclusions go against our overall understanding of the organism. After all, that is what many of us are tracking on. That thing we call common sense of which, our perceptions of it are being greatly altered by those who would blatantly go against the norm and rational tract of human existence. These people had, and currently have ulterior motives, and that is to make a name for themselves at the expense of the overall organism. Interesting the absence of any counter arguments to those defects of culture. Haunting to this author is the retardation of our common sense, logic and reason; building-blocks of self-control that maturate from our religious beliefs and help us determine what we will be as a species. As if our society had become enshrouded in sudden darkness, and who knows, perhaps that is what has happened. Whatever the case may be, when our sight returned, everything was changed, and we did nothing to make the organism called man healthy again. To do so, what needs to be done? Perhaps the time for a counter argument has arrived. Perhaps the counter argument should come from someone who is not a Ph.D. on the basis that our Judeo-Christian understanding for a well-refined education system has been milled to that of a social, psychological appeasement with absolutely no substance, well-defiled, and under the control of those who support a defective, disassociation of society.

WHAT IS GOVERNMENT?

CHAPTER 1

From the beginning of communal living, we have been erecting some form of social regulation; and whether it be workers or leaders, neither can exist without the other. One cannot identify itself without the other. Just because we say a government must be comprised of certain things, means nothing without something to govern. Therefore, we ask ourselves; *where does government begin?* We cannot understand ourselves unless we can determine where the idea of government begins. How many levels should it be, and what would be its nature. Yes; our Founding-Fathers had to contend with that very notion when formulating a social governing mechanism for these states that we call united because what they were proposing had never been done before.

When looking at government; for instance, in the United States of America, the first thing that comes to mind; is of course the national level. A body that bonds all of the communities together under one cohesive infrastructure for the benefit of the greater human condition. We all interact with one another either directly or indirectly whether we realize it or not. What one person does on one coast affects another person on the other, and all points in between. Therefore, we require a national mediator as a source of litigation to avoid misunderstandings between the communities. Oddly, the national government does serve another purpose; and that is to compel the people on a subconscious/conscious level to focus their anger towards that body of legislature instead of on one another. That is how human nature works; unite against a common cause to keep the unity intact, resulting in that all too familiar phrase; *Of the People, By the People, For the People.* Perhaps, that is the nature of government after all; to become the hated thing in order to unite a thing. A government designed to be the focus of social anger, and to absorb the hatred, so, that individuals will not become the focus of hatred and fragment as other communities have done in other parts of the world. The biggest controversy is of course, our understanding of state governments, and how they relate to one another on a national level. Many citizens believe that individual states should possess more power than the national government. This may be true, that is until you consider the power of the many over the power of the one. At the founding of the nation, there were two ideologies on what the United States of America should be. One idea was, that the individual states were independent of one another, but would work together for a mutual benefit towards a common goal. The second being, one nation with a collection of states that was viewed as nothing more than a successive level of government for regulatory purposes. Let us dig deep into the importance of knowing our history. We are a country born of thirteen separate English communities who just happened to be next door to one another; regulated by a single source located in London. From the point of view of the Crown, they were simply the colonies of the new world. What the colonies did along the Eastern Seaboard, south of the St. Lawrence River, was to start working collectively. Something the Crown was not prepared for at the time, and probably did not want. In fact, the Crown probably worked hard to keep the idea of colonial independence amongst one another, of which, resulted in a backfire. Pure speculation of course; there is no actual proof of this author's words; however, thanks to unforeseeable circumstances or sheer fate, those New World Colonies were forced into action. Not necessarily in the form of combat, but in coming together in more of a philosophical understanding. Again, something no mother-country wants from its colonial interests. What Mother-England did not realize is that the experimentation of new ideas could be enterprised without censorship in the new world, and a great many of those enterprises were religious in nature.

Enough of the history lesson. Let's get back to the advantage of being united. A single person may climb a mountain alone, but should there be complications; say, falling rocks that break an arm or a leg, then what does he do? It is nice to know that you can call upon your neighbor for help after you have just spit in his eye, or a middleman who can assist you with seeing the beauty of your neighbor's yard without it costing you the farm. Imagine having to require a passport to go from Kentucky to Tennessee or from Rhode Island to Massachusetts. We called the battle between the North and the South a Civil War, but the reality is; it was just two stubborn brothers with different ideas, duking it out. As-much-as we hate our fellow countrymen; we cannot imagine our country without them. Though we may not admit it openly until a natural disaster strikes, we truly do love our fellow Americans, especially the good-looking ones.

After the state level, there are counties (parishes), towns, cities, neighborhoods etcetera. So, where does government begin? The individual? No. We must examine the very roots of our religious values. The Book of Genesis establishes the core elements of government that are grossly overlooked. Government begins with the family. You begin a government; *Of the People, By the People, For the People* at the man and wife level. Now, we are not speaking of the elements of an existing government body for voting purposes or of voicing concerns, but the source for the administration of government. Anything else does not hold the same meaning. People whom engage in like-gender relationships form nothing more than partnerships or are a collaborative effort with the intent of an exclusive, complacent physical and financial delight that results in no form of communal contribution. It can even be viewed as a cooperative business sense; however, true marriage or what was originally known as a man cleaving to a woman, is a process of unifying what was initially two parts, and making them whole on a level that is apparently beyond our understanding. The first to be governed is she; who is wife. When beginning the governing process, you must have rules in place to establish an understanding of wants and needs in order to avoid misunderstandings as to ensure a smooth; effortless operation of the relationship. Before you govern she; who is to be your wife, you must make clear what is to be expected of her. If you do not say what you want, then how can she see to your needs.

Unfortunately, the very basics to social interaction is always taken for granted. As though community leaders do not tell their people what is expected of them. They think that implementing laws is enough to establish an understanding of an objective. When in fact, laws do absolutely nothing more than establish an agenda. In this modern age of the early Twenty-first, we have lost our perceptions of the true meaning of law due to an agenda of trying to be accommodating to every person and group's needs outside of the terms and understanding laid down by the Constitution of the United States of America. Retarding the process of achieving the overall community objective. Imagine the captain of a ship trying to be accommodating to each individual crewmember. Would the ship achieve its objective? Not by a longshot; and considering that the *state* is being, so, obliging to the feminist and homosexual communities, they fail to realize that those groups are the very cause behind the social disruption; the communal breakdown, and all of the chaos. They want empowerment over nature itself, even God. Unless in the service of God; man, woman, children is how you begin government; *period.* Everything else is self-serving.

The result of he; who is male; masculine; man, and she; who is female; feminine; wife, brings new substance to the model. Something that did not exist before. Something amazing to the environment that would result in a contribution to the community. A process strictly for the benefit of offspring resulting in a collaboratively beneficial effort. Yes; a man and a woman can come together under that same partnership notion without the intent of bringing new substance into the model, but the reality is, the potential still exists for such an action. Yes; even if either is infertile, does not preclude the fact that male and female are the natural components of reproduction.

With the idea of government originating at the family level opens up a whole lot of possibilities previously overlooked by scholars, philosophers and even parents. Something worth examining in the future. In the meantime, to be a basic government, you must have something that binds it together. Something with meaning, that you; the man, and she; the woman, both believe in with all of your heart. Yes, a man and a woman can create new life without the need for marriage, but what truly bonds the relationship together? Gives it foundation? What is it that gives the overall relationship purpose and meaning? Remember, animals create offspring all of the time, but they do not organize themselves in such a way as to benefit the whole of the community. In other words, they do not prevent starvation or put out fires, or evacuate from floods. In the animal kingdom; children, and the elderly are culled by predators and the elements. They cannot see beyond their own environment, and speculate on what is out there. They are simply left to the hands of fate. Then again, perhaps we should ask ourselves; what is marriage? Not from a religious standpoint, but from a common-sense point of view. What purpose does it truly serve? These are the questions that we as a modern culture require answers to when considering that, so, many couples are coming together in a cohabitation dynamic to bring children into the world, without the intent of a life-long bond or consideration of the meaning of a civilized existence. Separating is not an action to be prevented, but simply accepted when difficulties arise, and we all go through difficulties in a relationship. The question we never ask ourselves is if there was even an attempt to develop a relationship to begin with. Realistically; people meet, make a declaration, and then jump into bed. We ask ourselves why is the divorce rate, so, high in this modern age of the early Twenty-first? Ask yourself; what is the measure of our philosophical education, and you will have your answer. Marriage is a ritual to announce to nature for our appeasement, that we are something greater than that of nature itself. That something within us, sets us apart from the natural world. That we; the sapient life-form of this world, requires some form of process that is fundamental in setting us apart from other forms of life in this existence, so, that our offspring will not be leisurely feasted upon by those lesser creatures. Once the idea of marriage was conceptualized, a process was required that clearly defined its meaning; rules and regulations; guidelines for the proper institution thereof, and thus you have religion. Now, you have to ask yourself; what is the pinnacle of that religion? This author cannot answer that question for it goes against the idea of free will. You; the reader, must decide for yourself what that idea is, for the path has already been laid out for you. All you need do is choose, but choose carefully or you may not like what you find in the end.

In the Catholic tradition, that blossoming government begins with three; a male, female and a bonding agent, to ensure that nothing can pull them apart. Of course, if the two sides begin a civil war, then it is the bonding agent that always pays the price. The squabbling couple call Him liar, cheat, promise breaker. No; not in, so, many words; of course; but they say these things in their hearts; and they mean every word of it because they built their new government not on their religious virtues, vows, and values, but on physical pleasure, bedroom-play, sexual intercourse; *plain and simple*. Even dirt would be a more preferable bonding agent than sex because it's always there, and it washes off with ease. Over time, sex gets old and useless, and no matter how hard you try, it never washes off. Oh, sure; for you, the young female whom happens to be reading this, who thinks it goes away, ask yourself; ask any female for that matter who has allowed the engagement of premarital sexual intercourse, and it is something you never truly forget.

Therefore, should you; the male of the species, choose the path of family life. Then stick to it, and with the same woman. For you represent the very basic building blocks of government. Without you; the male thinking along family lines, there can be no law, and subsequently no order.

Now, when you look at the household as a government, then only one representative from a household should vote in any form of election, not those who are of voting age living under the same roof. Man and wife discuss the various representatives to determine who would best represent the needs of the home government. If both he and she conduct a vote independently, then it kills the overall notion of marriage. A man cleaves to a woman to create a new framework. That means they become one person. How can the idea of one person cast two votes? That is why in the past, women were not allowed to vote. There was simply no need to set a precedence to define the separation of man and woman after being bound together in matrimony. The reality is; men and women were simply never meant to be independent of one another. We; the male shape ourselves for the world not as a man, but as men. Women shape themselves not for men, but for a man. She is man's conscience, his compassion. Everything that he is not, she is, and when they become joined, the construct of man is complete. That is why the Church uses language such as: *What God has brought together, let no man put asunder.* The result of that male part of man, and that female part of man are parts for another couple with parts of their own. This is what man is all about. Therefore, laws are not meant for the woman, but for the man, of which, she is not until she is joined as such to the male of the species. Therefore, woman must have a wide latitude in regards to daily living due to the hell she goes through in life. It's not easy being woman; *period,* which means that being a popular woman is much more difficult. Considering as such; we men should be doing everything in our power to ensure that women are living in total bliss on the basis that a woman's life is a living hell. We men must ease her burdens; therefore, why should a woman be governed by laws that are designed to regulate a man's behavior? We the man, build the world around us for the benefit of the woman. Note: More than likely, the first man went about taking possession of or creating a domicile in order to store within it, his most cherished assets. His first; of course, being his wife because they were and are such a rare commodity. Now; when woman participates in the creation of that special something; it takes away the meaning of what is trying to be accomplished. Even the motivation; the reason for building anything just goes away. A gift has no meaning when the person that it is meant for, assists in obtaining it or flat out obtains it for themselves.

Now, whether the wife or the man conducts the actual process of voting should not have a bearing on the overall voting process. Only that the house makes a vote. For our forefathers to once say that only a man could vote was ridiculous on the basis that she too is man. Would you; the man, say that your left hand cannot hold the cup of coffee? That the right eye is forbidden from reading the print on the page? Woman is the most powerful part of your body, and yet, the most fragile. Perhaps the reality is that she should conduct the actual process of voting at all times. Not that she is smarter or wiser, but that she simply possesses a better intuition of communal needs.

Another point to consider is that by establishing a specific voting age is an insult to the very sanctity, and even the integrity of a democracy. Perhaps the voting age should not be an age at all, but more of an ideology. This would, of course, change the overall dynamic of an election. On the other hand, there is a downside to this notion. All those whom are not under a household should be able to vote whether married or not. There is no disagreement with this idea; however, this author also said that a government begins with a man and a wife. Look at it like this: A son or daughter is attending a university or even living on their own. They would be nothing more than a family-level absentee ballot; which would, of course be of no concern to any higher level of government. In the meantime; as-long-as no law is passed that would interfere with the process of a man seeking to establish a government, then concern over the legislative process should be eliminated, while he is seeking the creation of such. In other words, he is having faith in his fathers to make the proper decisions for him, that will ensure the continuation of their way of life. Naturally, if there is no faith, then there can be no culture, and just in case this author was not clear; offspring whom understand the electoral process would be subject to a form of family level electoral college system until establishing a *house* of their own. This has a great benefit to our current perception of the voting process. It places into practice an understanding of why the Electoral College is an effective tool for electing officials. Note: Do not assume that your child lacks an understanding of social concerns when deciding on a political candidate. You would be amazed at just how flawed our culture is, just by listening to your child. Their insight usually points to the obvious things that we; as adults, overlook.

CHAPTER 2

Deciding where government begins can be an ongoing process; however, ask yourself a question: If no one is at home, then is the government working? Imagine the Legislative Branch working in a factory from 9to5. Would the government be running during those hours? Would the government ever be open for that matter? Can a person truly conduct two different thought processes at the same time? We see people driving all of the time, conducting a conversation, with either a passenger or on the phone. Though they may think they are doing a good job with either one, it is usually everyone else on the road who is making that person look good. For it takes a lot of mental energy to generate creative thought, let alone engage in dialogue. Therefore, bureaucratic responsibility has to take an immense amount of mental energy, and if running a government is like that, then running a home has to be equally difficult, for no politician has to clean up the kitchen after the fact.

Consider a man who owns a home, and has a wife who manages that home very well. She is up in the morning and breakfast is ready, nothing fancy; toast and coffee. She knows his habits, and, so, anything else is just a waste. Saturday; breakfast is a little more filling; pancakes, eggs and bacon, just, so, he can keep better track of what day it is. His lunch is ready; fruit, sandwich and a beverage trussed up in a brown paper bag or lunch box and ready for him to take. She starts dinner; everything is homemade. No ready-made meals for her. She relaxes a bit, perhaps by afternoon she touches up the place. He comes home; kiss, and they have dinner, spend a little time bonding, and then go to bed. Saturday; she is in the supermarket. By Sunday, she is getting her man and herself ready for church, because no one would dare wear blue jeans in church. Yes; we are talking pure 1930s stuff here, but to continue; a crisis takes place: The hot water heater breaks. She calls the repairman, and he shows up to fix it, and soon everything is back to normal. Her man has no clue of the crisis until he reads the repair bill. Of course, a bad man would be upset that she did not wait until he came home or that she got a bad deal on the repair. A good man would just be happy that the home is ticking like a clock when he returns and praises his wife with a kiss and perhaps flowers. Yes; this author understands that the previous is pure fantasy, but that is the reason for this book, to remind you; the man, to express a positive attitude, for that too, is required to keep the home ticking like a clock. Do you happen to be someone who remembers when the shopping centers and grocery stores were closed by six or seven in the evening? Stay at home mothers took care of business during the day, so, that no one had to work long into the night. Monday through Friday, perhaps Saturday was the name of the game, and Sunday was sacred to our well-being. We had a rhythm once in this place called the United States of America, and now, there is just noise, or is this author the only one who sees this?

Now, let us add a few children to the equation. Mother is the bugler, getting everyone up and ready for work and school. Breakfast has meaning. She has laid down the law, and pa has to set the example by sitting down at the breakfast table. The wife feeds the baby, takes the children to school, and then works on the house. Her domestic life is tougher, but she manages accordingly. A crisis occurs: One of the children is hurt, urgently requiring her attention. The child is cared for. Through all of that, she still manages to have dinner;

cooked from scratch, hot and ready at the end of the day. Everything moves like clockwork, and no one is the wiser. In fact, the whole process becomes second nature, and when things become second nature, they are taken for granted.

Time to examine a house with a career woman working outside of the home. She is walking out the door with her husband or worse, she is walking in the house as he is heading out. He has Mondays off, but he works nights, and to boot, he is working twelve hours because his wife makes more money, and he feels that his responsibility is to make more money. She works days with Sunday's off. They may have some form of meaningful interaction sometime in the week. There is food in the refrigerator, but it finds itself in the garbage faster than it does in their stomach. Eating out or readymade meals is the norm. The hot water heater breaks and there are two choices. He can either go with very little sleep, risking life or limb on the job or the repairman can accommodate them by being open on Sunday. Why not, the husband is too tired to go to church anyhow and she; the wife does not want to go by herself. The repairman cannot go because he is working the seventh day to fix things because there is no one home during the week anymore. He will have to find a way to accommodate the Lord on some other day; perhaps. The interesting thing is; that everyone has time for the NFL.

Let's throw the one and only child into that situation, for both of them figured, that they could only afford a single child, though the household income can easily accommodate five. Not to mention that along with the wife's predisposition for having a career outside of the home, she is also not a baby-making machine. Now, he has a choice; lose valuable sleep and taking unscheduled time off or hire a babysitter. Most people are more than likely going to drop the child off at the daycare center. That will happen until preschool and/or kindergarten begins, and *they* will become the babysitter. Yes; let us be honest, that is what our public-school system has become, a state funded daycare. Next; waking up in the middle of the night to feed the baby causes her to lose sleep. In the meantime, she is pushing the child off on the man because she wants to lose the baby-fat, and shopping is a must because she has to dress nice for her job. The man is forced to cut his hours, making him feel like a house mule and the arguments begin. He gets less than 3% of her attention. They take vacation, but the child is a fifth wheel for they chose a vacation spot geared more for couples, even singles instead of families. He and she are party animals, and only know places best suited for lively adults. There is an interesting point to make, and that is, even with the hectic work schedule, life always finds a way; however, nothing is happening because she is taking her inoculation to prevent the disease of pregnancy, for she likes the idea of empowerment. On a conscious level he does not want children either, of which is the one thing they have in common; however, his natural instincts are working subconsciously, for the subconscious mind has a closer connection to God. What is the mandate from God? Be fruitful and multiply, but that is not happening, and the result is conscious/subconscious conflict. Nature is calling, and he is doing that ol' too human thing of controlling nature, and it is driving him crazy. Ask yourself, why is the world going to hell, and you now, have your answer. Eventually he decides to start a relationship with another woman whose availability is more practical on the basis that he sees more of his co-worker than his wife. Not to mention that she makes him feel wanted, always asking him for help. We live in a culture where the *state* forces employers to hire women. This coed workforce interacts more with each other than a man does with his wife. On the other hand: She is growing a close relationship with her boss, and works late hours with him. Deep down she believes that a man should be able to take care of the woman; though she would not admit that openly. Still, the child is a fifth wheel. Neither, interacts with the child. In fact, subconsciously neither one of them wants the child. When a dilemma arises at school, who tends to the child? He doesn't want to lose hours. Therefore, she; whom claims to be actually working two jobs, is tending to her second; *or is she?* Wait; who is doing her job at the company if she tends to the child? If she tells the child that she will be there after work, then is she being a mother? How can a woman be a mother and career employee?

By the fifth grade the child goes Goth, hanging out with troublesome kids; gangs, drugs, guns even prostitution. The point is; the child is seeking how to be a human from someone who has absolutely no experience at being a human; namely other children. Someone's income is paying for therapists, psychologists, court costs. Finally, the couple has had enough; and divorce is the only alternative. When they first met, they just knew they were made for each other. In the courtroom, they are both hoping the other would simply die. The reality is, that people go to divorce court, not to end a bad relationship, but to start a new one. The interesting thing about divorce is that the woman almost always wants custody of the child, but not with the intent of raising the child. Like that fantastic music collection that you spent your entire life building, she knows what it is you like, and knowing you no longer have it, is her way of saying; *Ha!* The one thing that society forgets is that the child is not hers, but yours; the father. Doubt this author's words? Then consider this; ever know a woman who wasn't a packrat? They keep everything. Even buy things without the intent of using any of it, and then stuff it in the place of the forgotten. When it is theirs, they have a difficult time parting with it, and yet a great many women support abortion. Look; if the child is truly theirs, then why do they have no qualms about destroying the child in the womb? Let a man give her a pair of fine shoes, how quickly she tosses them in the trash. He gives her a really nice dress. How fast does she take a pair of scissors to it? Give her a baby, and off to the abortion clinic she goes; however, when a woman has a child on her own via; say, an invitro clinic, or some other method, then the rules suddenly change. *My plumbing works!*

Back on track: The previous example is extremely superficial, but as a man, this author believes that you understand the dilemma of a two-income household, and that it is only beneficial to the woman. You say that you do not have enough money for multiple children, but the reality is you're gearing up for psycho-failure. For celebrities have conditioned you into believing that surrendering instead of fighting to hold a relationship together is the better part of valor. Take a look around in the place where you live. Is your place clean because your wife cleaned it or do you have a maid service? Are you eating homemade food by a hired nutritionist, or do you eat out, or heat up readymade meals, or are you eating homemade food prepared from scratch by your nutritionist-wife? Does your wife wash the clothes or do you have a laundry service? How are your children? Does your wife interact with them? I say children and not child because the modern family seems to have a problem distinguishing between dog and cat and human beings. Do you have more than three cars? Why? You spend, so, much money on yourself, that the children become background noise, so that you do not feel alone. Or are they the topic of discussion at some social gathering? We forget that the whole point for coming together as man and wife is to build a family; to bring children into the world; something meaningful to the community. Children are the focal point of society, and the whole point of existence. Not to prove that a woman's plumbing or your own plumbing works, and then cast the result into a pile of collectibles, but to know that our way of life will continue. If the children are disorderly, delinquent, violent, sexually enthusiastic, ignorant with low morals, foolish, unwilling to absorb useful, beneficial data; then what is to become of the establishment? What will happen to the system established by our forefathers? What would be the point for the continuation of human existence?

So, the reality is, if you make a good wage, it is not impossible for a wife to maintain the home-front as she has always done. In fact, it is practical for her to remain at home as a benefit to the community; to the children. For there is no greater feeling then knowing there is someone you can count on when things do not go right. A child is happier when they know mother is waiting for them at home. Someone who will kiss away all of the bad things that happened in school. Career mothers want everyone to leave them alone, so, that they can rest after a grueling day at the job. Homemakers know that their life is like the human heart. So, as a message to you; the man, take care of your heart, or it will fail, or are you that blind to the goings on around you?

YOUR RESPONSIBILITY

CHAPTER 1

Many of us are unaware that as the male of the species, we have a great responsibility in this world in regards to managing the community; however, where does that community come from? It does not appear out of thin air. It must be created, and two men engaging in fervent lust for one another does not do it. Two women engaging in fervent lust for one another does not result in offspring either. Only when a man has a passionate physical relationship with a woman is there a result. Everything we do, must serve a purpose to our existence; the ground, the sky, the water, plants and animals; all of it exists for a reason; has purpose; is beneficial to the whole of life. Everything we do must have purpose, a reason for doing, not for ourselves, but for the whole or it is nothing and results in nothing.

As the family grows into a tribe, and eventually expands into a nation, disputes between family members will occur, and someone is required to settle those disputes. Every organization requires someone to render a decision to end any, and all stalemates, whether it be government, athletics or religion. Especially in regards to our religions affairs. Without that someone; disputes between parties would never be resolved in a civil manner, and would fester resulting in out-n-out violence. Thus, we would never progress intellectually. For those of you who may site some form of council, panel of judges, or a jury, the result is always the same. It usually comes down to someone breaking the tie. That is why a panel is made up of an odd number of people or at least should be an odd number. Unless a unanimous decision is required; however, unanimity can result in a failure to achieve a resolution; resulting in a failure to progress as a culture.

Before the male can manage a community, there must be some form of educational process put into place. Rules must be set down.

Clarity of purpose must be distinct. Guidelines to purpose must be identified in order to establish a harmonious relationship with the whole. In other words; order is being formed out of the chaos. A natural aspect of the universe. Something that just doesn't happen on its own. Those whom do not accept the existence of a higher power believe that things happen by chance, and yet they send their children to the same schools as those whom do believe in a higher power. They drive down the same paved street, walk into the same buildings. Interesting what order does to a chaotic environment. Makes life comfortable. On the other hand, when the young are allowed to playout their ideas without the intervention of higher authoritative involvement, then you get school shootings. A child requires an adult to form them, shape them, make them work, and if that is the case for a child, then would it not make sense for all of the rest? Somewhere out there is a higher being shaping us, making us work, so, that everything else works. We in the religious community call Him; *God.*

Obedience to God; first and foremost. You must have a nearness to God that does not lead to a self-destructive state of being. Bond with God with every fiber of your being, for everything you are, depends upon it. Without it, life itself has no meaning. There would be no sense of remorse without a belief in God. We would simply be about individuality. Saving ourselves instead of others. The RMS Titanic Syndrome. A situation in which, the number of passengers whom should have survived, actually died due to indifference. Hurricane Katrina, Operation Castle, and most importantly, every planned parenthood in existence. Of course, you the reader can think of others, but the point is, our low regard for human life is proof positive to the kind of thing we are, in contrast to our Judeo-Christian beliefs. By ignoring God, then you do not respect the very sanctity of life, including your marriage or those around you. Thus, your children are meaningless to you. If your children are meaningless then you are worthless on the basis that you have little concern over your immortality, and are not a contributing factor;

having absolutely nothing to offer to the whole in the here and now, or the future for that matter.

We hear, and sometimes listen to certain people who say that the belief in a higher power; in God, is a primitive superstitious notion; however, this author; now, says to you, that not believing in God is a primitive state of mind. Before human beings could form communities and gather knowledge, they first required a belief in something greater than themselves as a means of motivation to a sophisticated state of mind. Resulting in the transposing of those beliefs into a new social activity that we term as religion. A temple of some kind was erected and a community developed around it.

What is religion? A set of guidelines rooted in tradition with a uniform practice designed to inspire people in such a way, that results in the harmony of free will to desire a belief in that, which is greater than themselves. You cannot evolve without that basic concept. Notice that the further we get from that basic fundamental ingredient of civilized conduct, the more prone we become to our social hostilities. Running off pure predatory instinct. There is no specific criteria or identification for true civilized behavior. For even an aristocrat or monarch can behave barbarously. No need for proof of that. Social conduct and morality are not well-governed under man's law. In fact, morality is all, but removed from man's law in this modern culture of the early Twenty-first. Not by means of enacting certain language as such, but more of the interpretation of existing law. Allowing the citizenry to behave as such that is contradictory to our perceptions of civilized, responsible conduct as to maintain an orderly productive environment.

We have forgotten that only religion can set the criteria for what it means to be civilized. Religion is the source of our human values, and we have taken those values for granted; and cast them aside on the basis that we are all grown up, but are we? No man; no government can accomplish that. All a government can do is create more laws as new bad behavior manifests and becomes intolerable to the community. Religion checks bad behavior at the onset, before it can roost. Not that it will prevent it, but that the conductor of it will pause and consider, before conducting an unrecoverable action. Without religious views, a person behaving poorly believes that what they are doing is actually proper or they simply make excuses for their poor behavior. They even convince the masses that their improper behavior is in fact proper behavior, so, that law enforcement cannot properly institute a form of action beneficial to the community. In effect, driving even police officers to commit bad behaviors, and perhaps go just a bit insane to the point of suicide.

Even if we regain our religious values in full, we; the parent, who instruct our children on daily living always seem to forget one crucial piece of information. A detail, so, basic that it has been taken for granted due to the assumption that it is somehow imparted into our very genetic structure; sewn into the very fabric of our DNA. An instruction that can have a profound effect on the daily lives of our entire species. Tell your children to remember to teach their children what you; the father, are teaching them, and without abridgment. As men, we make the mistake of believing that our children already know to pass on instructions and even the methods used to, so. That they somehow, got it during your rudimentary explanation of life. That is a woman-thing; assuming that a person will simply get it or understand what is being said. A foolish notion to abide by. Children; especially; require a detailed explanation of the information in order to; *get it.* Yes, some do appear to get it, but the biggest problem plaguing our society is the assumption that all of us simply; *get it.* Presupposing that we are all the same in regards to daily living, including our very structure, and the components within.

CHAPTER 2

As a father, you cannot simply educate a man-child on the finer points of life. That is a mother's responsibility. You must explain the relationship of the education to daily living. The Church uses an instructional method to help understand scripture from not just a literal sense, but a spiritual sense as well. Under that spiritual sense you have the allegorical; how does it relate to Christ. Moral; how does it relate to my conduct, and the analogical; how does it relate to eternity. This idea can be easily transposed into other aspects

54

of basic education. We apply mathematics to daily living through story problem, and English is simply a necessity in regards to social interaction, but what of the rest? History; especially, requires this method in order for it to have an impact on our daily living. Approach history from a secular viewpoint and you lose the pupil. A proven fact by the author: David Barton. Ask any student what they think of history, which is an oddity when considering that all forms of education is in fact, history, including religion. Yes, that includes math, science and even athletics, but in regards to history in general, without the aspects of religion, it is completely useless. Religion makes life interesting; *period.* Now, science is the true educational conundrum that almost always results in egotistical; arrogant and narcissistic behaviors. Unlike a religion, it does not allow the layman to simply join, and yet, in its own way, it is a religion unto itself. Funny; how with the passing of time, something can metamorphosis into something entirely different then its intended meaning or understanding. Did Judaism begin as a form of science? Mathematics is interwoven into its very meaning. The old scientific methods being overshadowed by the modern unattractive scientific methods; *perhaps.*

Math and science have no true rudimentary guidelines for the average person to follow, but is more of a state of understanding for that, which is always changing. Reason being, they are the other part of the tree of the knowledge of what is good and evil. Consider that evil is not necessarily bad, but more of a state of constant flux resulting in the manifestation of bad. What is good simply balances itself out from the constant change, from that, which we call order. People who follow math and science are simply trying to make orderly that, which is not designed to be order. Chaos is, what it is, so, that we can define what is order.

CHAPTER 3

Why can't a woman teach the relationship? Well; actually, she can; however, it goes to that little process of mental stimuli overload. Females allow themselves to be easily distracted. Not a bad thing, but a necessity due to the more important things in our lives. Namely;

our children; however, since entering what was initially a male orientated higher education sector, women have done absolutely nothing to teach the relationship. They simply upload the details much as a computer programmer might do. That is why women make great grade school teachers. Passing on details as a child would understand it. Then by the junior high level, the data can be used to render some form of ambition. Unfortunately, this cannot happen in our current circumstances. Which, may explain why the system is failing. Since women have been in the education sector for, so, long, they have passed on this rudimentary practice of asymmetrical input to men, whom are now, subsequently insufficient in their instruction of pupils. Without a relationship to something, you are essentially creating a piece of furniture with no quality. Doubt this author's findings? Then try explaining all of the teen suicides in not just this country, but the world as a whole. Sure; people have always ended their own lives, but examine our lifestyle since the rise of the Feminist Movement. Look at our social edifice since the days of the Women's Suffrage Movement. What do you notice? People do not appreciate the difference between what is proper conduct, and what is improper conduct.

What is that relationship? A connection with God through His Church. Our entire way of life must revolve around that very basic concept or our whole existence has absolutely no meaning or even purpose. Doubt this author? Then why is violence the social norm? Once applying religious values to daily living, then all the basic mechanics of living makes sense, leading to purpose, and the violence subsides in all walks of life. Including public education.

As fathers, we are required to mentor our children, especially our boys, in how to be the male of the species under the doctrine set forth by God. Religion, history, and rhetoric are academic principles that should never be abandoned. They are what bind a community together, giving it purpose for maintaining culture. Traditions to better follow, and understand purpose. To assist with that maintenance requires the complexity of musical composition. As a species, the orchestra is an absolute necessity to our existence. The works of

Bach, Beethoven, Mozart, Strauss, Tchaikovsky and all of the other great composers, including modern composers such as John Williams should never be abandoned, and are a must for daily listening and teaching in order to maintain a stable sense of intellectualism and social harmony. Add to that the enforcement of social traditions because once we men find something that works, we stick with it. For *we* do not like to fix things twice.

THE MISSION

CHAPTER 1

Now, that we are aware that we have a mission, let us re-identify the mission parameters. Develop a game plan; what direction your family will go in its existence. Everyone requires a game plan. Coaches, generals, the Church; all have game plans. Yes, and even Adolph Hitler had a game plan. So, you must have a game plan for your family that must correspond with the whole.

Next; you must keep your wife and daughters in line. A daring statement, but reality dictates that gender equality is a myth. Man has dominion over woman based on our perceptions of orderly productive conduct and religious principles. Search the source of your Judeo-Christian beliefs, and what do they say? In the book of Genesis, man gave names to all of the animals in the garden, and he named the woman: *Eve.* God called the man; *Adam,* so, that He would have power over him. That is why we name our children, so, that we may have power over them. Not the kind of power that would be viewed as destructive, but constructive in its means of execution. Protecting those whom we dearly care about, and, yes, sometimes people need protecting; especially from themselves because life can become overly complicated.

You; the man, must keep womanhood as a whole, in its place. Again; putting woman back in her place does not mean demean her in anyway; though, there may be cases when you must cut her balls off. Sometimes people forget who and what they are, and have to be reminded of why they are needed in a specific position. A soldier may fall asleep, while on guard duty. A baseball outfielder maybe too close to the infield. A commercial airliner maybe flying too low. A toddler is running for the busy street, do you stand by and watch or intervene? In the past, women were not put in their place, and now, all of civilization is on the verge of collapse. Men have failed to regulate a woman's desires. As you cannot give a child all that they desire, nor should a woman be granted all that she desires; however, when you give a child all that they desire, they come to expect it; wanting more. No longer earning what they get, but expecting it to be provided, and when they don't get it, they throw a tantrum. Sound familiar? Now, some of you may view this idea as a negative contiguity, but consider this; the universe is not perfect. All things require being put in its place or perhaps a more appreciable term would be a calibration, and someone must perform that calibration. Women have a propensity to do things that go against the grain. They are a different kind of man. She; whom we call woman is more than the sum of her parts, she is magic made flesh. In fact, let us look at her; the female, from a different perspective. Not as a person, but more of a state of mind or perhaps a behavior. She; who is woman is the very definition of sex; the very epitome of sexuality. In layman's terms, she is sex in its truest nature. She is what makes sex what it is. What makes sex work. She is by any other name; sex incarnate. Sex made flesh. The *only* behavior that is an identity. Everything about her is geared around sexuality. This is not a flaw, but a requirement of our species. Without her, sexual attraction is nonexistent, resulting in sexual intercourse becoming null and void. Without her, there is no compassion. Without her, there is no passion. Without her; there is no joy to what is pleasure; a reason to live. Without her, man, has no purpose. Without her, life has no meaning, just hate; hostility; violence, pointless living. Most importantly; without her, there is no procreation; man ceases to exist. She is the reason why advertisers say: *Sex sells,* and then model a scantily clad or even a nude, sumptuous, voluptuous, woman who has been through some form of beautifying method to create an effect? No; an illusion, in order to get your attention, for a woman can be naked even with her clothes on.

Man's very existence is based on the need for her; for sex; however, that need can grow beyond the confines of its purpose. It can be a distraction to the community. We see sex in every aspect of our lives; our modern culture. Whether it be the food that we eat, the clothes that we wear or the church that we pray in, everything is becoming sexualized. Sex is a selfish act, pleasing her own selfish desires. Given a job, and her earnings go towards making herself sexier before all else. Patriotism has no meaning to her. Tradition is a nuisance, and the status quo is a methodology requiring constant change, no matter how well it works. Sex likes to contradict our understanding of what is norm to suit her needs. One example of this is that sex can dress as provocatively as she wants as a means of expression, but a man cannot express his opinion on the abhorrent sexual display? Sex will refuse to be fruitful. Sex will even defy God in pursuit of her own personal gains. Even inventing a god as a means to an end. This has all come about in our current social standing because we; the man, have failed to perform a social calibration. In fact, it is way overdue.

What have we done with sex in the past fifty years? We have sex in our legislature, workforce, police departments, fire departments, and yes, even the military, and our schools and universities. We have sex in the judicial system. Journalistic community, and, yes, even in our places of worship. Parents, specifically mothers, allow their sons to have sex in their home. NASA has sex on all levels without consideration of its destructive force. It is easy to forget just how addictive sex can be in regards to a mistake in judgment. Something to consider in the aeronautics and space industry when conducting an inspection of the hardware or programming a computer to avoid the misfire of a thruster when landing a probe on Mars. A NASA employee must ask himself; *is my mind on the work or on sex sitting next to me?*

Doubt this author's prior assessment? Let's do a comparative analysis of our social construct for the past 50 years. What do we have? To be physically beautiful, a person must act selfishly to achieve a standard of living that pleases no one but, themselves. Fathers are no longer regulating their daughter's wants and needs. Therefore, what happens when a daughter strikes out on her own? She becomes feral. No longer a part of a family; however, she may bond with others, but not of a kind possessing true warm feelings. Feral females have always existed, but are generally ignored in regards to their movements, but not their presence. As with defiant boys; overly accommodating parents evolve their lifestyle around illogical-logic. For a daughter it is far worse, due to the feminine emotional complex. She changes into something unrecognizable. Sexual intercourse becomes a necessity, and she will more than likely be addicted to drugs, especially marijuana. She only gets into trouble on her terms. Social grace has no meaning, and politeness is nonexistent. The oddity is, though she is behaving very unladylike, we still treat her as such. This author believes that modern women call that; *empowerment.* Now, look at the effect the independent woman is having on our overall social construct. We are a far more selfish culture by nature in this modern age of the early Twenty-first than we have ever been since the formation of the country. This is not to say that men are not selfish, but that when a man goes too far, other men will come down on him; however, with a woman, legality becomes an issue in order to protect her apparent *rights.* Allowing those *rights* to flourish beyond sustainable sociological norms. *I am beautiful. I feel beautiful, but keep your comments to yourself because I am not in the mood.* To cope with her fluctuating emotional state of mind, selfishness is now, running completely out of control on all levels, including the Church, and if you doubt that little conclusion, then what of all the school shootings? Promoting marijuana, faultless lawsuits, same sex marriage, prochoice. All of the MDK is based on the desires of a selfish culture.

Sex will use cunning and deceit to keep the truth from you. What is the truth? That sex went through a metamorphosis. Sex is no longer fresh and new, but fruit that has been bitten into, and she has turned that part of herself away from your eyes. Made the apple look red and ripe with a makeover, but what you do not see is the huge bite taken out of her. Sex is the fine cake with a finger-smear across the layer of frosting all the way down to the bread, and she has filled herself in with glitter. Only an unblemished cake looks good at the party; however, when the frosting is smeared then everyone wants to touch it or leave it alone. Sex is a car with 200,000 miles, and a new paint-job. You've worked hard for a new car, so, why do you settle for a used one that has had many repairs? When you go to the supermarket, do you spend your money on the package that is already open? Sex, in today's world is an uncaring addiction that requires feeding. A vampire seeking that, which makes you; the male, strong. Taking your manhood and giving you nothing in return. Sex uses the only asset left to her to attract a victim, and that is her physical attributes. Her clothes exemplify her frame of mind. So, treacherous is sex; that she even allows her offspring to dress and behave as she. What kind of a creature is sex? A creature, so, dangerous that she could bring an end to all life on earth. It is a thing to be kept locked up for the good of the community, for the continuation of civilization.

For years we have used the word addiction to describe a state of mind that can be anything, and a whole lot of things, depending upon the strength of the brain itself; however, what we do not have is a grasp of what an addiction is from a physical sense. Oh, sure, we think we do, like the idea of love: We say we know what it is, but do we really? Perhaps a more appreciable term would be a psychological hunger. From that point of view, then how would we imagine addiction?

CHAPTER 2

Let us put addiction into a more familiar comparison model. Think of your brain as the North American Continent way back before the invention of water. Just a simple body of land made up of rock and dirt. This author thinks you get the picture. Then one day, water appears. A bunch of little streams, a few brooks, even a spring. Now, something gets your interest; ice cream, a funny cartoon, playing with toys, and the few streams get just a little bigger. As you get older other things get your interest; video games, sports, certain academics are as other streams, springs and brooks that join in forming a few small rivers. All repetitive actions are an addiction. Eventually, what you will get is the overall addiction resulting in a Mississippi River carving its way through the barren wilderness; wide and deep. No matter what we do with that water, it will always find its way to the Mississippi because it just grabs us. We must experience it.

Unfortunately, when we think of an addiction we limit ourselves to more familiar categories such as drugs, alcohol, and cigarettes; however, there is positive addiction and negative addiction. The difference between the two depends upon the impact it has on the environment. Based strictly upon this author's opinion; a negative addiction is a self-gratifying praxis. We love what it does to our person, and we seek it like a moth to flame. You are overweight? Then its food praxis. The smell triggers you, and all of the waters flow to the Mississippi. Lesser waters are the other aspects of life. Religious views? If you have them. Activities such as sports? If you have them. Some form of visual media, video gaming; all of it pales in comparison to your need for a piece of spicy chicken, smothered burrito or a large pot of spaghetti. Sure, you're a gamer, but you will find a way to stuff your face. Yes; you are dedicated to your office job, but you will find a way to stuff your face. A lot of us are addicted to the television. Specifically, certain television shows. No matter what, we will set aside everything to watch every episode, even take vacation from our jobs to watch the season on streaming media. Got a chance to see a beautiful sunset; *can't do it. My favorite television show is on.* Sex is another overlooked addiction. Whatever it is you do, you are going to get a fix, whether it be a living being or imagery; however, the difference with sex is that it is a living physical identity that is thrust into your face daily. Like a person tying you to a chair and forcing a needle into your arm. Some days you do not want it; however, you do not have a choice. There is an interesting point about woman of which, we men take for granted; and that is, when she reaches maximum arousal, she becomes the most powerful force on the face of the earth. It is difficult to describe what woman feels. The buildup of urges within the abdomen. That tingling sensation within certain parts of the mind. Sure; we attribute those sensations to raging hormones; horniness, even nymphomania, but realistically it is, so, much more than that. We are a people whom exist in a sex crazed culture. Therefore, when a woman's body begins to stir, it is a selfish need. She is making herself available for submission. Shutting down all aspects of independence, reason and logic. She is opening herself up to be controlled; adapting herself to another; presumably a male. It is a beautiful moment for her to be in that condition, but to the wrong man, it is an atrocity. The urge to physically interact with someone is incredibly overwhelming. What she feels is every known drug in existence swimming through her veins, and when a parent does not interact with her; specifically, her father, those urges will overwhelm her. She will do whatever it takes to sooth the savage beast within.

A woman's emotional state of mind is, so, potent at times that a man's only resistance is to simply get away from it. Get away from her, to include even a wife because dealing with the jumble of conflicting emotions; the whole feminine emotional complex as a whole, can quite literally drive a man crazy. There is no uniformity to the female frame of mind. There is no true understanding of her mental faculties. No satisfying a turbulent mind. Listening to a guy talk on and on is one thing; however, when a woman's voice comes into the picture; pleasing or annoying, withstanding, it is the wail of the banshee. Ever experience sudden anger and feelings of hostility for no reason? Think back; you were more than likely under the influence of an emotional female.

Then you have some addictions that have been thrust upon us as an identity, such as homosexuality. Then the need becomes, so, great that we learn to function with it to the point where it becomes second nature, such as an addiction to food, and thus we decide to associate it with an identity. Yes; there are other negative addictions out there, and you can just plug them right into the river model accordingly.

63

What we ignore are the addictions that would have a positive impact on our social welfare; such as being a workaholic. Yes; crazy, but consider that a person who is dedicated to a job; getting the product to market, so, that others may enjoy it. Making sure the numbers add up for payroll, so, that people can purchase their needs. Keeping the motor running, so, that the city has electricity. Those sorts of things are viewed with negativity; however, what makes them negative is the lack of appreciation from the company. You just loaded the truck in record time, and didn't make a single mistake. The supervisor says; *thanks,* but is that what you are looking for? A simple thanks? Works for some; perhaps; however, what you are looking for is something that is a little more tangible. Not necessarily money, but for the people whom will benefit from your hard work and dedication to know what you have done. You want to be the rock-star of your area of expertise. You want your customers to know that you brought joy into their lives because the alternative is bitterness. Go into a supermarket and your favorite product isn't stocked. Go to the movies and seating for the summer blockbuster is delayed due to a trashed theater. Expecting an important package? Where is it? Unlike that big celebrity we hear about in broadcast media; that one guy who stocked the product, got the theater ready on time, got the important package to its destination on schedule, gets no public recognition. When people know that you are the guy that made a difference, the parameters for work ethics change, and we are no longer concerned about the supervisor's pettily; *thanks.* You know that you made a difference in somebody's life, and that is enough for you.

Then you have addictions to horticulture; making an area look pleasing to the eye. Then of course, there are those of this modern era whom are addicted to limiting their carbon footprint.

What about those practices that could be the Mississippi, such as our religious obligations, but are treated more like the Colorado, downstream from the Hoover Damn at the Gulf of California? We blatantly divert the flow from there. Christian priests and Jewish rabbis have an addiction to their profession, though sometimes it can be swallowed by another river, but we would like to think that their Mississippi is flowing accordingly. On the other hand, what about the average Christian or Jewish person? What kind of river flows through their wilderness? Is it a stream? Is it a stream filled with trash? Is it the Hudson River; big and deep, but not as-long-as the Mississippi, or as the Los Angeles River; a torrid in the rainy season? Interesting how the very thing that keeps us civilized is the most neglected brain process of all.

CHAPTER 3

Now, regarding this author's previous notation regarding the imperfections of the universe; yes, that includes us; the male, and that is identifying, and regulating imperfection. That is the purpose of religion. Without religion, the calibrator can also fallout of calibration. Therefore, man must calibrate himself on a regular basis. What is the frequency of that calibration? Daily; with a more comprehensive calibration on the seventh day of the week. This more comprehensive calibration is conducted by someone who has made religion a profession. Now, of course we know that even those who have made religion a profession can fall out of calibration from time-to-time. So, who calibrates those whom have made religion a profession? Under Catholic guidelines, it is quite clear; from priest to Pope. Now, what about the Pope? Contrary to what you; the reader may think you know, or have even heard or perhaps read; though Popes have revealed flaws, Church Doctrine remains unchanged, which means that the Christ installed certain safeguards in the Church's overall architecture to prevent her from defectiveness. Perhaps that is why the Christ refers to the Church as His bride; a living entity, for she is a self-calibrating apparatus immune from social corruption. It would be next to impossible for a person to make a drastic change in Church Dogma. Furthermore; anyone professing that they have been sent to start another religion all together, or simply another Christian church because the old one is flawed would be in effect; a false profit due to these Christ-installed safeguards.

So, out of all of the religious entities in the world, why use the Catholic Church as the example? She has had two thousand years to refine herself. Not to mention that there is a clear and definite organization of intellectual progression. Oddly, now, that the Church has reached its pinnacle of evolution, you; the Catholic, refuse to acknowledge it, and those who have an opportunity to become a part of it, refuse it based on misconceptions and hearsay by; startlingly enough; Catholics themselves and journalists. Yes, she has been through a few ordeals on her path to refinement. Higher lifeforms begin as juveniles. They learn to understand themselves through mistakes, and over time, grow into something wonderful. In reality, the only way for us to learn is from our mistakes, and what she; the Church has done is establish a precedence for practitioners to follow, so, that future generations would not make the same mistakes as their predecessors. Countries such as the United Kingdom chose to ignore this valuable tool, as we too, in the United States of America are slowly ignoring it, and starting to slip back to a repetitive state of behavior. The Church requires her flock to sustain her. As a side note: This cannot be done by Catholic families of one or two children.

Now, the following too, will be viewed with great distain, but it must be said. Woman cannot share in the calibration process of man on the basis that she already has a mission of her own. Also, her propensity for change makes the very notion of calibration untenable. Females see life from a whole different perspective then that of the male, and should not be allowed in certain procedures regarding males. For example; the Constitution of the United States of America was designed by males to regulate male behavior, and even his desires. In other words, laws cannot reasonably accommodate both genders on the basis that it would become too complicated for anyone to remember, let alone, comprehend. The whole point for establishing laws, is, so, that people will *know them,* in order to obey them. All laws should be as our forefathers intended them to be; simple and to the point, so, that all people can have a rudimentary understanding of how to facilitate a smoother social interaction. If laws become too intricate, then the end result can only be guesswork and speculation

66

when determining social influence. In other words; if you do not understand the law, then how can you obey the law? That is until getting caught breaking the law and claiming ignorance, which is more than likely the truth, due to the complexity of our legal system. That is why in the past, females had to follow certain codes of conduct, regardless of social status due to the expectations of camaraderie and companionship. The law could not be applied to them due to adolescent interaction. Children do not understand social affairs and require guidance. To apply guidance, rules must be broken to align the mind. Besides, women should not have rights. They already have too many responsibilities.

Another point to consider is that laws should not work differently based on social status. Either they work the same for everyone, or they do not work at all. That is why we the people should not show favoritism towards a celebrity. In fact, they; of all people, should be held to a higher standard, and thus have a greater punishment outside of monetary value. They should be punished harder than the average person on the basis that they have such a profound influence on the general public. You; the average person, gave them their power; therefore, they have a certain responsibility that is not unlike a politician or monarch. The promise they make to the community is what all people seeking employment make; and that is to do their very best at what they are asked to do. You have given them power and your money in much the same way that a monarch acquires money. You want them to represent the best in you. You want them to lead you. So, do not give them a free pass for bad behavior because the money that you made could have helped you out of your bad situations; and instead, you chose to give it to them; the celebrity, and what do they do with your hard-earned money? Use it to conduct mischievous activities.

CHAPTER 4

Of course, there are those who will say that this author's words are those of a crazy man; and perhaps this author is crazy; however, this author is also a product of a lost culture. We listen to those who make comments such as; *he is crazy,* of which they apply no relevant explanation as to what it is that makes him crazy. This is something we must turn away from. Should someone say; *he is crazy,* or that; *he does not know what he is talking about.* Then counter them by asking; *how, so?* Oh, and please do not let them off with a; *because,* and have it at that, because, *because* stunts growth, retards evolution, prevents humanity from understanding itself. An explanation should always follow; *because.* You require a comprehensive counter explanation in order to make an informed decision, for both sides are entitled to a voice on the matter. Something journalists have clearly forgotten.

Ever notice a conversation where someone suggests an idea, but then someone else says; *that's stupid,* and you; the spectator, are waiting for an explanation as to why it is; *stupid,* but none is given? Notice how; *stupid* was the last word you heard, and, so, you try to manufacture a reason of why it's *stupid,* and just run with it forever and ever? That's because the person whom said it was *stupid* is someone who is more credible; part of the click, or is a close friend or relative and must know something. The reality is, the source of the idea is usually the best alternative in most situations, but you choose to avoid it. Guess what? After you have wasted millions of man-seconds realizing the idea was not *stupid,* the person whom actually said it was *stupid* repackages the *stupid* and reintroduces it as their own idea and takes all of the credit because they actually wanted to keep everyone's attention on themselves. People like that do not share power. They do not give praise to those with great ideas, and are the very embodiment of narcissism. Now, there is a rub to the whole scheme. The people who sided with that person whom said it was, *stupid,* shut out the original idealist when they try to regain credit for the idea, saying; *no; your way was different,* or; *she or he explained it better.* In the long run, when it becomes necessary to make adjustments, they can only make guesses. Even trying to hijack potential improvements offered by others, making amuck of something that could have been beneficial, and yet, no one seems to be bothered because, again, the thief has a certain persona that makes them, so, likeable. Allowing them to get away with murder. The reality is, those kinds of people are what this author calls; Distractive Hacks, and are extremely dangerous, and should be identified quickly. They distract; which is not difficult when considering that they are already popular with the crowd; until the time avails itself to run with the hijacked idea. Their kind make poor role models and leaders.

Then again, why is the man, or perhaps more accurately, the male of the species the calibrator? Males incorporate themselves into a community. Our initial laws were designed for the male due to our propensity for being loners, wanderers, individualist by nature. We gather knowledge and experience from varying sources to build our natural instincts for survival. Making us aggressive. Therefore, there must be some form of regulation for aggressive behavior as a means of a proper civil interaction in a communal environment. We men require rules to avoid misunderstandings; resulting in losing sight of why we are even socializing. We socialize out of fear for that thing called loneliness. When loneliness dominates, there can be no exchange of useful information, and the species evolves into a counterproductive state of existence.

CHAPTER 5

Let's go into a dark aspect of male/female interaction, and that is; he; the overbearing male, who comes down hard on his wife. Whom just blows up, when perceiving an apparent error on her part, that, from his point of view, seemed reasonably academic, without considering the difficulties she had to contend with in the home. The workingman, in this case, is an arrogant, career orientated male, who thinks that his job, is, so, demanding, that housework is nothing more than menial labor. Taking for granted the subtleties that makes for a smooth operation of any scheme. That squirt of grease, drop of water, or tightening of a nut. How unlikely it may seem that such a trivial thing would have such an influence on the greater mechanism. How easily forgotten that one person whom keeps the world from utter ruin.

The irony is, that whatever it was that required attention, was more than likely something he should have taken care of, to begin with, but instead he chose to ignore it, due to being involved with another woman; perhaps, or simply hanging out at a bar or a club or conducting some other form of activity that kept him from his domestic duties. Duties that should have included; of course, compassion towards his wife. She became neglected; denied the simple pleasures that motivates her towards her daily household routine. A disruption in finances interferes with pleasurable affairs outside of the home, and he becomes angry?

The reason behind the neglect is more than likely, the narrow mindedness of when the man was a child. Living at home with his parents; he probably took out the trash, perhaps loaded the dishwasher, and that was the extent of his perceptions of domestic responsibility. He probably didn't even keep his bedroom clean because it was irrelevant to him; therefore, his mother did that for him. His mother also served him his food, and, so, he came to expect these things of woman. In fact, he more than likely did not see his mother with great importance, except as nothing more than a servant, and even a source of revenue. Oh, sure he loves his mother, but does he respect her? Which explains his treatment of the feminine community as a whole. Now, the little boy within the man is using his wife in lieu of his mother.

Realistically, she who is wife never makes mistakes when it comes to maintaining the home; *period.* We the species of man, have a bad habit; perhaps the worst habit in the human condition; and that is to assume that everyone understands what life is all about. Sees life in pretty much the same way. Yes; perhaps we understand the key aspects of life; however, the next person may not understand. That is how life itself works. Some people see things better than others or perhaps better explained as; some people know, and some people are taught. Note: Those *things* can be anything; how a project comes together; how a mechanism works; the principles, rules and past practice of governing a people, even the simplicities of what is authority's relationship in regards to the understanding of power. This is what this author calls an act of God. A person with an apparent gifted ability is introduced into the social medium, to give

70

the human race a little intellectual, and even artistic refreshment. The irony is, that God does not discriminate in regards to where that prodigy will come into being, on the basis that He randomized existence. Consider how many gifts were born in what some would perceive as less than desirable circumstances, and was misunderstood as a freak of nature; a fluke, and simply put away. In any event, possessing a clearer perception for the complexities of life is no excuse for losing one's temper. That is why religious entities; specifically, the Church, places so, much emphasis on patience and understanding. That is the key to getting through any dilemma: *Patience.* Yes, this author is aware that it's easier said than done; however, patience is something that must be practiced not attempted at leisure because contrary to what some may say or think; life is not about one's self, but those around you. As the male; you must push yourself beyond reasonable, physical and psychological expectations to ensure social harmony with those around you, most notably your wife for she guards your immortality. A man's obligation is to the community, and the woman. A woman's obligation is to the man only; though she feels a need to contribute to the community as well. For those of you whom are wondering about the children. They come from her man, and, so, they fall under the pretense of a woman's obligation to her man. Women commune, and we men bring semblance to the community, so, that she can feel better protected, not from predators; which no doubt includes the man himself, but from the elements, from those things that she does not like; the rodent, the insect and yes, the serpent. Yes; she; the woman is the most valuable asset to the community, while children are the most valuable asset in the community. Without her, nothing is done, and yet, she best serves the community through her man. This is how marriage works. Not two people, three, or even six, or ten, but one person made up of three parts; male, female and God.

In regards to the overbearing male: When he comes across a dominating female, it will be a shock to him, and he will commit to an affair. For he has never been involved with a strong woman, and it is an unusual experience to him. Then before he knows it, his fortune is gone. His trophy wife will put him out to pasture, via a divorce, and he will learn the hard way that it is better to have a submissive woman, then to be submissive to a woman.

Let us make a self-examination of a man's responsibility to his wife. Number one, and this is the most important thing you must always remember, is to serve she; who is your wife, faithfully and unquestionably. You; the man, are a king, and as the king, your responsibility is to serve, not to be served, and that idea should apply to monarchies as well. By serving your wife, she in turn respects, and believes in you, and will do anything you ask of her. You are the captain of the ship, the policeman, the fireman, and the soldier. Your job is to serve and to protect. Many Christians follow the Christ; serving the people around them, and He is the greatest king. Notice that this author did not say, all Christians. Not all Christians respect the Christ. If they did; then committing a sin would not come, so, easily to them. Number two; you are required to keep her in high spirits, for depression is a very real thing for her, and so, you must make her feel alive. As alive as she did when she was a child, even more, so. Allow her to feed off your energy, gorge herself as a newborn on breastmilk. Remember, she is of earth, and thus always hungry for the energy of heaven. That is what we are; the breath of life, given to us by God in the beginning. She is the transition of life from heaven to earth. Again, she provides the substance for the breath to adhere to; vital to our needs in this realm. The happier she is, the greater her chances are for producing healthier offspring. Odd how first-borns seem happiest, while subsequent children seem more troubled; *coincidence?* Something as simple as a walk in the park can do wonders for she; who is your wife. Thirdly; you must be respectful of your wife, for she is the centerpiece of your house. She represents all that you have built. A stable foundation for your immortality to thrive upon. If she is trash to you, then your immortality becomes valueless.

A man who beats his wife and/or child is not a father, but a master. Do not mistake beatings for spankings in regards to children. A slave driver beats his slaves. A father encourages his loved-ones by explaining what they did wrong and providing them with alternatives to avoid future errors. A man who beats his wife needs a career change; say, at the forefront of a battlefield where his aggression will benefit the country as a whole. Remember, you; the man asked her to be your wife. Therefore, you can only blame yourself for her behavior. In fact, the problem is almost always your fault, due to your desire for a *sexier* woman. Work with what you have, for should you hit rock bottom, you would even settle for a mad man to comfort you rather than to be alone.

Be aware that since we have not put woman back in her place, it is having an adverse effect on our culture, and on herself. She is confused, going crazy, committing suicide. She is hurting inside, she is in pain, she is waiting for us; the man to do what we are supposed to do, and that is to simply tell her; *no*. Something we have been failing to do since the opening pages of Genesis.

Another mission parameter that is necessary for the survival of our species, is perhaps the most confusing parameter of them all, and that is, you as the man are required to serve your fellow man. Specifically, the female of the species. You should be prepared to give your very life, if need be, to help another, whom you do not know. For it is easy to give your life for someone you do know; especially if they are near and dear; a wife or child or close friend or relative. The real pinch comes when you have to die, for even an enemy. That is why a woman should be prepared to give her life for the child in the womb, whom she does not know. The ultimate act of selflessness, and a sign of true civilized behavior.

Do not attempt to be a bachelor, unless your intent is to be celibate and presumably serve God. Contrary to popular belief, you cannot serve God, and be a sexual deviant. Being single to engage in sexual intercourse with every woman on the face of the earth is unnatural, immature, inhuman and socially irresponsible. How can you be a calibrator if you are the one contributing to the social disruption? Being single and celibate to serve God is a supernatural act. You;

the Christian male, have purpose, and that purpose is to serve the Christ. You serve the Christ, by serving your fellow man, and yes; that includes woman. You serve woman by giving her what she needs, not what she wants, and what she wants is a sense of strength, confidence and social fidelity.

The last mission parameter is the establishment of laws that would accommodate freewill. The idea of freewill is a vital part of us. Without it, we are nothing. Yes, even homosexuals have a right to practice their behavior under the guise of freewill, but they do not have a right to impose their behavior on others through means of a sympathetic judiciary system bent on circumventing the very notion of what is identity and what is behavior. Freewill is a natural state of being, given to us from God. It allows us to be self-aware, but not sentient. Contrary to what the scientific community might say, we are not born sentient. Do sentient beings, kill each other for the sheer act of killing? Do sentient beings, deny the rights of others? Do sentient beings, horde valuables? Do sentient beings, pervert the flesh? Do sentient beings, systematically destroy the environment? No; sentience is a complex state of being that can only be achieved through a careful practice of patience, obedience and tolerance.

CHAPTER 6

Now, for the woman's mission: The man is the sperm, and the woman is the egg. As-long-as the two are separate, they are two different beings; however, when the sperm impregnates the egg then you have something else. Woman is now, a mother. Within her, is a creation from God through the man, dependent on her for survival in this realm of existence.

Human life does not begin at the formation of the fetus. It does not begin at birth. Life begins with the intent of sexual intercourse. The intent thereof when attracted by the feminine form. Your mind may be thinking in one direction; however, the mechanism has a misunderstood attribute, and that is; preservation of the species. Consider that before the construction of a thing, its design begins, where? Mathematics, science, even war begins, where? Ask an artist where their creation began. Before a person picks up a pencil, pen, paintbrush or stylus, he or she may not create a masterpiece; however, the overall imagination; the very thought of the act begins the art.

The male carries the breath of life given to him by God, and the female is the substance for which, the breath can adhere to in order for the human species to exist in this physical realm, and thus becomes subject to natural law. This is woman's true career, not trying to be something else. When her attention moves away from this process, childhood development becomes faulty. The children run wild. We the man are capable of being mothers in crisis, but social compassion would suffer. As a child needs a mother, a woman needs a man. Without this order, problems manifest themselves in the community. This is why premarital sexual intercourse is frowned upon by the Church, for it is an act based on instinct. Animal behavior, instead of a reasonable level of self-conscious, self-control and logic. Again, there is an order to all things. Break that order, and the process fails every time.

To make clear certain conditions and understandings of life, this author will remind prochoice advocates that the person within the woman is not the woman, for if it were the woman, then she would not require a man to begin the process of mitosis. This is the selfish contradiction of feminist thinking. That a woman is exclusive in the creation of life, and thus giving her the right to terminate a living presence. That life within the womb is the construct of both a male and herself; for her to have the exclusive right to terminate that new human being is not only an offense against God, but an offense against the very moral fabric of the Constitution of the United States of America. Termination without representation. Even a person who is not a U.S. citizen is entitled to legal-council, and yet, a U.S. citizen within the womb is denied? Well, if that is the case, then under the same rule, a mother would have the right to terminate a child at any stage of existence outside of the womb as well. Obviously, that would not happen based on the *state's* interpretation of law.

Reasonably speaking, no person; male or female has a right to terminate a process begun by God. Exclusivity in regards to life is strictly of God's domain. Whether you believe that or not is of no consequence. Why is that? The action of what we perceive as existence has been put into play. You live, and, so, the coming of new life should have that same opportunity. Killing another is the worst kind of prejudice in existence. Especially in cases of capital punishment. A maturating person, whether unaware or simply refused happiness has the right to the pursuit of a fruitful life under the terms set forth by the XIV Amendment to the Bill of Rights. No person has a right to deny another person that right, whether that situation is accidental or deliberate.

Consider; as the developing human is dependent upon the woman for survival, so, too does the newly emerged human from the womb depend upon the woman. Additionally, the developing child within the womb can be easily looked upon as a feeding; nursing being who is dependent on another for life. A process that continues outside of the womb, but simply at a different stage of development. *What?* Did we forget that human development does not cease at birth? The mother continues nursing the child. Without technology, how does the infant obtain nourishment? Yes, there are means; however, we are a people dependent on the familiar, are we truly capable of rediscovering the basics to life? Outside of the womb the child latches onto the mother's breast for nourishment; again, another stage of development. You see; as we age we are supposed to ween ourselves from the need for food. Within the womb; we gorge ourselves on the mother's sustenance to sustain ourselves. This is the source of the selflessness of woman. Once we emerge from her body, food is not a constant requirement. As we get older, the refining process improves depending upon our level of activity. Once the physical growing process stops, we should be cutting back even further, but are we? Gluttony is a very real thing in our modern culture, and though we make excuses, the reality is, food is readily available and, so, we pig out, but that subject is for another discussion.

CHAPTER 7

Take note of the importance of uploading data to the developing child's brain. Yes; a child can still be murdered if not properly educated. Ignorance is the biggest killer of man, and we ignore it like the air we breathe. Funny how we ignore oxygen until we do not have it. Is that not the same of knowledge? The reason human children take, so, long to reach adulthood is because the growing process involves a mental state of mind as-well-as a physical state. That is what makes us; the human being; an advanced life form. They both work in conjunction with one another because man is, so, dangerous. We, of the human species, live by more than instinct alone, but of logic as well, and for instinct and logic to work in concert, religion must be incorporated into the arrangement, so, as not to live by guesswork and speculation alone. Sound familiar?

Let us look at an example of the result of life. A woman allows a suitor to copulate with her, and he decides to end the relationship. Discovering that she is pregnant, she decides to do what is proper, and not remove the healthy tissue from the womb and give birth to a child. She gets a job, handing off the newborn to whomever she can, in order to take care of the child whom she is not taking care of. The child is learning the trials of life from a dozen or, so, different sources who are providing absolutely no result, but the child is still a good kid. Eventually, the child makes use of nothing, and the key ingredient of nothing is that it's cool to engage in premarital sexual intercourse with as many girls as possible, or to explore homosexual tendencies. He sees all of the girls and women wearing form-fitting clothes and does not understand why he is stimulated when looking at them. There is no one to tell him that it is a natural reaction for him to be turned on by the feminine form, and, so, he copes with it as-best-as possible. There is church on Sunday, but he does not understand, especially when mother, whom is not being a mother, chooses to go seldomly. When he is introduced to debauchery, for some strange reason those unusual feelings he has when looking at the feminine form briefly subsides. So, he sees the blatant display of the feminine form in body melding attire, on the television, at the movies, in the magazines, the internet, in his everyday life, and he starts pursuing females like a wild beast. They dress as though wanting to be engaged in sexual intercourse, so, apparently that is what they want. Eventually, he becomes licentious. Then one day he meets a fabulous young woman, gets married, and all is well, but due to gaps in his development, he pursues new relationships, for he does not understand the purpose of marriage; he does not understand what it means to be man. From his point of view, it is normal to be a philanderer due to the majority of his education coming from Hollywood, and the only thing coming out of Hollywood are stories about men who carry on affairs, not to mention that the actors and actresses do the same off screen also. His wife finds out, and instead of trying to get at the root of the problem, she simply divorces him because; again, that is what Hollywood celebrities do, both on, and off screen. Of course, if his mother had simply executed him in the womb, the whole ordeal could have been avoided all together, but consider that it was not the child who was at fault, but we do not view it as such. Choice is always the determining factor in any situation. Haste, poor time management principles and desperation, usually have an effect on choice.

LEADERSHIP

CHAPTER 1

In a world of social responsibility, there is leadership, and then there is motherhood. A leader is one with certain responsibilities that result in the success of an objective; however, what we want to focus on is the key aspects of leadership, and that is the necessity to place another in harm's way. Now, many of you reading this are thinking along military lines in regards to harm's way, forgetting that firefighters, paramedics, oil riggers, construction workers, miners, deep sea fisherman, certain athletics, etcetera, etcetera, etcetera, even a postal worker must face dangers, never forgetting, the biggest risk takers, and that is those in law enforcement. No matter the case, there is always someone who must compel others to face that danger.

In regards to motherhood, we again acknowledge the many responsibilities associated with being as such, but the crucial aspect of motherhood is to keep another from going into harm's way, and to even go as-far-as to sacrifice one's self in the process if necessary. That is why the male of the species is capable of being both leader and mother. Females think they are capable of this, but in fact they rarely face a hardship to the breaking point, and then face it repeatedly. That is because her hardship is to be a helper to the breaking point. Now, there are males who think they can assume the role of helper, but what they do not realize is that they are not following along the proper guidelines set down by nature. We are self-aware, and thus we know that sometimes we must compel ourselves to do what is right for the whole of the organism, no matter our feelings. If we do not commit to a selfless act, then the organism becomes corrupt and useless. Another point to consider are those females who are quick to sacrifice others for their personal benefit. Mean girls are a very real thing in our modern culture.

CHAPTER 2

Motherhood by default possesses certain leadership qualities, but is a characteristic designed to provide comfort, appeasement and compassion. Applying a happy medium for certain scenarios without a proper verdict in order to appease both sides, that may result in no true resolution. A mother tries to give all that she can; however, there are times when outright leadership must be applied in order to protect another from harm. A leader is not required to; and more than likely will not enable distinct motherly traits. There are simply moments when indifference is required to achieve a goal. An excellent leader has a unique trait of understanding humility, fidelity and dignity. Expressing cold fire at the proper moment, and yet allowing warmth when necessary, but is not truly motherly in any way.

What about fatherhood? It is a state of mind incorporating key aspects of motherhood and leadership into a single framework; however, fatherhood is not a full-time management system as is motherhood. Presence; though not frequent, is still necessary for the betterment of the family. A father installs restrictions and expects those restrictions to be adhered to accordingly. While at the same time, fathers must be yielding and adaptive in order to examine new ideas and determine their viability to their overall goals, and the goals of the community; and if necessary explain why the idea is, or is not viable. That is why fathers can also be mothers; however, mothers cannot be fathers, though some may perceive otherwise. That goes back to that whole notion of pushing oneself to the breaking point, and then some. Motherhood is a full-time responsibility on the basis that a segment of the population must have a point of understanding that is easily perceptible in order to begin a stepping off point for the interaction with others. A male must perform double duty in that regard, and still perform his task as father. No woman can do this.

Think of a mother as more of a catch-net for trapeze artists. A child goes through a routine; matters not if it makes sense, they are a child, and mother gives her full attention to the child. Note: that child, can also be you; the man, for we too on occasion place ourselves in precarious situations without realizing it. Now, the catch-net is always there, ready to protect, while the child goes about their exploration of the world, clueless of danger; however, if the catch-net perceives itself as something else, then confusion on the part of the child, sets in. She looks like a catch-net, sounds like a catch-net, and even feels like a catch-net, but then she pretends to be something else. The result is that the child becomes unsure of themselves. The rules of *exception* start to come into play unexpectedly. Some young minds are unable to perceive exceptions. Dealing with the basic account of life is difficult enough without the contributions of exceptions. In other words, you install exceptions as a means of confusion. Society places too much on a child's plate too soon on the basis that a segment of the population fancies the idea of alienating themselves from the status quo. We forget that we establish social familiarity for the benefit of our children, not for our selfish intent. The Flower Power Movement was the death knell in that understanding. Perhaps it is necessary to reinstitute pre-sixties social values and guidelines before we find ourselves in a state of complete social dysfunction and mental disorder.

CHAPTER 3

Yes; of course, there are some young ones whom are precocious and gifted, but to say they have an understanding of life would be reckless and irresponsible. We as a species easily forget that we must interact with one another, and that requires the talents of a mother. It takes every aspect of the human condition to carry out the act of motherhood. When dealing with a young mind, a person cannot carry on with other things that have no bearing with being a mother. Presence is crucial in a newborn's life. No person wants to be left alone, and yet, we live in a culture that believes that a child is best left alone to sleep, and in many cases these children remain sleeping even when they are awake. This author completely disagrees with the notion of leaving a child alone, on the basis that a person sleeps easier knowing that someone familiar is nearby. Consider, that whole bit about being empathic. Should a newborn be empathically sensitive, what would happen if they are abruptly left alone? They do not understand what being empathic is. All they know is that they sense life. Especially when considering that an infant spends nine months within the mother, before entering the world. Why change that familiarity? A sudden disconnection has an effect on both the mother and the child. Consider one of the punishments that is placed on a convict whom behaves poorly in prison. Yes; solitary confinement. God was well aware of the dangers of loneliness, and yet, parents do not realize that even in sleep, the mind is still tapping into the living world, which is why, so, many of us fall asleep in front of a television or radio. Strange things can happen to a developing mind when placed in an inactive existence; a *solitary* state of existence. Interesting how we often forget that Eve, in Genesis was created for a reason, and many women seem to go against that notion of being a helper, and mother to another.

CHAPTER 4

Leadership should never be looked upon as an adult exclusive medium, just as being an adult means nothing in regards to maturity, and yet a child can be a leader, but not be ready for adult interaction. For any intellectual to determine that a person should behave a certain way at a prescribed time is utter nonsense on the basis that cultivation can only exist in an ideal environment. That the two should go hand-n-hand in regards to the formation of life. Ideal environment should never be associated with creation, only direction; for hindsight determines what an ideal environment should be after life has taken root. Therefore, it would be completely irresponsible for anyone to deny the existence of God, for *chance* does not allow the impossible to be possible.

In any event, it is difficult to be an adult. It is a behavior that requires rehearsal; however, lots of people place great stock in being an adult, losing their sense of compassion. They become hard-nosed and insipid, without realizing that they are trying, so, hard to be mature that they are in fact behaving poorly, even immaturely. There is a fine line to correct mature behavior. Too far to the left, and you are a child. Too far to the right, and you are stuffy. To sum it up, we do not grow up, we simply grow older. We do not mature in the modern understanding of the definition. Our childish ways simply become a modification of our daily experiences, and are subdued. That is why it is, so, important that we teach the values of the Church first in childhood development. The child will have a moral functioning in society, and a foundation of moral conduct to build upon. The child will have a belief in a higher power greater than him or herself that will lead to honor and the meaning of telling the truth. Finally; the child will have a greater sense of need for restrictions in order to maintain a semblance of who we are as; not a people, but a species.

Maturity for us; the male of the species, is the ability to communicate in such a way as to result in a harmony that is beneficial to the whole. This can only be achieved by trekking through the quarries of infinite knowledge. Harvesting crucial aspects of useful material, and learning how to disseminate the information in such a way as to always result in a positive aspect that would spread through the whole, burning away the chaff of selfishness. Leaving behind a community dependent on the idea of helping others always, instead of helping themselves. It is knowing how to use compassion without sounding passionate or even being desperate. What to say, how to say it, when to say it. Looking into men's hearts; understanding with the compassion of a mother, but with the force of a father. Being able to put one's self into another's shoes to get an understanding of why something is or why a person does what they do and say. For you can never know what another has gone through in life, due to your own personal complications.

An immature person is not someone who plays with toys and watches cartoons, but someone who lacks empathy, patience, and humility outright. A selfish person beyond all recognition whom seeks the easy path in life. Concocting pointless excuses to deflect suspicion of inexperience away from themselves when conducting less than favorable behavior, usually in a covert fashion. False testimony becomes a way of life. They make baseless accusations to justify their petty activities. Lack the subtleties of compassion and social grace. Rush to judgment on others without thinking; basing evidence on one-sided testimony, and even personal opinion; supposition and a clouded point of view. Benefit-of-a-doubt has no meaning to them. Narcolepsy makes for a poor leader, and is the foundation for a truly immature person.

Another point to consider is that a leader should be of the hardest working, not those of the backstabbing, conniving weasel segment, who do very little, and still want it all. A person who was unwilling to commit to the job when they were the worker, but when given the promotion to be a supervisor, expect those whom were their coworkers to commit everything they have to get the job done. The reality of leadership is that a man must learn to follow, before he can learn to lead for no one is truly a leader in this existence.

The true marks of a leader manifests during crisis. When caught in a crisis, our internal clock seems to speed up, but in reality, time does not change. We have been placed into this idea that things must be done in an instant, but when you settle down, and take stock of any situation; nothing truly must be done in an instant. Case in point; have you; the employee, ever come across a supervisor whom drives you to finish a task or a project, placing undue pressure on you; and when you complete it, you discover that it is finished ahead of schedule; without, so, much as a thanks; job well-done. Not only is your end finished ahead of schedule, but that other projects associated with it are unavailable or are running late. Now, the person wielding the whip will not apologize for their needless harshness. As-far-as they are concerned, they were justified in their actions. They will make an excuse of; *at least we have something,* as a means of exonerating themselves from making some form of apology for their behavior. John Wayne once quoted in a movie; *never apologize, mister. It's a sign of weakness.* Well, that quote, is in fact unhealthy. Apologizing is a form of appreciation. It demonstrates to the workforce; the soldier, that you; the boss, are also human, and that only a responsible person owns up to their mistakes. People work harder for leaders who admit to an error, for to error is only human, and it is far easier to work for a human-being than a demigod. Besides, how does a person learn if they do not make mistakes? Note: the same principle applies to your wife or girlfriend. So, do not be harsh with her in any way should she make a mistake for the reality is; you make mistakes too, and she loves you more for it, and that is because you need that love to feel better about yourself after making a mistake. Especially when your mistake affects others.

Oh, and just, so, you will know; the primary element necessary for the instruction of how to be an adult, is responsible distraction. Constant responsible distraction is the key, and if you; the reader doubt this author, then consider what a child does to avoid responsibility when they are glued to their smartphone. The key ingredient to being an adult is responsibility. Ever meet a person who doesn't take responsibility for their actions or poor decisions?

There is a period in the human evolutionary process when male philosophical leadership must be applied to the overall masculine social complex ahead of any other forms of leadership. Yes, brute force does have its uses; however, the male mind thrives off philosophy, logic and familiarity.

CHAPTER 5

One of the most ridiculous notions that an adult can make in regards to a child who has done something mischievous or something improper or exhibited improper behavior, is asking that child why they did it. Why they did such a bad thing. You know; sometimes we have to use our common sense to understand that children do not understand the goings on of life. They do not necessarily understand the intricacies of what is proper and what is improper. Sure; they have a fundamental idea of proper and improper, but the application can be a different understanding to them. Carrying out the act of proper and improper behavior can be perceived as conflictive due to the contradictions in our society. It's okay to do wrong in one case, but not in the other; is a common practice that can be confusing to a young mind. Women; especially stir things up with their preconceived notion of what is different and what is not different. Also; women in positions of power; not mothers; are bending the child's basic perceptions of life, in order to suit feminist needs as is necessary to a malfunctioning society. So, children; male and female, become confused, making errors in judgment. You see, children, have not learned to arrest control of themselves. That takes time and training. Arresting the temptation of the inner being is one of those little details that we take for granted as adults; however, from a child's perspective, it might as well be the bottom of the ocean. Children feel the temptation to do things that go against the concept of what is proper conduct. Consider, that we were all children once. You; the reader; look into your own memories. Kick over the plate of food, hit someone; even hurt the family pet? Note: Children will follow through with the temptation if they are not taught proper ways. Children do cruel things, and depending upon the situation they will be given the benefit of a doubt. The dog suddenly bites, and the dog is punished. That is how it used to be. Today, the family pet is given the benefit of a doubt, for the child has been dehumanized. Many children have been brought up without Christian fundamental values. Even deists and atheists cannot deny the need for Christian values because no other party teaches a person to take it on the cheek, and then offer the other, not even the religions of the orient, Islam or Judaism. No instruction of what it means to be a good child. They are simply given birth to, and then they are allowed to rip and run.

Then you have those foolish parents who say; *I have a good child. I do not spank them because they are good;* while in the meantime, their child is committing more unscrupulous acts against other children, and even adults. The foolishness of human society at work. A good child would presuppose a perfect child, and anyone with the slightest bit of common sense knows that no one is perfect. Therefore; as a parent, you should presume that your child is malicious to better cope with the unexpected. Constantly reinforce the teachings of the Christ; kindness, respect, and goodwill. Most importantly pay close attention to the child's attitude to determine if those teachings are sinking in; for if they roll their eyes at you, then they will roll their eyes at others. Remember; you; the parent, are in charge, not the child. That child represents not only themselves, but you as well. Make sure that they have brothers and sisters, so, that they will have a sense of responsibility, and set a good example.

One of the greatest errors we make as parents in regards to our children is that we do not teach them thought-to-speech restraint. Knowing when to speak your mind is not something you figure out, but must be taught, and yet, we take such a subtle action for granted. Consider the impact that words have on the world. Speaking is crucial to society. Speaking is everything to humanity, but there is another aspect to the formula often forgotten or perhaps never taught; and that is; a man must learn the proper institution of words, and have insight into their use. The very act of speech itself is something we utilize on a daily basis with one another, with ourselves, even in our dreams, and it is grossly neglected. The constant altering of

86

meaning due to ignorance of; not the uneducated, but of an overall deteriorating intellect of the well-educated whom take for granted those small details necessary for social harmony. Yes, you may know the proper words, but speaking those words is a craft unto itself. What kind of society are we in this modern age of the early Twenty-first? The abuse of language is rampant in our modern culture in the United States of America. We do not maintain an effective social cohesion. Our social interactive décor is an awkward; clumsy culture of broken grammar patched with harsh expletives, lacking anything remotely familiar to social grace. Contrary to what you may think you know, in regards to speech; words and how we speak them, fall under two distinct categories; masculine and feminine. Notice how some words have a certain softness about them, while other words are more robust sounding. Notice how some people stress sentences in a certain concave manner, making them sound feminine or submissive in their tone. Whereas a masculine approach results in a certain level of hegemony in its tone.

Ever open a controversial topic and there seems to always be someone whom instantly interrupts before you can finish your thought and to make matters worse, that someone is usually not even a part of the group. Their thoughts are, so, restless that they do not consider proper thought composition before transposing thought to vocalization. Usually, when discussing controversial topics, we have a tendency of generating a rebuttal before the person who opens the discussion can even finish dispensing their thought. This results in gaps in the reception of the information, or if there is a dislike of the subject matter from the onset. Then we simply block out the remaining testimony and only a part of the initial topic is discussed. Then the point of the argument is missed due to holes in reception as a result of the constant interruption. Arrogance is someone who reaches a conclusion that they understand the topic from just a few words of the opening testimony. Arrogance is seeking to break the train of thought of the proposer due to a lack of intellectual discipline or simply a dislike of that person.

On the other hand, there are those whom relish the idea of directing discussions into more familiar territory. Such as... *sports*.

Then there is you; the person whom showed interest in the topic, but you do not react. Why? You make the mistake of trying to join in the discussion with calm, instead of telling the emotional person to simply; *shut up,* with great emotion yourself. The atmosphere should be cool and calm. The floor open for any topic of discussion; however, many people, mostly female, speak forthright without thinking. Raving opinionated nonsense with strong emotions to the point that you cannot get another word in edgewise. A person not of rational mind. Unable to hold a discussion on a civil level. Using emotion to evoke shock and enmity to apply a socialistic ambience, which leads to difficulties in our social nature. Revealing the overall truth of the situation. What gives a person the right to institute a totalitarian authority on a democratic system? We do! First; by allowing unstable behavior to be the norm. There is no way for the average person to recognize other subtle, unstable behaviors that are more than likely due to, two possibilities; insufficient educational methods and/or immigrants from countries whom have instituted social restrictive policies. Unstable becomes the norm and we think that democracy is adapting, when in fact it is eroding. Democracy only works in accordance with self-control and a rudimentary understanding of social grace. Unfortunately; however, those things are apparently an alien concept in this modern age of the early Twenty-first because we have allowed the *state* to suppress the obvious and institute an impolite frame of mind. The oddity to the whole affair is that we do not challenge due to fear as a result of our unwillingness to sacrifice basic comfort. In the end, you are left with a world of headphones and silence.

CHAPTER 6

Take control of your children early on in their lives. Children do not call the shots. At least not until they have gained some wisdom, and you have lost your mental faculties. The best example of fatherly responsibility from a Judeo-Christian standpoint is Noah, Abraham, the Prophet Sirach and of course, the Christ. Parents take charge of their children, and bear the full responsibility of their conduct; not lay blame on the child or society or make excuses that absolve themselves from failing to be parents. When a computer programmer inputs data improperly and the machine fails, do they blame the computer? So, why does that concept not translate over to parenting? Children are just computers to be programmed, and if not properly programmed; well, this author thinks you get the gist; and yet parents either forget or simply avoid properly programing their precocious little mech. Then when their precious little mech conducts mischievous activity, the parents make the excuse of not being able to control their children's actions?

There is such a thing as bad parenting. A proven fact. Whether it be ignorance or the foolish notion that a child will find their own way. Selfish parents bent on self-seeking glory, wealth or simply life's little pleasures are the focal point of our social decline. The parent; no one else, is responsible for the child's conduct. Not a teacher, relative, babysitter, daycare attendant or priest; just you; the parent. More specifically; you; the father, are responsible. Sure; mother maybe the primary caregiver; but you; the father, are the final authority to your child's welfare. So, do not even point the finger at she; who is the mother/wife, for you are the captain of the ship, of which, you are responsible for the conduct of your crew.

When children are preteens, they want parental guidance to achieve the goal of higher intellect. When becoming teenagers, they want answers because there are always unforeseen obstacles, while charting a course through life, and those answers must come from you; the parent. Not their relatives and wayward lost friends and classmates. While honing the man within the boy, teach your child what is expected of him at a young age. Plant his feet on solid ground, so, that he can grow to be confident, competent and respectful adults in this thing we call the United States of America. Again; you must temper his resolve with Judeo-Christian teaching. He must learn what is expected of him in accordance with your faith. Without this teaching, he will be devoid of a conscience; nothing to tap into when he goes out of control; and do not fool yourself, we all lose control. Without that failsafe, jail or an early death is guaranteed. In any event, he jeopardizes his very existence in the eyes of the Christ.

Oh, and by the way, if your child is not communicating with you, then you have made an error in your parental responsibilities. Your child should be able to speak to you about anything, and without trepidation. If either you or your wife are unavailable, then guess what; and just, so, this author is clear on the matter; being present is not necessarily the same as being there. Constant interaction is mandatory. Even if the child seems uninterested. Again; you are the parent, not they. Sometimes you must push them into doing something they do not want to do, and as-long-as it does not violate any moral grounds, then, so, be it.

In order to succeed at child-rearing, a child must have the traits of the father, and that includes the daughters. Without it, the child becomes lost and confused. Daughters who have sexual relations with males adopt the traits of those males, and is one reason why we say females are sluts, and males are not. Since daughters are of their father's body, these traits are readily accepted through a physical presence, without sexual contact. That is if those fathers are available to her. Once a suitor takes possession of a daughter through marriage or cleaving, his traits should adhere to her. Interesting the use of the word cleaving or cutting into something, for that is what we; the man, are doing to a woman's body when engaging in the process of sexual intercourse. We are cutting into her; both physically and mentally. Perhaps when we look at sexual intercourse with that regard we can get a better grasp of what it means for a woman to be a whore. How many times can the meat be cut? Yes, the knife can become dull, but it can also be sharpened. Once the meat is cut; however, it is cut. Yes, the meat can be stitched back together, but there will always be scars. We can also take that idea one step further in regards to why men, who lay with men as they would a woman is not an acceptable practice and quite definitely not an

90

identity. There is just something disturbing about cleaving the cleaver that doesn't sit well with this author.

As the father of a burgeoning teen-female, you must be familiar with the world from her point of view. Being propositioned by boys, and men alike, even being coaxed by friends to give in to their desires. This is the serpent-effect; e.g. being constantly tempted, making life tough on her. Which is why a mother must be present in the home. The daughter must be afforded some form of protection from the creatures whom lurk about the world, and given an explanation as to their existence, and the reason behind their behavior.

You must have an active role in her romantic lifestyle; at least in the beginning. If need be, conduct active surveillance. Yes; what this author is suggesting is absolutely absurd, but consider that the technology exists, so, why not? It's not expensive, and it serves a dual purpose, of which neither involves the suitor. It gives you; the parent, an idea of the effectiveness of your teaching guidelines. Were your methods viable? Did she adhere to your sense of reasoning and logic? The other aspect, is that sometimes daughters get it in their heads that they have to lock in the relationship by copulation. They fail to realize that they control all of the cards, and that they have already locked in their suitor's heart. Therefore, she may need protecting from herself. Remember; there is no privacy issue in regards to your children until they have moved out of your house. On that same note: Do not be concerned with the suitor's choice of language. It is your daughter's responsibility to direct the conversation accordingly. Afterwards; you can discuss the situation with your daughter if need be, and point out the tells of a potentially good or bad relationship. Again; all of it sounds completely absurd, but how else does a child learn to communicate unless there is direct involvement from the teacher. These are treacherous times, and we require new, and extreme measures in order to protect our children, for trust is a difficult thing to come by. If you; the parent, are satisfied with the situation, then cut the safety line, for her suitor has already caught her. Oh, and face the fact, that teens like to sneak out. Sometimes they have to know if they are ready to take on life; handle themselves without direct observation. They want to put your teachings to the test; however, should they be overly confident, then set a trap. She wants to be caught, and by not doing, so, reveals in her mind that you are an uncaring parent.

CHAPTER 7

The miscalculation that many Catholic Christian and Christian denominational parents make when raising children is that they don't guide them on a path of becoming priests or nuns. Raising a child to be a priest or a nun bestows a high sense of moral conduct on their young minds. That way if the child does not choose religion as a profession, they will still have the benefits of strong religious guidelines to keep moral ideas intact at all levels of existence. That is how greed is kept in check. Nothing wrong with achieving wealth, only how the wealth is achieved.

Let us take a moment to examine one aspect of failed Catholic adherence. Catholic doctrine, instruction, understanding, is not adhering to the young, for they are learning what is good, while being mischievous. It would be like trying to paint a wall covered in grease. You may succeed, but when things get hot, the truth will quickly manifest itself. This occurs when there is a lack of parental supervision and guidance. The *bride* cannot do it alone.

Why are Catholic fathers not teaching their children how to be good Catholics? To be good people? Many Catholic fathers dabble in improper conduct, believing that failing to adhere to Catholic Doctrine bars them from teaching their children Catholicism. That a person must be perfect in order to explain Christianity to anyone, especially their own children. Be realistic, if Christians waited until they reached some form of enlightenment like the Eastern religions, then how many people would be lost to ignorance. Just a small piece of Christianity can have a profound effect on a person's life. Christianity is a teach as you learn medium. Let us be realistic, you tell yourself that you will do better, but you have been immersed in certain pleasures for a very long time, due to your parents not going into the details of the Church. Catholic school loaded you up with information, but never explained how to apply it in your daily

92

routine, or you simply chose to ignore that part of the lesson. Pay attention to your life. You keep the dirt hidden, but leave the clean out to be seen. You are already showing signs of wanting to do what is right. Take it one step further, and simply explain the very details. Just telling your children to be good and respectful of others could get the ball rolling to send your immortality on the right track. That is what life is all about, after all; getting yourself right for final judgement.

If you are a Catholic man, and you know 25% of what it means to be Catholic. Then teach your children what you know because 25% of something is better than nothing. If you are a Catholic man and you know 10% of what it means to be Catholic. Then teach your children 10% of what you know because 10% of something is better than nothing. If you are a Catholic man and you know 3% of what it means to be Catholic. Then teach your child 3% of what you know because 3% of something is better than nothing. If you are a Catholic man and you know nothing of your faith, then learn before your child reaches kindergarten age. If you are a Catholic man and possess the knowledge of the priests, and you do not teach your children, woe on you, for you are worse than the fallen one.

To you; the Catholic Christian father, you must be mindful of your children around Protestant Christian children and adults. Not that they are your enemy or that they are against you in anyway, but that their understanding of the teachings of the Christ differs from yours. It is far easier for a Protestant to sway a Catholic than it is for a Catholic to sway a Protestant. Therefore, you must make sure that you double your efforts when guiding your children along Church traditions, or your children may find themselves up against insurmountable odds in questions of faith in their later years.

CHAPTER 8

Let us review the aspect of rewarding. If a child behaves, and another child misbehaves, but you reward each child equally, then the incentive for either child to behave is lost. Then what is the point of the reward? The same can be said for any form of activity designed to bring out the best in a person. If a person is rewarded for minimal or no effort at a task, then it taints the process of doing. Takes away the purpose of something. The point of the issuance of an award is to generate motivation from a group of people in order for them to strive even harder to not only succeed at a task in a satisfactory manner, but to push for excellence. Bestow a certain level of success in order to apply a sense of achievement within the child-psyche, so, that as adults they will pursue a communal task with great vigor, to identify those worthy of leadership.

Just, so, we are clear about the idea of competitive success. We; the man, base leadership on outdoing the other man in some form of competitive vehicle in order to establish some kind of an interactive social structure. To identify that success, it is natural to issue a form of accolade to those who accomplish a goal ahead of others as a means of verifying experience. When a contestant brags about winning, or rubs a competitor's face in insults, they reveal that they are unworthy of leadership or of honor. Achieving a goal is only part of the process. A man must reveal honor when achieving success. Whether a soldier on the battlefield or an athlete on the playing field, you do not truly win unless you have won the hearts of your opponent. For fame is not taken; it is earned, and once earned it is kept through the use of proper language and behavior. Oh, and just, so, we are clear on one other thing. Success is based more on the mother than it is the father. So, when certain people claim that there are no successful women in history, this author will remind them that success does not come on the backs of pigs. She makes a man's abilities, and in almost every situation regarding a hardworking man, there was more than likely a hardworking woman in the background to make it all possible.

Just as a side note in regards to athletics: If you are an athlete who utilizes some form of muscle enhancement that results in an unnatural increase of physical performance; ask yourself this one simple question. Was it you that achieved the goal, or was it the enhancement? You may hold the gold medal in your hand, but did you truly earn it?

For my fellow Catholics, we forget that our priests are leaders of faith, and the source of greater knowledge and insight on social conduct. In the old days when you needed an answer to a question you went to someone of higher standing for that answer. We still follow that process today. If you required a question to be answered, and you knew a smart person, then you probably would ask that person first, even before interfacing with cyberspace. That's because the natural process for the exchange of information was from person-to-person. It was the way we stayed on top of information; kept our traditions alive. Verified our humanity. Now, we depend upon our technology; devices of some sort to seek information. The problem with that medium is that it restricts the mind to just that detail. When you gather information from a human source, they more than likely will expand on the topic leading into other areas of discussion. We no longer exercise the very notion of our thoughts and our memories, and, so, they deteriorate. Isn't it interesting how Alzheimer's seems to coincide with the advent of the modern computer. What will be the outcome of smart-phone users? An even better question would be; what will happen to them if our ability to generate electricity is suddenly lost? If you cannot build a fire than you shall surely die; and to build a fire you must first have the capabilities of seeking the Lord, so, that He can show you how it is done. So, perhaps it would not be such a bad idea to dismantle the internet, destroy our cell-phone towers, and go back to the way things were. All we may need do, to fix ourselves is to simply rediscover something, we have lost.

To be a true leader of men, a person must conduct himself in such a way as to benefit the whole, and not himself. To do this, a person must have an excellent means of communicating.

A definite sign of someone who is poor in their vocal expression is their use of the phrase; *you know what I am talking about,* which can easily lead to guesswork, speculation and eventual failure on the part of subordinates. When that happens, excuses arise because the leader is never wrong. Which is true, in regards to how a plan is to unfold, but one of the most difficult measures for any person is communicating vision. Therefore, you; the man, who has gained the trust and faith of those he has just outdone, and would send others into dire circumstances, even surrender their lives for the cause, must master the craft of speaking. For if you cannot say what you mean, then you can never mean what you say.

CHAPTER 9

Since we discussed the behavior of the successful man, let us take a moment to examine those whom were unable to surpass the successful man. In the past we called them losers, but what is a loser? A loser is a person who does not give it his all. A loser is a person who does not strive to be better. A loser is a person who gives up. We often forget that as men, competition is based on determining leadership in battle, and in traditional fields of battle a leader leads from the front. There are cases when a leader will take his followers into battle, but may fall. Someone must take his place. Where does that other person come from? To achieve success, another must push him to that success. That takes great skill unto itself, and that is why you; the person who was second, must return to the field of competition, for without you to push, there cannot be true success. When charging into battle he is trusting you to be right behind him. So, as you can see, trust is a two-way street. Trust to lead, and trust to follow. You may not have a trophy in your hand, but without your perseverance that trophy has absolutely no meaning to the winner because no one truly likes an easy win.

This may or may not work with the woman-child. The problem with the woman is feminine emotion. The idea that everyone wins defeats the idea of striving for perfection. It falls onto the feminist idea of equality. Imagine a world from a woman's point of view where everybody wins; there would be no progress. Remember, when one side wins, the other side searches for ways to overcome the winners in the next engagement. Thus, the progression of humanity throughout the ages. Imagine an existence where a person says; *I discovered the electric light or a rocket into space or even another continent;* but then someone else says; *no; we all discovered those things;* and everyone places their names on the discovery. Not even communism is that shallow. Eventually, there would be no incentive to get ahead because we as a culture like the idea that someone achieved a goal in order to give the rest of us inspiration. Without that inspiration, there would be no point of seeking the goal, and we would simply become stagnate and wither. Another interesting aspect with women, is the notion of packing it in before the task is actually complete because they have a child to tend to or a family to get home to. A man in the same circumstances will engage in conflict with his wife in regards to the career outside of the home and who should tend to the children. That is unless they have the finances necessary to hire a fill-in parent, but then what would be the point of having children if someone else is going to raise them? Your child is a continuation of yourself, so, make sure you choose the proper woman to be their mother. A woman who adapts to your ways, so, that she may teach your children a proper understanding of life in order to better continue your immortality.

Lastly, it is imperative that you remain within the context of manhood. Should you go outside of that context, then she; the woman, will fall out of context of womanhood, and children will fall out of context of childhood. At that point, society will have no relevant meaning or understanding of purpose leading to complete deterioration of the whole. The child will find other ways of getting answers to questions, and again, some of those ways end with the barrel of a gun.

REGARDING EVE

CHAPTER 1

After placing, so, much emphasis on the importance of woman, it now, becomes necessary to refresh an old idea that may seem offensive to modern woman-hood; and though as unfortunate as it may sound; as harsh as it may be, a woman's place is in the home.

97

In fact, we use the term, homemaker to describe a stay at home mom, but this is actually an improper description of a woman's true nature. To remain in the background. To maintain the children. To take care of the home-front. She is never meant to be out in the open. What is meant by this? Her care and love is for her nuclear family; her man and son, or sons. A woman's place in society is to keep a warm house, for no one likes to come home to a cold house. This is not a demeaning state of being, but proper social procedure, that is older than civilization itself. An example of what this author is describing; think of the Charles Dickens classic; *"A Christmas Carol"* when Ebenezer Scrooge arrives at his home. All is cold, dark and lonely. To sum it up, he is very uncomfortable. If you are the first person to open a shop, how does it feel when you arrive? Ever arrive at an event, when no one else is around? There is just something about a place with someone already there that makes you feel more comfortable.

CHAPTER 2

Women also have another great responsibility they can no longer fathom, and that is being more than a wife with a family, but a mother to the community. A necessity to the continued existence of the community. Mothers determine if a community is safe for a child to dwell in. If there are ample safety measures in place to assure that worry is kept at a minimum. While at the same time there is a certain level of challenge, and even controlled danger, for proper mental stimulus. True fun only occurs when there is a certain level of danger. Not to mention the resilience of the human body. We learn by our bumps and bruises; by falling down, for if we do not hurt ourselves, then we lose our perception of what being alive is all about.

Unfortunately, we live in an urban setting geared for adults, with children being nothing more than an afterthought to the social décor. If our children are treated like a piece of scenery, then what would be the point of existence? Children prevent us from being just that; a machine. It is they whom cross the line of neighborly reluctance. It is they whom go out and find the fun. It is they whom

98

motivate us into reacting. It is they whom bring a smile to our faces, and what do we do with them? Neglect them due to our own fear of the unexpected, and need for certain pleasures.

A child going to school in complete fear for his or her life is not indicative to a thriving culture. To make matters worse, the child returns home, and is burdened by worry, and despair, and even wonders what to eat? What to do? How to cope with the basic frustrations of life? They are alone when the questions arise because mom has been conditioned by the Feminist Movement into believing that her responsibility is to bring additional income into the home. Compete with a man; her man. Another aspect of the domestic chaos is that by the time a parent gets home, the child forgets the questions they wanted to ask in order to get a better grasp of life's little turmoil. Crucial questions that are beneficial to a child's development. For the child that all too familiar feeling of being safe and secure is absent. They will never know that feeling of nothing can ever hurt them at home. A two-income household does nothing more than feed the corporate pockets to the point of evolving into a single income with two people fighting to keep the truth from coming to light. What is the truth? That if warmth, compassion, concern, and sensitivity are not engrained into the human heart at a young age, then we become nothing more than a component in a pointless, lifeless existence. No progression of the overall social dynamic in such a way as to say, we are something better than what we were. We become stagnant. An evolutionary dead end, showing no true useful contribution to the universe. We are, as the people of Noah's time were, before the flood; a thing to be expunged from existence. Warmth, compassion, and sensitivity are basic tools of social existence. A necessity for achieving a sentient existence. For those pieces come from the woman, which is why you; the man, cleave to a woman; marry a woman, and before doing, so, you must insure that she has the necessary building blocks and qualities for constructing a reliable future. For your immortality requires it.

Children are the key to a successful community, and that success cannot be achieved without a mother, but we have misconceptions between what is mother, and she who has given birth to a child. Pursuing an occupation outside of womanhood before keeping her obligation to motherhood is not a wise decision. What many women end up doing is waiting too long to be impregnated, and thus missing that physical and mental sweet spot for conception. When a woman gives birth to his child in her later years; usually after establishing a career, she is no longer a mother, but a grandmother, and the positive parental focus falls short. Mothers spank bad children as a means of strict behavioral indoctrination. While grandmothers try to reason with bad children, spoil bad children, thinking that giving them rewards will garnish good behavior, and in some cases even gaining their approval. When in fact, what a child is looking for is a great sculptor with a hard chisel to shape them into something of worth.

It is the woman who makes a man's success possible, not him. Good or bad, it is she, whom changes the world through her son and/or her man. The success of the man-child she gave birth to, is what makes her great by default; however, a good mother knows she cannot share in the spotlight. She must remain in the shadows or her success; which is reserved for God only, would be ruined. Contrary to what you; the reader may think; it is the mother whom the son reflects upon the world. The mother's traits that makes him what he is; from conception to death, it is a woman's input; a woman's skill; a woman's power that makes a man great. That is why there are, so, few great women in history, and those whom do exist have a limited or no prodigy. Why it is safe to say, that a mother seeking fame and glory is a selfish woman, going against the very nature of what it means to be a mother. The son of a good mother wants to be able to say to her; *I can now, walk on my own, mom.* Failure comes in the form of a son who still lives at home, and turns it into a bordello. Failure is allowing a son to remain a child, and suck at his mother's breasts even when he is capable of picking up a cup and drinking from it. Failure is when he does not have a home of his own, and kicks his mother out, instead of taking care of her when she becomes too frail and burdensome. Every convict has/had a mother. Therefore, why are they convicts? A bad mother says; *I cannot control my child's actions,* after being vacant from her motherly duties, and part of those duties is determining what is, and isn't a proper man for her and essentially a father.

Therefore, tackling motherhood and being employed outside of the home, regardless of how you spin it, is an impossible endeavor. Gearing herself for a career outside of the home, and key aspects of mother-hood suffer. Specifically, in matters regarding child-welfare. This is a result of engaging in a sexually deviant lifestyle or basic romance without the realization of the expectation of pregnancy. Modern employed females get, so, hung up in their careers, that they fail to sense that mysterious link that occurs at the moment of conception, preventing them from understanding certain aspects of the person whom she will give birth to later.

Motherhood is a woman's true occupation. She cannot serve two masters. Being a mother does not imply pregnancy, giving birth, baby-proofing a home, remodeling a room or purchasing baby necessities. Being a mother does not consist of taking the child to the babysitter or daycare, so, that she can be a part of the workforce. A woman thinks that pregnancy is about preparing the body for birth; however, once aware of conception, it is an unprepared surprise. A complex state that we know, so, little about. A frame of mind that takes a considerable amount of mental prowess of which a woman must begin placing herself in when she is a child. Thoughts must be focused at the moment of conception. What is involved? Sure, we are familiar with the physical aspects, but doesn't the mental state come into play as well? Yes; children feed off a mother's thoughts; her brains; what she is thinking. Taking in more than body nutrients is a factor, but we must also consider mental nutrients as well. Every aspect of who and what a woman is, comes into play during the gestation period.

Negative emotions impact the world like a wrecking ball to a building. The wrecking ball just keeps whacking away until the building is a heap of ruble. Apply that analogy to a wife and child or any person for that matter. How long can a person hold up to such abuse? On the job, in the home, at some public setting; a ballgame, bar, even a school. Whatever the case or place, abuse can only be tolerated to a certain extent. Science has proven that living matter such as plants and animals are affected by negative emotions; hatred and anger. What we do not consider though, is whether or not it is negative emotions that destroy or the actual intensity and impact of sound that is the culprit. Perhaps it is the combination of the three, but whatever the case, we know that a violent, hateful environment does have an impact on any and all in its vicinity. Yes; that also includes the animal kingdom. Our negative emotions are driving them to react with hostility. We are forgetting that whole Garden of Eden stuff. Emotions are part of the natural equation.

Long before the birth of a child, positive emotion must be whole, and this can only be achieved with you; the man. A woman is doing more than simply providing a stable platform of growth as a mother, but the bonding process as well. As a man; now, father, you must see to the comforts of she, who would give birth to your immortality. Contribute to the bonding to make her feel safe and confident. Push yourself to the very limits of your physical and psychological capabilities, and even beyond. If you; the father, fail in this endeavor, she; the mother, will become uncertain, and uncertainty leads to apprehension, and apprehension can lead to anger and resentment. You do not want your prodigy to have any discrepancies. You must greatly lower the overall risk factor.

Why is she avoiding her responsibility? She is apprehensive about who, and what she is, and the effect the world is having on his child whom she has given birth to, not to mention the effect his child, whom she has given birth to, is having on the world. She fears being a mother, and, so, she tries to avoid it. Perhaps thinking that by waiting, she can gain some form of motherly wisdom from an unforeseeable or unconventional source or that a stable income makes for good parenting.

102

It is imperative that the child or children get the full attention of the mother; or what this author perceives as motherly support, and that includes when a child is not in her presence. Motherly support is far more crucial, in regards to the child's welfare, than parental support, on the basis that part of the father's responsibilities are to the community; to deal with the mundane things in life. A full-time mother and a father part of the time, augmented by the bride compels the child to do good first, so, that instructions about good things can be better understood and adhered to during the child's psychological growth. That is why the Church says the teachings of the Christ must begin in the home; however, parents cannot teach, if both are seeking careers outside of the home.

Teaching is a fulltime responsibility. Imagine a school teacher slipping out of class to work at another job. Would your child get the best possible education? Wouldn't the instructor be simply passing along information and telling the pupil to figure it out on their own? That is what many parents do. Parents often forget that they are a child's first line of instruction; mentor; guidance, but why is the female best suited for this function? She; the mother, has that 9-month bond with the child. A period in which, that squirming little person within her is actually indoctrinating woman into motherhood. Every action a woman commits; how she moves, the ambient environment; all of it shapes the child both physically and mentally on a level deemed acceptable to the whole. In becoming a mother, she indoctrinates the new person into humanity. After birth, the umbilical cord may be cut, but there is still an attachment. No one knows a child better than the mother, which means a mother should not simply cut off a child for any circumstance. They are dependent upon her. In need of her. They need to know that she will catch them when the bow breaks because if the child hits the ground there will be hell to pay. Especially for the boys.

CHAPTER 3

There are subtle signs that hint of a female in need. For their fashion choices are not by accident or ignorance. The cosmetics, body movements, even where they travel, are all part of the routine of attraction. Constant wiping of the hands on the thighs, toying with their hair. Some females will even go as-far-as initiating first contact. Impatience is a natural part of being a female in need; again, not a weakness, but a necessity. A necessary part of the preservation of the species; to give us; the man, a sense of purpose. As with a man, rigorous physical activity; sports, is the best remedy for this; however, any activity that is not sexual in nature will work. Thoroughly distracting the mind is a must, and yet, how is this accomplished in such a highly-provocative environment? Just imagine what is going on in the workforce, where both genders are employed. No place of business is safe from the raging hormones of a female in need.

Now, this author is not going to pretend that the craving for sexual intercourse does not affect virgins because it does; however, on hot summer days, a person stays away from things that make them thirsty. Should they eat something salty, then it is preferable to drink cold water rather than a sweet soda. It is much easier for a girl; and yes, even a boy, to control the urges of sexual intercourse when their virginity is intact. So, as a parent, give them only water because sugar can be very sweet to a thirsty child.

CHAPTER 4

A woman's devotion is to the male of the species, while a man's devotion is to God. That is why man and wife is the proper terminology for marriage under Judeo-Christian values, instead of husband and wife. On the basis that the language removes man's obligation and devotion to God. Husband and wife, establishes the idea of two beings, of which is saying that he is no longer devoted to God, but to the being known as man; his wife. Whereas man and wife clearly reveals her desire to rejoin the being known as man, and his willingness to be obedient to God.

Beware that every child born outside of wedlock places mankind closer in relationship to the very animals we are supposed to have dominion over. We treat marriage as a farce; something with no meaning; as though it were some form of board game. In fact, many of us have brought the childish notion of a high school drama to the idea of marriage. *She's my girlfriend one week and the next week I have found someone else.* Do we even know what marriage is anymore? This author believes that we do not. Therefore, it is imperative that you; the Judeo-Christian male, obeys the edicts, rules and laws of God to the letter, for it is necessary for her to remain joined to that being we call man. Break the rules and it jeopardizes the whole of man, and makes it a partial species.

Indeed, there are those of you who will question the Church's rule of a priest not being allowed to cleave to a woman. There are always exceptions to those who have made religion a profession. A priest's responsibilities are astronomical in comparison to even those in the medical field. There is verification of this in the Old Testament. The Levites did not take possession of any land in Canaan due to their obligation to the priesthood; however, they did take wives and start families. On the other hand, a Catholic priest's obligation to the community is far greater than any civil authority, leaving no room for an ideal parental obligation. No man can serve two masters; for there would be conflict; chaos in regards to whom comes first during moments of family crisis.

EQUALITY

CHAPTER 1

What is this thing we call equality? A state in which, two sides are either alike or, so, close in resemblance that any differences would be negligible. Not worth mediation over the details. Manufacturing or harvesting methods are designed to generate equality amongst specific products. We, as creators, institute quality control to ensure equality; however, what of nature? What items in the natural environment can be deemed as equal? No point at making a list, for we know that many things would be equal in the natural environment. What we are concerned about are those things that are of the same group, but not equal. Notice for yourselves, the more advanced the organism, the greater the difference. We, as a living being standout from all others on the basis that we can control our physical appearance, mannerisms, strengths, and our weaknesses. We can literally guide our evolution, shape our physical structure and mental characteristics for the needs of the moment, and yet, human nature can be such a tricky vehicle in our overall existence. Even confusing in regards to relationships. Not our families, or daily interactions as men, and not man to woman, but males to females. We familiarize ourselves with certain aspects of what is male and what is female, and develop ourselves according to who we are. Even establish guidelines to define our very being in regards to gender. Many females expect a certain something out of us. Want their males to be a certain way. While a great many males want their females to be a certain way. Some prefer a certain skin tone, and are attracted to a certain vocalization and physique. All of the senses; yes, even this author's proposed sixth sense of empathy, plays a part in the attraction. Ideally, we all want our mates to be smart; however, equality just does not stretch that far, and that is the whole basis behind this subject. Equality begins with the brain. That complex device that we take for granted as a species. Consider the power of the human brain. It is capable of figuring out life on its own. Doubt this author's words? When we are born, we go from a liquid environment to a gaseous environment, and the brain makes the adjustment. Yes, science explains the process, but forget science, and think about the transition from a basic point of view, and you cannot deny the amazingness of the transition. In the religious community; we call that transition miraculous or simply a miracle. Now, as life progresses, the brain makes interpretations of its surroundings, using basic sensory input to make adjustments accordingly. The reality is, our environment determines what and even who we will be, and part of that environment includes other people. The more advanced the life form the greater the need for the institution of regulation. As a species, we require regulation to better understand ourselves, and even our reason for being. Rules help us to relate, and sometimes those rules can seem unfair when looking inwards. Now, here is the tricky part. Greater complexity requires a balance of simplicity. Should complexity dominate, then confusion sets in. Examine our current social setting, and what do you see? Social confusion. Should simplicity dominate, then progress diminishes, and what do you see? Social dysfunction. Interesting that both exists in our modern culture of the early Twenty-first. Now, associate complexity with hard, and simplicity with easy, and what do you get in regards to the human condition? People striving to go beyond the confines of earth, and people without jobs and homes wandering about the Earth. For the complexity and the simplicity to work reciprocally is motivation; however, like all mechanics; motivation requires some form of fuel. In this current age of living, money is the fuel. What is money? A mysterious dynamic that bends our perceptions of morality beyond all accepted tolerances in the form of greed, selfishness, desire and anger. The end result is violence. How did money become the fuel? The answer is, so, simple that we have completely overlooked it. Basic comfort is the answer. If you don't want to be hot, cold, hungry or thirsty, you will do whatever it takes to keep perceived discomfort at bay. Comfort evolves into desires because we always want more of what makes us feel good, and thus we have creature comforts. Wood is okay, but I desire natural gas because it ignites, so, easily. Water is okay, but I prefer beer or wine because it tastes better. I like the sound of a violin, but I want an orchestra. Wind may bring the scent of honeysuckle to my nostrils, but I would rather hold the honeysuckle in order to smell it at my leisure. She is beautiful, but her hips are too narrow. He is cute, but too short. In a simpler time, our religious values were the fuel for the motivation, and for some people it still is, but again, it is all about balance. Proper religious practices result in social balance. With religion comes patience and logic, you cannot have one without the other. Note: In regards to religion there is actually no cap to its absorption, and practice, only the potency of its dissemination to others. Only one specific religion makes cross-social ideologies innocuous. Do your own research to determine which, and you will begin to delight in a world gone mad.

What is equality; exactly, in regards to human existence? This author will explain it as nothing more than a confusing state of mind.

As a culture, we become, so, preoccupied with the idea of wanting equality, that we forget that arrogance, stubbornness and ignorance is the driving force behind the need for equality. Of course, there is always room for sarcasm. We always forget that life is not about equality, but purpose, and all human beings have purpose. Including those whom are gestating within the womb, but are they equal? Culturally, our pursuit of equality has blinded us to the finer aspects of inequality. If that is the case, then perhaps we should make a closer examination of inequality to better understand equality.

If everyone had a say in daily affairs, then nothing would get done. Should a supervisor be equal to the workers? Why isn't the person who changes the tires on a car equal to the engine mechanic? Do the workers who pour the concrete for a building's foundation view themselves as equal to the building's architect? Is a colonel equal to the privates? Is the quarterback equal to the offensive linemen? Those people realize that purpose supersedes equality. Imagine a team of ballplayers having an equal voice to the coach. For the team to work there must be a leader. You as the man are that leader. The house is your house. The game plan is your game plan; therefore, she; who is your wife, must follow your rules. She is your wife, and she must support you in everything you do; short of your defiance of God. That is why a wife cannot testify against her husband in any earthly court of law. She agreed to this when the both of you exchanged vows and said; *I do*. Those of us whom are religiously orientated are well aware that equality is in fact, nothing more than a distraction in life. Beginning with Adam, Noah, and Abraham, the Bible is full of inequality; and women would appear to be unequal to men across the board, or, so, it would seem; however, Eve had purpose. Many women in the bible were not equal, but they had purpose. We; as a species, have forgotten that a woman's purpose is not to seek equality, but to be a helper. Now, those of us who are familiar with the book of Genesis are aware that we have covered this. A dog or cat, bird in a cage or rat, does not make for a suitable helper to neither man nor woman. She cannot separate herself from he; who is man, no matter how much she wants to, for males and females are joined together under the symbiosis, which we call man.

CHAPTER 2

Reasonably speaking; females should not be equal to males when considering that males are not equal amongst each other. Males and females are equal as human-beings, but as genders, are completely different creatures of the same nature. To equalize the genders would result in a great loss in both. A man has a specific purpose as does a woman. Equalizing them results in social confusion and dissolves the purpose for which the natural order of man works. That is why men and women are, so, different. It is those differences that offsets our faults, making the relationship between male and female work, but when you have a woman that behaves more like a man then you run into problems. Woman is not meant to be independent. She is not meant to engage in sexual relationships with multiple men; however, the feminist movement would like you to believe otherwise. That woman is somehow liberated when she behaves as a man. This is the thinking of the witch, and she has taken on a new form and description. Feminists are what we call them now. Feminists have an obsessive need to equalize the genders. Why is that? Are they ashamed of being women? Do women hate being treated like women. If that is the case, then how do they want men to treat them? Like men? Interesting, that when we do treat them like men, how quickly they fall back on social etiquette in regards to the treatment of females when they get into trouble. There is absolutely no defense against feminine emotional needs.

Perhaps, they dislike what it means to be man, or is it something greater. Perhaps the very defiance of God, or at least the idea of a male orientated deity offends them. Deep down, they believe that God is a she, but if that were the case, then sexual pleasure in any form would be the focus of God's plan; and acceptable in all settings; to include domestic animals, the beasts of the wild, and yes, that includes homosexuality, but that is not the case based on our knowledge of any of our mainstream religions. Again, she is the very definition of sex, and though, it is the male whom, in fact

109

generates the attraction, it is she, whom generates the stimulation. Take that away, and you have no reaction; just perversion. Women are overly compassionate towards animals beyond the scope of the rules set down by God's Law. They are quick to cast off tradition under the belief that it keeps them in bondage, without consideration of the consequences. They place absolutely no restrictions on sexual expression with little or no concern over the effects it has on society. She is the ignition and he is the fuel. Human emotions are the accelerant. The end-result to the original concept of male/female adherence is lost in the noise, and the idea of bringing about new life is viewed as a disease instead of a blessing. Birth control inoculants, and abortion, completely contradicts God's plan; and yet, both practices are necessary towards the foundation of female empowerment. What does God say in Genesis? Be fruitful and multiply, and feminist say, that God is what gender? Oh, and for those of you who say that there are men whom support birth-control and abortion. Well; there are also men who lay with men as they would a woman. Not exactly thinking like a man. So, before continuing; let's get one thing absolutely clear in regards to God; though not visible; He does exist, and that He is in fact a He. The Bible is clear on that fact. This is why a woman should not try to be like a man, do what a man does, behave as a man does, dress as a man does. She must be different, so, that the human species may endure. Making subtle changes through sons to avoid the disruption and harmony of the community. When women take charge, they can be too radical and selfish; focusing on nothing more than women's rights instead of culture as a whole. Girl power and women lead, leaves the boy to figure things out on his own. The previous system worked. We; the man, simply forgot why it was put into place. Women belong in the support role. A term that apparently has a negative connotation for some people. That is until we examine the military complex, and then a person has a clear understanding of just how important the support role is; however, in a sociological setting, the support role is simply an action of some kind that provides for the process as a means of continued existence. A helper;

110

a friend; one who makes it not, so, lonely in the world is in a support role or in some cases, being supportive. It is a title of a specific purpose. Neither one can survive without the other. Consider that a building's shape, materials and even its color make it something to be looked at, but without its *support* structure what do you have? Of course, the outer material serves a purpose; *protecting* the support structure. Sound familiar? That is why the support structure has to be strong. Where does the support structure receive its strength? From the encouragement, love and care you bestow upon it. You think an army can win a war without support? Imagine a soldier going into battle without bullets, food and a uniform. We treat support as if it were nothing. That is until you need it, and that is when the whole world just opens up to all kinds of possibilities; and not all of those possibilities are good.

Now, what would happen if the support structure wanted to be the outer structure of a building? Would you have the same effect? How about sharing the job? Possibly; but then there would be weaknesses, and it would not take much to bring the building down, much like the twin towers of the World Trade Center of 11 September 2001. Think of what people have to do to bring down a traditionally built building. Isn't it fascinating how men and women compare, so, well to a basic skyscraper? When the two work together there is no height they cannot achieve. Just keep building; however, take any part of it away, and it collapses.

What happens when a woman takes the feminist path? What are feminists really conditioning her for? Oddly, not even they know the answer to that question, because if they did, there would be no conflict between the genders, and just in case you do not know; we are in a serious conflict. Males and females are at each other's throats. In fact, it is, so, bad that we are just a few cruel words short of a major war, and to think otherwise would be reckless and irresponsible. Now, the feminists do not have the answers because they are busy with the agenda. That is the whole point of feminist thinking; always putting the cart before the horse. *After achieving the agenda, then we'll figure out a goal.* The result will be strictly from a feminist point of view; and like all of their other agendas, it will be a pointless gest. Making no sense to even themselves; but no worries. They will simply force themselves to understand.

Perhaps the reasoning behind the conditioning is due to feminists guiding unsuspecting women to be more like men; however, what does it mean to be a man? Women want what a man has, but they do not understand what makes us a man, or what it takes to be a man. Look at what is going on with women all across the United States of America. They make mistakes, and instead of owning up to their mistakes, learning from their mistakes, they cry foul. Ever listen to a woman when things go wrong? *That's not fair!* Men on the other hand, simply eat it, and drive on without dwelling on it. Note: A man should never say; *that's not fair,* for nothing is ever truly fair in this world. That is except for those men whom are trying to fill a woman's role in the grand scheme of things, and instead of being bothered, she is supportive of their encroachment in her domain? *Go figure.* A woman cuts in on another woman's action and she gets upset? A man cuts in on her action, and she is… supportive? This author calls that; social interactive shock. She feels sorry for him due in part that she cannot cope with the unnatural act of what is going on. Again, being conditioned by mass media, celebrities, even family and friends into believing that her unnatural competitor is some form of victim; and in all respects, he is, but that does not give him the right to cross into a woman's territory? Consider he; who butchers a half dozen people, and there are women just lining up to be with him. The strangeness of feminine behavior when it goes unregulated, and quite simply put; women do not regulate, which is why law is being twisted beyond all recognition. Choose to kill the baby in the womb; legal. Choose not to wear your seatbelt; illegal. The good-looking guy staring at her butt in those tight-fitting jeans; perfectly okay. The nobody guy who does the same; a pervert? Demanding equal pay for equal work; justified? Failing to do equal work for equal pay… justified? What a truly interesting world of equality we live in.

Of course, when things do fall apart, we; the man, conveniently blame the woman for what is actually our lack of fortitude in taking charge. Remember, if you; the man, run with the woman's idea, it becomes your idea. So, when things do not work out, do not blame her for you adopted her idea instead of formulating your own. Part of being a man is allowing your creative juices to flow. To take charge; but this does not mean forsake the female's wisdom, for she is a helper to you for a reason. You the male are not supposed to take on life alone; therefore, her helping you is a necessity. A woman does much for us; more so, than we realize. She is the flower in the desert. She keeps the thirst from our lips, and the heat from our backs, and when the time comes to water the flower, we choose to drink it ourselves, even though we do not need it. We take, take, take, and give nothing in return. This is the behavior that has driven the woman away from us; the man. Just look around; woman has begun her rebellion, and all of society is paying the price. Our children are becoming unrecognizable. Do we; as men enjoy acting as agents to the fallen one?

By serving God, He rewards us with His gift. What do you often do with a gift given to you from your parents, friends, or even your colleagues? Do you trash it? Perhaps some of you would; but more than likely, you would put it away for safekeeping. Unfortunately, when you put things away to keep them safe, you often forget about them. Oh sure, the gift is safe, but at the same time, you are neglecting the gift without realizing it. In your endeavor to preserve God's gift, you in effect, also neglect the gift. Even as-far-as taking the gift for granted. God's gift to man should not be locked away, but displayed with great pride and happiness, made happy and never sad. The gift in this case is a living breathing being that requires even greater care than yourself, and your possessions. For woman is a completely different being than yourself. Her behaviors, mannerisms, build, even her actions are completely different from that of a man, and yet, they are the same. They bind together through social structure; everyday interaction. We men bind together through beliefs and ideas. As independent beings; we men, like to establish social rules of engagement to avoid conflict, for we are, so, territorial and even possessive. They are the purpose for which to live; breathe, fight, build and yes; destroy. Without them we cease to exist as a species. It is they as to why we are not considered the same as the beasts in the wilderness. We have constructed our entire society around them, shared our inner desires with them, and even killed for them. They are not unequal to a man. They are the reason for why being a man is, so, great. They are not subservient to men. They are the mother of man. It takes a great mother to make a great man. They remain in the background for their love is not meant for men, but for a man. Their duties and actions are not meant for men, but for a man. Yes; there is truth behind a woman being a superwoman, but even someone who is super can overburden themselves. Women are prone to doing just that, and your purpose as a man is to regulate her burdens; ensure that she does not take on too much at once. Take care of your woman and she will take care of you. Not advice, or necessity, but a requirement. She is the key to the survival of man. Fail woman, and you will lose paradise. Without her, all fails.

CHAPTER 3

The reality is, the best we could hope to achieve as a species is fairness, but never equality. To be equal, in the true sense of the word, we must be exact in principle, nature and physical makeup, and no one is exactly alike. We are all randomized elements, and yes; that goes for twins as well. There is always a factor that makes us different in some way from our neighbor; whether it be physical, mental or active, we all have varying degrees of differences. What is similar are certain physical characteristics and traits, but notice that a man's physical traits are far different from that of a woman's. If that is the case, then how can men and women be equal? To take it one step further: A woman's emotional state of mind will always set her apart from a man. The downside in our society is that we tend to listen to the wrong people when we try to figure out who we are. The upside is; we love each other's differences, and in some cases, quite literally to death. Now, imagine an equal world. Absolutely no differences between male and female. Again, let's take that idea even further. If society decided that all of us should think alike, talk alike, same inflections, pitch in our voices; our eyes would be alike, lips the same. The overall question would be; big breasts or little breasts; fat body or skinny, tall frame or short? How would you ever choose a companion? It is those differences that help us make up our mind when choosing someone to be close to us. What some people may find unattractive, others may find extremely attractive, except that they would be removed in order to maintain an equal environment.

CHAPTER 4

What happens when you seek to equalize a specific medium. For instance, career fields. When woman dominates a sector, she applies a heavy emotional state of mind, of which there is absolutely no defense against. What she wants is what she gets. Whether hot-headed or apparent innocent victim; she; the woman, gets what she wants, and she will demand special concessions. Needs that will help with job performance. Once granted certain allowances, is the idea of equality still there? Consider that nursing was a man's profession, now, dominated by women, not because they could do it better, but on the basis of a woman's emotional state of mind. Secretary was once a man's profession that is now, dominated by women. Same notation. The interesting aspect of that particular profession is that we can see the evolution of a female's emotional state of mind in real time. Females view the occupational title with a negative connotation, thus replacing the title of secretary with assistant or something that is more gratifying based on her image. Woman no longer wears the kind of clothes a man would wear if he were a woman. Otherwise, when considering the corporate world as a whole; "Mad Men" is about as accurate as it comes and nothing has truly changed.

A plainer more recognizable example of her emotional state of mind is visible in regards to cheerleading a ball game. An activity once conducted by men. How did men conduct the task of cheerleading? Rallying the fans. Leading the spectators in a spirited voice to motivate their athletic contenders against a competitor. Now, that women dominate that sector, what has it become? A vanity issue? Perhaps even a burlesque of distraction. One thing is for sure, and that it is no longer a matter of leading others, but a means of attracting attention to themselves. Oh, not the pretty little skirts showing off those big beautiful thighs; no. Whether the team wins or loses, the idea of sexual pleasure is always at work in the background due to the understanding that sex makes it all feel better. This is the notion of empowerment at work in plain view. The most potent drug in existence. Something about her voice that makes us want to look. We then see the body and the face, which all says something about who she is. It becomes a pleasing discomfort, and we can never get enough of that. This idea applies to all career fields, activities, ways of living, interactions, and our very existence as a whole.

Oh, and by the way; just for the record; cheerleading is not a sport. It is a rallying activity designed to inspire and command the loyalty of supporters against a competitor; however, when in competition itself against others in the same field of endeavor, then it falls more along the lines of perhaps synchronized gymnastics. They are competing against others in their field, of which this author believes, would qualify as a sport.

CHAPTER 5

Sure, women profess inequality and even unfairness; however, realistically speaking, she gets what she wants, where she wants, when she wants because, quite simply, she is the very definition of attraction, stimulation and delight. Sex is that powerful, and she places the man at a greatly disadvantaged position in regards to social affairs and academic fields. Their mere presence, let alone certain attire is a distraction to a man. Allowing females to feed their pleasure center with the thought of knowing they can tell a guy to get lost when they; themselves are trying to concentrate on their academics, and then charming him when he is trying to focus on his own studies with a tender alluring voice, placing him into a submissive state of mind. Knowing they have that kind of power over the male is a relishing aspect to her; the woman. This is why males were traditionally kept apart from females, for there is no true defense against her allure. With female presence, males cannot maintain a practical overall academic focus.

There is a fine line between competitiveness and companionship, and yet with woman comes sexual competitiveness. She makes change to what works for her. Goes against tradition. Disrupts proper social conduct in her liberation from man, and yes; God, including the practice of a male orientated workforce, the military, and our education system. They truly have an unfair advantage against males when allowed into any scholarly challenging environment, such as public education and higher learning. A certain kind of woman has been allowed to propagate in those arenas, interfering with a rational understanding of what is logical in our daily routine, and in situations whose effects may vary between the genders, resulting in the stifling of male esteem, and even his physical strength. We; males are geared for the marshaling of strength. There is absolutely no limit to our stamina, even our strength, short of retardation as a result of rules and regulations specifically geared for male behavior. For a man to experience his full potential, he must have certain allowances to achieve his goals. Most importantly a woman cannot participate in the pursuit of strength. Even being aware of her presence changes all of the parameters of pursuit. Male orientated institutions were designed around the marshaling of strength. There is always a time when *boy* needs to show his presence in order for that full potential of what is male to make itself known. That certain familiarity we come to expect when looking at a man. Especially in regards to military academies, of which, were once male orientated fields of endeavor. Where a male could experience his full potential without reservation; however, once women were allowed into these institutions of learning, their traditional masculine harmony was disrupted. His overall masculinity became retarded. The general notion of what is male has grown weaker since the inception of females to male orientated universities including West Point, Annapolis and the Air Force Academy. The military idea is an institution for boys to become men; to learn what it means to be man, based on religious convictions, honor and teamwork. To expand the mind beyond the confines of all existing reason and logic; however, the team can only be as strong as its weakest link. Part of being male; even in this high-tech world of mechanical contrivances, is still physical strength. Yes, intellect plays a part; however, in crisis, it is the male's strength that prevails when all else fails. A male's longevity has no boundaries, provided there are other males to spur him on. Pushing the limits of mental endurance, so, that we; the male of the species, can develop the confidence necessary to overcome any obstacle, which is crucial to human survival on the basis that technology is fleeting. Again, feminine distraction is preventing male cadets, midshipmen and combat trainees from tapping into their full, all around potential of what it means to be male. Though some men may attribute it to women getting tougher. The fallacy of that notion is whether or not females were ever truly weak to begin with.

CHAPTER 6

Even periods of relaxation and unwinding are retarded by the presence of females. Doubt this author? Consider this; when we males relax, what do we like to do? What do we like to talk about? Sports, technology, automobiles, more sports, and the dirty little delights we would like to do to women. No restrictions; no worries about any form of earthly reprisal. We can actually be men without following-through with our illusory ambitions, of which in turn allows the buildup of aggression. In most respects, aggression acts as a wonder drug in maintaining train of thought in challenging situations. That works for all levels of education; by the way. How, so? Aggression is the driving force behind success, and what is the source of male aggression both on a physical and mental plain? The pupil is forcing himself to focus on absorbing knowledge. Directing his increased testosterone levels on his confidence. Invigorating his brain with more testosterone, increasing his ability to memorize; to retain and recover detailed information. Yes; your testosterone is more than a thing for sexual combustibility. More than the key to your muscle mass, strength and stamina, but key to your mental mass, strength and stamina; your intelligence; and overall thought process as well. Perhaps now, you can see the true reasoning behind coed everything. Strip us; not the male, but the male community of our testosterone, and we fall by the wayside in regards to academics, and even physical prowess and leadership.

Now, be advised that the act of absorbing data is an extremely delicate process. Therefore, what do you think will happen to you, when a female is suddenly tossed into the mix. The buildup of testosterone that you have been fighting, so, hard to keep under control when her tight little body, sensual hip movements, pleasing voice, long hair and that great makeover gets hold of you. Your synapsis will scramble like a dozen eggs in a hot blender. You have just lost your ability to maintain complete focus. From that point on, sex is always in the mind's eye. We; the male, cannot focus; cannot concentrate on the crucial elements that keep our social infrastructure relevant and intact. What is it like today in the early Twenty-first? We are a sex-crazed culture that is out of harmony with reality, and every single thing is coming apart or does your smart-phone have that much control over you?

Male students must keep their academic focus. An impossible task since the inclusion of females in the overall academic process. She; who has made herself an attraction has become a distraction from the functionality of our entire civil and social infrastructure. Naturally, many of you reading this will probably disagree with the previous notion, and that is understandable when considering that you are the subservient male, or perhaps the male who can do no wrong in a female's eyes. When you speak; your words are music to her ears. The way you look, smell, and walk spins her thoughts into a euphoric state that makes interactions with her easy. Females call you sexy, and males call you cool, but all-in-all you are a person who lacks the ability to understand that not every guy can be you, and why is that? Because females say, so.

Consider; that most of our current colleges and universities are coed; a recipe for bad vibes between males and females. Centers of higher learning are designed to be competitive institutions, resulting in a gender paradox. A woman is not meant to compete with a man, but to be his helper. In our modern universities, there is a high state of dislike between the genders, but on mostly a subconscious level, which easily translates into inefficiency that leads to conflict in the social infrastructure. Oh; and let us be realistic; the whole sex-game plays the biggest part in the division between male/female relationships. Imagine that: The very thing we need to perpetuate the species is the cause of our resentment towards one another. That cannot be normal. Let us address that issue. Female copulates with male. He happens to be less than appealing on a psychological level; treats her like trash, and the whole concept of being a helper is in jeopardy. Premarital sexual intercourse continues with subsequent males furthering her bile for the very thing that she is meant to help. This translates into an unhealthy social system, and needless conflicts in daily life. She will be unable to cope with males in a productive meaningful lifestyle, and worst of all; she will never fully trust her man, should she reach that social evolutionary process. In fact, she may resort to a life of being a lesbian, something we; the male, do not want in regards to a traditional family setting. Furthermore, the bedroom becomes a competitive field. One side trying to dominate the other, for women are trying to be independent. Part of being independent is to overcome the world, and to do that, a person must be domineering. What women have forgotten more than anything else is how to be that indomitable force to be overcome. Instead of standing like a mountain, she lays flat like bulldozed earth. Woman was once like an ocean, but instead, she behaves more as a puddle of water in the street. His whole point is to get her to fall in love with him, and her whole point is to prove she can love him without the need for physical enticement or interaction. As it seems in our current social setting, she is more of a person who asks; *can you make me feel good?* Nothing no longer exists in regards to a mutually beneficial place for the continuation of the human species as-far-as civilized beings are concerned. Just sexual waste.

CHAPTER 7

Okay; she wants equality, and yet she wants to maintain the difference. She wants to keep her uniqueness intact in the grand scheme of things. She wants to maintain all of the gratuities initially afforded her as a woman prior to the great change. Notice that women have not given up a single thing in their pursuit of equality short of their vestal ways. All she has done is take more. This author asks the question; what is she willing to yield to achieve this thing we call equality? Beware that it is not equality she is searching for, but the removal of man's way of life. What is man's way of life? Everything.

Perhaps there should be equality, but it should remain within the genders themselves, and not taken out of the context of its meaning when trying to combine the aspects of different things, for it is easy to forget the truth of reality. That life must follow a certain pattern for the betterment of our sanity.

A final word on equality, in regards to our pets. Those of you, who are religiously orientated are the biggest fools in existence when allowing your pets to utilize furniture meant for a person. Allowing that big dog onto your couch or bed basically makes a statement. For those of us in the Judeo-Christian community, we have forgotten that humans were given instructions by God that allowed us to eat animals due to growing too close in relationship with them. Accepting them as equals, which can lead to profanities such as sexual intimacy with them. Sure, we say there is no harm in letting your dog share your couch or bed, but what of the next generation who are not, so, clear on that prospect? Do not assume for a minute that our future generations will simply understand. Certain interactions become precedence, and later generations lose objectivity to what is proper and improper homo sapient behavior.

Now, there is nothing wrong with having a close association with your pet; however, animals, such as dogs were given short life spans, so, that each subsequent period of your existence can be invigorated with a kind of newness that encourages an inspiration to be happy. The old pet is replaced by a new pet and it's time to live anew. Therefore, let the old guy go, so, that the new guy can experience your love and care.

HATRED OF CHILDREN

CHAPTER 1

So, the question is; do we hate our children? The answer to that question is an unequivocal; yes. We hate them until they become corrupted. Mentally and physically abused, sexually assaulted, after of which, we suddenly feel compelled to show them the affection they should have received prior to the application of the corruption and the abuse. Why do we not love our children? They have a certain nearness to God that we as adults slowly shed over time. We are guilty due to our selfish desires, ideas and beliefs. We have established a way of life that is contradictory to God, and, so, our children are confused. Since they have a nearness to God; a fresh connection to Him, they know that what we; adults are doing is wrong. Therefore, we allow that innocence to be corrupted, and yes, they are highly prized by the perverse for their innocence. Now, there is a little-known secret that many of you reading this do not know. God is innocence in the truest meaning of the word, and form. We are all God and have the potential to be like the one true God, but we become corrupted. How does this happen? Why does it happen? The answer is quite simple. The disease of want. Not by our children, but by us. We make the idea of want, look, so, good in the eyes of a child that it sets in and corrupts them. On the other hand, what would you get if you protected your child with every fiber of your being? Taught them to be kind and giving; respectful to those around them. To never turn away a person in need? They would truly be the golden child of society; however, if you do not care for your children, then they will grow up like the lion or the gazelle. In either case, they will survive off instinct, and that is something that will not work in a complex culture.

All of our behaviors are a matter of want. We see, hear, smell, touch and taste things that we want. Add to that, this author's proposed sixth sense of empathy. Ever get the *feeling* that you must have it? All of which, is a direct effect towards our behaviors. Every aspect

122

of this reality affects us in some way beginning at our very conception. That need to live, to thrive.

Behaviors are nurtured during a human being's physical and mental development. The world we live in, immediately impacts the infant both within the womb and outside of it. This is why mothers, not fathers are crucial to childhood development. The mother has established an integral bond with that child, beginning with conception. Why break that bond after birth? The father's duty is to provide a sense of safety for both the mother and the child. He provides the nest, the food, the sense of bond-ship. In other words, to protect and provide, of which we; the male cannot be present in their lives all of the time; however, if we are, then that too can have an adverse effect on the child. Too much male intervention can lead to gaps in the masculine/feminine complex.

The mother's responsibility is exclusive to the child's existence on the basis that childhood-development is, so, fragile, and requires a level of attentiveness that maybe distracting to a point that nothing else matters in the world. Do not get the preconceived notion that your child is a gazelle or a bison. We; the human, are a higher life form with greater complexity then that of the beast of the field or of the wild. Another way of saying there is something special about us; making us standout from other living things. Religion calls it a soul. Therefore, a human mother does not simply allow the child to start off on their own, not in regards to the physical development of the child that is, but more of the mental development, for it is our mental faculties that gives us a sense of existence; however, like the gazelle or the bison, a mother should be close to his child; your child, constantly, even in their adult-hood. Remember, that child is a continuation of you; the father. They are you, and they are God, and yet they are neither, based on the understanding of free will, allowing for individuality. Without freewill, we could not call ourselves human-beings. What is fascinating about being individuals is that we are designed to work as a whole, which explains the purpose of Judeo-Christianity. There is a difference between a team and a herd. Perhaps our modern cities have become a refuge for the herd without us realizing it. We are a species that preys upon itself without necessity. We are both herd and predator. Notice that there are times when we will hunt in packs. We as a species must break the cycle of going everywhere, and yet going nowhere, by becoming a team. To break the cycle requires a book of directions. This author can think of one book that would be perfect for this understanding of ourselves.

CHAPTER 2

Unfortunately, we know for a fact that parents do not raise their children properly; especially if both parents have a career outside of the home. Raising a child is not some mediocre task. It has to be a well thought out, and never-ending process. Children are not some machine that a person can simply turn on and off or set loose at a whim. They are a living breathing being, and if not constantly tended too; they have the potential to be more devastating to a society than any bomb. With constant proper parenting; mentoring children can develop together, but that would presuppose an ideal environment. We do not live an ideal environment because children do not have constant support in the home, and women who could provide constant support choose not to give it; and those women who want to provide support cannot because of the displacement of men from the workforce by the career woman or the unfortunate result of premarital sexual intercourse or divorce.

The problem with our culture is that we have abandoned our religious views for a secular lifestyle, which, is nothing more than a collection of ideas from various sources with an understanding that everyone can have it their own way to some degree; however, this course of action is doomed to failure. Ideas from different sources do not work because they greatly vary in almost every area of understanding. Judeo-Christian philosophy is tried and true, and yet because some people in our society choose not to believe in God, we have to do things their way? This is an improper course of action in regards to maintaining a prolific civilized environment. A person can choose not to believe in a thing that works for others. It is their prerogative; however, if the majority is fine with how
124

something works, then why bother it? For the minority, more often than not, is made up of a conglomerate of trouble makers anyway, and they simply want to feed off the very chaos they create. In all accounts, an atheist is nothing more than a dissatisfied person. If everyone said that God did not exist, they would simply say; *He does exist,* just to maintain the psychological conflict within the community because that is human nature. Twist the screws to see what it takes to break the status quo. Agents of chaos, and we allow them to rip and run throughout our community due to our lack of understanding the application of Constitutional Law?

Could steroid use be the cause of, so, many males being born with autism? The breath of life passes through the male of the species, and taking steroids may be tampering with that delicate biological processes. Something to consider when attempting to push the body beyond its limits through means of a drug. What makes a male attractive in the eyes of a female is not something that can be overlooked. She wants the cream of the crop, not product subject to quality control. With particular want comes unrealistic expectations in regards to the synthesis of genuine warm feelings for another. There are lots of autistic male children, and there are lots of competitive male athletes seeking female desires. Again, she is sex, and we want it, and logically speaking we do, so, much to the human body to get it without consideration of the long-term effects, and yes; that includes the kinds of food that we eat, for if we are what we eat, then perhaps parents should reconsider their dietary choices when making plans to expand the household. Ponder on a kosher diet for the benefit of your offspring's mental development. Just a suggestion from this author, not a must.

CHAPTER 3

Why are our children killing one another? Could we be placing undue pressure on them at too early an age? Not in an academic sense, but more of contending with daily interaction with others on their own without guidance. With secularism currently dominating our culture, everyone is running with opposing ideas and beliefs. No matter how chaotic the idea, we allow it to thrive, and the young mind latches onto it due to the parent failing to apply a functional state of moral conduct from the onset of mental maturity. Think about the internet. You surf the web, and it's easy, but imagine someone surfing the web for the first time. No one to explain the intricacies, and tricks to find things of useful interest. To find anything for that matter, but they are absorbing something. Interesting how we take the subtleties of daily living in much the same way. We know it; forgetting that someone taught us how to use it. In the past when more women stayed at home; mothers could take their time preparing children for the day, and for life in general. There was no need to rush, with the possibility of leaving them to fend for themselves. Depending upon them to motivate themselves into going to school on their own, or wherever they had to be. Now, that more mothers have careers outside of the home, they have applied their work schedule and ethics onto the child. Effectively placing their career-burdens on them at an age when all they should have to worry about is their schoolwork. Now, they are under the pressure of mother's employer for mother's sake, for the feminists have set the standard, or she simply made a poor choice in allowing a bad man into her existence. So, in effect, we are immolating our children without realizing what we are doing to them. Our immoral conduct is a holocaust, and though we pretend to care, we truly do not. We are a culture working, so, hard for feminist's rights, that we are *sacrificing* the very thing we need for a continued existence. Truth be told, social systems do not fail from the outside. No one simply walks in and conquers a thriving community. Failure comes from within due to the populous taking for granted their social stability, laziness of human enthusiasm and lack of creative motivation. In other words, a civilization's comfort and vigilance falls out of balance. They let down their guard. Interesting how the one thing that cancels out the comfort is the thing we strive to avoid, and that is *war!* We are not talking about the conflicts that are kept at a distance, but a major world war that smashes everything. Takes away the comfortable environment, so, that people will be on their guard for the unexpected.

When civilization is gone, then we see the truth of gender interaction, and its overall purpose in the grand scheme of things.

Another point to consider is the effect a negative environment has on a developing mind. With that in mind, why is it, that we are not more understanding of those who may have been consumed by a negative environment during their growing years? A time when a person should be at their happiest, but instead experience the negative impact of life. Oh, not a situation of hunger due to a lack of food or clothing. No; we are speaking of the negative impact of foul language and behavior that may be construed as being proper by a young mind. A mother with a child in her womb, who is constantly being bombarded by hate and insults. How does that affect them? Think about a man who is always angry; yelling at those around them, especially at children and women. What is a child to think? Children do not comprehend the intricacies and delicacies of social interaction. So, when harsh expletives are tossed about in their presence, he or she absorbs what they hear and run with it, and what do we have today? Negative emotions overwhelming the positive social disposition, even in a benevolent environment, resulting in hostility increasing exponentially. Even more abstruse is the effect that certain kinds of music have on a child, both in and out of the womb. A harsh, hateful environment does impact our surroundings, affecting both living and nonliving matter. Sound shapes the mind and evokes emotional response. It influences compassion, determines behavior both within the womb and after birth. Sound is capable of sending a child into a positive or damaging sociological state. Sure, you may hate jazz, you may hate an orchestra; however, soothing the mind cannot be achieved by the *boom*. Violent sounds. Dark sounds of hatred and disrespect of a worsening kind. Hostile language that usually focuses on those who depend upon us for protection, and sure, a woman complains about her treatment in society, while shaking her ass to the very thing that demeans her very existence? Yes; we say there is nothing wrong with it, while the hatred increases exponentially within our communities. An artificial tone that can only degrade the mental state. Steal away mental energy, and lead to mental decay. Sure; we may say a rock is not affected by negative emotions, but are we sure of that? Strange things happen around us. Machinery fails for no plausible reason. What else can it be? Especially in regards to a piece of electronics; a car or appliance. Consider the choice of sounds we immerse ourselves in. As with the movie; *"Ghost Busters 2"* emotions do have an effect on matter.

CHAPTER 4

Look closely at our modern culture here in the early Twenty-first, and asked yourself; are we stripping our male children of their innocence? Their self-esteem? Of what it means to be a male? When a man-child says, he does not like girls, does it mean he is on the path to homosexuality, or is he simply seeking his manhood? Perhaps; and while in his pursuit, he does not want girls getting in the way. Boys do not understand the purpose of girl, and learning what is girl, interferes with learning to be boy. That is the point of sex education; plain and simple. We are forcing boys to be accepting of girls, understanding girls, but are taking the boys for granted on the basis that girls are not required to understand boys. Freeing her to pursue her goals, and many of those goals cross over into what should be male territory. Boys want to be men; however, so, many mothers are riding the homosexual bandwagon, that they apparently, do not understand what it means to seek that, which we the male of the species call manhood. As if mothers think it's cool for their boys to be lovers of male flesh, or does it have something to do with women dominating our society to the point of stripping away a man-child's opportunities?

We live in such a fragile social infrastructure, that when you take under consideration that *feminine* is the baseline for human behavior; then it takes a step up to make someone masculine. Look at boys and girl from babies through adolescence. There is a point when the masculinity kicks in on a boy, but be mindful as the father, for the boy may not realize that it is kicking in, which is why we; the male of the species, requires a rite of passage. Sure, it is hard being a girl; however, it is harder for a boy to develop masculinity. Sometimes a boy needs to be told that he is male. Girls; whom are maintaining
128

that boy within them, require clarity of conduct. Consider, that if a woman does not ween the child from breastfeeding, would she continue to allow that child to suckle until the age of eighteen? Not that it's possible for a woman to produce milk for that long, but under the pretense that occasional variations just do not register; and if it does not register, then it may take a little kick in the pants to get it to register.

Children; usually boys go off their rocker for whatever reason. They shoplift, spit, cuss and say the damndest things at the most inconvenient moment, and naturally you take the necessary steps to prevent them from building upon that kind of behavior. That is unless you are a foolish parent whom allows their child to do whatever they want; a term now, referred to as affluenza. So, to you; the rational minded father who claims to be a Christian and is aware of what is proper and what is improper, what gives you the right to override the will of God? Your responsibility to your man-child is to guide him along the paths of manhood no matter what. Not tell him that it is okay to bend another man over a table or to allow themselves to be bent over a table and pumped in the anal cavity by a male sexual appendage. By you allowing this kind of behavior to persist, begs the question of where the true problem lies; the person who exhibits homosexual tendencies or the parent, relative or friend that allows it to go unchecked?

Consider a Boy Scout leader speaking to your confused man-child who happens to be asking questions about relationships, and instead of guiding him along the path of heterosexual thinking, masculinity, and being tough, he tells him instead that he is gay. That it is okay to get in touch with his feminine side. Now, do not get the wrong impression from what is being scribed by this author. Getting in touch with your softer side is perfectly okay, but only after you have identified *boy* first. You cannot identify one without the other. For males, we must discover our masculinity first, and the same can be said for the female, accept in her case, femininity must be identified in order to restrict her aggression. Makes you wonder if fags are qualified to lead men and boys. It would become a means of covert recruitment into the ranks of the perverse.

A man-child has every right to know what is expected of him. Do not assume he understands the social game plan. These are confusing times. We are no longer a male orientated society. In the past, everything a boy did and heard was male, and, so, naturally, as with everything else, we men just assumed the male orientated infrastructure would always be there. Look at the world today and what do you see? A female dominated society. Therefore, you; the father must tell your boy that he is a boy; and at the proper time, guide him along the lines of understanding the purpose of a woman as a means of achieving a harmonious, productive lifestyle. Teach him how to be a man, not a boy, and you will be surprised at the result. Most importantly, stop listening to and/or seeking advice from those, whom support immoral behavior. For they are agents of the fallen one, purposely designed to mislead you and your man-child down a different path. A man-child is hungry to learn what it means to be a man. He wants to grow up, so, that he can be counted as part of the overall human mechanism. Part of the team.

No man-child should be denied the right or rite towards seeking his full all-around potential. If we hand off all of the things that a boy needs to be a man, to a girl, then what are we left with in regards to being a male? A girl? Flip-flopping the genders like some toy? One day she can be the boy, another day she can be the girl? That is what you get when feminine values govern a civilized culture. Erosion of the genders, resulting in absolute adolescent confusion. This is a result of the Flower Power Movement. All of that free love stuff. Many couples created children out of wedlock, for in their minds, they had to break with the status quo. Anything goes, a person can do anything they, so, choose; however, we are learning the hard way, that idea does not work; even in a democracy. Let us call that idea; *The Foolishness of The Human Animal,* and since we are in an unacknowledged Dark Age; let us institute another new term to help us define a boy's behavior: *The Beaver Effect;* for boys who do not want to interact with girls. The 1950/60's television show called; *"Leave It To Beaver"*. The lead character; Theodore or the Beaver; had a dislike for girls. This is, believe it or not, normal behavior for a man-child. A built-in mechanism; if you would, for dealing with the gender interactive process. Preventing children from prematurely engaging in sexual intercourse; however, the modern feminists are disrupting this mechanism. Once we started instituting sex education in our public schools, things went horribly wrong. What is sex education? A method of integrating a feminine understanding into the will of man without the concept of marriage to regulate the process of maturity in regards to she; who is sex. In other words; telling a child to be accepting of sex. To be mature around a female. In effect, canceling out the Beaver Effect, so, that girl can dictate the overall social interface. The subconscious is the place where innocence thrives. Let's call that area of the mind, God's little com-port. Our understanding of sex education as it stands is a practice that is nothing more than an abomination. A means of conditioning culture to the point of complete disorientation. Becoming more of an encouragement to a thing rather than an understanding of responsibility. Why did this happen? Examine the patterns of social change. First; gender integration of our classrooms. Next; regulated education on a national level, and the secularists got hold. Again, seek the writings of David Barton for further insight into that travesty of human endeavors. Next; when mainstream careers opened up for women, academics became more of a competitive concern, rather than a medium for crossing the threshold of the unknown. In other words, feminine demands have driven academics to gear itself to her needs. Affixing itself more on the programming of the mind, instead of the intellectual creativity for understanding purpose. Sounds crazy? Then ask yourself one simple question; why are more boys dropping out of schools than girls? Of course, boys could be suffering from sensory overload due to the constant burlesque. Since no useful academics is being absorbed, they fail to make the grade, and what, stay in school for the rest of their lives looking at the burlesque? Oh, and let us be clear on one other matter; sex is everywhere. Even where it shouldn't be. What is the public education system today in the early Twenty-first? Havens for teen suicide? Drug dealing, and even gang activity? Gratis prostitution zones? And where there is prostitution, there is violence. Fact of life, and people say that we need to institute better gun control measures? This author has an idea: Institute gender segregation and a strict dress code. Oh, and just in case you; the reader, haven't noticed, many high school students exhibit the signs of homelessness whether they are doing well in school or not.

Look; the movers and the shakers of free love, inherited the world, and they incorporated ideas that were defeatist in nature. Getting all of us to believe that; *our children are going to initiate sexual intercourse anyhow, so, let us institute safe sex practices instead.* Just as a side note: We talk about safe sex practices, and yet allow our daughters to show off their hot little bodies in public, thinking they are just little girls, but what we fail to realize is that; let us call it; *Clothed Nudity,* is the pouring of gasoline onto the fire. Every person develops at a different rate on both a physical and mental level. Some female children have a certain physical aptitude that casts them right into the league of extraordinary pageantry, while still in junior high. Should describing them as being a *minor,* be deemed as proper language in regards to those with an adult build? She plays the part, so, well that she is capable of fooling even adult females, and it is *he* who is punished? The power of our mental competitiveness at work. You want a certain look, you will achieve that look, but what of those adults whom are not physically ideal, existing at the opposite end of the mental spectrum of insecurity? Think about that from a psychological standpoint as a man. Again, having to *figure* things out when your body is being stimulated by a female walking down the street or in our halls of learning.

The point of the Beaver Effect is due to the fact that sex is an immature behavior; *period.* A boy is seeking maturity. He does not want to be involved with the very notion that will hamper his efforts to becoming a man. How do we know that sex is an immature state of mind? Reaction; plain and simple. Distraction. How do people behave in a strip club? How do you behave when a hot bodied female passes by? Do you view sexually illicit material in a public setting? Why not? Those female intellectuals profess that sex should be taken maturely; *right?* When your children do something immature, what do you do? How do you react? What do you say? Your child jumps up and down on the bed; what do you say to them? Playing some form of ball game in the house; what do you say to them? Trail mud into the kitchen; what do you say to them? Tormenting the siblings; what do you say? Simply being a plain annoyance; what do you say? For all of it, you tell them to stop. When children conduct any form of immature activity, you tell them to stop. If viewing sex generates immature behavior, and those female intellectuals tell males to be mature in regards to sex, then perhaps we need to be mature in regards to all immature activity, and at all ages. Ever have a woman tell you to grow up? That usually occurs during a sexual encounter of some kind. Ever watch a circus clown in action? He is behaving immaturely; *why?* Ever see a comedian throwing out insults? He is behaving immaturely; *why?* Do you know a person who collects toys? He is behaving immaturely; *why?* We do immature things to break the monotony of life. When we are children we run from immaturity; however, when we become adults we seek it out. Sometimes we just want the joy of feeling happy, and there is nothing in this universe that makes us feel happiest then a hot looking babe clothed in the nude. Now, isn't it funny how we say that reacting a certain way, to a certain thing makes us immature; and yet, projecting something that generates immaturity is acceptable? Unless it's the wayward kid that shows illicit material to the other school students in the school lavatory.

CHAPTER 5

What is the process for developing positive masculinity? Ideally, he; the man-child, requires a sex-free environment. Though many people will disagree with the previous, it must be said. Females truly restrict a man-child's abilities. His masculine potential, and the overall masculinity process, which is an extremely delicate process. What he wants to do is go inside of a box and come out with massive biceps, triceps and a chest that belongs to a super hero.

He wants to feel ten feet tall. Unfortunately, children do not develop evenly. We know this for a fact. Some are born with greater courage, while others have a propensity for intellectualism. Therefore, parents must train their man-child how to fight. Fighting does not necessarily denote violence, but simply a way of life. It is how we males toughen the sinew, build confidence, and help us to better serve the female. He needs this for when he is tested by the bully. Remember, winning or losing a fight is of no consequence to what it means to be man, but simply expresses the willingness to be aggressive; to embrace his masculinity. What the bully wants to see is aggression. Applying masculine affection. A state in which men fight each other. Sometimes after the ingestion of an inebriating material to see if the other meets the criteria for masculinity. He is simply another male who wants to know if your boy is someone he can be friends with. No tough guy wants to be associated with a wimp because it makes them look like a wimp. At some point during the masculine affection, the intellect prevails instituting the male bonding process towards friendship. At least that is how it used to be. Explain to your man-child to not be ashamed of losing a fight. Standing up against an aggressor is what is important. Tell your boy the secret that you were not taught, and that is; he must get mean, but remain in charge of his faculties; his self-control. Let his opponent know that he means business, for he must earn the right to be called a man. It is not given. This is not a new concept, but proper masculine conduct that has been around since the beginning of humanity, but is now, stifled by the feminists. There is also another means of fighting an opponent, and that is, with the use of words. Words can be used to hurt or to gain trust. A true leader of men must use both; strength and words honorably, to be accepted by his peers. Females have disrupted this male growth process, and it clearly shows why women do not belong in a male environment. Yes, you have girls who exhibit a higher aggression than a man-child, but this should not preclude the idea of letting her take the lead. He has every right to realize his full potential. It is his right as the male in pursuit of manhood. Again, a girl loses absolutely nothing if she is prevented from being boy. Just because a girl has the urges to be boy does not mean a father should allow her to be boy. She must be guided along the path of what is girl.

We have gone away from the moral understanding of what is masculine and what is feminine in regards to our daily living. A gender-neutral environment conflicts with our need to maintain simplicity in an ever-expansive social existence. The ability to define a thing based on the existence of another is paramount to our overall understanding of anything; existence itself. A feminine is required, in order to identify what is masculine. Without that aspect of life, you cannot identify one without the other. That is the very notion of man. Without that difference, a total breakdown of everything is assured. The man-child must come to understand the purpose, need, and importance of the female. Explain to him how she plays a pivotal role in our society, for without her, we; the male cannot identify ourselves. We are nothing, and as previously scribed, we are just half a species. Our whole being in this realm is to protect her; and yes, that includes even the promiscuous ones, the harlots, and the adult performers because even they serve a purpose in our culture; however, to do, so, we must deal a firm hand to the witch and the warlock.

Next, as we separate males and females in the classroom, the key thing we must ask ourselves as males is what of the purpose for females being educated to begin with? Yes; a straight slap in the face of womanhood, but we must accept the possibility of some men requiring an answer to that very question. Human-beings require clarity of purpose in order for the implementation of social procedure to occur. Retarding a person of knowledge is a primitive state of being. At the same time; incorporating the female into the daily social function of life is an error. Her knowledge is not meant to be collaborated with the overall social infrastructure. Yes, this author understands that women have great ideas; we do not call it father of necessity for a reason, but the problem comes with the complexity of her mind. Ideas and information treks through her mind as bugs around a nightlight, and with great emotion, comes impatience, the clouding of reason and judgement. In other words, she is, so, different from the male of the species in regards to the overall thought processes that we are compelled to wonder if she is even of this world. Whatever the case may be, her psychological complexity is crucial towards keeping man atop the food chain. Constantly developing her intellectualism; advancing the human machine. Pushing the threshold, so, that we do not stagnate into a useless collection of repetitive mechanics. Look at animals. They stick to one process. Humans; on the other hand, advance by means of introducing new ideas and concepts, but within the guidelines of tradition. How is this realized? From a specific perspective or angle. Yet, there are multiple perspectives to build upon. Why not others? Simple; that is how the male works. From the perspective of a child; *simple*. You cut the board in one direction in order to get a smooth edge. Easy to understand. Easy to follow. Introduce additional saws at the same time, and you get chaos; however, from a feminine perspective it is viewed as art, and ever since their ideas entered the communal process, social evolution ceased almost immediately because their first agenda was to kill the child. The one in our hearts and the ones in their womb. It was by no sheer coincidence that the sex education initiative, *Roe-v-Wade* decision, and the feminist movement happened together. To switch from a collaborative system to a self-serving system, you need those three to work in conjunction. Nobody is willing to make the sacrifices anymore to make the system work. Everybody behaves as the feral woman; vain, and self-serving. All aspects of life focus around being self-serving, including our children. Which explains why the Church does not fit into the new social order or perhaps a more appropriate application would be, chaos. One: It represents order. Two: It represents self-sacrifice. Three; and this is the one that is completely missed: Not to fear death. The Church is an institution that prepares a person for death from the very beginning due to life being such a precious commodity, of which under feminist needs, is viewed as nothing. Forced means of survival of the fittest, except

136

it is not by natural choice, but by a woman's choice. Explaining why we are unable to expand our minds, in this modern era of the early Twenty-first. Our existence is simply an extension of what has already been established or a modification that has simply been rearranged. That's what women do: Make rearrangements, so, that the same looks different, giving them a sense of something new, but with a certain affinity or need for the old. This is a result of focusing on her agenda of equality instead of social progress.

CHAPTER 6

Since we do not allow our children to be involved with the adult film industry, are we in fact dehumanizing them, still? No, of course not. We know, or at least should know, that as parents, it is our responsibility to guide them on a proper course of behavior, and not allow them to make a decision that would lead to jeopardizing their sense of what is proper, and what is improper. A child's mind is a jumble of ideas, dreams, and what ifs. In a nutshell, their thoughts are pure chaos, and yet they have a certain nearness to God that we take for granted in our later years. That core programming that identifies what is proper and what is improper. They require guidance to bring about order to better understand core values. Consider that if a child spent just one or two hours a week learning their academics, how much would they learn? So, why is it, that you; the parent, make it a point to spend one or two active hours with your child at best, and expect them to understand the basic mechanics of life? To interact with others? To understand what society is all about? Note: As the child ages, the less time you spend with them. If you; the parent, spend more time at the job than with your child, then your child will seek advice from those whom spend more time with them. That is why it is necessary for both parents to raise a child. You must spend huge amounts of time with your child for them to get it. If school takes all day, then you should be spending the equivalent with your children. Impossible, you say? Summer, fall, winter and spring breaks, and the weekends. Do the math. Children spend more time out of school, then they do in school.

If you; the reader, happens to be Catholic Christian, non-Catholic Christian or Jewish, you must teach them about God first and foremost. Not math, not science, but God. A child requires religious input from both of the parents in order to fully maturate the conscious and subconscious mind to an understanding of religious principles and obedience to a greater power. How this is applied is determined by daily household activities, but must be applied no later than adolescence, and is ongoing for life. Adhering to doctrine without question. This gives the child perspective in a world of infinite possibilities. Understanding of who they are, so, that they may have a sense of moral identity and presence when firmly planting their feet on the path of purpose. Once they have purpose, they will develop confidence and achieve sentience. This is what a young woman will be looking at when deciding on whether or not to accept a potential suitor or accept the proposal of a potential suitor.

Another point to consider is that asking a chaotic mind what it wants is completely illogical. As a parent, it is your responsibility to bring those thoughts into alignment. Guide their decisions and choices. Give the child purpose; direction, specifically, the man-child. What you; the father, will find most difficult is aligning the thoughts of the youngest child. The one child whom needs you the most because they are dealing with a whole slew of variables such as older sibling rivalries and the feeling of inferiority in wanting to be a part of the daily action. They are cast outs due to youth, until they mature to a point of where they can engage in the daily adult routines of life.

Foul language is perhaps another thing a child picks up on. If you use it, then he or she will use it. He or she will not use it, if other people use it, but if you use it, then as the chief instructor, he or she will get the impression that it is okay for them to use it. Furthermore, the use of expletives in dialogue are not required either. A person can express dissatisfaction and anger without the use of foul language. We all experience pain. It is simply a part of life. The use of expletives is not.

A crucial point to make in this age of the early Twenty-first, in regards to our children, is that teaching homosexual behavior as being okay; is in fact, improper. Teaching about sex is improper. There is a time for such things, but those necessities for a proper productive lifestyle should be taught when there is a better understanding of who they are as a living being.

Be mindful of using siblings in lieu of yourself; the parent, in regards to rearing of children. Big brother and/or sister must have the admiration of the child before doing, so, and there can be no divergence from this idea. They must also possess a high sense of responsibility. You cannot simply thrust responsibility upon them, unless they have a clear understanding of Church doctrine. This will help them later in their lives when instructing others from the perspective of leadership, perhaps even their own children.

Once accomplishing the task of gaining your child's attention, you bestow your legacy upon them. Remember, your children are an extension of yourself. Whatever they do in public and/or in private reflects upon you, so, make sure that you align them well to the overall needs of the community. Make them aware of your expectations of them. Do not give them an inch for they will take a foot. A child has no privacy under your roof. Their bedroom is subject to inspection 24 hours a day, 7 days a week, and yes, that includes their social gathering areas; basement, garage, treehouse or wherever. They do not choose what to eat; once they are hungry enough, they will eat what you have cooked. They are your slave until they get a place of their own; dirty little cuss, but essentially the truth. This is not a bad thing. It is a necessity, in order to prevent social-disruption. Oh, and those of you whom are thinking that disorder and chaos are the same thing. Well, let this author put it to you like this; we are currently in a state of social disorder. Chaos occurs when complete ambivalence affects all levels of society resulting in the complete breakdown of the public infrastructure.

Dealing with the woman-child is not as difficult as it may seem. She must learn kindness and humility. What she requires is lots of attention. If you; the father, do not give her that attention, then she will find another who will, and that person may not share in your ideas or beliefs; however, you must make sure to remind her of who her parents are. Give her power, and she will become a serious nuisance. There is nothing worse than an obstinate daughter whom is seeking to be the dominate force in your household. Mother will be the target of her aggression. Worst of all, she will become a harlot, and all of it will reflect upon your failure as a father.

Another point that is being grossly overlooked, and that is a man-child whom is bonding to an older boy or even a man, does not denote homosexual behavior unless the older boy or man institutes it. The man-child is searching for guidance, purpose; verification of truth. He is searching for reason. He is extremely vulnerable and incredibly impressionable in his preteen years. So, you; as the parent, have to be extremely careful with him. He is bombarded by sex. The display of the feminine form is impacting him on all levels of existence. Women ignore this because they think that man-child will adapt. Do not deny the facts. We are not adapting. No one is, for she is always changing the rules and the jails are overflowing.

When a person engages in homosexual activity, we say, or to say the least, there are people who say; *that is the choice they made;* however, if they are not shown their options then is it truly a choice? A child grows up in an antithesis of what was taught by previous generations then are they not being denied an opportunity to carry on the ideas, beliefs and traditions set down by their forefathers? If a mother is not guiding that man-child along the lines of what it means to be a boy or that woman-child of what it means to be a girl; even a very basic understanding of what is proper male or female behavior, then what options do they truly have? You cannot allow a child to make crucial sociological choices in a delicate environment such as this; the United States of America, on the basis that we are a peoples secluded, and yet bonded by an idea. What has kept the country together is the fact that people whom cannot see one another have faith enough to believe that the ideas are still the same. Unfortunately, there are parents whom kill that notion

140

when saying; *that is the choice that my child has made,* but then when it comes to choosing a partner to commit to a physical interaction, for example; an adult male, then that same parent will say; *that's wrong;* and with great fervor. *That's inappropriate.* They will call it rape, and as-far-as they are concerned, that older man is a pedophile, a child predator? Yes, and the same can be said for a girl. Notice, how some parents will say; *the child is capable of choosing their own path;* and when the child makes a choice that does not set well with them, they abruptly intervene? Their child's choices are suddenly unacceptable? These, so-called parents allow their children to choose their sexual orientation, and even when to conduct their sexual orientation, but then intervene when the child's choice of whom to engage with in that sexual orientation? View it with contempt and negativity? View it as inappropriate?

We should be saying; *no,* to our children, repeatedly, in regards to that, which is unhealthy from a moral standpoint; however, we; the parent, become easily frustrated, and simply stop trying. Look; we are stubborn creatures, and when we really want something, we push ourselves until we get it. That includes sculpting our children. Stubbornness is a part of the human evolutionary process, and a child's stubbornness is like a great chasm. At first glance it may seem to be an impossible obstacle to overcome, but persistence is the key. Especially in regards to homosexual behavior because in reality none of us who understand moral living figured it out overnight. You did not learn it in an instant, but you expect others to figure it out right there and then. Again, we are a lazy species by nature, and often forget that it takes time for the details of conformity to sink in. Looking at history in milliseconds instead of understanding it in accordance to the natural passage of time. That is how you get your point across to a child, not giving in due to controversial social perceptions.

Let us make clear that the idea of a child finding their own way is a ridiculous notion. Parents must guide a child's decisions from the onset of life. You must set them on the path of your choosing. Condition your child to your wants and needs and expectations before society gets hold of them; before their so-called friends get hold of them. So, that they can have a baseline to build upon, and make changes if they, so, desire. You teach your child to walk because that is what you do. You teach your child to talk because that is what you do. You teach your child to use a toilet because that is what you do. So, why would you wait for your child to make their own choices about life in general? Do you give your child a choice to attend school? Why not? If your toddler is about to walk off a cliff, do you let them? Got news for you; the parent reading this, that is exactly what many of you have done over the years. Perhaps the philosophy is; *you have to break a few bones in order to find your way in life.* Look; the truth is, you cannot start teaching your child the choices of life when they are teenagers. Contrary to what you may think, or what you may have heard or may have been told; children want guidance, they want to be told what to do. Even if you are unsure of yourself as a parent, a partial guidance is better than no guidance in order to get your child going in life. You can both learn together as he or she grows and matures. They want to be spanked when they are bad. They want to be told that they did something wrong, in order to help them fit in and do the right thing, not for society, but for morality's sake. It is a sign that you are a caring parent. Do not run from parenthood, for your child is an extension of yourself. They are the key to your immortality, so, it is important that you teach them when they are young because a child wants to bond with their parents, not with someone else. That is why it is important to marry a woman of like-mind. Yes, it may be difficult to find her, but not impossible.

Could autism be the result of a lack of constant motherly attention? Perhaps not; however, it is something to think about, especially when considering that human mothers are more than likely prone towards leaving his children, especially the man-child alone for extreme long periods of time. Not necessarily after birth, but in their daily lives and rituals. She; the mother, must show the child constant love and attention, especially during hours of sleep, and most importantly, a non-hostile state of mind, or that spark of joy just fizzles. Naturally, it is assumed that growth and development ceases at child-birth. This is a myth. Growth and development does not end until the death of the body. We are creatures whom require constant social interaction and activity. Preferably; positive interaction. Without that interaction and activity, we wither and die. Not physically, but mentally, and when the child is dead, they will take others with them.

There was a time when doctors would spank a newborn to induce tears. Perhaps as an understanding of somehow waking the child to a new world. Could this action have been a preventative measure for autism? The sting of pain, wakes the brain.

CHAPTER 7

Now, withal said, would you let any harm come to a child? If you see a child about to run into traffic, would you prevent them from doing, so? Not your child, but someone else's child; and yet, you intervene; *why?* You know in the deepest fiber of your being, that you have a communal responsibility to all of the children whether you have children or not. If you see one child harming another, do you intervene or do you sit by and watch? Are you the kind of person whom encourages a child to fight, perhaps even kill another child? Some of you probably would, but for those of you who behave on a more civilized level, consider this; what does a young mother do when she walks into an abortion clinic? She is bringing her unborn child to a person to be judged. Yes; that child is being judged by another, and is immediately deemed unworthy without proper representation. How does an abortion clinic doctor know the crimes of a child to warrant an act of capital punishment? The idea of those who are versed in the medical field have a responsibility to save lives, and yet we clearly have a *secular* contradiction at work in our midst.

There are those whom ask the question of; *why do people show, so, much concern over abortion?* The answer is, so, simple that even those whom fight against it often forget why. As abolitionists fought for the rights of a people in the United States of America prior to 1860, those exact same questions regarding human rights have arisen yet again. Are our unborn children entitled to the same inalienable rights under Constitutional Law as with any person? Yes; women fought long and hard to get from underneath a man's thumb. A man's wants. A man's needs, in order to achieve their individuality, and yet, that very thing they hold, so, near and dear to their hearts; that individuality; that sense of liberation, they deny to that child developing in their womb? The right to the pursuit of happiness? Does not a child have a right to even discover what happiness is to begin with?

Let us be realistic. The idea of prochoice is a Constitutional paradox when considering that law is designed to protect, not just a person's rights, but their very life because if there is no life, then what use would there be for rights? Even in regards to homicide, it's not, so, much about rights, but justice. Roe-v-Wade is clearly unconstitutional on the basis that before law can protect a person's rights, it must first protect life, for you cannot have rights without life. Hence, the XIV Amendment is actually being interpreted in such a way as to violate that, for which it was designed to prevent in the first place. That particular paradox of law proves that logic and reason are unsustainable in regards to gender versus life. Such as the institution of slavery in a country proclaiming freedom for all. Do not deny the facts. The United States of America is a country of contradiction that has gone insane, which proves that like the recent same sex marriage decision, some topics are simply outside of the domain of the judiciary at all levels.

CHAPTER 8

She; who is woman, presents a unique constitutional reality, and that is, she is the key to the creation of that, which the XIV was established to protect to begin with. Not just a person; but the very sanctity of human life itself. The Constitution of the United States of America is a document created by people for people and nothing else. Therefore, when the XIV Amendment to the Bill of Rights defines the word; *life,* in its framework, its intent is all, but clear. Denoting the act of human mitosis within the womb will not result in anything, but a human being. New life is entrusted to woman by

144

nature. To clarify the relationship between woman and the XIV Amendment; it is the only amendment of which the flesh was made word. The XIV Amendment are words that identify the very act of feminine nature, and that nature is the preservation of human life. Her *natural* duty. An evolutionary process of which there are now, additional persons seeking life, liberty and the right to happiness; and the Supreme Court's decision regarding Roe-v-Wade? That a person, who by nature, with a unique and exclusive quality has a right to abandon that quality? Would a reasonable analogy be; *the ship is sinking, but we are not going to deploy the lifeboats because we choose not to?* Of course, there are options. Perhaps another ship can come to the rescue. Woman was designed for a specific purpose, and for her to refuse her part of the natural process of human existence results in a disruption in the overall process of existence. Nothing more than a serial killing by the organism; man. In this case, the human organism; not the individual, is the predator. Note: that when examining the idea of prochoice, we forget the very notion of what choice is, in regards to a child's right to choose life over death, but then some states allow a person the right to end their life. Yet, we deny the complete opposite to someone who wants to stay alive? Naturally, there are those of us who will ask the question of how do you know a child wants to stay alive? The answer to that question is; again, simple. In an ideal environment an organism thrives. The process of life is a natural state of being, and once begun, only an outside force acting upon that life can result in its ending; *snuffing it out.* Guess we could call that; *The Inertial Life Factor.* Except that once stopped, it cannot be restarted. That is, unless we look at human life itself as a whole; as one great organism. Then snuffing out one of us diminishes the whole. Therefore, we are back to the initial setting. Killing one unborn child can have a profound effect on the entire species. A child that could have prevented the Columbine High School massacre was aborted. A child that could have prevented 9/11 was aborted. A child that could have prevented John F. Kennedy, Martin Luther King, Robert F. Kennedy, Elvis Presley, Michael Jackson, Prince's untimely death, was aborted. A child that may have prevented World War I from occurring and subsequently the rise of Adolph Hitler was aborted. A child, whom could have prevented the Titanic from sinking, was aborted. Now, some of you are saying; *there is no way to prove that an aborted child could have prevented, so, much tragedy;* however, we are aware of the child who was not aborted because you are currently reading these words. Amazing how thankful you should be that your mother did not pay a visit to the sanctioned executioner to have you tossed out with the morning refuse. Then again, wouldn't it be nice if the child in the womb could simply transfer to another ship?

When conducting a more comprehensive analysis of human development; there is perspective with regards to a child outside of the womb, and yet, we express great prejudice in regards to the breakdown of a child in the womb. Therefore, when we say a child in the womb is not a person; then what are they? A car, or a horse? When defining them as not a person, would that be fetal prejudice? Maturation discrimination? Hate towards those seeking a right to life? Denying them a right to have a birthday? Let us look at the truth of the XIV: An amendment that was designed to clarify certain aspects of law to benefit those whom were seeking *life* when being systematically exterminated due to the color of their skin; *who they are.* Therefore, this Amendment was not designed to give woman the right to treat a person with such contempt, or for homosexuals seeking to expand on their relationship.

Makes you wonder what that little person in the womb truly did to warrant capital punishment? For nine months, a person is doing something pretty amazing that we all wish we could do for just a day, and that is, feel alive. Sure; people cheer when a child is murdered in the womb, but are in an uproar when a child is murdered in a school. If the child in the womb brought it upon themselves to be killed, then the child in the school must have also brought it upon themselves to be killed.

Interesting how certain lawyers are capable of overlooking human rights through means of manipulating our perception of mitosis.

Defining a pregnancy as nothing spectacular. Just another part of life. Therefore, making the argument that: *A pregnancy is being terminated. She wants to end her pregnancy.* Stating a process in such a way as to incite depraved indifference. How does apathy take root? Secular conditioning to the point of suppressing all sense of natural compassion that is the source of understanding the true nature of God. Let us clear the air: Pregnancy means gestation of a living being within the body. *The woman is with child,* is what we used to say to clearly define the existence of another person. Now, we simply say; *pregnant,* and have it at that. No longer associating a word to a phrase in regards to the warmth and compassion of its true nature. The physical development and growth of a child begins at fertilization and continues until into their teenage years, of which the brain continues. This author would call that impressive. Wouldn't you? And yet, we take that miracle of development for granted. In fact, we take a whole lot of things for granted, do we not? For us to say that human life begins at some point after basic cell-division or even outside of the womb is not only arrogant, but irresponsible. Who are we to determine when a person is a person? Ask any scientists; would examining some form of microbial animation on another world, be life? There are certain factors at the cellular level that even we; the human-being require, in order to survive on this world. There are even tiny microbial things that are quite capable of killing us, and yet certain people are allowed to make the rules of when someone is human, and when they are not? Sounds eerily familiar with such people making similar decisions in regards to people of African blood and/or descent. Jim Crowe South, when negros were denied the right to live due to white supremacy or maybe females aborted from the educational process. Nazis deciding that those who were Jewish needed to be aborted from the overall social directive. What these philosophers and scientists did not consider when rendering their opinion is that, if any part of the human species is inferior, then the whole is inferior, and that goes for our association with human cell division. This author wants to know; does a child have the presence of mind to commit suicide? If not, then shouldn't the establishment wait until a child actually has a reasonable understanding of life to decide for themselves if they even want to end it at all? Then again, the expectation of wanting to live has to be the proper exception because if it were not, then life would not have begun in the first place.

CHAPTER 9

What true crime is committed by a developing child when their life is abruptly ceased after fertilization? Contrary to what some people may have you believe, it is not her body once the fertilization process begins. The woman's body becomes our body from the point of view of the child, and yet, the selfishness of they who want things to go it all their way, say otherwise? These are the same people who protest the very notion of a man seeking custody of *his* child, not our child. When a man attempts to retain possession of *his* house, not our house. *His* car, not our car. Again, that child in the womb is not regarded as a child, but a pregnancy, easing her emotional recourse; *it's my body,* thus avoiding the truth of the matter in regards to finishing her thought: *Not our body.* We often hear people speak out against bullying, but funny how we do not think of a newly fertilized female, whom walks into an abortion clinic as being an accomplice to bullying. Why is that? A government that permits human abortion is a supporter of bullying; *right?* The developing child did not choose their predicament, she; the mother, made that choice for the child when she copulated. Oh, and for those cases of rape; this author will apologize for the fact that life has begun, and as mentioned earlier, only God has a right to terminate human life. Besides, let us be realistic, and that is, in most cases of rape, a woman places herself in an easily avoidable circumstance due to poor judgement. There are certain rules of nature that no law can restrain, of which, forces women to behave accordingly. A man drinks to destabilize his sense of will, to unwind or perhaps he drinks for courage. When a woman dresses provocatively, and then takes a drink of alcohol, what kind of a message is she sending? *I'm wearing this to get your attention, and I'm drinking this to relax. Now, come, and help me unwind.* By morning she realizes that something
148

is not right, and there is regret? Later, she discovers that she is pregnant, so, to preserve her reputation, she declares rape, and pays a visit to the government sanctioned executioner, via the authorities, so, that she can tell her abridged accounting of the facts because no female ever tells the whole story, let alone the truth, do they?

When she errors in regards to copulation, resulting in pregnancy, the natural processes of life, is not a mistake, just unexpected, and most importantly, not unmanageable. As a man, this author is not going to pretend that he understands or even knows what pregnancy is all about, or what it is like for a woman to give birth to a child. As a writer, the best that he can ever hope for is to imagine as-best-as possible, and that is it; however, as a new mother reading this; consider the following; as a woman, your body was designed to give birth to children. Being afraid is obvious, but fear should not be a factor in regards to the child's outcome, for there is a community who is prepared to be there for you at a moment's notice. Give that child a chance. You will not regret it; this author promises you that. What you will regret is the aftermath of what ifs, should you decide otherwise. There is nothing worse to the human senses than evicting someone who did nothing wrong when they are living under your care. No pregnancy is an accident. Every child has purpose; is a lottery ticket, and a mother has the power to make that ticket a big winner, but she cannot win if she does not play when the moment arises.

CHAPTER 10

Time for the six million-dollar question. Why shouldn't she abort a child within her body since the man is unwilling to be a part of the child and her life? A man whom makes a child with a woman, and then abandons her, makes it clear that he has a total disregard to the very sanctity of what it means to be human. He leaves his immortality to random chance, and to the unexpected dangers of human behavior. Not to the man's offspring, but to those around that child. To sum it up, if he abandons she whom would bear his child, then he abandons his neighbor even his country. The child is his child, and yet he does not want his child; therefore, we have to ask ourselves; why would the woman want his child? Why

149

shouldn't the woman get an abortion? Just some of what's on the minds of prochoice advocates. Interestingly enough, those same certain people and groups encourage a young woman to surrender her virginity to begin with, and then deal with the consequences later. As a side note, this author will explain to you something that those of the Free Love Movement will not tell you. No matter how disciplined you may be in regards to contraception, whether male or female, the need to reproduce will become overwhelming. The more you engage in sexual intercourse; the greater the need for reproduction, which will grow exponentially. Again, why the Church says; *no,* to premarital sexual intercourse. Keeping virginity in check, or practiced abstinence is the only true method to keep the reproductive urges at bay. If all else, she; the woman, should perhaps keep her legs closed to the point of bringing about the end of human existence. It would be preferable to the self-destruction we are currently facing as a society. Yes; she should end the cycle of human existence through a natural means. If we; the man, are unwilling to take on the responsibility, then why should she bare the burdened alone? It makes absolutely no sense to this author for us to continue making children with the sole purpose of perpetuating the species with no intent of perpetuating the understanding of what it means to be human. We will not be there for the child; teach the child; ensure that the species will remain dominate in the world. To bestow a destiny on the child. Explain to the child what it means to be human. To perpetuate and maturate the human species to a higher intellect. To leave this task solely to a woman is pure lunacy. Our current social standards in regards to sexual intercourse is exactly what the animals do in the wild; stick and move. Oh, and for those certain groups who say; *let a person be what they want to be. Let them live their life the way they choose.* This author's reply is; then why do we have courts and jails?

CHAPTER 11

Let us briefly examine the man and wife who take scientific action to retard the reproductive process or perhaps a question would be more appropriate. What do you do in old age; when your body is broken, and you can no longer fend for yourself? Ever factor that little nuance of life into the equation? Sure, you have retirement communities, and in-home care; however, do you ever crave the attention of family in your existence? To see your prodigy reach a certain goal that you dreamed of? Oh, and if you should happen to have a million dollars, and a few nieces and nephews lurking about with some free time, then good luck. Just consider that some parents have a difficult time at getting their own children to take care of them in their old age, and some of them are quite wealthy. The point this author is trying to make is; the higher number of offspring, the greater your chances of being cared for by family, or to say the least, spreading the burden out.

Children play a pivotal role in our social decor on the basis that they bring happiness and delight to the community. They are the very essence of a thriving culture. Establishing connections that bind us together, making it possible for social interaction. How can such a simple person do what adults avoid? They give us hope and motivation based on the realization that life will go on. Even those whom are in the twilight of their years, feel a certain happiness when knowing there are children playing about.

Now, consider a community without children. No matter how happy the people may seem, the gloom lurks. There is despair, hopelessness, and even fear of knowing that death looms like a vulture over the community. This idea can be applied to unhappy children for if they are not happy then can we call them children? Imagine a world of immortals. Are they happy? Children bring happiness. Notice the plural; children, and lots of them together at play. Watching them interact in the art of joy brings a certain something to the community. Realistically, immortals would have no sense or need of children. Even the Greek gods had a child here and there, and when you examine the details between even Apollo and his twin sister; Artemis, clearly two is not enough. Have you ever been in a park without children? Big difference in atmosphere. Besides, immortals would fear pregnancy because it would mean that their immortality would be in jeopardy.

151

Death should be a delight to the old when knowing you are making room for the new; however, look at our modern culture of the early Twenty-first, and what do we have? The old unwilling to let go. So, selfish are we about the idea of not wanting to let go that we sacrifice the new because as this author scribed, new life threatens immortality. Could that be the truth behind the Pro-choice Movement as a whole?

Each successive generation should be better than the previous. Ask yourself; are we a better culture today? Not technology wise, but more specifically, on moral grounds?

SLAVES

What is a human slave? A person who is pressed into service against their will, and managed accordingly, without explanation, compassion or upbringing. Paying someone a wage does not absolve the pretense of slavery. In the modern world, corporations use many tools for maintaining a covert slave mentality, but that is for another topic of discussion. Over time, slavery evolves into a state of oppression, when a person is refused advancement in a culture in regards to certain fields as dictated by their oppressor(s).

Children begin life as slaves; doing chores, going to school, eating what you feed them, and wearing the clothes you buy them. Well; perhaps not, so, much the last two for many of you. Then there is keeping their rooms clean, etcetera. The idea; however, is that you are there at every moment of their lives; teaching them and molding them into an extension of yourself; guiding them out of a state of slavery to become productive law-abiding citizens in order to maintain a productive meaningful society.

If you are not there for your children, and say; you are always at the job or at the bar or philandering, whatever the case maybe or excuse you may have as a father; then what becomes of your children? Of anyone's child for that matter? You come home and make your child do their chores, inferring upon them, not a slave-like mentality, but an oppressive-state of being. You do not teach

152

them, you do not guide them, and yet, when they error you come down on them as if they had lost the family heirloom to some confidence trickster in a shell game. From a child's point of view, there is nothing on the horizon, though they hunger for purpose, and the outcome will eventually lead to rebellion. There is a difference between slavery, and oppression. The interesting thing about slaves is that they are not always oppressed, and those who are oppressed are not always slaves. It is a matter of nature for the oppressed to rebel against their oppressor. Oh, and buying your child toys and electronic devices to occupy their time is another form of oppression. The worst kind of oppression because you are a drug pusher. Addicting them, and they will turn against society when they reach adulthood. Everyone around them will be a toy. Furthermore, do not use the adage of; *I provide a roof over their head and food in their mouth.* Zookeepers provide animals with roofs over their heads and food in their mouths. You use that excuse to justify your lack of presence. Now, as a father, you do not have to be there for your children at every moment, but you should manage your time accordingly. Newborns require a mother at all times, even while they sleep. A mother who leaves a child alone thinking they are safe is the biggest fool on the face of the earth. Placing your newborn in a separate room, thinking they need to begin some form of parental weening process or that they need to sleep, or whatever mundane excuse a modern mother uses to separate herself from a child; may be asking for trouble down the road. There are strange forces in our existence that we do not fully comprehend. Certain phenomena that maybe viewed as out of the ordinary, that a newborn might be highly sensitive to, whether you believe it or not; and, so, the presence of a parent is required at all times to interfere with those certain unexplained phenomena.

You, as the father begin the weaning process of your boys; leading them to a state of independence as they mature, but it is a precise technique, that must be carefully administered. A mother; on the other hand, is bonded to the children whom she has given birth to, for the rest of her life. It takes the strength of a man to;

153

not, so, much, break her bond, but disrupt her bond when the child wants to go into the world. That is why mothers should be cared for by the community when they become widows as prescribed by scripture, and yet, in contrast, certain single mothers allow their sons to remain at home, even allow them to turn their homes into brothels. Completely normal for an abnormal situation, for there is no father to break the mother's tie, and there was no father to wean the boy from his childish ways. He went from reading Playboy to becoming a playboy, and again, this author says, if you do not enslave your child, they will rebel against you or worse, rebel against society and/or enslave you. The sign of bad parenting is a spoiled child. Again, toys and electronic devices are often given in lieu of parental guidance to occupy a child's day, but what a child wants and needs is a parent by their side guiding them, explaining to them; teaching them the ways of life. Again, contrary to popular belief; it is not a roof over the head or food in the mouth that a child wants, but a father who is present in their lives.

THE QUESTION OF SEX

CHAPTER 1

What is this thing we call making love? Is it making someone fall in love or making ourselves love someone? How do you make love? Not the coitus allegory, but the actual rational attitude based on its meaning. Oh, we can make a baby, but how do we make love? It is this author's opinion that *making love* is truly a bad use of language resulting in the eroding of the spirit of its meaning, including the compassionate/emotional lines between what is male and what is female in regards to true harmonious companionship.

Now, some people say there is such a thing as love at first sight. Perhaps that is true; however, what we are sure of is lust at first sight. Another fact of love, is that it is often put to death, and in many cases in the most gruesome of ways. So, the question we must ask, is, are we experiencing love when we meet a woman? The answer

154

is; *no.* The feelings you have for the woman, is lust. The overall attraction for a woman cannot be put into words. She drives us; the man, to do the craziest of things to gain her attention. That is what we; the man, like to do. That is not immaturity on our part, but simple desire. Interesting thing about desire is that it has nothing to do with the true perceptions of love. Therefore, you cannot be in love because love is an evolutionary process. How do you know the difference? Easy: If you *desire* intercourse, then it is lust. If you *desire* her company, then the evolution of love is beginning. Love is very much like a human embryo. It requires time to grow into something wonderful.

Once gaining her attention, what she wears, and how she wears it, determines the direction of the conversation, and essentially the direction of the relationship. Her choice of clothing has induced an arousal within us; the suitor, and thus only natural for us to direct our feelings along those lines. *You look sexy, so, let's talk about sex,* or to say the least, you guide the mingling process along those lines; however, you are required as a man, to stave off the lust until your wedding night. Then you may have a chance at something real. That is, if you are a serious minded male. Note: This does not mean running off to Nevada just after meeting a woman. If you have engaged in premarital sexual intercourse with her, then in the back of your mind, she is nothing more than a harlot. A slut, a sucker, and not really worth more than a casual moment of bedroom play to ease the burdens of life. Remember; women desire attention above all else, and that want, drives her to array herself accordingly. To compete for your eye, and yes; the competition is very stiff. When one woman attires herself in such a way, others will imitate, but differently, based on; *competitive demand.* Do not take this author's word for it. Examine history. When feminine competition stiffens, clothing is the first tool in the competitive arsenal to go through a metamorphosis. Women want to show that they are more than just a pretty face. Though many do not realize how beautiful their facial features are until they have crossed the line of what is proper and improper feminine conduct. She, whom likes to go out on the weekends for fun: Does she get upset when a guy with sex on his mind approaches her? Consider her choice of evening wear. She wears the sexy. Looks in the mirror saying to herself; *I am sexy,* and that she can even feel the sexy, and what? When a guy who is thinking along those same lines approaches her, she becomes bothered? She tells him to get lost? Let us be clear about the matter. She is not telling him to get lost because his mind is in the gutter. More on the subject later.

The time has come to ask the crucial question in order to address the biggest problem, by far, that is plaguing our society. A problem often mentioned in this book. That is staring all of us right in the face; and that we, perhaps can attribute to the evolution of culture. We have made great strides in curbing the amount of pollution being discharged in the environment; and though we are still far from perfect, we would like to know that we are making progress. Attempting some form of remedy; however, is it not odd how we are unable to see another kind of pollution flowing freely into our existence in this modern culture of the early Twenty-first. Images of the old factories discharging vast amounts of waste into the rivers and skies was appalling, repugnant, disgusting, and yet we are swimming in sexual euphoria 24/7. Experiencing an overdose of sexual delight, that is leading all of us in the wrong direction, and of course, we choose to ignore it. We don't even care how it effects our children, and we call ourselves civilized? Honestly; is this author the only one who has taken notice of the highly provocative nature of feminine fashions? The skinny jeans, running tights, yoga-pants, leggings, body melding slacks, and all other forms of stretchy material; open or closed toe withstanding, are nothing more than dense pantyhose, that greatly emphasize her smooth contours, while concealing skin discrepancies that may result in beauty disillusionment. Then there is the summer attire that is more akin to casualwear for the bedroom, and shirts that are as socks for the upper body, and yet all of it, is delight to our eyes.

There was a reasonable balance between a female's attire, and the effect it had on a male, and up until the mid to late 1960s, the

156

balance was relatively close, that is with exception to; of course, prostitution. With the rise of the Sexual Revolution, that balance began a subtle, but noticeable change. By the 1990s, crazy swept through the female population like a California wildfire. Now, this author is not proposing that women did not adorn the provocative pre-Sexual Revolution. We are speaking of majorities here. You see a cluster of beautiful girls whom are prim and proper, and they are what they are; however, she; who is wearing the form-fitting apparel, gets your eye, for she is the bad girl, and we do like our girls bad. In this modern age of the early Twenty-first, the majority is form-fitting everything, but the problem is, they are not all bad girls, they are simply adopting an odd perception of what is fashionable and what is reasonable in regards to the effect they are having on the social medium. You must realize that as a man, a woman will do whatever it takes to garnish your attention though she may say otherwise. Form-fitting is now, the norm, for like the weapons of war, we did not understand; not necessarily that the tactics did not keep up with the technology, but more of the understanding the effect that the technology had in a real-time environment. In the past, when the bad girl wore tight or form-fitting fashions, she knew how to handle herself; what to expect, and being preyed upon by hormone raging guys was a delight to her; however, the rest of the female population did not get that memo when tight-fitting became all the rage. That is a bad habit of human nature. Seeing something that works for one person, and then assuming it will work globally, without consideration of how to handle it in a real-time setting. Not to mention the consequences of having it, or doing it. Stubborn nature drives us to try to make controversy work when we should be admitting to ourselves that it simply does not work for everyone. *It does not work for me, but I will play along anyhow because that's what's popular.*

We have always worshipped the feminine form. It is pure delight. Pleasing to the eye. Which explains why pagan beliefs seemed to place such great emphasis on female deities. We find the body-melding attire tantalizing; alluring; stimulating; mouth-watering.

Especially when they cram their smartphones in the back pockets of their skinny jeans, as if a means of gauging the bounce in their stride. We thrive off the feminine physique when it plays risk in a public setting. The certain degrees for which, her body concaves and convexes the material helps define the *curve* appeal; and yes; we do like our girls curvy. Her *clothed nudity* is far more appealing than being out-and-out naked. Placing the mind into a euphoric state that is not unlike drugs. Even affecting women who view other women, and even those who look at themselves in the mirror. For the splendor of her body is, so, incredibly powerful that even she cannot resist its allure; she is not immune to even herself. It is a form that men would like to possess, and women strive to become because it is true earthly power; a motivator that makes us; yes; both men and women alike, feel extremely good. Imagine her behind a silhouette screen; *is she naked? Is she clothed? Does it matter?* Her figure delights and excites the pleasure center of the male mind. Especially when revealing those regions of the lower body, inner thighs, especially the gluteus, and perhaps the most enticing display of all is the pubic gap. Those parts of the female anatomy, not her upper body, are the true stimulators of male desires. Why is that? Her lower body denotes her level of activity, her liveliness. Beauty is truly in the booty. Now, should a woman wear pantyhose in public without a dress or skirt, it would be deemed as exposing herself, and please, do not make the excuse of the sheerness of the material due to our perceptions of reason, logic and the law. Dresses and skirts are woman's mainstay in daily fashionable living. It places before man a more serious tenure than that of attire that reveals her entire figure in a single glance. Add to that a thin waist, and there is an explosion of hot sexual delight in the mind of a male, while practicing the fine art of girl watching.

What about a woman's breasts? Whether large or small, they are an attractive feature, but not, so, much a distractive feature, unless displayed as such. Consider that there is only, so, much sexual stimuli the human senses can handle at any given time. Displaying portions of her figure, and men can manage accordingly; however, her mere presence is enough to drive male hormonal levels through the roof. Distracting him from responsible activities, and even his self-control. How do males behave around females in the animal kingdom? Add to that the *clothed nudity,* and we; the male side of man, are reverted back to a primordial state of being. Bringing out that aggressive nature of competitiveness. This is not a flaw on our part, but a natural part of being human. There are no corrective measures or controls that can be administered for such behavior, but there is a means of curbing the craving, and of course it involves she; the woman.

Females also have this aggressive side, but it is not as prominent in them as in us; the male. She prefers to use illusion and/or covert treachery as a means of purging the competition. Ever notice how a girl can be treacherous one moment, and the innocent little fool the next? Females; even the inexperienced ones, are exceptional illusionists. The difference is that some of them master the art of illusion quicker than others. Some are careful about their skill, and use it to benefit those they are serious about, while others use it for personal gain. Regardless of what you may think, we are creatures of body-language not of words. What she projects is what gets our fluids going.

CHAPTER 2

Another point to consider is that the Christian woman whom dresses excessively expressive, while attending places of worship, is an affront to God's authority. A direct offense against Him. She wears heels and cuffed dress-shorts, revealing, so, much thigh in God's Temple, that she can practically go swimming. She even dares to wear the running tights, perhaps making the excuse to herself that she has a marathon to attend afterwards or perhaps something has abruptly changed her workout schedule. Of course, if that were the case, she could have just as easily slipped into a nice maxi-dress, but they do not do that; *why not?* In regards to the Church; they use their sexual prowess to distract men from the celebration of the Christ. Covet their vanity instead of covering it during the celebration as they once did in the past. Unwittingly piggybacking the worship of Asherah onto the celebration of the Christ.

Interesting, how some people treat going to church as just business as usual, but attend all other formal affairs wearing their finest. For the teenager going to homecoming or prom; what do you wear? Blue jeans? For those of you who do not get it; going to church is the same as going to a formal dinner engagement, homecoming or prom. You are attending a fashionable outing. An event as big as a wedding. The excuse of; *it does not matter what you wear as-long-as you show up;* is a poor one. That is an excuse for those who have come upon hard times, but for most people whom celebrate their religion, they possess formal clothing, but simply choose to treat the occasion as unimportant, but for other events, those same people slip on their finest. Especially in regards to representing their favorite ball team after church; and when a person dresses a certain way, then they behave a certain way.

Fact of the matter is, women love to distract men; especially in regards to their religion. Though she would not openly admit it, her intent is to challenge God in His own temple; plain and simple. She wants to be the goddess Asherah, of which gives her empowerment. Placing herself ahead of God. *I will get men to pay attention to my butt instead of paying attention in church because my empowerment makes me feel good.* Whether it be her intent to do, so, or not is of no relevance. It is a subconscious act that places her in a highly dubious position. She expects the man to behave maturely about her shapely display. Though she likes to garnish the attention of men subconsciously. Consciously, should he react, then he is behaving immaturely. From her point of view, he is wrong, and she will place him in check in order to exonerate herself from any wrong doing. That is unless he happens to be Arnold Schwarzenegger circa-1975, and single. Well…

If that were not the case, then women would be mindful of what they wear at all times. Truth be told, there was a time when a respectable woman would pay close attention to her attire, even her mannerisms; certain physical actions that were deemed inappropriate,

160

were avoided in a public setting regardless of her status. Mothers would properly guide their daughter's clothing practices, and mannerisms at all times as they once did; however, in today's culture, all bets are off. What defines a woman from being either promiscuous or modest is now, greatly blurred. Of course, the million-dollar question is who decides what styles are in or out? The need for difference is what guides the overall idea of change. This is the foundation of feminine contradiction. She likes the other woman's style, and yet it has to be different; for women hate to be uniform. Kind of makes this author wonder why women are allowed in the military.

CHAPTER 3

Perhaps what many of us do not understand or fully understand or more accurately are unaware of in regards to basic feminine anatomy is that a layer of fatty tissue overlays a woman's muscular structure, giving her that smooth outline that we; *normal* male's, find irresistible. Her shapeliness is designed to incite our desires; to attract and to stimulate. Her every action generates a reaction from us; the male of the species. Without that aspect of nature, there would be no reason for the man to react to the woman. A necessity for the preservation of our species.

Clearly, we have been conditioned into believing that females dressing in the nude is the way of things, and that there is no other way. What a person projects, is what is perceived by the casual observer. Form-fitting fashions reveals to the casual male-eye that she meets the feminine physical criteria; and that she is comparable to the next woman. Perhaps the oldest illusion in the book of seduction. Interesting how a prostitute arrays herself in certain fashions to reveal to potential shoppers that she meets those physical requirements of her profession, and what? Frame of mind defines the difference between she; whom sells her body for a fee, and she whom gives her body for free?

When a woman wears body-melding fashions what kind of a message is she sending? *Look at my body, not at me, for I have something you want.* If a woman wants a man to look at her for who she is, then why does she imitate the prostitute? They justify their choice of attire based on certain attitudes. *I can wear formfitting clothing because I am exercising or that it makes me feel good. I am not wearing it to attract men, but to compete with other women;* of course; that competition is for the attention of men. That little point they leave out. Be that as it may, a man's impression is that a woman's behavior guides her choice of attire: *I feel like a slut, so, I dress like a slut, therefore I am a slut because that is what men want; that is what men expect; I am a walking, breathing, living, blow up doll ready to entertain any man in whatever capacity is asked of me.*

Her whole selling point is her body, not her intellectualism. She displays her body without realizing that doing, so, interferes with a man's thinking process; his rationality. We have packaged this effect into a little convenience that we call; prostitution. Virginity is a onetime use thing meant for a man not for men. Once gone she has nothing else of value, but her shapeliness and seductive skill. She will use that as a means to an end. Money or any other form of barter makes no difference. For a more comprehensive study on the subject, seek the works of Dr. Janet Smith.

Interesting that when prostitution is obscured, then controversy is usually at a minimum; however, when visible, it exists in settings that are usually violent. Does open prostitution exist in non-violent neighborhoods? In the suburbs? And yet violence is everywhere. *Everywhere!* Ask yourself; what else exists everywhere? Fully clothed nudity. Females have a tendency of sending the wrong message when it comes to fashion. Perhaps the worst places for this kind of affectation are our institutions of learning. Our public schools are scenes of some of the most violent activity in our modern culture. Therefore, consider what else is going on in these institutions? Feminine teen-attire is highly ebullient. *Coincidence?* Not by a long shot. Especially the colleges and universities, which, happens to be the demographic where a lot of sex crimes occur. Women believe that they have a right to dress as they want, where they want, when they want, with the attitude of; *I dress as a prostitute, does not mean I am a prostitute;* that boys and men must

162

contend with, on a daily basis. Whether it be an institution of learning or on the job, she; the female attires herself in the nude. Do not deny the truth. You say to yourself; *I would like to meet her,* and what is it that drives you to this frame of mind? The reality is, she mimics a prostitute who chooses her customer; and since you do not meet her expectations of an ideal male, then you cannot look at her in an impious manner? You dare not look at her. She says; *do not look at me in that way! I am not a slut!*

CHAPTER 4

What is the practice of Asherah? A play on the mind with the intent to entice the vulnerable into a state of intemperance. For those of you whom are religiously orientated; how are the women in your church or temple attired? If your eyes are paying more attention to their backside, instead of the Lord, then the delights of the goddess Asherah have captured you; drawn you away from the Lord. Contrary to popular opinion, all pagan gods are real. They are simply a physical depiction of our behaviors to help us better understand ourselves; why we do what we do. Remember the First Commandment; "You shall not have no other gods *before* Me." The meaning of that law refers to an obsessive need that becomes, so, great that it takes on a life of its own. Reaching a point to where you cannot distinguish between responsibility and desire. Nothing else matters. At that point, a person severs themselves from the truth. Literally worshipping that obsession; now, a deity; first and foremost, to a point of even compelling others to join. Creating images of their feelings, to solidify the whole concept into something more real. Yes; that includes worshipping certain forms of entertainment, including athletics. An interesting point to consider is, do all of our modern, so-called Judeo-Christian celebrities encourage the following of God? Why not? They want you to worship them. That is how they make money.

CHAPTER 5

When considering a male's propensity towards the worship of the feminine form; restrictions become necessary to keep ourselves focused on the proper social directive. Again, look at what is going on with your own eyes. Woman is given free reign, and the cosmetics, the clothes, her very attitude is creating a torpid environment. We are going nowhere because she is that powerful. We are locked up in a sexual jail cell with little hope of escape. Women do not understand the need for restrictions. The idea of rules is an alien concept because they believe that rules are designed to go against them; and in most respects that very notion is quite true. Why is that? She represents the pinnacle of our very desires. Not just sexual, but all physical desires. Once obsessed with her, nothing of true useful substance gets completed. We; the male, realize, that without restrictions the purpose for life becomes unrealized, even sterile.

While on the subject of attire, let us be clear that when a woman wears what a man wears, she sexualizes it. When a woman adorns clothing designed for a man's profession, it loses its professional grandeur; its meaning and respect. It is no longer professional, but burlesque. As previously mentioned, she is the very epitome of sexuality. Therefore, when a woman wears an adaptation of men's clothing, it is normal for a man to react accordingly; to fantasize, and thus when the opportunity presents itself, to, hit up on, or make a pass at her. In this modern age, we call that kind of behavior *sexual harassment*; however, from a male's perspective, he is simply being gay towards the feminine form, for there is just something about her wearing our dress-shirt and/or service cap in the bedroom that is, so, appealing to us.

Notice that sex does not wear fashionable complexity for her wedding ceremony, which hints of her frame of mind in regards to the overall marriage process. Sex wants to disrobe quickly like a street walker on her wedding night. No patience for a cheap thrill because the courtship was nothing more than a test drive anyhow.

The removal of the gown should be a ritual unto itself. Sex is a special gift, of which she should have placed great effort into the choice of clothing and accessories. Her gown is the wrapping paper for which, you; the man, should patiently unwrap as you flatter her

164

with delightful words in regards to her very being. Maximizing her arousal, which will lead to an unforgettable passionate experience. That is why sex should lose her virginity on her wedding night. Not on her prom night, in a car, her parent's basement during the house party, that secret alcove at school or some other dank, forgettable place in the world. It should be a special moment through-and-through. She cannot experience the full potential of that special moment on her wedding night if Billy, Bobby, or Bradly was her first gratis john. You; the husband, should be the first man she knows, in order for the bonding process to begin. Which is why headstrong sex does not work in a relationship. Intercourse for them is the center of the venture, not the bonding of two people into one.

CHAPTER 6

Let us examine the day in a typical male's life. He leaves the house to go to work, and there's the beautiful jogger wearing the running-tights and bra passing him on the street. Then comes the teenage girls, apparently dressed for a harlot's convention, when going to school. Upon arrival to the job, and there are the female coworkers, who's wardrobe apparently consists of; *fit me tightly, baby because I feel sexy today.* After making it through the day with the looming dark cloud of watch your mouth looming over his shoulders, he goes to the supermarket to pick up a few things for dinner, where he bumps into the woman wearing leggings and a tank-top. At home; he is surfing the web for a picture of the planet Jupiter for a project he is working on, and an image of a nude woman pops up instead. In fact, no matter what you search for on the web, from Aardvark to Zebra, you will get explicit material of some kind. Makes you wonder if Ma-Bell was still running things would the web be better regulated. Good idea or bad? Who knows?

How much of the internet is a valid medium for gathering information, conducting research, and a form of entertainment that compels the mind to imagine? Or is it a source of exploitation of the desperate, forsaken and the greedy? Where entertainment fails to allow the mind to think for itself. The internet is without a doubt the nuclear bomb of sex fatigue, and perhaps even the cause of our downfall as a species. People, whom once had a fighting chance at arresting their forbidden passions can now, explore them without restraint on the web. Unfortunately, this exploration can escape privacy, and is perhaps another reason why, so, many women have given into their lustful desires for little boys. Not that she is incapable of making the first move of what is perceived to be a sexual predator. A segment that is predominately male, but more of a misunderstanding of the attributes of true social needs.

CHAPTER 7

Does this mean that every woman is promiscuous? Perhaps not; however, men have been conditioned to view the display of the feminine physique as an invitation to intercourse. Is that what a woman wants? Is that what a father wants? Is that what a brother wants? Note: for the woman who is reading this; if your first impression to a man is the display of your body, then that is what he'll expect of you. There are ways to dress attractively or should this author say, cleverly without sending the wrong message, but why do that when you can simply adorn nude fashions to instantly get his attention, dealing with the consequences later. A result of living in such an impatient, and even a lazy culture. Therefore, we are back to our original question: How does a modern male cope with the fully dressed nudity? The answer is; *he doesn't*. Male intelligence is on the decline, resulting in a continuation of immaturity in what we deem as his adult years. Remember, sexual intercourse is a reality in the youth segment. If a person is not maturing out of their youth, then sex continues to be approached from an immature state of mind. Nothing more than candy. If that is the case, then what is the point of furthering the mind? Dropout rates for boys are at an all-time high, and we expect our teen males to pay attention to the class instructor with teen prostitutes in the classroom? Again, a male student whom drops out of school is simply a child who is no longer progressing their mental faculties, and the irony is, it's not the child's fault, but the laziness of culture. The education process should do more than institute a mental programming aptitude. It must delight the child's imagination. Draw on a child's need to know; stimulate the process for the need for knowledge. You do that with religion, not secularism.

It is hard for some people to understand what it means to be a boy, and what it means to be a girl; man, and woman; male and female. Therefore, as the parent; you cannot leave a boy to his own vices. He must have guidance along the lines of how to be a man. This does not mean doing manly things with him such as taking him down to the gym and teaching him how to box, wrestle or play football. No; he needs a more direct approach. Something to guide him towards that goal; a baseline towards manhood. The whole academic principle must be taught from a male perspective, so, that it can be approached from a male point of view, but not in such a way as to utilize the female in some illicit abstract or negative connotation. Woman should be explained to the boy as a precious commodity to be protected and nothing more. The man-child needs this in his development in order to fully grasp the notion of what it means to be the male of the species of man. There are parts of the brain that control masculinity; helps a male to achieve a status that is ideal to the continuation of the gender as necessary. To insure a healthy masculine architecture, and a beneficial role in the communal setting as prescribed under natural law. A woman can only give a basic understanding of what it means to be male, and some are very good at it, but only a man can give a man-child an understanding of what it means to be male. The inputting of a female way of thinking, which; by the way, is not necessarily done by the female instructor, but the female students, contaminating the process, interfering with male development. They bring about female values; a female's way of thinking into the male educational process. Disrupting the whole idea of the male-thought process, resulting in a pause in his masculine growth. Oh, and just, so, we are clear on the whole matter of interaction; her very presence is enough to bring pause in any form of setting, especially in school.

Yes; a male-way of thinking is completely different from the female learning process. Lose the male way of thinking results in a blending of genders in such a way as to confuse the man-child, sending him far afield of what it means to be masculine; a strong male, to simply be a man. In other words, the mind starts to blur the lines between what is male and what is female resulting in gender confusion. The boy feels like being a girl, and then he will be a girl. A girl feels like being a boy, then she will behave; not as a boy, but more of girl lacking feminine regard. The difference is, the boy becomes a girl, whereas the girl almost always remains a girl, and thus, you lose the male, and we become half a species. There would be no counter balance to the genders. No counter, to her way of thinking, her emotions, her needs, and eventually it will lead to civil unrest and our extinction. In the past, we dealt with this kind of behavior; however, due to the female's involvement in our social policies, we've stopped dealing with abnormal thinking. For some reason, we got it in our heads that a person should be allowed to project their lifestyle on a general setting. We have dispensed with the idea of social order, so, that social unrest could propagate in our culture. This author wonders what group benefits from all of the chaos? That is why it is, so, important that a homosexual does not raise a child. Not from fear of any sexual interaction, but on the basis, that the homosexual whether male or female does not understand what it means to be male. They do not understand how to bestow masculinity on a man-child. If they did, they would not be pursuing like-gender relationships. There is more to being a man than just reproduction and physical pleasure. There is a certain understanding of what it means to be willing to sacrifice one's self for another. That life is not about one's self; not about wanting to be pleased. That is a feminine urging. A woman's way of living. The woman has a right to be pleased on the basis that she must be prepared to sacrifice, so, much, even her own life if necessary for the continuation of man. What does a fag sacrifice in human procreation? Nothing; for homosexuality is a selfish need for soothing certain urges of the body, and nothing else. There is no communal benefit from the anal copulation. Only risk.

What homosexuality does as a whole is blur the lines between what is man, and what is woman; including the purpose of a man, and a

168

purpose of a woman. When men assume the role of women, then there is a disruption in the order of nature, causing an imbalance in the natural state of the world. Man was created for a specific purpose, whereas woman too was created for a specific purpose, and the question is; *do I have the right to defy that purpose; and when doing, so, what impact do I have on nature?* The human condition requires the familiar, in order to work. When things become unfamiliar, then confusion sets in; no longer recognizing the very purpose of existence. Social order began as male and female, man and woman, mother and father, obedience and defiance, law and order, right and wrong, appropriate and inappropriate, good and evil, so, that we may elevate ourselves beyond the state of the animal-condition, and truly call ourselves sentient. Therefore, it is imperative that we remain a culture of two distinct genders with an understanding of what it means to be man and woman. Those differences in ideas and behavior are what give human beings an edge in nature. Yes, there are cases of men whom experience unusual urges, and the same can be said of women; however, there is a point in all of our lives when we must take on responsibilities; take control of those urges because if we do not, then we are allowing the body to take control of our will. When it is our strength of will that should be controlling the body. A child is allowed some leeway in regards to mischievous activity, but as they mature, they learn that improper behavior is unacceptable in an adult environment. She experiences masculine sensations; wants to be one of the guys, and yet as she matures, she comes to understand her responsibility. A boy; unlike a girl, needs to be told he is a man, and even in some cases he must be shown how to be a man. If you do not tell him he is a man then what does he become? He will have to determine that on his own? Makes you wonder, how many men would be normal if it weren't for the mother who said; *I sensed my child's sexual preference when they were an infant.* Now, isn't it interesting how we associate child abuse to the physical aspects of human interaction, but rarely in regards to the psychological. Oh, sure we know that harsh words hit as hard as a fist, but sometimes it is the soft gentle voice that is the most dangerous in our culture.

CHAPTER 8

Of course, a lot of people will disagree with the previous notion, but consider this; we are currently living off the residual of the old ways, but when you keep cutting off that, which feeds the process, it will cease to exist. The human species cannot exist as a mono-gendered species. If the male identity dissolves, so, does humanity. There is a reason why we call the human species; man.

In any event, guide your daughter's choice of clothing along a less distractive path of destruction. Challenge the status quo in regards to availability of feminine fashion. When you do not reveal your concerns, what are you saying? What do you say when you attend family gatherings, and your wife and daughters adorn the risqué fashions? Are you aware of the effect they are having on their male relatives? Is it fair that they have an effect on their male relatives? When a woman or girl attends a family function they should be beautiful; like something worth protecting, not explicit, something to be philandered over; drooled over, coveted. Do not hesitate to think that incest is not a common thing in the U.S.A., let alone the world because in reality, it is as common as cancer. Especially when considering the presence of alcoholic beverages at most social gatherings, and that some adults permit teenage consumption of such beverages. Oh, and should you happen to be a person who finds this author's last statement disturbing or even offensive, then you are naïve and in denial to the realities of life. If you are a person who happens to agree, then open your mouth because remaining silent supports the problem.

The irony is that women as a whole are waiting for us; the man to disapprove of the available choice of fashions in today's world of the early Twenty-first. Why it's safe to say that they; women in general, are begging for men to say enough, but we won't; *will we?* We are hopelessly addicted to sex. This author will tell you; the reader a secret. Civilized men want women to behave with restraint in a general setting whether he realizes it or not. We are growing

170

sick of the sexual innuendo. Starving for the long dress and the shrug. The prim and the proper female whom charms with her eyes and words instead of her body. The woman who says; no, to sexual intercourse, and holds fast to her virginity like a raccoon with a shiny object in its hand. She; whom makes an effort to be less revealing of herself in the public eye. We as a culture must address how, what, where and when, in regards to feminine fashions. Her attire should fit the form, not be form-fitting. For it is her figure, not her nudity that we men find alluring.

CHAPTER 9

Why do women like to display their physical structure, while we men, like to obscure ourselves? We are different creatures of the same nature. Different in our perceptions and approach of passion based on our understanding, that it is a whole different experience for either gender. She approaches it maturely because; again, she is the very essence of sex. We men are highly insecure of ourselves due to the child within us, whether we want to admit it or not. Being treated as substandard does not sit well with us. We do not like being scrutinized to the point of being ridiculed in some way, and yet, the kind of females we prefer are devilishly unforgiving in regards to a less than physically substantial male, and that is due in no small part to our being unforgiving in regards to her shortcomings. This reveals the conflict that exists in our desires for one another, and yet, it somehow balances itself out or at least it used to until the advent of birth-control.

So, who is wrong, and who is right? In reality, it is the man who is correct in this matter on the basis that women have a tendency of being immature in their thoughts from time-to-time. She follows the man, but is trying to please the child, and, so, she arrays herself accordingly for the man, with the idea that she is competing with other women, but what is she truly competing for? Not to say that men are not childish in their ways, but that we take a more general approach to life, and sex can handicap that process. What we; the man, do not realize is that woman is not doing anything that is out of the ordinary. As previously mentioned, she is required to slip into a childish state of mind in order to better interact with children, and yes, that includes us; the man as well. Of course, we men can also be a bit rigid in regards to her natural adaptations, due to our understanding of who and what she is, in regards to man. This childish adaptation of hers works out later in life as the child within us matures into something more appreciative. Therefore, go easy on she; who is woman when she happens to behave just a little childish because our children need this psychological nourishment, and, so, do we; the adult male, from time-to-time.

CHAPTER 10

Let us take a moment to examine the various sexual drives of a woman. There is attractive, sexy and sleazy. Now, let us examine the three, and see what we get out of them. An attractive woman wants you to look at her as a serious, but beautiful woman. A sexy woman is going out of her way to get your attention because she is perhaps going through some form of crisis, and that she would like a relationship that is more substantial in order to stabilize the uncertainty in her life. A sleazy woman is letting you know that she is in need of a man for physical pleasure, and that a one-night stand is okay with her. Don't worry; as previously mentioned, money is not required, for the company she works for is paying her fee. The modern woman conceals her sleaziness under a thick coating of sophistication. She is in denial of who she is; a harlot whom provides sexual pleasure at the expense of the company she works for, but only to those who know what code words to use or what buttons to push to get inside of her safe deposit box. Unfortunately, that box is full of a lot of emotional complexes, and is a confusing mass of conflicting notions; suffering from bipolar, and multi-personality disorders, and flat out rage. Not necessarily at you or herself, but the world in general. So, when dating a woman whom suddenly flips out for whatever reason, you will understand why. Of course, the virtuous woman is capable of flipping out as well, because she is called stupid or childish for being self-conscious about her body.

Now, a great many of you are probably saying B.S., and that's understandable, but let us examine the facts. When a male lives an independent lifestyle or choose to live the single life, how does such an activity relate to the other gender? He wants to hustle females into the bedroom. It's about sex. The pleasure of what she has to offer on the physical side, but without the intellectual side.

Now, let us examine a female living an independent lifestyle, even choosing to live the single life. How does she relate to not just the opposite gender, but to the community? Before continuing, you are probably wondering; why has community been added to the equation? She; who is woman, is the community. What makes a community? Consider that females form herds, and males roam freely; therefore, when the herd takes a static existence; in other words, form a settlement, then how does an independent minded female affect the idea of the herd? She is thinking like a male, but nature says, she belongs in the herd. So, how is she going to behave? Be a lesbian? If not a lesbian lifestyle then what? More than likely she will want to hustle too, but what does she hustle for? Bedroom with a man or with a woman? Perhaps; however, she is seeking that, which requires money without using her own earnings. No secret there. She is seeking males for their money; however, he will more than likely not involve any form of financial gratuity for very long without some form of reciprocity, and, so, she has to decide her next course of action. Surrender herself in the bedroom, or move on. Should the guy have money, she will do what is necessary. In that case, guess what? We're back to square one; prostitute. Except now, she has a high paying job to offset her income. A family-supporting career with no intent to start a family. The best of both worlds, and that eager guy who would love to marry and start a family? That young woman who is eager to settle down to domestic life; waiting for a man to take her away from all the misery of daughter-hood; well? Both of them lose out.

Let us examine certain aspects of male/female interaction:

Passive intercourse is usually some form of initial meeting; her movements, eye-contact, vocal inflexions that initiate the arousal between the two of you.

Indirect intercourse: Touching; e.g. holding hands, arms, waist, even the touching of lips to cheek, lips-to-lips.

Direct intercourse: The touching of secluded areas of the body. Use of the tongue, fornication; utilizing the arousal of the human senses to maximize physical pleasure.

Oh, and by the way; saliva exchange is perhaps more intimate then sexual intercourse itself. Direct fluid exchange is an exchange of information. Think of how sensitive your taste buds are when eating food. The subtle differences between what is tasty and what is nasty. The joy of relishing what is sweet over what is bitter. Ever notice how you feel whenever you have a dry mouth? Quenching the thirst; even water changes the overall outcome for the moment. Fluid exchange is a crucial part of a relationship, and yes; that includes even her vaginal fluid. We forget that our mouths are the insides of our body, and it is very delicate and sensitive in there. Now, isn't it interesting that the only other natural entry into the human body is her vagina. Everything about her exists between her legs. That is why it is important for her not to engage in premarital sexual intercourse. Moreover, her providing you with oral pleasure should not be a necessity, other than benefitting a smoother physical interaction. Again, every interaction between the two of you is to benefit her alone. She is entitled to be selfish in her pursuit of pleasure on the basis that she is required to be selfless in the final result of the interaction, for the benefit of your immortality, for which, she is to be extremely generous.

CHAPTER 11

Withal said, what is going on with the overall mingling process? What is it that the modern woman wants? Let us again come to grips with the truth. She wants to impose gender filtration. The ultimate in selfish behavior. She adorns a certain kind of attire, in the event that she does happen across that one guy who stirs her loins. To

174

garnish the attention of a certain kind of male, of whom oddly enough, is someone whom seems to never be interested in her on an intellectual level. While in the meantime attracting the attention of several dozen males, whom she finds less than appealing, thus giving them a polite, but rude brushoff; however, once he sees an alluring female, the genie is essentially out of the bottle. At that point, there is nothing she can do. Even changing her clothing style will not work, and when he does not refrain from being attracted to her enticing display, she will get frustrated. File a complaint with the establishment. Then when society does not comply with her complaint in a suitable fashion, she will become irate; assaulting him, either physically or verbally. Claiming sexual harassment, seeking legal or journalistic assistance; pushing for laws to be changed to increase her edge in society, resulting in eventual hostility, which could lead to serious punishment for the man. To include even jail? She, in effect, becomes a bully. Using the powers that be to enforce her will. Since the implementation of sexual harassment policies in our social decorum, there have been women and even some men whom have allowed its use in a cart-blanche style for every little social interactive nuance. The idea of having space between their perceptions of rape and empowerment can be solace and yet absolute. The problem is that crazy is a very real thing in the feminine community and yet, female psychiatrist, perhaps psychiatry as a whole has erased a man's perceptions of what a rational thinking female should be.

You see, life for a male is about trial and error in regards to understanding human nature. We determine action and reaction in order to make an informed decision and this is accomplished through our interaction with the environment. Discussion tickles the mind. Makes the social edifice interesting. Discussion is a necessity for sanity. Our sanity can determine life or death. You never know when a conversation may impart a piece of useful information to determine a proper course of action.

Crazy or what this author likes to call possessed females, interfere with that process. Crazy exaggerates the facts and her ability to tell a lie is phenomenal. The most dangerous aspect of all is how she can behave, so, rationally when seeking an agenda. The oddity to the whole affair is that it is usually she whom directs the conversation towards becoming offensive and we must cease being human to accommodate the crazy? We currently live in a culture that allows crazy to be a part of the social diorama and you challenge her sanity and the judiciary comes down hard.

Are there any of you reading this familiar with terms such as inquisition or witch trial? Oh, and beware that courtrooms were the settings for many of those processes and instead of stepping up, you have chosen to step back and allow this American masculinity inquisition to continue. Missing the one important question that is never asked, and that is, should a man be held responsible for his behavior due to a lack of self-control in an overly sexualized, yet masculine suppressive environment? His and her behaviors are completely different all together. Have we forgotten that the *state* forces males and females to interact with one another in the workplace, and then punishes the male for behaving according to what was given to him by nature when expressing his desires for a female colleague. He is behaving as a man. Reacting naturally to feminine presence. She is attracting, and he is reacting. To tell a man to simply switch off his natural instincts towards being attracted to the woman would be like asking him to stop breathing. The repetitive view of facial beauty and curves on a daily basis is just another form of PTSD. Telling a man who has lost his mind to a hot-bodied female to just stop, is not enough. Would telling a soldier, suffering from PTSD to control his anger, be enough? Then why would women wearing body melding attire expect a man to stop being attracted to them?

He should not be harshly punished for reacting to the feminine form. When people jump down the throat of she whom cannot hack it, we tell them to back off; however, he whom cannot hack it, is disciplined, loses his job or goes to jail?

Once integrating the woman into the workforce, the expectations of proper conduct should not be an enforceable issue. Stress is a very real thing, and it is a natural human reaction to generate expression to stave off the beast of stress. Natural to keep the mind in high spirits, especially in the most difficult of situations. Take away that means of doing, so, and what do you get? Pent-up rage. Consider that everything about a woman is sexual. No institution can bar her from being as such. The modern American male must except her stimulating effect, which means that she must tolerate certain male attitudes; Chauvinistic Pride.

Why are we, so, harsh to men who are bombarded by sex on a daily basis? Again, that balance of sexiness is at play. If women were restricted on what they wear in public, would they; the casual female that is, behave differently? Ease the sexual burdens on the male population? Could certain feminine apparel be the catalyst for, so, many sex crimes? Any crime for that matter? How does a male deal with the constant sexual subliminal messaging? Let us be realistic: We know why she wears the formfitting attire, and we know the excuses she makes for wearing it in a public setting, but does this truly give her the right to say; *don't look at me like that,* when it does not suit her? Understand that we, the male, are dependent on a female looking at us as a *hint-of-interest* in regards to initiating relations and how is that done? By looking at her.

Let us examine the darker side of gender relations. Sex fatigue is not recognized as say; battle fatigue, for we men do not have a clear perception of what a woman is doing to us on a conscious level. Unfortunately, we bring it upon ourselves due to our delight of her shapeliness. When you are constantly bombarded by a thing without a chance of avoiding it, or recovery from it, then the result can be an overwhelming factor that is not unlike PTSD, or simply suffering from a drug addiction. In the case of sex; her presence, whether in motion or stationary affects us; the male of the species, like some form of sexual inertia, but mostly subconsciously, though, there are moments when we may react consciously.

Naturally, there is a difference between attraction and arousal. Her presence is the attraction. Her overall appearance; clothing, cosmetics, hairstyle; determines the arousal. For example; she wears

177

a long dress, and simple blouse, nothing that would make her standout; however, if her top happens to be a form-fitting half-shirt, and the dress happens to be a low rise or mini, then all of the variables are changed. She becomes more than an attraction, but an arousal. Prostitutes have been doing this long before the change in clothing style in our modern culture. They are also aware that revealing a portion of skin can have an added effect to the overall sensation. In the past, her choice of apparel had a definite effect on a man's conduct; however, in this modern age of the Twenty-first, there are apparently no exceptions.

CHAPTER 12

Now, the way that we approach sexual intercourse is not logical or reasonable; not in the least. It does not jibe with our perceptions of being human. Sexual intercourse is not a recreation, but a responsibility. The greatest drug in our existence. She is stimulant, depressant, pain-killer, manipulator, and will-breaker wrapped up into a convenient package that can be found everywhere. Far more potent than the combination of all the drugs on the face of the earth, and the interesting thing is, they all have a relationship, but with one applicable difference. Whereas other drugs hit the mind first, then the body, and then the spirit, she; who is sex, is capable of destroying the mind, body and spirit in one felled swoop.

Sex has purpose, meaning, and even responsibility, and yet we treat it as some casual plaything, as though it were nothing. Logic dictates that everything has purpose; everything has reason for being. Therefore, the only reasonable explanation for our treatment of sexual intercourse in today's society is truly illogical. It makes absolutely no sense. Not only does it not make sense, but it is a conflicting mass of emotions that is not unlike a child. Truly a curiosity when considering sex's relationship to immaturity, and how college professors, specifically the women of that profession want the general populous to believe that such a circumstance can be approached maturely, but this is not the case. Sex is an act of childishness, and yet they degrade male behavior for not practicing restraint when female behavior goes unchecked. This action unto
178

itself is childish, for one side cannot practice restraint unless the other side does, so, as well. A woman dresses to garnish attention. Then she and/or other women will insult a man for looking at her in what they may perceive as demeaning. Of course, without the immature behavior how does a woman know that a man has an attraction for her? Interesting how it is only immaturity when the man is less than physically substantial in the eyes of the female. Oh, how we; the man, miss those subtle markers, in regards to our understanding of the relationship between what is sexual harassment and what is sexual inappropriateness. Especially when contending with an on-the-job investigation. Accusations made against a man that jeopardizes his position in the company. Punishing men for being men. It is our natural instinct to behave accordingly, based on feminine presentation, and yet our culture has made it a dirty thing to even look at a woman. Using even our religious values as a justification for their reasoning; however, looking at a woman is not sinful. Desiring a married woman is a sin. A man can look at a woman and comment on her. A man can look at a car, a rifle or automotive tools and comment on them. So, what makes a woman different? Certain individuals have conditioned us into believing that looking at a woman and commenting on her appearance is some form of sexual harassment. This is in fact a lie. A woman has a right to dress as she sees fit; however, you the man cannot look at her? She dresses to attract your attention and because you do not measure up to her standards you are expected to stifle yourself? Simply, look away? Shut off a million years of evolution? Talk about unfair, unequal, and unjustified.

Men are already aware that sex is an immature state of mind on a subconscious level. Sex is not meant to be a part of the daily routine, but kept concealed. Which is why we do not allow people to simply fornicate in a public setting. If it were a mature act, then people would not hesitate to knot in the park under the afternoon sun. When children behave immaturely, it is accepted, but when adults act puerile, they either conceal themselves or are confined. Prior to the full and proper maturity of males; and as a majority, depending on the level of their physical, and mental aptitude, they view sex as a game, and thus approach it immaturely. That is why males conceal it under the mattress, the pillow or ceiling panel. Perhaps women should not be college instructors to men. You cannot approach sex from a philosophical point of view to men under the age of 30-35. Most men do not have a grasp of the fire within themselves, and more often than not resort to violence, even war, or to say the least an all-out street brawl, to overcome the need to be fed upon. Good thing someone invented sports.

CHAPTER 13

Before continuing, let us be clear about certain aspects of human sexual interaction. Incest is when both sides are closely related, and the intercourse is consensual. Rape is a situation where one party uses some form of influence to overcome another person's will. A boy can rape an adult female using childish-charm or words to entice, that play upon her motherly instincts. A woman having sexual relations with a boy is not rape on her part, but simply the sign of what can only be perceived as a weak-will. A woman whom brings a boy sexual delight is bringing to reality his biggest fantasy, and he will not say no to her, on the basis that it is in a male's nature to be curious, to experience everyday things to their logical conclusion. Especially in cases of interaction; e.g. his pretty school teacher whom he is more than likely fantasizing about anyhow. An old thing for those of us who remember our youth. In fact, a woman who engages in an intimate relationship with a man-child cannot be viewed as statutory rape unless he is of a state of mind that is incognizant to the understanding of the overall purpose of such activity. Oddly enough, even the woman would not understand the purpose of such an activity on the basis that pleasure is not, so, much a purpose, but more of an activity to incite a reaction that may or may not result in a purpose that would be contradictory to our correlation with nature. This is not to say that there is not the occasional man-child who does not want to be with an adult female in that situation, it is just that a great majority of male children have an attraction for older females due to all of the sexual innuendo in our social edifice.
180

Other than that, a woman is designed to be exploited, and that exploitation can be from any source. Let this author be clear that exploitation is not always of sexual intent; however, the potential for sexual exploitation can result in the long-run, if not properly regulated and understood. We all require behavioral training from the onset of life. Where does that training come from? Again; in days past, there was a mother in the home. If you; the reader, do not see the implications of a mother who is rarely in a child's life, then put this book down, and never pick it back up. Mother behaves a certain way, and daughters imitate that behavior. If mother is not present, then whom does the daughter imitate? Or perhaps you want your daughter imitating others? Strangers for whom you know nothing about; capable of activities that go against your better nature. Of course, imitating you; the father is not, so, bad, but realistically, what you want is a princess, and to have a princess, you must marry a princess. If all a female can do is lay on her back, then what can she teach your beautiful little girl after giving birth to her?

Back on the subject of why a boy is fantasizing about his school teacher or any woman in his sphere of influence for that matter. Boys are becoming sexually stimulated at a much younger age, incorporating sex into childhood industry, but then are forced to retard that stimulating feeling that is roasting their loins. While females; on the other hand, continue to push the sexual-envelope beyond the limits of reasonable expectations; proving the existence of traumatic sex syndrome in our culture. A serious dilemma that is being ignored in our society. Better yet, let us call this ignored behavioral phenomena, OTSS: Ongoing, Traumatic Sex Syndrome because no matter what we; the casual observer sees or do; we can never get away from sex in any form.

Human evolution and child evolution are not, so, different. There was a time of social innocence, when the populous was naïve in their daily routine. When happening upon the amazing; they desired it. An attractive adult female is like a goddess to a burgeoning man-child. She is mother without being his mother. Naturally, the first woman a child has an attraction for is his own mother; however, she subconsciously prohibits those fantasies from manifesting and eventually, nature kicks in to stabilize the man-child's mind; that, and of course our religious values. Understand that it is not a bad thing for a man-child to have a sexual attraction for his mother for he does not understand himself yet. That is why parents must instruct their children on what is proper and what is improper at the onset of life. Oh, and just, so, we are clear on one other overlooked aspect of our social décor, and that is, mothers whom array themselves in sexually enticing clothing, while in a private setting are fueling the fires of lust that are just beginning within him; the son. He is a little boy, and she is thinking, he will adapt to her enticing display. That he must adapt because these are the times, and women have rights. What she wears, and what your daughter; his sister wears, is the same thing that promiscuous females are wearing. How we attire ourselves determines behavior. She dresses a certain way; he behaves a certain way. He sees the eroticism online, in a magazine and what is the boy supposed to expect? Even a strong forceful mother will be seen as something of an alluring nature. He is trying to figure out on his own what is going on with himself, and no one is explaining to him the natural biological reaction of attraction. By the time he is hitting his teens, his hormones are a nuclear furnace. Oh, and just one other item that he may not be learning; and that is, how to be charming, respectful and kind. He may be developing into a lustful cold, methodical predator. A passionate rapist or skilled philanderer or an abusive rapist. Which is almost always the case for those who have a questionable understanding of their own level of education. If he should be big and tall, then he will become a passionate rapist due to low moral feminine self-esteem. She will fear him, and simply give in to his needs. If he is short in stature, then he may break, becoming brutal in his assessment of females. Which is why mothers and sisters should conceal their sexuality in the home. Males need a period to rest from all of the public sexual innuendo. What? He gets home and must continue to be immersed in hot bodied females? Is that fair to him? Sure, there are moments when a woman wants to look and feel sexy, but not every moment of every day.

Let us briefly sidetrack. You have a son that exhibits sexual desires for his mother, and the explanations are evidently not sinking in. What do you do? Psychiatrist? Therapist? A medical doctor who can determine a physical impediment? If your son exhibits bad behavior in general, you seek specialists? If you cannot get your son to listen to you, and there is nothing physically wrong with them, you don't spank them? If your son is defiant when a child, then what will they become as a teenager? What will they become as an adult? We see people in our modern culture who were more than likely never spanked as a child. They feel the world should revolve around them. That laws, even those of heaven, do not apply to them, and many of them are upper middle class and rich. We now, identify them as; *affluenza.*

Therefore, should we be punishing adult females who get caught up in the intimacies of human interaction in regards to a man-child? Incarcerating she; who is woman for submitting to the desire of innocence lost? Doing, so, is pointless. Again, look at our culture. How do you punish someone who has been subliminally conditioned into accepting leisure sexual intercourse as a normal circumstance of the human condition? The little details of the human condition that have been discarded thanks to the feminist movement. Simple things that are required for a female to maintain her dignity, self-respect and self-control, that have been replaced by language such as liberation, women lead and equality. What are those simple things? They are things that exist on the very twilight of her subconscious mind that are easily shed in the face of becoming liberated; however, what is she truly liberating herself from? The answer is, so, simple that it could be construed as satirical by design, resulting in sheer tragedy in the end; and that is her obligation from mother-hood. Do you; the reader, recall this author's mentioning a woman's ability to reduce herself to a child-like state to better interact with a child? To literally become a child to effectively impart certain details that would otherwise be ignored if they were communicated any other way? Without this little detail, children would never mature. Doubt this author's words? Look at our children. Do they not behave as adults, but from a child's perspective? A woman requires an adult male; presumably a husband to bring her back from this immature state of mind. As with the child behaving as an adult from a child's point of view, what will happen, should the adult female not return from her immature state of mind after interacting with her husband's child? When sex becomes a part of the adolescent scheme of exploration? The innocent curiosity evolves into taboo. How about the adult female school teacher who does not have an adult male to bring her back from her immature state of mind? Yes; a malfunction will occur; and what is interesting is that it is not her fault. Again, our modern culture as a whole is in a state of complete social malfunction! Sex has been introduced at too young an age, and the child cannot cope, and, so, what happens to that adult female who is unable to revert to an adult state of mind with all of that child-hood sex roaming about? Full circle in regards to student/teacher sexual relations. Which may explain why male homosexuality is, so, pervasive in our existence, and why fags should not be instructors, to the young in any form.

Girls; on the other hand, who are caught up in the same situation have a cutoff point when experiencing those same feelings about their male teacher. Even in cases of a strong emotional attachment. Whereas males are naturally curious; females; as a whole, are naturally cautious. A man has to put some effort into convincing her to surrender her virginity, it is a failsafe mechanism built into her construction by God. That is because females have more to lose in a relationship whether it be successful or not. Naturally some of you are going to say B.S. That there are girls who are more than capable at seducing an older man; and in many cases, with ease, but the reality is; if these girls are no longer virgins; precociousness is, what it is. She is not blatantly looking to surrender herself to the act of intercourse, but simply imitating life due to culture being, so, irresponsible about sexual interaction to the point that she has no clear perception of proper social rapport. All children want attention; especially the females, and when they discover a new means of getting it, they will take full advantage. Think of the sick-child routine. A child sees their sibling or even another child getting the attention of their parents or adults when they are hurt or sick, and, so, they too, try to get hurt or sick. This occurs; especially in children who are given lots of attention. Now, apply this idea to the woman-child who is used to getting all of the attention. What will they do to keep that attention? They will go as-far-as sexual deviance to attract attention to themselves. Yes; the same as the street-walker. So, as the adult male, it is your duty to put the woman-child in check, and with great prejudice. We, as a society must beware of she who is scorned by the adult male who is putting her in check. She will use devious means of; again; getting him out of the way in order to continue her little scheme of attention-getting until someone actually calls her bluff. We do not want her to discover the truth of life the hard way because deep down she is a good girl.

Even worse is that feminine attitude is having a profound effect on our overall social lexicon. Modern parents have become indolent in their duties as to who is essentially in charge of the household, allowing their children to call the shots. This is a common occurrence in most American households in this present day of the early Twenty-first, and requires addressing. For you; parents, who allow your daughters to reveal their shapeliness in a public setting: Many of our children can reach physical maturity quickly. In fact, there are many girls, even under the age of fourteen; yes; youngsters, who could easily pass for adults. We can say that this may be due to the chemical additives in our food, or perhaps it's genes, or some other nonconformity to the human machine, but reality dictates that the competitive spirit for attracting attention is extremely high in our culture. Not to mention that human-beings develop at different rates. In regards to females; that difference is having an adverse effect on society as a whole. Case-in-point; one girl views another girl attracting attention, and it must be the skinny jeans. It flips a switch on in the brain without her realizing that her body is not developing at the same rate as the other girl. Doubt this author? Ever catch sight of a little girl wearing skinny jeans? Kind of gives you the impression she is wearing dance tights without a tutu. Obvious that she is a child, and yet, she is imitating a woman, and no one is telling her that she should not dress that way because we live in a culture of social fear. Say something about what she is wearing, and you are accused of being a pervert. The parents or some other person would challenge you with words such as; *Why are you looking at her like that?* Now, this author understands that in the old days when girls dressed and behaved their age, it was necessary to deal with those with an affinity for young flesh; however, in this modern age of the early Twentieth-first, your average fifth grader dresses like a seventies-streetwalker. Now, we men scold the boy who is a nuisance to the girl, but say nothing of her fashion choice, which is sending the boy's hormones into overdrive to begin with. *Get away from me you pervert!* is the attitude a boy may experience from these females. How does the man-child cope, let alone the adult male? Apparently, those males who cope with the open displays of sex become sexually insensitive. Those males who do not adapt become sexually insane, and usually end up in jail or amount to very little in society. Do not take this author's word for it. Turn off the television news and other forms of mass-media, and look at the world around you. What is going on with our children? What do you see? Does what you see jibe with what is being said in the media; by celebrities, journalists, even politicians? He is attracted to the girls, and he is reacting to the girls, but then forced to control the impulses he is feeling for the girls. Are you; the parent, helping a selfish, one-sided generation force male children to adapt to impossible odds? Your son is losing his mind. He is in a state of confusion. Can we view his situation as fair? Clearly a social double standard, for she has absolutely no problem with the jock who pursues her in the same manner, but the average run of the mill boy needs to behave? The guy who happens to be like Arnold Schwarzenegger circa 1975 can stare at her backside in those formfitting everything? Which brings up a key question. Why do women wear running tights when they are going for a leisurely jog to stay in shape? They are not competing against anyone, but running for fitness and health; so, wouldn't it make more sense for them to

186

run in baggy sweats; clothing that catches the wind for resistance for a better workout? What is the purpose of the running tights? Logic dictates; they are seeking to draw the eye of the male because contrary to what some women may think, running tights are not imbrued with magic to keep them shapely. They want acceptance of their sexuality, and let us be realistic, females are not dressing sexy as they like to put it, but sleazy, and we do not even realize it for the lines between what is sexy and what is sleazy have been greatly blurred or we; the man, prefer the sleazy and dress it up as sexy as an excuse for our faults.

Okay, let us put an end to the social fear once and for all. People crack for whatever reason, and locking up every man who has an affinity for the feminine form is untenable, and yet, that is exactly what we are trying to do. Weaker willed men are looking because their minds are more than likely stuck in adolescence. Again, a male's sex drive is being switched on at too early an age for many of our children to cope. How they perceive sex as a child remains with them into adulthood without considering that there is no mature understanding of what sex is from a mature state of mind. That is, if there is any true baseline to determine what is adult to begin with because the understanding of mature behavior has not been imbued with what it means to be an adult.

For the benefit of our children, we must address inappropriate attire on the basis that in their later years they may be unable to cope with the presence of a female in daily living. Reality dictates that males will still feel like children, even when becoming adults. Therefore, *he* cannot define the hot bodied girl from the shapely woman because he is still viewing her from a child's point of view; and let us accept the fact that it is next to impossible to distinguish between what law perceives as a minor and an adult in regards to human nature. Again; between 12 and 30, it is truly a toss-up, and a lot of our young females truly grow up fast.

Rebuke the person that asks the question of; *why are you looking,* and do it with great emotion. For you are not looking out of want or lust, but out of concern for a child's frame of mind, and not necessarily for the child's sake either, but more for the parent's benefit because we men see the world in panorama. Though there are those who would like us to utilize some form of tunnel vision as they apparently hint of doing when going about the community. Especially in regards to the woman staring at the gorgeous, hot bodied male passing her on the street.

What is interesting is why do we look at females who are under the age of eighteen as minors to begin with? For a very long time, the states allowed females who were under the age of eighteen to marry, but today we view these laws as antiquated. Why? Were our forefathers, perverts? Dirty old men who viewed females as social tools to be used or was it something else? Our country was once a religious dominated society. Which means that our religious values set the social standard for gender interaction. We allowed our common sense to determine when she was ready, and no, it was not perfect. Nothing ever is, but we are a secular dominated society now, and things are really great in regards to minors and men; right? Another point to consider is that boys grew into manhood at an earlier age, but not due to mortality rates. Fathers in the early U.S.A. encouraged intellectual maturity with their man-child because they understood that their children represented their immortality. Gaining experience rapidly was a necessity on the basis that no one in the U.S.A. wanted a repeat of what was going on in Europe at that time. Ignorance was a dangerous thing, and still is in today's world. The idea in the days of our Founding Fathers is that all people should have a shot at reaching a certain standard of living. Females, on the other hand, though restricted, were compelled to keep up. Not from a competitive standpoint, but due more to social status. Though historians would have everyone believe that females were viewed as nothing in western culture, the reality was, and in some cases still is, the opposite. For most families and communities, it was more of economics, and the needs of the house. Look at the facts; those aristocratic families educated their daughters. Furthermore, girls were being pushed into woman-hood faster than they are today. It was not uncommon for a much younger female to marry an older male. The story; *"Gone With The Wind"* is fiction based on fact, and is an accurate depiction of life, not just in the South, but across the entire social spectrum. Females imitated their mothers because their mothers were constantly present in their lives, and gave them a working model to follow. Now, consider what happened to daughters when their living example was no longer present. Oddly, going into the workforce made things more difficult, but it was not the beginning of the loss of the living example. We have to peel away the decades to see what was going on in the U.S.A. that led to the destruction of the family. This author sees *Prohibition* as the breaking point for daughters and mothers. Yes; the problem-daughter was not a new thing in the early Twentieth; however, with the speakeasies came something new that few saloons had up until Prohibition. A place for those under-aged girls to show off their precociousness. Do not allow Hollywood fiction to cloud the nonfiction narrative of those types of places. There may not have been any Shirley Temples, but perhaps there were quite a few Judy Garlands.

Another possibility is that the chances of a still-born infant was extremely high, and, so, too were the miscarriages. Both are still a very real possibility in this modern medical age, therefore, as a husband; a man, you viewed the female as a fragile creature, prone to mechanical failure. Obsessed with the need for females to take care of themselves. Avoid stressful situations, that; yes, included seeking an education because from his point of view, schoolwork was difficult. No doubt about that. The pressure to learn in the old days was extremely high, but not today. *Wonder why?* As man is perhaps the most adaptable creature ever conceived, it is no wonder those of the religious community say that he is a likeness of God, and the female simply adapted accordingly. You see, it is natural for the human brain to remember via all senses; however, we refuse to trust our memory. We are capable of remembering what a person says, exhibit, exchange, do, and how they feel. We simply do not exercise that aspect of ourselves as we should as a whole. Females were forced to trust their memory, which is an act that comes naturally to all of us. The amazing thing is, that she was capable of doing this, and keep her feminine abilities intact. Do females today keep their feminine abilities intact or simply throw their sexuality in our faces? Interesting how females have a greater trust in their memories giving them an edge over us; the male, in regards to academics.

As academics opened up further for the woman, boys were no longer pushing themselves to the intellectual limit in regards to the very fundamentals of social philosophy. There is nothing more distracting to a boy then a girl; *fact!* The idea of maturity waned, and we as parents noticed that our boys were maturing later in life. Again, there are those whom will say, that in the old days, people did not live as-long-as we do today, and that they had to grow up quickly, due to less advanced medical practices. This author calls that; science overshadowing our perceptions on life. Observe for yourself how long a person lived in the past. Specifically, in the U.S.A. Now, it is natural as human beings to say, that when a person is not ready for something, then we need to hold them back until they are ready. Fathers in our country's heyday sensed when their boys were ready to take on the world, even compelled them to do, so. Over time, fathers yielded to their educated wives whom felt that their boys were not ready, and, so, what happened? The idea of a child not being ready for adulthood overshadowed male common sense, and now, we have laws that say; 18 is the age of consent, but let us be realistic in regards to a mature state of mind; 25, even 30 is fast becoming the new 18, and even older for boys. Parents are refusing to allow their boys to grow up. Fathers are not pushing their sons to grow up because they are simply not part of their son's lives, and how does that immature state of mind relate to sexual intercourse?

Again, sex is an immature state of mind, and as previously stated, woman is the very epitome of sex. She is an immature creature who is holding back the development of the man-child. Even her focus has changed on being more like that of the male, placing her in an even more immature state of mind, and thus our children are remaining children later in their lives. There are certain behavioral conditions a woman must ascertain to define herself accordingly with the delicacies of communal interaction. Those conditions are nonexistent, and all a boy sees in today's schools is the clothed nudity. Until we come to grips that a woman's choice of attire has a definite impact on the world around us, male academics will continue to decline.

CHAPTER 14

Let us be realistic. We are easily distracted by the greatest enemy to our very reason and logic, and yet it is a necessity for our continued existence. A necessary pleasure that loosely shares its lineage with sin. As a culture obsessed with sex, the only way to get right, is to place a tight leash on the female. Specifically, her choice of attire, while in the public eye. To deny her the right to provocative attire during daylight hours. Sex wants to flow freely. It's how she maintains her hold over man and society as a whole. We must change our view of society to get a clearer perception on life. Not an impossible endeavor. If we can overcome mountains, the bottom of the sea, and reach out to other worlds...?

We require a daily balance of gender interaction, much like a daily balance of vitamins and minerals. This does not imply sexual intercourse of any kind, but simply the pleasure of a woman's presence. Sex needs to fall back into the arena of responsibility and not recreation. Placed on a high shelf, so, that when encountered it becomes unreachable until we are sure of what it is; for love and lust share a common understanding and a common ancestor. We must remove the sexual innuendo from the environment, as we would a pollutant; however, when doing so, we must remember what sex is, and be compassionate about her removal. It is a substance that must be contained, so, that we can go through sexual withdrawal. Recover from our sexual euphoric state of mind, in order to focus on more important things, and realize just how destructive sex can be on a civilized society.

Girls and boys should be separated in schools, no later than the 4th grade. Sexually suggestive advertisements should be removed accordingly. Television journalism is more in common with a fashion show. All entertainment that displays a woman's sexual nature should be treated as adult-only content. Pornography should only be created

191

as a means of a teaching aide, and be respectful of the practice of good gender interaction; hugely taxed and well-regulated to include barring it from streaming, broadcast, cable or satellite, and kept in the realm of prostitution, and thus treated like a firearm's dealer would store guns. Why, legalize prostitution? For the simple reason that it can never be done away with. Besides, to deny its use in a constitutional culture violates the very idea of the democratic process. A person can live a deplorable lifestyle to clearly identify those in need of God the most. They should not be locked up. This act would be a waste of tax payer dollars, but instead, given assistance to break the habit like any other drug.

Feminists must be identified and dealt with directly along with their witchcraft ways, and remember that a warlock is a man who is subservient to sex; allows her to dominate him; usually, but not necessarily, through physical gratification. A woman has no right over a man, and a man has no right to abuse a woman. In this modern age of the Twenty-first, you do not stone the witch or burn them, you simply ignore them. This is by far the worst kind of punishment that you can bestow upon a woman. She does not like to be ignored on the basis that they are designed to be, vain; attract attention, and garnish praises. Deny them this, and you have done worse than kill them. You have killed their power over you.

MORE QUESTIONS OF SEX

CHAPTER 1

Let us dabble in the greatly ignored taboo of child-hood sexual intercourse. Realistically, males should not be experiencing sexual pleasure before the age of 21, and females should not be making themselves sexually available before the age of 13. Talk about sick; however, in regards to the male; his virility comes from his testosterone. Nothing should impede a man-child's masculine growth, for at least his first twenty years. The greater his natural strength, the healthier his seed. A man-child requires a clean

192

palette from which to paint his masterpiece of life, and that is not something that can be done overnight. For if it is not beautiful, he would be unable to attract a suitable female for which to cleave to when his time comes. A male child's body is growing, developing, changing; and, so, the last thing he needs, is an excessive loss of his seed during his physical development. We; the male, need our testosterone to toughen the sinew, and strengthen the overall aspect of what it means to be male. In fact, when a man takes some form of drug to enhance his masculinity, then he is exchanging his natural testosterone for pollution. Doubt this author? Look at boys today. They are sex crazed maniacs unable to take a moment to figure out who they are; their purpose in life. What they should be doing is gaining an understanding of the true nature of woman. Why is that? Sex gets hold of them early in life, and like a Pitbull; does not let go, and over time, she literally drives him mad because as is typical with a child, he has access to a thing without an understanding of a thing. To him, it is, but a toy to be played with. To make himself physically, and mentally powerful, he should, one; keep his virginity. Two; prevent genital pinch. Three; avoid the sexual innuendo as-best-as possible. Four; and perhaps the most important is to align himself with Judeo-Christian values.

In the case of the girl, it is quite the opposite. It is natural for the feminine body to engage in sexual intercourse, even during her developmental stages. Sexual intercourse does not impede her physical development, but it does affect her mental development, of which, to us; the male, is far more important than her figure. For a crazy woman can devastate the best laid plans of civilization. Furthermore, pregnancy is also a natural part of who she is, and does not affect her physical development either, though feminists, and perhaps some in the psychiatric and medical communities may say otherwise; conditioning our entire culture into believing that teen pregnancy is a bad thing; which is of course, a lie. Actually, it is premarital sexual intercourse that is improper. Her womb is stronger at youth than it would be in her later years. Newborns benefit from a younger viable motherly body rather than an older one. A lot of the physical problems that mothers and newborns experience may be remedied by women simply giving birth at a younger age. You also avoid the mysteries of sudden infant death, and a woman's urge to kill the child. These things are more than likely one and the same, but as this author has adeptly titled this book; *"I Am Not A PhD"*, then the previous statement rests strictly on opinion. Youth does not experience the same urges as an older woman, and perhaps the reason behind that is due to an unnatural process of existence. The modern female is retarding feminine nature in lieu of her impression of what is male nature. Taking on the difficulties of society, the natural world, and just plain living. She is focusing her attention on *everything,* and trying to be a woman as well, resulting in anxiety; discomfort; apprehension. The buildup of tension is disassembling her psyche. Not to mention the constant allowance of sexual intercourse, which is causing the mechanism to behave in an irregular manner. In other words, that whole equality thing is turning into a real social nuisance, and since behaving more as a male; in that brief instant, she lashes out without realizing what she has become; a man without the male. She becomes the very thing she is supposed to counteract, and that is independence. Casually crossing the line of what is male and what is female, she actually does not want the loneliness that comes with being independent, and, so, whom does she seek to remedy that burden? The gender that is specifically designed to handle such burdens. Naturally, a lot of women will disagree with that notion, and even some men, but if you pay close attention to our current social standings, you will clearly see that something is off. Why would this author say that something is off? Our children are dying; plain and simple. Teaching a child at a young age about sexual intercourse is a fool's errand. The reason that children are discovering sex at an inappropriate age is due to idle parenting. If there are doubts, then consider the term of child-proofing a home. Distraction is a very real part of life. In the old days, when a parent gave a woman-child a baby-doll, that child would treat that doll as if it were real. We knew then that the woman-child was on the path of motherhood. She wanted to be a mother. What do

194

modern parents purchase for their woman-child in this modern age of the early Twenty-first? Barbie? Some other vanity dolls, or nonconformity to the natural processes of femininity, of which, reinforces feminist's ideas? Toys geared more for independent thinking? They say; *stop the brainwashing of our girls, and show them that they can be anything they want!* Yet, in regards to being a mother; no cultivation. Sure, looking out for our children is crucial to the survival of our species. Interesting that when a child is lost due to male negligence it is the rape of the civilized world; however, when a child is lost due to female negligence, it is a tragedy brought about by social neglect. Again, that little feminist double standard. That inability to see the truth, due to feminist standards, and the social neglect of our children has increased exponentially in the past fifty years.

CHAPTER 2

Time to ask the question of where did the sexual addiction in adolescence come from? Perhaps the sex education programs in our public school system. Sure, sex education was okay when women dressed less tantalizing, but mix in a little free love with the form-fitting and/or skimpy outfits, and an explosion was bound to occur. Now, there is a problem. The explosion never diminished. It simply got worse. Therefore, teaching sex as the world currently stands in regards to a child would be like encouraging a child to take drugs. Again, sex carries the same behavioral aspects as any drug. Beginning with a little, until the addiction sets in; becoming an overwhelming force. Indifference will be all the addicted knows when trying to obtain it. That is why we have pretty-little liars and child-hood rape. Girls and boys sneaking out at night. Boys resorting to trickery and lies to evolve into a philanderer. While girls will do what is necessary to be with Mr. Popular. What would happen if a five-year old started drinking alcohol? What kind of a person would they become once they reached adulthood? Doubt this author? Take a look around and ask yourself what happened to the prodigy of dream builders? They are not even trying to push forward with far reaching innovations, but simply doing the bare minimum to provide us with the illusion of progression. They are as lost as a jungle boy in the heart of Manhattan. All they know is greed and nothing else. So, the status quo is to make it better and charge more. All in the name of sex; and when a drug gets hold, you really are not in the mood to do much of anything else.

The remedy to the explosion was, and still is the self-imposed vaccination of our girls. To prevent the disease of pregnancy, of which Feminist call, being liberated. What about the consequences of that liberation? No one truly factored in the emotional conflict between what is motherhood and what is whore. Every time she allows a man to engage her in sexual intercourse, nature taps her subconscious mind expecting a result. What happens when a person is exposed to something repeatedly? What happens when a person is constantly beaten? What happens to the subconscious when constantly viewing an advertisement? Passive torture is a very real thing in our modern culture, and is why we behave the way that we do. Treat it as though it does not exist. Torture has never been about the physical effect, but more of a psychological device. The torturer applies physical force to distract their victim in order to enter that part of the mind that consists of the core programming: Awareness of proper from improper, logical from illogical, reasonable from unreasonable, safe from sorry. In computer lingo, that would be the factory settings. Something we do not want tampered with, for if that fails...

The one thing that sex education never explains to a child is that sex is not a recreation, but a responsibility. Going out and losing her virginity to some hormone raging boy or a lesbian trip is not a rite of passage, but a pathway to mindless convictions. If she gets an urge to shoplift, and she is told that shoplifting is wrong, then she fights the impulse no matter how strong; *right?* Over time the compulsion subsides, and she learns to focus on other things. More important things. Can this concept be applied to raging hormones? If no one tells her that shoplifting is wrong or even worse; that shoplifting is actually okay, then she will continue to shoplift; plain and simple. What we have forgotten, and pretty much ignored is that females have a unique capacity that boys just do not have; and that is their ability to stave off those urges and raging hormones. Provided that she understands why it is happening to her in the first place, and that she has not been prematurely activated by her kith or kin or worse; a complete stranger.

CHAPTER 3

Now, for the big question. How do we keep sex away from a boy until a minimum of 21 years of age? Seems like a hopeless endeavor with all of the sexual exhibition in our culture. To deal with the problem of adolescent sex, we must segregate the genders. Dirty cuss; but to fix the state of emergency that we are refusing to accept as existing, is, to gender segregate our education system, so, that a boy may learn what it means to be a man without distraction. To understand life from a male point of view. Without sexual presence, what becomes the motivation for the anger and violence in our halls of learning? What? The "A" science student would evoke rage and anger from his fellow classmates? Perhaps, but unlikely. What is the one thing that leads to the anger of a teenager? Rejection. Yes, no one likes rejection, but it is a part of life, and we learn to live with it, but until we reach a level of understanding that; *a person can never have it all their own way,* then the path becomes a long and difficult one. Feminine rejection for a male teenager will have a life-long effect, and she can be quite brutal in her rejection of a suitor. Some females do not purposely brutalize a potential suitor with cruel words. Sometimes it can be frustrating for her to be innocently attractive. In other words, some females need not do much to reveal their beauty, where as some females deliberately display their attractiveness on a level equivalent to that of a prostitute. These are impatient females whom are in a rush to meet a guy and are blind to the truth that beauty comes from the heart, not the mirror. The worst-case scenario that plagues this society greatly is that they have more than likely been switched on by rape. An action involuntarily introduced at too early a stage of her development. She does not understand what has been done to her, and she becomes competitive because the very thing that she is, dominates her life. We view rape as a crime, no doubt of it being, so; however, the reality is, when her

197

rapist abandons her, it results in a double shock, and that is in fact, the true rape, and the tragedy of the whole affair. There is no compassion or warmth. Just cold meaningless penetration, leaving her lost and confused. She must have done something wrong because he has abandoned her after the fact, and she holds herself at fault for not being able to express compassion. Seduce his heart; a sense of wanting to be his helper. The truth is, her rapist is abandoning her, for he is afraid of facing the true warm feelings he never received as a boy. The victim did not understand the mother within, to show warmth and compassion, so, that he may face his fears. She simply reveals fear of him; feeding the frenzy of his lust. Regardless, if she is at fault then she will not speak to anyone about it. This is where the truth behind proper and improper parenting reveals itself.

We must reinstate our religious values. Our belief in God must return to the forefront of our livelihood. Teach our children to love God inside and out, and should they discover love of each other, then that love will be more real than life itself.

Religion aspires and inspires social interaction. Provides an educational foundation. The idea behind the Bible is to reveal to us our inability to pass on to our offspring our understanding of beliefs. The only logical conclusion to the application of academic stimulation is to further male brainpower.

We must also take a closer look at the judiciary in regards to the male who may simply lack an understanding of the truth of their circumstances in regards to male/female sexual interaction. A man whom has abruptly fallen into the hole of wrong doing. Not in regards to the sociopath. He; whose mind is closed; the out-n-out predator. No; we must consider, how many young men have been incarcerated for simply not understanding the truth of culture?

THE ENEMY

CHAPTER 1

The time has come to reveal the enemy of sex. Yes; sex has an enemy, and that enemy is massive in scope to our perceptions of what big is in the world. That enemy is; of course, the, so, called field of adult entertainment, and yes, that field is, so, broad that it easily crosses over to the mainstream film industry. Ever watch a movie at the theater and wonder why, so, much emphasis was placed on a sex scene. Let alone why there was even a sex scene to begin with? Over the years, many movie producers, directors and writers have felt it necessary to reveal a couple, going through the motions of sexual intercourse in order to achieve a certain effect or arousal? Comparable to that of the adult film industry. Why? There are countless ways of tastefully expressing strong subject matter without the facets of unhealthy viewing. Let's be reasonable; true art is when a person creates an expression that compels a mature mind to work on a subconscious level to formulate an opinion, based on a point of view. For those of you involved in the movie-machine; art is not just how two people conduct a performance. All levels of the film industry must be artistic or you lose the artistry of the whole. For even the easel, palette and brushes are an art form in their own right.

Now, for the obvious enemy of sex: To begin; let us be clear, that; yes; pornography is a form of expression; however, should it be allowed to freely express a notion that is clearly not designed to promote healthy living? What is pornography? A recording of some kind, of a person or persons conducting an activity that is considered an art form, performance, theatrics, resulting in a perversion of what would otherwise be sacred in the confines of human awareness, sanctity and sentience, for the preservation of the very essence of humanity. Trashing human pride, dignity, and most importantly, morality, sensitivity and emotions. Legalized rape! Yes; someone is always being forced, dominated, abused and humiliated; which usually; in the case of the sexually orientated movie, is the victim; and a financial gratuity is supposed to make it okay? Saying its consensual makes all of the difference? We forget that pornography is a heinous activity that rapes the very essence of society; decays the moral fabric of humanity, and prevents the progression of human motivation. Serving absolutely no purpose, other than to humiliate the human condition. Devalue a million years of evolution. Devolving a superb piece of carbon engineering back to a primitive state of existence to be preyed upon by lesser creatures. An institution of blatant sexual harassment, and yet, allowed to thrive in our modern culture amid the feminist hypocrisy that is polluting our moral objectivity. Perverting the very facet of woman-hood to its core. Anything, and everything a woman does to just be a human being is made a sexual mockery. Sacrificing a part of the female populous to further feminine guile and deceit; *perhaps*. Or; perhaps, it is something that is far more dubious. Perfectly okay for females to exploit females. Nothing wrong with that; *right?*

Just, so, we are clear; sexual harassment is not something you simply apply to a single plaintiff. It can also be associated to an entire gender when you really get down to the nuts and bolts of the matter. When women were barred from voting, not all women had a problem with it. We called it; Women's Suffrage, and the law viewed it as affecting the gender as a whole. Businesses refused to hire women in peacetime, of which, not all women had a problem with that idea, and we called it discrimination. In both accounts, subtle changes in language were used to throw off our thought-processes, thus ignoring the blatant harassment of womanhood as a whole in regards to the adult film industry. Perhaps there are unforeseen forces at work here with a greater agenda.

Let us revisit the idea of rape. There is passionate rape, and then there is abusive rape. Most females are victims of passionate rape because they are sexually active, and it does not take much to turn them on. Especially when they are not in the mood. Which begs the question: Should a female be allowed to scream rape when it suits her? She is groped; molested into a stimulating, enticing mood, usually during moments of hot romantic lip caressing. Then when all is said and done, and her mind clears from her euphoric experience, she files charges of rape? She showed little resistance; nothing in the way of a fight for her sexual decorum, and she

200

complains? Usually, years later, when that man, who was more than likely, sexually enticed by her provocative display, suddenly rises to a position of prominence. That's not rape, but revenge, due to the feeling of being taken advantage-of. A little-known term in today's social circles that has been conveniently put on the back shelf of forgetfulness by the feminists. Now, those men, who are excellent manipulators of the heart are simply accused of being rapist, and punished due to females who want to go it on their own? This author does not know a female whom did not get into trouble when experiencing something for the first time, and that includes getting involved with a sexual shyster. A man gets burned for his mistakes, and he deals with it accordingly. A woman gets burned for her mistakes, and she wants justice? Sometimes, decades later? Would that be called equality without fairness.

Let us probe deeper into our understanding of being taken advantage-of. No matter her level of education, the female frame of mind is devised around the need to live a fantasy relationship, and it can be overpowering for many of them at times. This is not a flaw as the feminist may have you believe, but more of a necessity to keep depression at bay. Strangely enough, she may get lucky, but not always. In any event, what is going on with our sisters and daughters is that they are trying to intertwine lifestyles. Why females do this is a mystery, even to this author. She wants to be the innocent little girl, but play the adult in a bad world, thinking that perhaps her knight in shining armor will come to the rescue before the evil villain can get his claws into her, or that she will rescue her ideal male, who is stuck in the muck and mire of civilization. Whatever the case, they will become involved with what they perceive to be their dream man, missing the subtle hints of risk when confiding too much information about themselves, either directly or indirectly. Then after all is said and done, some of these women whom happen to possess degrees in higher learning, will refuse to believe that they have fallen victim for such an obvious scam, and try to rationalize the whole affair. Even continue to allow him sexual intercourse with her. Now, some psychiatrists will call this act Stockholm Syndrome, but that is not the case. This is the foolishness of an intellectual woman's refusal to accept the fact that she has been taken advantage-of. The well-educated woman, whom is truly in denial about being dominated; macked; turned-out by a man who has geared his entire lively-hood towards that sort of practice. In a woman's mind, she believes that a university or college degree makes her immune from such scenarios, for she is not some naïve high school girl. No, she is a grown woman, and grown women do not fall for such shenanigans, but feral females do. She will convince herself that she is not at fault, and that the issuance of vengeance is in order. Seeking legal actions. Claiming rape. Generating lies of somehow being doped or drugged, to justify her actions without; of course, disclosing the fact that she is perhaps a party-animal; alcoholic or suffering from some form of substance abuse. We are all familiar with the college atmosphere, and how wild things can become sometimes, but all of that is ignored in the cases of declared rape.

The stark reality is, a lot of men reveal themselves for what they truly are, and in the most obvious of ways, even before they open their mouths, and these, so-called, educated women blind themselves to the obvious. Usually out of desperation because again, those kinds of women cull the herd for the prize bull.

Now, this is not to preclude the fact that a man is justified in conducting deceit in order to engage in sexual intercourse with an unsuspecting female; however, conning people is a way of life in the United States of America. We live in a culture where deception is an accepted practice, and goes mostly unchecked. Doubt this author's words? Ever look at a fast-food advertisement? Does what you see ever match what you buy? What about those products you see on TV that seem, so, impressive that you have to have one; and to really make your mouth water they offer a second one for free, adding to that a bunch of free side items; of which none ever live up to expectations. Items that eventually get tossed into the drawer of forgetfulness. In the past, a person would listen to music on the radio or in their favorite nightspot? Then when they bought the music, it was completely different? Radio broadcasts and public venues such as clubs and dance halls were just another form of advertisement that played upon your ignorance. Our legal system allowed the music industry great latitude in regards to what is called a radio or club edit, which is nothing more than a spiced-up version of the original song. So, like fast food, it was juicier to the ear instead of the eyes, in order to compel you to buy the plain version you did not want. Therefore, as you can see, there are many things in our environment that do not live up to the hype. Including people, and when considering that all human beings are different; then sexual predators can exist in many forms, and on many levels. Now, here is the interesting thing about them. Some are honest, and some are dishonest. Some are specialists, leaving their *mark* with a smile on their face, while others are not; leaving their *mark* resentful. They will use words as a means of trickery and treachery to get it their way. Some of those words can seem harmless and even pleasurable. While some words can be harmful; for the truth of the matter is, words can hit as hard as a fist. We've heard that before. He may use tenderness or be brutal when seeking sexual deviance. Being conned by a simple swindle results in anger. When artistry is applied to the swindle, of which, in any case the result is always the same for the woman afterwards, she is content in her anger and simply moves on. With a single exception. She works to convince herself that everything will be okay, but that is a lie. No matter the attitude of the man, she; the woman, will always have regrets, either subconsciously or consciously, especially when, and if she meets mister right. Life was, so, much simpler in the old days when smart girls simply stuck to their guns, and said; *I'm not that kind of girl.* Whatever the case; does this give a woman a right to get it her way when she fails to pay attention to the obvious? Perfectly okay for a woman to take advantage of a man out of; not always financial gain, but perhaps sheer convenience. She will even file charges of rape when she is caught engaging in covert sexual intercourse. With her, there is always exceptions to our perceptions to certain scenarios; no matter the case, but the reality is our laws just cannot be a subject of perception or points of view. There will always be a difference of perception in life between the genders. Of course, feminine hypocrisy will say that taking advantage of a man's wallet is *different* than taking advantage of a woman both physically and psychologically. That no man should be able to take advantage of a woman, and get away with it. Under legal precedence, genders cannot be interpreted differently, and yet, that is exactly what is going on with our state of mind in the U.S.A. Gender equality, with a separate understanding. This author believes that idea was once called; *separate, but equal.* Perhaps the true nature behind planned parenthood is, so, that females who were hustled into the bedroom will feel better about themselves after the fact.

In any event, should a man be punished for using trickery, treachery, or some other means of deceit at his disposal for getting a woman into bed? After all, women wanted to make a go of it on their own. Allowing her to choose her ideal male on her terms? That is what is truly going on; *is it not?* Being able to pick and choose on her terms: Empowerment. Though many females are either not meant to go out on their own, or not ready to go out on their own, is not the case. They simply want an edge when they do go out on their own. Life is about living and learning, and women should know that they have a lot more to lose from the onset of making such a choice, than men. That is when failure sets in. The nice thing about failing as a man is that there is always a slim chance of meeting a good woman who will get him back on his feet. Not, so, easy for woman, for certain men like to use women as stepping stones, and that sometimes includes, when getting himself back on his feet. This very act of male depredation has made the female angry and evil. So, thanks to our recent forefathers; the average woman will lie, cheat and steal to regain her pride. Therefore, make sure that you have an effective escape plan when you engage in lasciviousness. Of course, there is no escape plan in regards to a sympathetic legal system bent on ignoring the fact that there are just stupid women in the world. Oh, and by the way; a stupid woman; is a woman, who thinks the world is a safe place. A stupid man; is a man who, thinks the world can be made safe for an independent woman.

CHAPTER 2

Journalism reports rape in universities, colleges, in the home, even the Church, and yet they are hauntingly quiet about the rape of women and girls in the adult film industry. What? They; whom agree to bare their bodies before the camera; record their sexual intercourse into visual media are exempt from the understanding of being raped? When someone is offered money to do something that goes against the natural state of rational thinking, they go into temporary insanity; *fact of life.* We associate temporary insanity in more familiar terms such as homicide. A state of desperation, if you will, but then excuse it in moments of people debasing themselves before a camera? The reality is, temporary insanity is always a case of unexpected shock of conscience morality. That, which tells us the difference between what is proper and what is improper behavior. That we are not animals, but respectful of the world around us. When a person becomes addicted to a thing, and an institution or individual takes advantage of that addiction with some form of gratuity, that addict will always give in to their need; their addiction. Apparently, journalists conveniently turn a blind eye to the voluntary insanity, and yet the college girl, whom gets drunk at the frat party; leaving herself wide open to be taken advantage-of, and then yells rape after the fact, is newsworthy? *Interesting.*

There is no doubt that there are a lot of women in journalism, and yet they do not speak out against the exploitation of women in the adult film industry. Could it be that performing sexual acts in front of a camera is one of the few careers that women are paid more than a man? Or could it be that female journalists are cold, heartless methodical individuals whom do not really care about young women and girls renting their bodies out cheap? Going back to that high school notion of; *who cares about them, they made their choice, and they are stupid anyway.* Perhaps they think of it along these terms: *Every girl whom goes over to pornography is less competition for me in the real job market.* Let us be realistic, women; people in general, whom have a career in journalism are never scrutinized, they are quick to report the vices of others, but what about them? They come off as being perfect, but they are not perfect, and yet, they have wiped out marriages, reputations and fortunes. The difference between them, and a killer is that they have a free pass to get away with their apparent indifference. Perhaps we should be paying closer attention to that pretty little face on the television screen, for they have lots of secrets that may be news worthy.

Another point to make about the journalistic community is their apparent disregard to report the little-known darker side of the adult film industry in regards to females whom are compelled to engage in sexual intercourse with bisexual males. The little-known truth behind the females whom self-destruct due to those things that drove them to their predicament to begin with. That beautiful gift from God calling out for help, whom abruptly and even conveniently passes away due to unusual circumstances that are beneficial to the industry. Must be more important to dig deeper into a Catholic priest's lifestyle then to go after something that destroys a female before she can actually get a grasp of what life is truly about.

A note for you; the female sexual exhibitionist, that you should be aware of when you experience feelings of being compelled into any situation with a bisexual male: and that is, a bisexual male is a representative of the LGBTQ+ in regards to financial contributions to that organization. That organization has its hands in everything, and do not believe for one second, that they do not have their hands deep in the pockets of the adult film industry. The two of them are the best of bedfellows, whom live by a code of proper immoral conduct. If a Catholic's donations can be given to a person suing the Church due to certain conduct, then would it not make sense that donations to any organization conducting intimidation can be sued as well? Remember, temporary insanity in regards to immoral conduct does not mean suspension of rationalization.

CHAPTER 3

Do not assume that those who view prurient material are not humiliated. The psychological ingestion of such imagery crowds the logic centers; perverts the senses to such a degree as to literally rot both the conscious and subconscious mind to a point of which, everything that a viewer interacts with becomes sexualized. No matter what a viewer of such material does, sees or hears; conjures images of sexual situations relating to daily living because the adult film industry is notorious for incorporating lascivious fantasies into real life scenarios, accordingly. A need to visually experience the effects of OTSS as a means of further feeding the addiction.

How would a person know their brain is rotted? When nothing else in their life matters, but sex. No matter what they look at, they are reminded of a sexual situation played out on the video. *I do not see the woman. I see the perverse things that can be done to her. I do not see the man, but a threat to my satisfaction.* Again, the porn-industry is all about sexual indignation and sexual deviance. Its purpose is destructive, not constructive, and thus not a freedom of expression, but more along the lines of a freedom of perversion. A means of exploiting the ignorant. A vehicle of manipulation and exploitation in order to addict a human-being to an intoxicating experience that interferes with reason. Cultivating a sense of fear, that eventually incenses the human mind, inevitably destroying the will, preventing beneficial creativity. It is an institution that is not deserving of protection under the law on the basis that it harms the body. Harms the ignorant of mind. Harms what it means to be human. We have laws that tell a person to wear a seatbelt. In effect; protecting a person from themselves, but then use law to allow the adult film industry to harm a person's mental state of being. An institution that harms our children. The very sanctity of life itself. *I have a right to give my body over to a physically abusive, demoralizing act; that has a damaging impact on our social infrastructure; however, I have to wear a device that results in no harm to anyone outside of the vehicle that I am operating.* An interesting contradiction is it not? The result of this is to bring about a chaotic state of what would otherwise be an orderly well-kept society, and thus requiring the application of our common sense when determining its handling under law.

The worst bit of all are those whom are addicted, and in denial, or simply ashamed that they view such material, allowing it to drive them to commit violent acts against those whom they see as a violation to the conformity of civil behavior. In other words, they view an interracial sex scene, and it taps into a certain sense of racial purity standards or they happen to be a man who is having difficulty garnishing the attention of a charming, insightful young lady of their own race. Pornography dresses up the beautiful white female whom would be viewed as the girl next door, and then matches her with what would be perceived by some to be a hip hop gangsta'. Now, consider the lonely white male shunned by the beautiful white female. Finding the imagery iniquitous, and over time, after repeated viewing, may become disgruntled and react accordingly. People once denied their alcoholism due to shame, and were sometimes violent. Pornographic addiction needs to be confronted, and treated with compassion to help those who may be unaware of its effects on the conscious, subconscious and the conscience. Both sides are unaware that they are victims and may have lawsuits pending against such practices.

Now, some people will say that you can rot your brain on other things. That is true; however, sex is the one human application that can be self-administered at anytime, anywhere and with or without a partner. Drugs and alcohol can be taken away. Murder, death, and killing, you are a participant or a witness. If you do happen to apply MDK to yourself, well, you can see the end result of that. Sex is by far the greatest overlooked addiction in the world. It is an addiction forced on our families, children, and even animals. The general populous would rather ignore the problem; however, when you ignore a problem, it manifests into something beyond recognition. Sex is a self-generated drug that has led us to believe that it is the norm, and, so, we have adapted our lives around it. We've been told or have told ourselves that it cannot be overcome, and, so, we deal with it. This is, of course a lie. So, when we say that pornography is an art-form are we truly making any sense?

Then in that case, murder, too, is an art form to some degree, and the creators of such artful renditions have many followers.

Oh, and, by the way, for those of you in the movie industry who say that religion has no right dictating how a movie maker creates a film or that the Hays Code was an industry nightmare. Remember those words when SAG-AFTRA dictates how you create a masterpiece on film. Good thing SAG-AFTRA did not exist during the days of Rembrandt, Van Gogh or Monet. Credits would cover the art from top to bottom because everybody wants to know the name of the guy who cleaned the toilet after production.

What about the average follower? Even more unusual and perhaps even disturbing is why the average person would want to break their backs at a 9to5 job; even as much as twelve to fourteen hours a day; struggle and fight to scrape together funds to live a comfortable life. Then give it to an organization that has absolutely no interest in them or even those whom are employed to conduct such activities in front of the camera. This author would call it acting, but acting is more in the relationship of faking it, creating an illusion for the audience, thinking that someone is engaging in a specific activity, and anyone who has viewed pornography knows; *they are not faking it.* Therefore, why is it called acting? Perhaps our culture is too lazy to come up with a more appropriate word; or, to simply utilize the appropriate word necessary for its proper identification, say; *prostitution.* The perfect example of the double standard in America is the acceptance of porn, and the denial of prostitution. One is accepted as illegal; perhaps under the basis of a lack of medical oversight, and the other is legal; under the basis of freedom of expression under the arts. Therefore, copulating or perhaps more accurately; humiliation in front of a camera for all to see, is artful. Copulating in a back alley or a hotel room is not. In both situations, there is an exchange of money, the individuals do not know one another personally, and in most cases, a middle-man is involved. The interesting thing to consider is that the porn industry will even portray prostitution in front of the camera and call it art. The irony is that the participants, in any case, lose. So, the real question is; who is truly benefitting from all of that sexual combustibility in front of the camera? Indeed; properly classifying the industry's activities would compel the courts to act accordingly, something they are apparently not in the mood for. Therefore, suggesting to you the reader to stop feeding the porn conglomerate would be futile because like oil, it is a needed thing that is killing us. Consider this when you are in that dark space stimulating yourself to the point of removing from your body, all motivation for living a real life. At least oil can be converted to a usable resource, and take you out into the real world. Pornography is a room without an exit, and yet, you can leave it at any time.

Try spending your earnings on something worthwhile. Better yet, involve yourself with something, so, risky, so scary, so interesting, that watching someone being victimized is the last thing on your mind. Just a suggestion, for when you are wondering what happened to your paycheck twenty-four hours after depositing it into the bank.

Then again; if pornography were acting, then why do the women in front of the camera garnish, so, little wage when compared with actresses in the mainstream movie studios. Top Hollywood actresses garnish millions of dollars per film, and yet not a single female in the adult film industry can earn a wage in the hundreds of thousands for an action regarded as a performance, let alone millions in an industry that garnishes billions in revenue. Makes you wonder what the female in porn is really worth? On the other hand, when it comes to sex, any foolish female will fit the bill. Nothing more, nothing less, and just as a side note; for you fathers who are not close to your daughters; you maintain an excessively high supply for the industry as a whole. You are absolutely no different than those fathers in the orient who have no qualms about handing their daughters over to unscrupulous people to alleviate the strain on household resources. The responsibility of the parent is to guard the children both male and female. Not toss them into the sexual sausage factory.

210

CHAPTER 4

Understanding that fathers whom forsake their daughters, gives us insight to the female whom pursues a career in pornography. They are in the greatest need of our affection, for they have placed themselves in self-imposed exile. They feel; perhaps, that they are unwanted or are not getting enough attention. Then again, it could simply be the money. In any case, what they do is no different than what many people are doing in today's world; they just do it openly. They must be approached with the greatest of care, and eased out of the drug we call sex. How does a person get sex to contain herself? The best technique for showing a person who is at their lowest is by using your eyes, not your mouth. More can be said just by how you look at someone one rather than what you say. Show them your sorrow. Your very presence is sometimes enough to show that you care. Remember, those who overcome other forms of drugs have a long climb ahead of them, and for some, it is simply easier to slide back into the hole. Once you have the attention of a victim you have a lifelong duty to them. You do not pat them on their back and move on. You must take them under your wing, and make them your child. When a woman loses her virginity, it takes a mountain of concentration to break the need. No other drug in history has ever been, so, potent. That is why it is important for a child to never be exposed to open displays of sex. Guard your offspring as if they are the gold in the depository at Ft. Knox, and perhaps we will be able to recover the future for them, and shut down a pointless medium that is corrupting our society to its very core.

OPFOR

CHAPTER 1

Over the years, thanks to the feminist movement; Women's Lib., Women's Suffrage, Sexual Revolution or whatever we may call it, a certain kind of female has been perpetuating certain views into womanhood as a whole. Urging females to incorporate more of a testosterone lifestyle into their daily routine, while encouraging the idea of empowerment via contraception, that resulted in an unusual stirring, deep within themselves. A tingling confusion between the mind, body, and even the soul, in what it means to be woman. *She, is trying to be both male and female, and it is destroying her.*

Pills and other medicines are designed to help when something is wrong with the body, and yet when a woman takes a pill to retard childbirth what is she saying? Think about that for a moment. A person taking pills even though there is nothing wrong with them? People do that sort of thing when inoculating themselves or they are addicted to a certain kind of effect. Therefore, what is a person saying; *childbirth is a disease. I have no faith in God's miracle of life. God is wrong and science is right for me.* Psychologists and feminists alike, use words such as empowerment, women's rights, and pro-choice to create a contradictory atmosphere that goes against the very nature of God's gift of life. When a woman retards childbirth then what is the preventative measure from all of the psychological effects that come with the loss of virginity and constant copulations. What about the physical effects of the removal of healthy tissue from the womb? The Church's position on sexual intercourse has always been one of reason and logic. In fact, in the matters of women's rights, the Church was first. Up until the arrival of the Christ, most men viewed women as nothing more than rubbish or bargaining chips at the negotiation table for an alliance. A means of maintaining the peace or a surplus population, and yet, the consensus amongst most people, especially women, is that the Church is a male dominated chauvinistic regime bent on keeping women subservient to men. The reality is that daughters are to be subservient to their fathers, and that wives should be subservient to their husbands, and no one else. So, in effect, it is not keeping women subservient to the male, but keeping female subservient to man. Now, realistically, isn't that how it should be? At this point, many women are probably saying; *no,* without realizing that subservience in this case, is not a matter of being someone's slave, but more of a symbiotic lifestyle. Even

212

much more than that, when considering the complexities of the heart. Teenage girls never consider, that being under daddy's house; under daddy's will, is not such a bad thing when considering the alternative. Trading one daddy for another is the worst way to go because the other daddy views her as something useful in the short-term, then discards her in the long-run when her youthful value subsides. Her true daddy will love her even when she is down on her luck. In any case, why would they say; *no?* Since the institution of birth control or should we use a more appropriate term, such as, *the defiance of God's will;* girls practice little; if not; absolutely no form of self-control in regards to her very being, whether it be the actual act of sexual intercourse or the blatant display of their shapeliness in a public setting. In fact, since the establishment of sex education, all levels of psychiatry has thoroughly conditioned parents with the idea that their children are going to engage in sexual intercourse regardless of what they say to them, and that there is just no stopping nature. Note: Funny how we do not consider nature's course in regards to a boy's reaction to the feminine figure. Apparently, it is easier to retard child-birth than it is to retard human nature.

Psychologist say; *go out and engage in sexual intercourse, just take measures in preventing disease;* regardless if it be infectious or procreative. That seems to hit home with the general populous rather than the Church's antiquated notion in regards to premarital sexual intercourse. Needless to say, the psychiatric community benefits from all of the premarital sexual intercourse. Propagating greatly over the years due to females trying to cope with the positives and negatives of independent living. Trying to live life on their terms, but in denial over their moral objectivity. Females trying to live within a parental lifestyle, but without their parents. Traditional understanding of independent living in regards to a man, is to seek a helper. In the past, suitors had a choice between good quality, living at home with their parents, and those whom were feral. Now, those females whom were feral weren't necessarily independent minded, but at the end of the 1970s, leading into the 1980s, the idea of the average naïve female living single was a blaze, due perhaps to being simply caught up in difficult or questionable circumstances. Over time, females simply adopted independent ways without realizing that being a good girl was not compatible with being feral. The question is, when she goes out on her own, what does she want to do? Have fun. Daddy's little girl wants attention; however, with feminine independence comes either prostitution or gratis prostitution. Regardless of how you spin it, the male petitions, and the female is petitioned. The john and the street walker by any other name, is still just a Rose. Therefore, we must look at independent living from a male's standpoint, not from a female point of view. For independent living is a man's domain. When a person goes out to have fun, they do not want to place great thought into it, but it does involve risk. The greater the risk, the greater the fun. Risk and fun are the opposite sides of the same coin. There is no figuring out who belongs and who doesn't; and restraint is not to be expected, but there are certain rules of engagement. Then the Feminist Movement entered places of carousing and wild fun, resulting in a huge decline in; not intelligence, but common sense. A female's encroachment on an independent way of living is geared more around her perceptions of what it should be. Her understanding of independence completely contradicts a male's way. Each female has a unique lifestyle mood due to her expansive set of conflicting emotions. There is never a fixed set of moods. One day she is one way, and the next day she is a different way, and yet, she expects those around her to adapt accordingly, and the result is women at the top of the intelligence bracket screaming rape? We think that since she is university, she must be smart, but the reality is, females have a very bad habit of stripping naked and covering themselves in pig's blood when going into the forest at night. Resulting in our perceptions of what could and what should, becoming blurred.

Females are the complexity of man, while we; the male, are the simplicity of man. Males do not like to engage in data overload, whereas females usually just crash when things get too demanding. Females will usually avoid a balanced social medium because they thrive in the feminist idea of empowerment. They like to cackle

214

like a gaggle of geese; seeking control, regardless if she has proven her worth. Flooding the conversation with fast talking white noise to confuse the issue.

Closely examine our modern culture of the early Twenty-first. We are accommodating to those in denial of the life they are living, and the psychiatric community invents new terms to justify the social confusion, so, that females; everyone for that matter, will feel better about their questionable ways, and the only thing it has succeeded in doing is making things worse. Keeping the furnaces of illogic stoked. In other words, they have cleaned up financially to the point that we cannot imagine a time without them. What they do not want you to know is that without premarital sexual intercourse, most of them would not have a job. So, sure, allow your daughters to go out and surrender their virginity. Lots of people obtain Ph.D.s in psychology, and they need jobs.

CHAPTER 2

Though you; the reader may not agree, the truth behind the feminist movement is to remove the equality of women amongst themselves. The signs of the witch are everywhere; in our very faces, and we; the man, choose to ignore it because they use good little girls as pawns, to shroud our reasoning. To keep us; the man, inline. Stronger women sacrificing naïve women to prostitution, pornography, and other illicit activities as a tool to further their agenda of just wanting more. The irony of it all is that those naïve girls would make suitable housewives. Mothers taking care of the home-front, attending to the first level of government. In fact, that is all they probably wanted, but instead they have been, so, conditioned into believing that being a homemaker is the greatest evil imaginable, that it would be preferable to seek a career in prostitution/pornography then to be a housewife. The very basic state of being, that allows for a liberated existence, and yet, even then a female is not truly liberated. That is because no career gives anyone true liberation, which may lead to the very notion that all women are prostitutes, in one form or another. Whether it be college tuition or the company she works for, having her choice of a john is currently deemed as empowerment to ease the burden of guilt. What is the guilt? The subconscious realization that she would rather be that innocent little girl holding her dolly again, then come to terms with the reality that there is no true empowerment after being involved with several dozen men, either in a private setting or in front of a camera.

The reality of the feminist movement is that it is more of a religious crusade geared towards the worship of who they are, and yet, rejecting the overall responsibility of their true nature, and that is companionship. Unfortunately, we now, live in a culture where sex dominates every aspect of our lives. She is designed by nature to attract the male whether she wants to or not. She is the catalyst in a male/female environment. Anything else is an abomination under the eyes of God, and yet unrestrained sex is the true nuclear bomb of civilization, not a missile warhead or jet bomber payload, and it has been invading every bastion of masculinity in the United States of America since the 1970s, and why is that? Are we saying that we; whom are the male of the species are not entitled to have exclusive institutions devoted to the focus of masculinity? To know what it means to be a man? To discover the principles of man-hood in our own way, through religion, academics, and the sheer aggressiveness of being a male? Of just plain having fun as men? That we; whom are the male of species cannot have a moment of peace from sex? To run free on the field of dreams?

In the old days, women were not allowed to possess property. A standard of living that gives a male individuality, position in society and most importantly, independence. The understanding of our Judeo-Christian beliefs is that woman is not an independent being because this would make her like a man; and that only when a man cleaves to her does she gain a form of independence under the being of man. When a woman did possess property, she usually lived outside of community affairs or outside of the community itself. Outside of community affairs, she may have been a prostitute, but not a guaranteed notion. Outside of the community itself, and she was usually regarded as a witch, but again, that is not a guaranteed notion. These women were like the modern

216

feminists; obstinate, individualistic and stubborn. A hardened state of masculine-femininity. Woman is meant to be dependent at all times due to her vulnerably to the forces of the unexpected. When woman is alone, she becomes susceptible to the whims of the serpent, and remember, a woman can be alone, even in a crowd. That is why in scripture an elderly widow is never meant to be alone. She must be cared for by the family, by the community. Strong lines of communication must be maintained or she will become lost in the silence of inaction. Even resorting to a state of lesbianism is not a bad thing when considering that loneliness is a very real and dangerous thing for her, and is why original scriptural language has no preclusions to feminine desires within their segment. Sex plays upon itself to maturate the pleasures of physical interaction. The male lives a difficult life and would like to experience the maximum level of arousal from the pleasurable input of a woman when the time avails itself because as science tells us, sex is the best stress breaker in existence, not a man.

Once gaining power, feminists and their supporters brought their way of thinking into the overall social construct. Dissected every aspect of male behavior. Implemented strategies that have practically annihilated the male from all directions of daily living. Compelling males to adapt to impossible expectation of self-control. Forcing men to keep their urges at bay to the point where masculinity has become all, but an illegal pursuit, so, that they themselves can run naked in the community, while keeping the male on erection no matter where he is at, or what he is doing. As a man, what do you see in today's world of the early Twenty-first in regards to the pursuit of being the male of the species? You have to practically run a gauntlet of legal opinions to achieve masculine success; to even feel like a male. Self-imposed desire-control. Like flooding a community with drugs, and then telling the people to just say; *no*. Fine and dandy when the drugs are kept hidden, but with a woman it does not work; for many are harlots, and that includes many of our woman-children. Oh, sure, we say that pedophilia is wrong, and yet we take absolutely no action at altering the perceptions of the clothing industry in regards to girl's fashions. Do very little to curb their less than genteel attitudes. Allow a machine to regulate social interaction.

Our seeking masculinity is the equivalent of a woman seeking more sexy, more beauty, more of who she is. Seeking more of who she is, has become the norm, and woman-power is striving for males to be sexier, but not from a masculine perspective, but from more of a feminine perspective; being more like them, while in turn denying us masculinity. Again, women do not realize that male sexiness comes from our masculinity; being rough and tough, not how we wear clothes and other accessories. We; the male, like to fight, get drunk and bloody, and then laugh about it in the end. Rutting antlers is what it means to be a man. If you have a power base that is denying a male from being a man, would that not be a violation of gender rights? Men and women call other women sexy. Women call tough guys sexy. Men call tough guys cool, unless they crave a phallus inside of their rectum. Try to be a man, and she; the feminist, will hold that against you. At best, she will tolerate your male ways until she can find a guy she can better manipulate. Mold into what she perceives to be an ideal mate.

What about the entertainment industry's need to dissolve the platform for building a male role model in order to strengthen feminine social values. The idea of a hero who saves the day, saves the world, saves the damsel in distress, is being treated like some moldy old bread. When it comes to substituting the hero for a heron; she does not save the day, she is nothing more than a feminist with an agenda: To prove that she can compete with a man. That she can handle herself in a tough situation. That she is better than a man. Respectfully, if the hero rescues the woman in distress, then logically, the heron's first order of the day would be to rescue the child, but in the real world, it is the heron whom destroys the child. Kills that for whom she should be trying to rescue. The idea of a heron is truly a farce in our perception of reason and logic. Man rescues woman, and woman rescues... Who does she rescue? Nobody. What does she rescue? Women's rights? Her goal is nothing more than to eliminate the idea for the need of a hero. The rules of heroism are about committing to a selfless act, and the irony is, that even a hero can be a glory seeker and lose all perceptions of what it means to be a hero. The end result for him is robber knight.

CHAPTER 3

Let us also be reasonable about an additional aspect of feminist intervention in daily living, and that is women in politics has been a calamity from the start. Their apparent goal may have been to lead the country into prosperity, and to do a better job than men; as the feminist movement, so, hailed back in its heyday; however, their overall goal was no more than a simple agenda; *women's rights first!* Everything else takes a backseat, and since taking the cultural lead, the only thing women have succeeded in doing is stripping away masculinity rights from men.

We are a society born of common sense of which, is not a woman's forte on the basis that she prefers to change things to suit her needs. In fact, during the late 1960s and early 1970s, women fought relentlessly to change the status quo. Changing things is what they do, and how we know that God is not a woman because the rules between heaven and earth would always change. Science may change our perceptions of what God has already established; however, it is woman, who questions what works. Repeatedly going through the whole process of trying to figure out what does, and does not work for them, and an interesting point to make is that we men have already conducted the trials and errors of what does and does not socially work; however, woman feels that she can make a process that does not work, actually work. In time, we, men, become frustrated by the constant complaining of unfairness, and eventually fail in the performance of our duties of maintaining male dominance across the entire threshold of society, and that's when things begin to fall apart.

Women overlook common sense in favor of the written word. They base their lives on what is written down for they are creatures of verification. Expecting the unexpected is an impossible acumen for her on the basis that it is a vade mecum for what it means to be

219

male. That is why when a female is hit with something that she is not expecting, she always cries out; *that's not fair!* This is a term that a male should never use, even in the event of the other side lying or cheating, for that other side is almost always a woman. Possessing great book sense, and a keen sense of detail are a woman's strongpoints. The problem comes when information is not written down, sending her into a confused state of insecurity. For us; the male, common sense comes into play when writing new law becomes impractical. First, there is common sense, and then comes the books, for it takes time to process the details of social practicality. There are times when the information may seem obvious, but clashes of understanding are always a possibility. Remember your basic history? The establishment of the United States of America was due to a different way of thinking brought about by a result of Thomas Payne's; *"Common Sense"*. Back in those days, ideas that were proposed had never been tried before; however, when women were factored into the formula later, our common sense was retarded, and we became depended upon strict book sense. Restructuring of society based on the reinterpretation of old ideas resulting in a contradiction of law. Accommodating those, whose ideas conflict with the natural state of existence. No common sense. No new ideas. Just reinventing the wheel over and over again, believing that a square, rolls better than a circle. We have become a society of believing that we can make better what already exists, instead of conceptualizing a new standard of living without infringing on tradition. The end result is a dark age; however, it is never a result of women gaining more rights that entails its arrival, but more of males failing to guard their own.

Since the inception of women in politics, our sagacity of what was once common sense has been quaintly reinterpreted by the courts. Sympathetic judges whom clientele to opinion instead of clarifying the obvious. Are our legislators instituting new law? And if they do, and it results in a more proper lifestyle, would not a judge simply declare it unconstitutional? What we; the male of species fail to realize, is that common sense cannot be reasonably legislated, it is simply a feeling or a gut reaction. Trying to place common sense into a judicial arena or legislative architecture would result in a paradox of social behavior. Actually, taking law beyond its context. Once atoning for bad behavior stops, the only recourse is to tell a lie. A thing that females do very well.

CHAPTER 4

Under Judeo-Christian beliefs, a man cleaves to a woman, literally creating a new being, a new gender; if you will; that we call marriage. She; the female uses her abilities to influence a male, and the man-child; and let us be honest, females have an incredible amount of influence on us; the male of the species; however, what she was never meant to have is influence over man. What this does is interfere with other womanly influences; namely a wife or fiancée. A woman is not meant to hold a job in the workforce for the same reason. Another man would have influence over her; quite literally, a pimp. Oddly, when women have influence over other women there is almost always a negative impact on society unless that influence comes from her mother. That is because most women who have gone out on their own, are getting away from what they perceive, as the bossy mother; in most respects not even a mother, but someone who is more of a challenge to her feminine mystic. If a mother is not constantly engaged in a daughter's life, it is only natural for the daughter to eventually see her mother as just another woman. For you mothers reading this; your daughters become your apprentices, so, stick to them like glue.

Male influence, on the other hand, is usually built on strength-of-will and endurance. Women cannot show aspects of strength as a man on the basis that it removes the passionate side of the human psyche. We, the people of Earth may seem like complex creatures, but realistically, that complexity demands simplicity. Woman is compassion, man is aggression. The simplicity of that idea is for the benefit of our children. Child sees woman, and that is a safe haven. See a man and beware. When a woman behaves as a man then it results in confusion in the mind of the child. The child does not know what to expect anymore. This confusion destroys a

221

woman's devotion to the child. She cannot serve a child and an employer. Someone will lose in the long run. Proof of that exists in regards to the *state* enacting certain measures such as FMLA in an attempt at balancing out domestic obligations with an employer. Forcing employers to be held hostage by domestic issues in an attempt at resolving the vacuum left by the absent homemakers. The *state* trying to be accommodating to the impossible. Clearly acknowledging the need for a traditional home-setting. A woman in the home. From the beginning of civilization, the system has always been, the man goes out into the world, and the woman maintains the home. Think of it in terms of baseball. He works the outfield, and she works the infield.

In all reality, businesses have a right to seek their maximum economic potential. A person whom is not regular in attendance interferes with that potential. If the *state* does not have a right to dictate how a person runs their home, then why does the *state* have a right to dictate how an employer operates a business? Sure; some companies employ thousands, making profit-loss negligible, but does that give the *state* the right to dictate terms to the employer. If an employee is spending more time dealing with personal affairs during normal business hours, then the business has a right to find more reliable staffing to achieve its economic goals. Not pass on the loss to the consumer. The Constitutional Understanding is that the *state* should not be responsible for employment of the citizenry outside of its own needs. Further details of the matter can be examined under the works of David Barton. Yes; and some of you will no doubt bring up that dark period of the Industrial Revolution when employers would conduct certain practices that would be viewed as barbaric by today's standards; however, you fail to take note of the opposite effect. When the worker pushes back too hard on the employer. Manufacturing left the United States of America for a reason. Another point to address is that sometimes it becomes vital for the *state* to umpire an understanding of fairness in regards to a hugely diverse populous. For even employers must adhere to the very fundamentals proposed by the Founding Fathers.

Men require constant leadership, and the corporate machine wants to keep production going, not an excuse for when the child gets sick. So, as a reminder to the company: Man-hours are lost when man and wife work in the factory. The wife maintains the home-front; acting as a company's passive mechanism to keep *your* component going. Motivating him, so, that production does not grind to a halt due to a low performing male. If she works outside of the home, then who pushes the male. She is either at work, or at home suffering from burnout from her employer or perhaps she is the boss. In any case, there is simply no push.

CHAPTER 5

Even with all of the social confusion, there are still just two sides to male nature in regards to a female, and that is impressing her, and protecting her, and as much as we try, we could not break that nature even if we wanted to. No big secret there; however, we; the man, would rather avoid the presence of a female when seeking courage on the hunt, for it is natural for us; the man, to go into that primordial instinct to protect, and as previously mentioned, we do not like to be seen in an embarrassing moment should the great beast get the upper hand. Like our attraction to the feminine form, protecting the woman is not something we can simply turn on and off, though some, especially Hollywood, would like you to think otherwise. Truth be told; woman applies too much expectation on us; the man, when she is present during the hunt. Expecting us to protect her, while she is proving that she can handle being on the hunt. Something about reading her mind; an action that many of us men find difficult to do when a situation becomes tense. Women do not understand that mind-reading does not work when certain instincts are active. Naturally, there are women whom can handle being on the hunt, but again, human nature kicks in like a disease. Other women see her success, and say to themselves; *if she can do it, then why can't I?* Then when the average woman fails at the hunt, she demands change. Seeks legal recourse on the basis that it is not they whom are wrong for the hunt, but that the hunt is wrong for them, and that is the concern of this author. The rules are changed, so, that those women whom are unaccustomed at doing a job, can do the job, greatly weakening the initial understanding of how the job should be performed. Implementing more femininity on the overall aspect of work-discipline resulting in a decline in productivity, ethics and awareness. Severely changing the overall social dynamic in the overall community.

As time went on, the natural woman came out, and instead of pushing herself to the cutting edge for a job, she adorned the tight-fitting attire, and then complained about the lack of gender equality to such an extent, that it prevented us from even thinking about asking the most important question of all in regards to a woman demanding equal pay for equal work; and that is, does she actually do equal work for equal pay? Which forces us to examine another problem that is, so, well-camouflaged into the very lining of our modern culture, that we simply accept it as the norm. Are men being jailed due to a lack of self-control? For simply having a weaker constitution towards a beautiful face, and a fine figure? The country spends billions to incarcerate men whose only flaw is that they are incapable at adapting to a woman's right to live an independent lifestyle. To be feral; openly express herself; her sexuality. These men have been hammered by illicit views of sex from the onset of their life, and do not understand why they react the way that they do. They are reacting to the attraction; and what they see is extremely stimulating. She is revealing her shapeliness, giving a sense of desiring passion; and why not? It is a beautiful, and wonderful thing. Part of the overall feminine package, and yes, we do love it. More than life itself. What we fail to realize; though, is that we can become obsessed. Then again, a man can only take, so, much sexuality, and many men have been locked up due to their weakness; or perhaps they are *different*. Yes; we understand that word, don't we; however, that difference does not correspond to a woman's needs or wishes, so, we put them away; shut them out of society. Could there be a great miscarriage of justice going on in the United States of America? Fifty years ago, many of those men would have been a rallying cry for masculinity. Now, they are an inconvenience to something that is untenable in the annals of human existence. Examine what we have done to make a feminine acceptable environment, and still they want more. You see, we; the man, are to regulate a woman's desires. Without that regulation, her wants and needs become unquenchable.

Most mainstream occupations were initially designed to make males stronger. Masculinity was imbrued into the functionality of work ethics and performance. Sometimes we men hated it, and sometimes we liked it; however, the reality, was that we had to accept it, for the benefit of the family, but knowing that at the end of the shift or the close of business, that the job had been overcome, gave us a sense of empowerment. A familiar word to those seeking liberation; however, feminine demands have disrupted the comfort level of what was once a male oriented workforce, resulting in a drastic modification to our overall social parameters, and a loss of manufacturing masculinity. A sort of feminine overload; *let's say.* A condition where feminine behavior hinders masculine presence, either physically or mentally, which may explain why, so, many males reveal feminine tendencies in our culture. There is simply no opportunity for masculinity to settle into the proper gender for an overall communal benefit, which leads to a state of social disobedience and rage. Note: That changing the occupational culture over the decades due to the female emotional complex was not a woman thing; but simply human nature at work. Again, it is natural for males to look out for the female, and help her even when she does not want it.

Of course, we have been, so, focused on the matter of whether she can, that we have forgotten to ask ourselves if she should. Do not take this author's word for it. Observe the social environment. When something goes wrong, it is never her fault, always someone else's fault. *The system is wrong, and needs to be changed because I; the woman, am never wrong.* Which may explain all of the; *blame the other guy* lawsuits. Naturally, we men do not like change. We do not even like to change our laws; however, should a law become obsolete, that is perfectly okay.

Let's briefly make a closer examination of the work environment in general. Females are easily distracted by, so, many things. It comes with being a mother. A purely natural reaction on her part to keep those around her safe. She wants to prevent danger, and thus, many employers are forced to prevent males from tapping into their full aggressive potential due to safety concerns; however, this author is here to tell you that employers apply certain safety regulations to benefit feminists, in an attempt to gender-equalize work performance. Inundating the work environment with, so, many safety factors, that no one can hope to remember them all. Males know by experience that safety cannot be a factor when meeting quotas. There are just times when risk becomes necessary. Bravery is a very real thing for males. When you; the man, want to apply brute force to a project, and your boss says, you will be punished, even fired when doing, so; then your masculinity rights are being violated. In a nutshell, it is sexual harassment, plain and simple; however, there is a catch. You cannot claim masculinity rights to your job, and then make a claim for an on the job injury. Naturally, there are certain extenuating circumstances that refute that notion; *I was lifting a heavy box, when the forklift hit me. Working in the laboratory; Dr. Doe's experiment malfunctioned causing a flask to break, greatly scarring me.*

Now, when this author is scribing manufacturing masculinity, he is not referring to just an assembly line, but the entire work ethic of any company. In regards to a male wanting to apply pure brawn into the actual application of the overall process.

We should also consider, that there are some jobs that not all males can execute. So, why alter the parameters for the benefit of those whom are not physically adept at certain labors as a majority? Of course, it is only natural for woman to adapt, and when she does, what is the physical outcome? Becoming butch, resulting in a masculine challenge, and we use the civilized environment to retard the natural process of gender identity? She starts to develop along the lines of the male, and then law says you cannot challenge her as you would a male because she is…?

It is only natural for males to rut antlers from time-to-time to ensure that male principles are enforce; however, when a female wants to partake in the rutting of antlers, what happens? When she behaves more as a male, it is only natural for a male to make a challenge. She wants to run with the boys; prove that she is capable. The problem is, she is being boy from a female point of view, and since she does not know how to approach him seductively, a narcissistic attitude manifests itself. *Do as I say or else!* Men have always challenged the man who is giving the orders, and that is nothing more than male fortitude in force; however, a woman will more than likely use another man or group of men to enforce her will. This leads to animosity, resentment and disillusion. He will never perform to his utmost for her because she cannot meet his level of accomplishment. *I can throw ten bales of hay in a minute, you cannot, so, why do you have say-so, over me when you have not proven your worth at the job or as a leader of men?* Also take note; that those whom show little effort when they are in the blue-collar workforce will make others work very hard when they become a white-collar employee. That is a good way for a company to lose profits and go out of business, or why many U.S. brands have disappeared or are no longer under U.S. ownership. Look at the United States of America since the rise of the feminist's movement? We attribute it to bad management, without considering the option that perhaps the reduction of productivity was due to the encroachment of females in a male-work environment.

Naturally with risky employment comes the need for focus, but when mothers entered the workforce what happed? The overall social construct; the interaction with coworkers, shifted. Jobs can be stressful, and a man did not have to think about what he was saying around the eager female employee; however, when a man has to put thought into what he is saying, it increases the stress of the job, and interferes with motivation and eventually productivity. Of course, some of those motherly employees wanted to fit in and, so, they adopted the ways of the foulmouthed male coworker, and thus brought that attitude home to the children, and what comes

227

out of our children's mouths today? If some of you remember; it was the stay at home mother whom prevented the use of foul language in front of the children, but now, she uses foul language as well; *coincidence?*

Realistically, a male can work with a female to a limited degree; however, when our social rules go beyond the degree of what is socially acceptable, then we lose what is real and live a lie. In other words, too many females in the workforce creates a dilemma that no man can overcome, and that dilemma is a woman's emotional state of mind. That little nuance of what it means to be female, that has gained control of the work environment, and even of certain activities resulting in the; *emotional dominance of the segment.* Dealing with a hardened state of conflicting emotions, and we have allowed those emotions to enter law enforcement, the legal arena, the general workforce, the military, bureaucracy, and yes; even NASA. Do women even belong in space? The reality is that men and women are two different beings of the same nature. Women behave one way, and we men behave in a completely different way; unless homosexual.

Oh, and by the way; the success behind "Rosy the Riveter" was nothing spectacular. It was simply an overabundance of workforce. Whenever a female employee felt overwhelmed, she could simply take a break without it effecting productivity because a colleague could simply fill-in. Under normal operating practices, it would have been cost prohibitive for any company to overstaff, and maintain a practical sense of what would be a reasonable earnings cap for blue collar employees in a high cost of living environment; however, a world at war is an obvious exception.

CHAPTER 6

On the other hand, why did the feminist movement seem to work in the beginning? Back in the 1970s, we were still dealing with more of a hardened male society; therefore, women entering the fray were more professional in their endeavor for liberation; like their male counterparts in every facet of professionalism. This author will give you; the reader a little forgotten insight into the early days of the fight for women's rights that has been long forgotten. Eager minded women determined to prove a point, dressed professionally. These early pioneering females also behaved professionally, and were very serious about who they were. They were gung-ho feminist made of stern stuff; prepared to face the male attitudes, and the harshness of the male ego. Deal with the blatant sexual harassment as it is called today, for it was to be expected. So, what happened? Necessity drove potential housewives into the workforce because men are essentially lazy beyond all recognition. Crossing the path of a well-employed bachelor was becoming next to impossible for the naïve young woman seeking to get from under the grip of her parents, and he is not taking the time to seek her out. He simply dates his colleague; resulting in potential suitors being scooped up by working women. Not necessarily due to affection, but more of a display of energy and financial relief. Two incomes are better than one when trying to exist in such a materialistic society. Oh, and if you happen to think that there is never enough money? Take a look in that dusty cobweb basement or attic, or the garage that has no more room for a car. How about that storage shed filled with all of those poor financial decisions or more aptly explained as; *psyched up to justify the expenditure of one's hard-earned cash-decisions.*

The traditional woman; being of a softer substance, had no enthusiasm in regards to entering the factory, and had no clue to the realities of the male attitude in the workplace, and, so, the emotions came into play. The oddity of the whole affair is that it was not the feminists whom complained, but other men whom took pity on those women who were not up to the challenge. How do men behave around the tender emotions? No; better yet; how do lonely men of power react to those tender emotions, the soft-spoken voice, and the eyes of helplessness?

As the feminists indoctrinated more women into the cause; these potential homemakers entered the workforce, bringing with them a more relaxed lifestyle. Why is that? How come a woman cannot simply dress the part? Lower earnings was the answer; or, so, it was hailed, but the reality was, and still is; it takes an exuberant amount of capital just to be her, before the necessary expenses are dealt with. One of those expenditures involved fashion. Male fashions were viewed as a social necessity. Feminine fashions fell more in the realm of social extravagance, for contrary to popular belief, females want to be fashionably unique. They require accessories, while males prefer fashionable uniformity, which means, assembly-line style; however, there are men whom like to step things up, and will seek a means to be properly fitted to make them look fashionably unique.

At first, dress codes were adhered to; however, working on an assembly line posed a different challenge all together. Certain feminine attire was just impractical; however, in regards to that area of expertise, feminine attire did something entirely different. More on that in a moment. Meanwhile, most fields of employment made it possible for women to look the part. There is just one slight problem. Women like change, and once breaking through the male orientated barriers, and given breadwinner positions, feminine behavior abruptly changed; breaking the male model of what it means to be professional in appearance. *Why am I dressing like something that I am not?* Became the new rallying cry. Even the Department of Defense has lost its sense of professionalism. With soldiers wearing their combat fatigues in a civilian setting, like some Cold War communist regime. For the military budget is being compliant to feminine wishes. Therefore, what was once considered to be a professionally dressed woman has all, but disappeared. Closely examine any form of visual journalism. She; whom is reporting the news, is very sexy. The idea of the fashion show beauty pageant in this manner, is the conjuring of the witch.

Eventually, the competitive atmosphere drove women to be more provocative in their choice of attire. Which; of course, spread into the educational sector. Sexy attire, and the boys drop out of school. Sexy attire on the job, and the boys are stripped of their enthusiasm to perform their duties. Some even quit and live on the street. Sure, hope that you the reader are seeing the eerie parallel. She is vain, and wants to show everyone that she's got that thing.

230

Oh, and contrary to popular belief, department stores are not going away due to online convenience. They were a concept based on the domestic lifestyle structure; the housewife passing the time by hanging out, whether to buy or to spy. Unfortunately, when the feminists got their way; and what was the primary department store demographic? This author thought he would never see the day when women would pay for garments without actually trying them on first. *If the clothes do not fit, then she did not commit.* Today, she takes the time to ship them back to the retailer, and who pays for that bit of frivolity? Well, not the seller. Apparel is more expensive than it should be, and women simply demand higher wages to buy them. Not unlike wives tormenting husbands for more money to buy clothes in the days of domestic living.

CHAPTER 7

Let us further examine the drastic changes that have occurred to the Department of Defense in the past few decades, in regards to the blatant casting off of military tradition to make room for ideas that do not play favor to those in need of a healthy understanding of discipline. The reality is, the original formula put into play was in fact the proper procedure. Defining gender difference is a necessity towards the understanding of not just military discipline, but social discipline as a whole. How can a male apply proper social conduct to she; whom is expecting such treatment accordingly in a nonmilitary setting, if women are not defined with feminine qualities as a whole? Trying to exercise male mental faculties to compliment, so, many different feminine complexes is not only untenable, but unnecessary. It sets a precedence of trying to solve for Pi. We men cannot simply flip some form of decorum switch. The attitude of; *you need to figure it out,* does not work. We the male, like she; the female, must cultivate a broad sense of functionality to keep an understanding of what is man. Adding her unpredictable emotional shifts to our functionality is not proper. She goes through a varied state of dynamic mood swings on a daily basis, and is given a benefit of a doubt in every circumstance, which clearly denotes that we are still playing on the old principles of social conduct. Fact of life; society does not concern itself with male functionality, only feminine demands, which clearly denotes her rights as dominate regardless of the situation. Therefore, why are males being forced to learn a female's functionality? The answer is simple. She is trying to be both male and female, which is having an adverse effect on her, and what the idea of what the military formula should be as a whole, and that is; a way of life that is geared towards the proliferation of testosterone, restrained and structured by strict masculine discipline in preparation for certain actions that require the sheer aggressiveness of a male.

As a whole, females serving in the United States military should always maintain certain qualities that define, and even refine her differences from that of a male, while keeping with proper military tradition. Furthermore, common sense should not be suspended for the U.S. military on the basis that the establishment of such, was to defend the very notion that resulted in the formation of the United States of America to begin with, and that is; *common sense.* In other words; there is just something wrong with females wearing service caps, trousers and being integrated into direct combat situations that conflicts with the very notion of common sense. We the male are responsible for protecting the female. Not sending her into harm's way. Oh, and to say there is no true sense of a line of battle in this modern age of warfare of the early Twenty-first, is not only ridiculous, but irresponsible. Drawing a line in the sand as a means of clarity of purpose is always necessary when motivating combat troops in regards to a particular situation. Imagine a ballplayer with no understanding of a line. If a combat line is not established, then a military leader has chaos, and nobody wins in chaos. Regardless, she should always be the last line of defense in any hostile action because her responsibility is to protect the children; the home. Logic dictates that if she is a combatant, then he and she turning on one another would become a normal state of existence resulting in the complete loss of species integrity.

CHAPTER 8

Okay; so, with the employer now, paying the tab for sexual favors to solicitors; a woman can be particular about her choice of men; *right?* Whereas a streetwalker could not be, so, particular due to clients paying directly. Something to think about as an employer when hiring a woman. She's allowing multiple men to engage her in sexual intercourse at the company's expense, and if the company doesn't think it costs, then it should take a closer look at the books. Work-ethics and performance, not technology, have always been the key to production. Her actions place the company on par with the porn industry; minus the cameras. The adult film industry pays a woman via the viewer's hard-earned wages to partake in some form of lascivious behavior. Just as consumers involuntarily pay for her pornographic activity when businesses inflate the price of their products. Allowing her to be paid in advance. Making prostitution free in the United States of America. God bless America for employers unwilling to pay 100% of your medical benefits, but are willing to pay 100% of your prostitution needs.

Let us take that idea to our colleges and universities. Grants, loans even the parent's hard-earned money has become advanced pay for sexual services rendered. Public schools: The tax payer's money is advanced pay for sexual services rendered to a lucky hormone raging male student, and to make matters worse; parents provide a convenient location for their daughters to conduct their promiscuity. Perhaps the Department of Defense should consider prostitution as a job specialty in the military. After all, they are paying promiscuous women to engage in moments of pleasure, and considering that it is a profession, as old as combat itself, why not take a page out of Hooker's handbook. Sure; soldiers may die, but they will die with smiles on their faces.

The interesting thing in regards to female employees is that they almost always make poor choices in regards to a relationship, and her employer is the one who loses, and consequently the customer. She goes into some form of emotional singularity, and thus the company has to initiate some form of adjustment. So, either profits decline or someone has to work harder. As a boss, you attempt to deal with her, and she gets offended, and rips you a new one, of which makes her the boss or to say the least; the senior-senior employee when she is not in the mood to work. The boss realizes what she is doing and threatens her with termination, and she pulls out those two magic words that gives her unprecedented job security; *sexual harassment.* Why has that phrase become a magic bullet for women? You have some women who have absolutely no qualms about sleeping with the boss as a means of getting ahead, and yet, when she and the boss are discovered to be involved, she will tell a lie.

Should a male employee be subject to disciplinary action when making advances towards a female colleague? The answer is a resounding; *no.* A man should not be punished for giving in to the seductive charms of she; whom is not his wife, and that includes the military as well. Engaging in sexual intercourse with a female under his charge is a two-way street. In today's workforce, a woman has too many tools for dealing with indiscretion in the workplace by her supervisor. So, if she chooses to have sexual relations with him, then she has made her choice. Besides, living an independent lifestyle comes with risks, of which, manifests the pretty little liar whom always seems to overrule the balance of power. *He placed me in a position where I had no choice. He is in a position of power and authority over me;* however, we forget that sex is an overpowering drug. When the need for it arises, a man will go through any lengths to acquire it. He will use guile and deceit to get that fix. A working male's biggest fantasy is to engage in some form of carnal pleasure with the mature-minded female co-worker. Especially if she is in uniform. Now, here is the rub. In the past, most employers resisted hiring women because they knew that the cost was too high. Therefore, the *state* stepped in, and compelled employers to hire women. Now, those of us whom really do not make it a point to conduct indiscretion have to ask the question; *I didn't want a woman in my sphere of influence due to how I or men in general behave around them. You; the state, forced my employer to hire women, and now, I interact with them as I would any man, and it is identified as sexual harassment? My physical needs overwhelm my sense of appropriateness, and when I have sex with a female colleague under my charge, I get demoted or fired? So, in effect, I am being fired for being a man?* It is normal for a man to be attracted to a woman. So, is that really an excuse to demote or terminate a man's employment or forcing him to retire based on his differences? We talk about behavioral differences in society, but then overlook that particular aspect of human behavior in regards to interaction and attraction. Do we even consider that perhaps sexual inappropriateness may have spurred his actions? As she can claim sexual harassment, his recourse would be sexual inappropriateness; plain and simple. When we think of sexual harassment, we think of it as a state of torment: *He is bothering me, and I want him to leave me alone.* Sexual inappropriateness are fashion choices, cosmetics, what she talks about, that all leads to a misunderstanding, and even a form of social duress. *What? She made herself attractive not to get my attention?* No; she made herself attractive to get the attention of a particular man or a particular type of man. This author's got news for you; the reader; you are not that male. She wants the male with all of the attributes of a man, but without the aggressiveness, the pride and distinction of what it means to be male. The kind of male who needs to allow his testosterone to flow freely. Do wild things to her in the bedroom, but then turn himself off when it suits her. I got more news for you. A man does not want a woman dominating him. If he does not dominate her, then he is, instead, subservient to her, which begs the question, is she existing in her natural state of being, or is she a contradiction to what it means to be man?

The idea of one man being acceptable and the other having to restrain himself is completely outlandish, immoral, hypocritical, prejudicial and cruel. She dresses a certain way for a select man, doesn't mean you have to stop behaving like a man to benefit her desires. Her attempt at attracting what she deems an ideal male is a risk factor she must contend with during the social exploration process. Then again, if the homosexual male is pestered for being himself, then it is a hostile atmosphere; however, he, whom has philandering tendencies is vilified? As a culture, we punish him. Embarrass him. Do everything possible to make him feel like trash.

We bully him because he likes the pursuit of women? Should we be saying that one emotional complex is okay, and the other is not? Some men have a stronger constitution than others. Some men are weak willed, while others are strong willed. Some men have excellent self-control, while others lack self-control; and what? Equality between males goes out the window to forge a stronger equality between genders? Are we conducting some form cultural evolution of behavioral equality, will-power equality, emotional equality? Should we be pursuing this avenue of equality, which dissolves the very notion of what makes he; a man and she; a woman? This author believes that gender equality is a far more damaging prospect to the human organism than it is beneficial.

Also consider that employers require male employees to keep their attention on the job, not on a woman's all too apparent glutes in those form-fitting skinny jeans. They did not hire them to engage in courting rituals, make conversation; to be sociable, and yet it goes on without retribution; *why?* Barring them from doing, so, violates the very nature of human existence. It is inherent for men to pursue women, but again, employers are not paying them to do, so. The power of interaction compels the natural forces of attraction to operate accordingly. This is a difficult thing to cope with for most men; especially in an environment where women have freedoms to openly express their nature. There is the big picture to consider and what a lot of women do not realize is that they are better in the home where they can apply their force of will upon the world through their husbands and his children. Yes, and that includes his daughters. The irony is, most women sense it, but are led astray by the words of the rebellious woman; the feminist; the witch of the community. Yes, it sounds like chauvinism; a dirty word, but nonetheless a true expression for those women whom would go against the natural order of man. You will always have women; whom go against the grain; however, difference is not always the best thing in an orderly productive society. The first sign of such a creature is her defiance of God.

236

Does this mean that sexual harassment does not exist? Not at all. What must be taken under consideration; though, is whether or not femininity is encroaching upon stalwart masculinity to begin with. Is she profoundly alluring? What we perceive as sexual harassment is a constant occurrence between males and females; children and adults, brothers and sisters, husbands and wives. A touch, a glance, a word, even a smell can all be perceived as sexual harassment. Besides, how does a man express his desires for a woman if he does not harass her in some way? As nature would have it, a woman's desires are clearly dominant. That little-known understanding is what determines sexual harassment, empowering the female in a state of social dichotomy. She chooses when the male may approach her; and when frustration sets in, she tells him to get lost. In contrast; when he does not react quickly enough, she simply wears more piquant attire, and of course, no one challenges her pornographic determination.

In any event, a man's Constitutional rights must be suspended in order for employers to demonstrate a feminine friendly work environment. As a male employee, examine your workplace. What do you talk about? Whom do you talk to? If law enforcement suspends your Constitutional rights, there is hell to pay; however, employers can behave with a certain autocratic impunity in the face of the very government whose mandate is to protect the rights of the people. Interesting how it would appear that the *state* actually supports those mini autocratic entities as a means of accommodating feminine hypocrisy. Our common sense tells us to be respectful of a female's presence, not law; however, law that is designed to regulate male behavior cannot reasonably; logically accommodate a woman's wants and needs without stepping on itself. For our common sense to work in regards to woman, we must be able to determine what is woman. There must be markers of some kind that clearly denotes who she is, but on the same note; she must maintain certain levels of conduct in order to clarify her position in the social scheme. In our modern culture, female employees fall out of the realm of proper conduct, but expect male employees to maintain certain protocols regardless. Therefore, what is truly fair and unfair in the work environment?

Let us step back to examine why a woman needs to feel sexy while on the job to begin with? Her very being is the driving force behind who she is, and of course, her success. If she is not feeling sexy is she truly a woman? Feeling sexy means she is feeling who she is. How does that idea play out on society as a whole? Why does she need to feel sexy at all? Competition is fierce, and not just from other women, but from the entire social edifice. Being sexy is who she is, and it is an absolute necessity to her very being because if she is not sexy, is she still a woman?

CHAPTER 9

Since the 1970s we men, have been allowing women into the mainstream of everything, and once doing, so, there was no longer any compromise. They no longer had to give up anything. The problem is, not only did they not have to give up anything, but in fact, they have demanded more, in order to live a lifestyle that literally contradicts the meaning of proper social conduct. Developing a mentality that society must adapt to her needs according to her varying moods. Demanding everything under the sky in order to feel socially comfortable. Why is that? Think about the needs of a woman when she is a homemaker. There are certain things she needs, to make her surroundings palatable.

Female employees were never meant to receive an equal wage to their male counterparts based on the understanding of gender interaction and the overall social dynamic. When their earnings are considerable; where do they focus those earnings? Closets the size of an average bedroom? Enough shoes for the population of a small city? Handbags galore to supply an army? So, much makeup that a department store could compliment their stock, and for what purpose? Then when a man approaches her with the intent of dating, being employed is simply not enough? He should possess other attributes that would be appealing in the eyes of a woman? Of course, not all men have that certain *thing* that makes them appealing to a woman. Therefore, she will not commit, and more than likely

238

his only saving grace is that he is good in bed? Should they get married, guess what? Considering that she makes an equal wage in a relationship, then surrendering her independence is not an option. She maintains the aspects of a woman seeking men because married women behave differently than single women; at least they used to; and for what purpose? All to make a statement; *period.*

Why are we in the current situation of equal pay to begin with? In the past, females did not work in the same places as males or did not perform the same functions as males. The *state* stepped in, and changed all of that; however, employers maintained the social practice of offsetting the household wage without considering her marital status based on the idea that her goal was to get married and have children.

A little overlooked bit of dark truth behind gender relations in regards to employment is that an employed woman will more than likely not accept the proposal of marriage from an unemployed man. When the *state* forced employers to hire women, did it take under consideration that eventuality? Now, we exist in a culture striving for a gender-equal workforce. What is the truth behind a gender-equal workforce? Female employees will only marry employed males, of which, logic dictates that half of the population would be automatically unemployed. If 50% of the population is unable to procure employment, then what of their housing needs, food, and clothing? Overall communal impact? Something to think about when seeing all of the tents popping up alongside the city streets. Truth be told, a housewife is not unemployed if she is married, and working girls are not in search of househusbands.

Are companies refusing to hire men on the basis of some form of male/female ratio? Waiting until enough women apply before hiring a certain number of men? Doesn't this force women whom do not want to work outside of the home, to seek employment? If that is not the case, then why are there, so, many unemployed men when employers are hiring?

Could there be a counterintuitive in our midst? Let us conduct a hypothetical situation: A not, so, popular guy whom is snubbed by the finicky beauty queen of the community, whom prefers the company of the popular guys. She meets that guy, gets pregnant, and then he abandons her resulting in her becoming a single parent. She needs a job to take care of the popular guy's baby, whom is not being a father. In the meantime, the guy that she snubbed, has his sights on a great prospect for marriage, but requires substantial employment for coalescing confidence; however, the woman running H.R. at the company he applied for hires the single mother whom snubbed him in high school instead, because her fatherless child needs a roof over their head and food in their mouth. Forget the fact that the mother will more than likely be spending more of her income on herself, than the child. She wants a life; a man, and that guy whom she shunned cannot get a first-rate job, and he gets to watch his dreams fade into obscurity as that great woman he could have had, marries that popular guy whom actually gave the finicky beauty queen a baby. His life falls apart, and he ends up living in a tent on the side of the road as that same finicky beauty queen whom snubbed him, resents the living hell out of him for not getting a job as she passes him by in her new car. Yes, highly speculative; however, the whole scenario is something worth thinking about. Oh, and that fabulous woman he wanted to marry, ends up being the third wife in divorce court with a fatherless child of her own. Always that one guy who gets to be the breeder.

CHAPTER 10

The other downside to employing women that has been well camouflaged by the politics is the fact that you; the employer did not hire her to get pregnant. She goes through a slow nine month-transformation that brings out sympathy from her coworkers, but the reality is, she becomes an inconvenience. Depending upon the labor atmosphere, she can become irritable. Some may display an outright nasty attitude, expect a change in duties, even extra breaks to cope with the physical and emotional changes; the mood swings. Making accommodations always has an effect on the financial overhead. Now, some employers say, it's manageable; however, what are the underlying circumstances that make it manageable? In reality, companies have been forced to accept this modern idea of the natural process of being a woman. Oh, sure, the pregnant woman says she can handle the stress factors, but liability factors are all too real. Then again, in a culture of child-apathy, mothers are not concerned about miscarriages due to occupational stress. Her career has primacy over nature and to entertain the prospect of a lawsuit is not an option. Perhaps the one instance when she does not blame the other party, whom is not at fault. In light of things, pregnancy is cost prohibitive in regards to being efficient, and yet, the *state* forces employers to accept it, and those employers whom cannot cope, either go overseas, or go out of business. Whichever the case; the whole suffers from the woman who says; she can do it all. What she; the feminist, does not understand, of which a man is all too aware of, but does not have a healthy respect for, is that no one can do it alone.

CHAPTER 11

Yes; many women have achieved success in careers traditionally held by men. Though their numbers are still not at an ideal level, it is a noble achievement. Women's suffrage can say that they have struck a huge blow for women's rights, but at what cost? Actually, radical women have won. The ones whom wanted to run wild, whom traditionally would have been harlots in another time. Of course, in every war, there are winners, and there are losers. Whom were the losers? Our children were the losers. Big losers! No longer are women fighting from the home front. No longer do our public schools have a mother's voice. Oh, and by the way, for those of you whom did not know; stay at home mothers molded the teacher to the needs of the community. Now, the school teachers are alone, running on guesswork, opinion, speculation and Washington Politics. No guidance from the community mothers. The house-wife/mother has been replaced by the career woman/mom, whom has questioned and demanded change for nearly every principle for a safe, civilized culture with little consideration to the outcome, which has led to the very social degradation we live in today. Sorry, but that's a woman's fault; plain and simple. Women were necessary for holding the fort.

Who holds it now? The Federal Government? The partying, sexually active teenager? The new powers that be, said homosexuality was okay. Said children should have a right to choose, but then imply that a developing child has no rights. Of course; *that's different.* They said; *I can make it on my own.* Truth be told, allowing women to live on their own terms was the opening of Pandora's Box. We have wasted trillions of dollars trying to make something work that does not work no matter how you engineer it. Women were just not meant to be on their own. They have changed the terminology of words such as policeman, anchorman, and congressman. Why should mother cook a healthy meal, when she can simply sue McDonalds into providing a healthy meal for her family. *I'll lock my kids away, while I am at work, and then give them pills to curb their excess energy levels when I get home. I'll leave it up to my public schools to act as babysitters, but bar that institution from disciplining my child when they misbehave.* Time-out is the name of the game because spankings are an assault against the child, not to mention that; *my child is not bad. I just can't be a parent to them the way that I want to be. Oh, and by the way, my freedom of choice does not harm the child because I provide a safe financially stable environment for them. The ones I did not abort that is.* Sure; since women have put on the pants, the United States of America has just gotten, so, much better.

Look; this author does not mean to be condescending about the whole affair; however, a two-income household makes a lot of money, but the parameters do not include the fundamentals of true adolescent kinship on the basis that the idea of helper is corrupted. Resulting in the parents being blind to their delinquent child. Even growing accustomed to their child's mischievous ways when going through their varying degrees of development. These children are allowed space by their parents; privacy to make their own decisions without parental guidance. When the child reaches a level of intolerance; that's to say, caught by an outside force; police officer, mall security, teacher or truant officer, then the parents use their fortunes to seek therapists, psychologists or the occasional calling of a favor at city hall. Quite an advantage over a single mother struggling to make ends meet whom requires that kind of assistance, but cannot get it. Of course, those families whom utilize babysitters, daycares, or nannies, or perhaps they send their children to boarding schools; fail to realize that their children are not learning the family's core values, but someone else's way of living. That is if they are learning anything at all. To make matters worse, the parents are unable to exercise any form of discipline short of having the occasional talk. More often than not, these talks do not sink in, due to the parents having missed their opportunity to bestow fear into the child. Yes; you; the parent, must bestow fear into a child not friendship in order for the child to behave properly when you; the parent, are not present. If the child does not fear you; the parent, then once reaching the teenage stage, they are a force to be reckoned with. Their minds have been filled with contradictory information from foreign sources, and deep down, it is you, whom fear them, and, so, you try to reason with them, negotiate, bargain, come to a happy medium, but there is no happy medium. They dominate you, without you even realizing it, for you are in denial about being a bad parent.

Another point to consider in regards to a two-income household is that your daughter is using her bedroom as a bordello. Why not? No one is at home. Your house that you worked, so, hard to obtain; made into something that you call your own, becomes a waiting room for potential clients. A sex haven. She is being the host for a Romanist orgy. Doubt this author's words? Install surveillance cameras in the common areas, halls leading up to her bedroom or around her windows outside; you may be surprised at what you may discover or are you the overconfident-father whom just knows he is in control? Consider this; did you spend quality time with her when she was an adolescent? If you are having a difficult time interacting with her as a teenager, then you probably missed out on her adolescent years, and now, Seth, Ryan, Billy or Ashton are speaking her language, and are more than willing to give her the attention she desires, and then some. They are young, handsome and popular, and most importantly, they are filling the vacuum created by you and your wife when you two devoted your time to yourselves instead of your darling little girl, for she was an accident to begin with. Free Love was/is about sexual recreation, not parental responsibility. Notice the thinking process of those protesting the Vietnam Conflict. They wanted an end to the killing, and those same people had absolutely no qualms about supporting the Roe-v-Wade decision. Those same people speak out about saving a helpless animal, but are hauntingly quiet about the helpless child in the womb whose only crime was being created by two self-serving people seeking physical pleasure with one another. Somehow, a female feels liberated when knowing she can stop a process she could have prevented in the first place; and no, not with contraception.

CHAPTER 12

After all that we have been through as a culture, we come to the realization that a woman's ability to look at the details of life; of human nature in general, and we could have perhaps prevented the dilemma we are currently experiencing in our modern culture. Let us go into the details of why the genders have a difficulty in regulating man. As previously mentioned, we; the male, are the simplicity of man. We generalize; look at the similarities of life. The social structure. The superficial things in a superficial fashion, which is the source for that, which we call; common sense. She; the female, is the complexity of man. She wants specifics. She looks at the details of life. The social edifice as a matter of differences; and at times she can be a bit analytical, even obsessive with the details. That is why when you discuss certain topics with women, the first words out of their mouths are; *that's different,* for they do not see the broad similarities, on the grounds that they are, so, focused on the subtle differences. Maintaining such complexity requires the creation of documents.

Seeing the world differently, results in confusion of laws and even conflicts of interest. For we are trying to adjust law to benefit a woman's wants and needs, which are many and mundane, and are always changing; serving no useful purpose to the overall needs of the community. Making the genders incompatible in regards to the day-by-day governing of society. Confusion is a very real thing when trying to obey the law, which explains the need for lawyers; however, amid all of the social confusion, we miss a very important point. One component is serving a specific purpose, and the other component is serving an entirely different purpose, and yet those purposes are similar in regards to the fabric of human nature. This is the beauty of the apparatus of man, and when those components come together, they form an indomitable force of will that is next to impossible for nature to overcome. Think of it along these lines. You; the male, are buying a house or a car, and you glance over the contract. She; on the other hand, scrutinizes the contract, and asks certain questions that may save you from a lot of headaches later. Provided that you utilized her keen sense of observation. Any woman can perform this function, but only a foolhardy man ignores it; however, only a devoted, closely bound wife can perform this function with great efficiency for she has a divested interest in the overall outcome of any situation in regards to his *house;* and not to mention that she knows her man well. As a wife matures, she will come to see the general similarities in life, but from her man's point of view. Where we run into problems, is that as a woman; who has assumed a position of public authority, will try to see the basic similarities from the perspective of many men. Feminists never see it because as they get older, life becomes all about women's rights. In the vernacular, they become set in their ways, for all they see, is a world requiring a woman's deft touch, of which exists in constant flux.

CHAPTER 13

Time to answer the million-dollar question of why this author comes off as being a chauvinist; a misogynist; a hater of the female being. Women are meant to be pampered and protected, not poked and prodded by the hardships of the world. We thrill off the idea of rescuing the damsel in distress; protecting her from the dangers of the world. Fighting off the hateful rage that has all, but consumed our society. She believes that she can go it alone in a world meant for men, but it is a cold world out there, and we men know that;

and we are best suited for it. When you see a female in trouble; rescue her, whether she wants it or not, for she does not always see the truth of reality or the dangers that lurk in the shadows, regardless of how much self-defense training she has had. Yes; the world is very cold and cruel, and truly we would like to know there is a place we can go, to get out of the cold, but as-long-as the feminists are allowed to dominate our culture, we; the male of the species, will never find that warmth again.

Look; if the Feminist Movement is such a worthwhile cause, then why after all of these years, haven't American women put an end to the adult film industry or organized themselves into some form of militia to free oppressed women around the world? They're always harping that they are going to show men how it's done, and yet, they take no direct action to spread the movement where it is needed the most. Fact of the matter is, though women profess they can go it alone; the reality is, they need a man to do, so.

So, how do we fix our society? We need to be separated from sex, in order to bond with that, which makes us a man. Perhaps we should remove woman from the day-to-day operations all together. Have her step back and see what is wrong. Put into perspective the damage being done. Woman is in denial due to modern feminist ideas and misrepresentation, which has locked her into a state of obsession that things can work, and if all of society crumbles under our feet; so, be it. Whatever it takes to prove her point, for she is stubborn. We; the man, have seen this obsessive behavior in the past, and have always put a stop to it before it went too far. So, why haven't we put a stop to it this time? Perhaps a reasonable explanation would be our unwillingness to accept the idea that we; the man, are the cause of her obsession. When we; the man, accept responsibility for our actions, then we can go about the business of helping her to help us put an end to the madness that has overtaken our society.

Therefore, we must kill the witch and propagate the stay at home mother, but this time we must remember the rules for successful male/female interaction; to not abuse the female in any way, except in cases of a woman behaving as a man would behave. Do not mislead or deceive the female, she has enough on her mind then to be worrying about a lie. Most importantly, never love a female more than God or she will come to dominate your very existence, and lead you on a path to failure. There is a reason why goddesses dominated our culture in ancient times; and it had nothing to do with the belief of a deity. By nature, men are loners, though *momma's boys* may contradict that notion, but men are designed in the image of God through-and-through. In the beginning, God was alone. When he created woman, He was creating for Himself a mother, so, that He could come among us in the flesh to celebrate this wondrous thing He created. Since we did not kill the witch in the past, the witch in effect is killing our mother, and if you doubt this author's assessment, then examine our children.

Now, killing the witch does not mean putting her to death. We do not want to adopt the brutal side of human nature in order to resolve the issue of the rebellious woman, because what creates the witch is our failure to protect woman. Even from herself. We must be able to identify the witch by her behaviors. Kill her means of control over; not us, but the woman whom has been blinded by the witch's selfish desires, and pointless goals. Remember, it is natural for her to bond to a man. It is a part of nature; however, when you, as the man, perverse that bond, then you become far worse than any witch. You compel the woman to seek other means of survival, thus the warlock-mentality; keep male and female from a natural civilized interaction.

THE BIGGEST CON JOB OF ALL TIME

CHAPTER 1

We the people of the United States of America have reached a point in our existence when we must decide if we are going to do what is popular or what is proper. Will we decide that what is popular is not always proper or just be one of many in the crowd? What will we do when the time comes to decide? Draw a line in the sand or pass the responsibility on to someone else? It is easy to join the crowd and hope for the best, but the real pinch comes when you have to decide whom to stand with, and whom to go against, but consider; he whom stands alone will be crucified in the end. What is often ignored is that it is better to die for what is right, then to live with the shame of supporting that, which contradicts your beliefs because when it comes down to the nuts and bolts of life; no matter the population of the earth, the galaxy, or the universe, God always possess 51% of the vote in all matters both visible and invisible.

Hence, there comes a time in a civilization's evolution when it becomes necessary to clarify certain standards of living for the benefit of its continued existence. A culture; any culture, has a propensity for taking for granted the ideas, edicts and laws set down by its founders in regards to daily living, without serious consideration of the social environment. The overall problem with the United States of America is its propensity of taking things for granted without consideration of the overall circumstances. Each subsequent generation cuts corners when teaching their children what it means to be human. That is, if they are teaching them anything at all. We assume that everyone knows what it means to be human. As if that crucial tidbit of information of what it means to be human is passed on through our genes. It is difficult to comprehend that we learn by the passing of time not by the passing of genes. In our later years we assume that we learned everything instantly, but the reality is, it takes many years to learn, and, so, we grow impatient and say; *We don't need this or we don't need that,* and yet the very things we feel that we no longer need is the very thing that we need to define who we are. In effect, what may seem like a trifle is perhaps the one key component that makes everything work, and we have gotten rid of it. Resulting in our entire existence having absolutely no purpose, no reason or meaning.

Yes; we are all mired in the muck, gunk, and goo of the social evolutionary process, now, gone awry. As more people receive degrees in higher learning, the greater the noise becomes because they all believe that a degree in higher learning gives them a pass to social superiority, and that the world should listen to them like some child that has just learned their A,B,Cs and 1,2,3s. That they have the answer to what is rotting our moral infrastructure, while pursuing their doctorates. All of them have taken for granted the very basics to the essence of life. What are the basics? We are all born heterosexual by nature, and that all other behaviors manifest themselves from that initial blueprint. To sum it up; as we age, we modify our behavior due to social ambiance. This modification begins at childbirth. What is a newborn's first experiences when emerging from the womb? Light? Sound? Touch? Temperature variances? To be alive? That tingling sensation we all feel when touched unexpectedly, by either a physical or psychological encounter. Whatever the case, the newborn is experiencing the world outside of the womb and begins implementing modifications accordingly. With each stage of development comes a form of modification to the human-construct; both physical and mental manifestations, and of course the finishing touches to give us individuality. Each process is delicate in its own right, and must be properly nurtured for a more efficient end result.

Now, here is the interesting thing about newborns: There is a basic rulebook for boys and a basic rulebook for girls. Whether or not some of you want to believe this to be important, is of no consequence on the basis that you will find doubt in everything anyhow. For the rest of us; the reason for two different rulebooks is simple. Each gender serves a specialized function in the evolutionary process of life. Both are essential in ensuring the continuation of the species. Let us call this reality: Gender Exclusivity. Drop a man and a woman anywhere on Earth and they can begin the reproductive cycle. Two men cannot do this, and neither can two women. Not even fire is that simple, and yet fire is as common in our lives as the pollution it creates.

CHAPTER 2

Let's not prolong the obvious any longer, and get right to the heart of the matter. What is homosexuality? Specifically, that all exclusive and inclusive male affection for another male? Not the dictionary term, but from a more comprehensive analysis of the activity itself. A situation in which, two peoples of the same gender interact in such a way as to provide for themselves a physically stimulating experience through means of an unnatural process. Who, is pleasing whom? That is the question. People whom dabble in the unnatural, want us to focus on them in order to divert attention away from what they do. They have legally created an amalgamation of wanting public acknowledgment of who they are, while maintaining privacy in regards to what they do.

Perhaps the problem that is plaguing the overall social process is that we are all looking at this from two different points of view. One side is looking at the harmful effects to not only our society, but to our species as a whole. These are the people whom embrace Judeo-Christian values. While, supporters do not see the harm, and yet some of them even embrace Judeo-Christian beliefs and ideas as well. Therefore, let us discuss in plain language what is a same sex or like-gender relationship. Let us disassemble the very idea into its core elements.

Oh, and before we begin, we must first nullify that, oh, too used phrase of; *It is, so, much more than that.* All situations have a pinnacle to their function. There is no such thing as a relationship being, so, much more than what it is; unless you have introduced something supernatural into the process. In today's society, a man meets a woman; takes her out on a date. They exchange details, and as they continue to interact, they develop an understanding for one another. Then at some point in the relationship, sexual intercourse comes into play. They continue to date, hangout, and copulate. There is nothing else. Nothing special. They are two people going through a physical exchange. They date, copulate, date again. There is nothing more. In fact; the physical interaction compels them to make bold declarations of being soulmates, and, so, they decide to get married. This author is willing to bet that the interaction between like-gender couples is no different.

250

Secondly; beware that if you are a homosexual reading this, you are not the object of persecution. It is to make clear that you may be simply a result of bad parenting. Though no one wants to acknowledge the existence of bad parents, the reality is, they do exist; more, so, than the most prevalent disease. The sure sign of a bad parent is the behavior of their children. A child reflects the parent's conduct. If parents are doing nothing substantial with their child, then that will be the child's conduct.

Let us examine a specific form of homosexuality for what it is. Men kissing? Men holding hands? Men whom love each other? Have a certain fervor for one another? Fondling one another? Anal penetration in the bedroom? Oral pleasure after the fact? Now, that's something to think about. He will probably say; *my partner wore a condom.* What? There is a barrier between him and his lover? Look; a condom serves two purposes, and one of those purposes is just a little hard to come by for a man. Proving that homosexuality is about what you do, not who you are.

Interesting point about heterosexuality is that it does not necessarily imply an action or any specific attraction. Only the proponents of homosexuality want you to think, so. When a man assumes a physical relationship with a man as he would a woman, he is homosexual. A man whom does not engage in sexual activity is heterosexual by default until choosing a different course of action. A male infant is not homosexual, but heterosexual by default. Again, only his passage through life determines what he becomes behaviorally. For a mother to say; *I sensed that my child was born homosexual,* would equate to saying; *I sensed that my child was born a murderer;* and yet, they do not guide the child along a path of being a murderer? So, if they teach the child that fagging is a harmless act, then why not allow the child to carry out such activity in front of others? If it is; after all, so, benign, then what is the harm of one man penetrating another man at say; a family function, a restaurant, the half time of a ball game or on a public beach?

Also consider that we as a culture are struggling to cure a disease that is a result of an unnatural process, so, that those whom like to partake in penis to anal copulation can return to a state of relief and reassurance when they do not adorn a prophylactic in order to experience the touch of flesh-on-flesh delight.

CHAPTER 3

Time to do something that no one would dare attempt, and that is to define social chaos by scribing the following:

Sapphic is an activity that denotes the equality between two, or even more females seeking a physically pleasurable interaction.

Lesbian, is a dominate female providing a physically pleasurable interaction in lieu of a male. Though both parties may share in the pleasure, one will always be dominate, which denotes the need for the replication of a male appendage.

Male-on-male copulation or let us simply use the word; fagging, for the use of the word gay in place of such, is actually designed to mislead the general populous into believing that there is some form of joy in the physical process; which in any case is a state of which, a male experiences urges of femininity. He possesses feminine desires. He wants to be dominated; assume a female's role in the relationship. Interestingly enough, his partner may be bisexual. A male seeking to be served, and he will attend the first person willing to serve him. For the dominate male, it is about power and control, and sometimes knowing that he has control over that, which is designed to have power over another is more desirable than a proper gender relationship.

Down-low, neither male is surrendering his masculinity, though he may exhibit an unintentional, submissive reaction. Males; in effect, have a need to dabble in illicit risky behavior, and are almost always married in the traditional sense of the word.

Now, there are some readers who will strenuously object to the previous analytical. That this author has no right to place his own interpretation on a lifestyle; and that; of course, is understandable; however, the reality is, we require some form of semblance to the overall differences in certain behavioral aspects of human nature, to make some sense of it all. By stirring up the pot there is no way to get a clear understanding of what is going on; thus, furthering the

252

conditioning of the populous in accepting an activity that is unnatural to human existence. It is only natural for the human mind to try, and understand a thing, but those in the homosexual community are doing everything in their power to prevent an understanding of why. They are moving, so, quickly that there is no time to see the truth. Ever come across a fast-talking salesman who is trying to sale you something that you really don't need? After you've been swindled, how do you feel? Empty?

CHAPTER 4

Man cannot be a receptacle and a giver. By nature, a man gives of himself to a woman in order to perpetuate the species. She receives him as a promise that life will continue. When a man gives of himself to another man, there can be no perpetuation of the species, therefore the promise cannot be kept, and thus the relationship becomes a lie.

When a woman uses a likeness of the male appendage, it is a sign of her willingness to return to his trust when he is done being foolish. Sapphic relationships are a false sense of trust, want, and need of a woman's desires. She wants a man, but she craves love and affection more. In most cases a man cannot provide a woman with the level of emotion she is seeking, and more often than not she has to suck up and drive on as-best-as possible from what she cannot get. The terrible truth is, that not even another woman can quench her thirst for sexual affection because what she has done is opened herself up prematurely to an activity she does not fully understand; e.g. premarital sexual intercourse. Once they have had a taste of a hundred men, they want another hundred. The same goes for the man, except that he will want to experience more perverse acts because in his frame of mind, the natural state of sexual intercourse gets boring. Remember, men are risk takers, and women are cautious. Men will have no qualms about the threat of a sexually transmitted diseases. That is why HIV/AIDS spread, so, quickly through the general populous. Specifically, and most unfortunately, to our women and children as well.

CHAPTER 5

Male-on-male copulation is not about affection, compassion or even love, but domination; conquering a male without any form of true benefit to either party, other than the self-satisfaction of knowing that one party has dominated the other. To dominate something that is supposed to be a dominating force gives a high sense of satisfaction, but it is not beneficial. Dominating a woman is not a conquest unless the intent is just to engage in sexual intercourse, and since men cannot give birth, then the result is clear or you; the supporter of the behavior, is someone whom is in denial about the obvious. Once a male has been perversely dominated there is a loss of pride, dignity and self-respect. What has been done is that we as a culture have justified those losses, allowing them to be acceptable in society in regards to those whom are practitioners of said behavior in order to feel better about their choice of physical proclivity.

Sure, those of the homosexual community say, that they do not lose their pride, dignity, or self-respect, but the reality is, one of the males in the relationship has to be submissive; to be dominated. Women usually fill this roll to feed that overpowering need to submit to a man out of compassion. She does not experience the loss of pride for she has her vanity. From her point of view, she has seduced the man. A man loves to be seduced, and a woman loves to be dominated; however, a man cannot seduce a man, he can only be dominated. When we speak of compassion in this case, it is not, so, much as emotion or feeling, but more of a natural duty; self-satisfaction to fulfill the utter craving of procreation. For a man to assume the submissive role is nothing more than a transgression into the female's domain in order to satisfy the carnal lust to soothe the craving fires of anal penetration. A need to blatantly defy the very rules of God and nature.

Contrary to popular belief, there is such a thing as an interactive malfunction. We all have some form of mental malfunction; however, we learn to overcome that malfunction. We call that malfunction; in some cases; a perversion. Determine for yourself the purpose of the anal cavity. Yes; expelling hard waste from the body. A singular purpose, and any doctor should tell you that; and they are strangely quiet about the subject. Why is that? Psychiatrists, on the other hand, will support anal penetration under the pretense of stress relieving benefits that comes with an already twisted culture. So, ask yourself this one simple question; *what the hell is really going on?*

CHAPTER 6

Lesbians on the other hand simply cross the line of what is male and female, but men destroy it. How do we know this? Look at society for yourself. Do you see men whom behave as women? Look like women? Want to be women? Now, examine a woman whom behaves like a man, and then call her a man. She may take offense. That is because they are not searching to become men, but applying a personal perception on what it means to be female, which, unfortunately is resulting in a casting off of that, which identifies being woman. Naturally that is the overall contradiction of feminine thinking. *I am proud to be a woman. There is no shame to be a woman. I am a woman; however, I just do not believe that the established identity or behavior for woman is grounded in stone.* Well; the contradiction is, if you are not doing what it means to be one thing, then you are trying to be the other thing, then you are that other thing.

Let us look at what is going on with the destruction of the gender barrier. The woman crosses the line in order to perpetuate feminine behavior in a man-child. Conditioning him to destroy the barrier between what is male and what is female by convincing him that he is female. Look at one side of homosexuality, and what do you see? Males whom behave as females. We are not speaking of those whom dress like a woman or wear heavy cosmetics; the drag queens, cross-dressers or transgenders. No; what we are looking at are those males whom behave as females emotionally; whom are overly compassionate, overly gentle, extremely feminine in their actions. These men dress as men, groom themselves as men, and in some cases, behave as men; however, what they seek is male copulation. The feeling of mushy butt syndrome. The oozing of fluids from their anal cavity that gives them a feeling of bonding love with their partner. Yes, too, much information; however, if the dirty details are not brought to light, then the truth of what it is can never be realized. Kind of like the truth of war. Censored-vs-uncensored. Which is better? To deal with the slaughter, the truth has to come to light, and let there be no mistake, fagging is slaughter.

What is interesting about the lesbian is that she does not have the same social impact on the community as the fag. On the basis that females in any event require constant passion. As-long-as females conduct the natural process of passion without the use of tools that mimic the male phallus, then is there truly a problem with females quenching their thirst for passion? She is not only sex, but the source of passion as well. Romance is the material that makes her what she is. Females teaching one another the intricacies of romance, is not; perhaps, something that should be viewed as irregular. How else does she learn the intricacies of conducting a proper kiss? She's not going to learn that kind of thing from a male and maintain her feminine integrity. This is how passion works. Love is a heavenly thing; however, romance is of earth. For that, which is of heaven to interact with that, which is of earth, the female must institute the process of romance. When a female makes the initial move, she does it, so, innocently, so, beautifully, that it can seem heavily in its origin, and in fact it is; however, it is the male whom makes a mess of the interaction. The female must regulate; literally conduct an on-the-spot class of how to initiate first contact. If you; the male, have been busy building yourself up, mentally and physically, you may have never had a chance to figure out the intricacies of passionate interaction. Of course, the only real way for males to learn how to apply romance to a female is to actually involve themselves with a professional woman. Interacting with a woman prior to marriage could result in going too far. The controversy of real hands-on experience in its truest form. Interestingly enough, initiating passionate interaction with a female is not much different than that of first contact with a male, based on space and vocal expression.

Realistically, we as a species find it difficult to initiate first contact with those of our kind in any forum, and it's only getting worse. This is a result of a secular dominated society, for it is better to keep to ourselves than to be picked apart by our lack of proper use of language.

CHAPTER 7

We live in difficult times when a lack of communication and exchange of information prevents clarification of disputed matters. Up until this time, this author finds it disturbing that opponents of fagging have been denied a right to explain their point of view before the masses. This has been accomplished by proponents using terms such as hateful, and bigoted, so, that the discussion of why fagging is wrong, can never be fully addressed. It is a means of preventing opponents from voicing their concerns. There is another term that can best explain what is going on; and that is subversion. A prelude to conditioning. Is that how a democracy is supposed to work?

Therefore, we accept homosexual behavior because we do not see or hear about the results of the act of homosexuality. There are a lot of murderers, rapist, and thieves, but you get a firsthand account of their activities; however, homosexuals conveniently keep their activities under wraps or we simply avoid looking at two men puncturing their anal cavities with their penises. Therefore, this author asks just one simple question; is the insertion of the male sexual appendage into the anal cavity of another male a normal biological function of the human body? Another simple question that seems to never be asked; is the ejaculation of sperm into the anal cavity of another male a normal biological function of the human body? If we do catch two men fagging each other, we simply say; *keep quiet. We cannot speak of such things, openly;* but we can acknowledge something without knowing what it is all about? Kind of reminds this author of a person whom invests in a real-estate scheme without conducting any form of research. Of course, when a family discovers their child has been fagged, we do not attribute that action to the whole group because it has been conveniently isolated into its own substructure. Then as certain tendencies manifests in the child, the parents simply guide him along that path, and say; *he was already gay, we sensed it when he was born. So, we have learned to support his choice of being attracted to boys.* Bad parents make this excuse due to their failure at being proper interactive parents. Between the money and other personal needs, the child was sacrificed. Too bad their child never got a chance to know what life would be like as a man. Sort of like supporting a daughter who is raped and then decides to become a porn slave or a neighborhood nymphomaniac. No mother would ever allow that, or would they? What kind of a society are our children truly growing up in? Oh; and by the way: A question to those mothers who say; they sensed the man-child was homosexual after giving birth to them. If the man-child became sexually involved with an adult male; would you put a stop to it? We protect our daughters due to the risk of pregnancy; however, if you have already determined the man-child to be a fag when putting a diaper on them, then what further harm can come about, when an adult male anally copulates with him? If you bar him from the relationship are you truly being supportive of his identity? It is not like he can get pregnant; *right?* Realistically, you are living in a state of denial of what is male and what is female. He exhibits feminine behavior, and, so, you treat him as such. In your eyes, he is a girl, and that is how you see him, and treat him. It never occurs to you; the mother, and perhaps even the father too, that simply saying; *you should not do that,* is, perhaps all that it takes to make him a boy. Sometimes our children simply need someone to speak up. Give them attention. Give them direction. Is that not what you do when they are about to throw their food on the floor; chew on the wet toilet brush or make a public nuisance of themselves? You stay on them until they stop doing that, which is socially counterproductive. Apparently with all behaviors, save, but one. Why is that? Somehow, someone determined that a behavior can be an identity? That is what is better known as social conditioning. We have been programmed by certain people who have gained power in our daily lives; in our mass media, to accept something that goes against all conventions

258

of reason and logic. Just because someone who is successful in life says it's, so, doesn't mean, they are right, on the basis that you would be amazed at what a celebrity does to achieve success, for no one ever tells the whole story; *do they?* Once categorizing what was once a behavior as an identity, affects your approach on child-rearing. Perhaps subconsciously it is perceived as a physical defect rather than a mental defect, and thus, you; the parent, adapt.

Now, we cannot simply say; that is how it is, or, that is what it is, when dealing with a person's behavior. Especially in cases such as; *why do they do that, or why did they do that?* Acts that are beyond our control and warrant such an application are; *why do hurricanes occur, or why did the tornado destroy our house and not theirs?* In regards to human behavior, it is a matter of control; not presuming the occasional birth defect or the person who snaps. Otherwise, we do acknowledge that we can control our behaviors and regulate them, but not the earth, the air or the water.

CHAPTER 8

Whatever the case, there is no greater need for proper vocal communication then to our children, for when they see something that their underdeveloped intellect is unable to comprehend, they are compelled to ask you; the parent, what is going on. The reality is, if we have a difficult time explaining heterosexual behavior to our children, then how do we; as parents, explain homosexual behavior? Interesting, that for hundreds of years parents had no problem explaining the varied racial identities in our country, even from a bigoted stance when associating behavior to color. Today, we know that applying a behavior to skin color is completely illogical, even unacceptable. In the past, Jim Crowe Laws restricted a segment of the population to specific behavioral traits unnatural to human psychological growth due to the laziness of past cultural practices. In regards to a behavior now, elevated to a state of an identity; how does a parent explain to a child without utilizing its behavioral aspects? Explaining skin color, is relatively easy. Why people kill one another is difficult. Explaining a religion can be like ice-skating on Lake Michigan in July. If you don't know to wait for the water to freeze, then you just don't know. Think of it along these terms: Elevate racial bigotry to a state of an identity. How would you explain it, even justify it? When a police officer is in uniform, that is the identity, and, so, you; the parent, can explain what they do. A construction worker wears a hardhat and toolbelt, and, so, you explain, what they do. A postal carrier walks with a bag on their shoulder, and you explain, what they do. When your child sees two men fervently passionate for another in the park, do you explain their actions as an identity? Your child sees a person crossing the street; is that an identity? Your child sees a person spitting on the ground; is that an identity? Your child sees a bunch of people playing in a public water fountain; is that an identity? Your child sees a woman slap a man; is that an identity? Social confusion is a very real thing in our modern culture, and it is something that cannot be overlooked. Many people, specifically men have been incarcerated simply due to social confusion. Is that how things are done? This is not a good recipe in regards to the creation, and enforcement of law or the regulating of extemporaneous ideas.

To avoid social conflict; communication is everything. Without it, there is misinterpretation and misunderstanding, which leads to social overload. Communication is a crucial mechanism for social harmony that begins at childhood. Not in school or with an infant, but in the womb. Parents imprint who they are on a child at the moment of conception. Everything that we are is communicated on a subatomic level, and no scientist should dispute that fact. Communication is what makes being alive, work, and to say that a maturating soul within a woman is not in communication is completely absurd; no, it is an atrocity. Everything a mother experiences in life is imprinted on the child growing within her. Anger, hatred, happiness, pleasure, all of it is communicated to the child in the beginning. Which is why it is, so, important for a mother, to have a good man, not a father to the child. The mother plays off the gentle aspects of a man's presence to ease the burdens of pregnancy.

CHAPTER 9

If your child decides that they want to be homosexual, then you must make sure, that you; whom are also a supporter of it, explain everything that goes with it. As sex education is a comprehensive understanding of females, and their relationship to man, or at least that is the theory, then you must figure out how fagging fits into the male/female equation. Case and point; if she, who is woman, is the very epithet of sex, then how is the emotional accord of man achieved without her? How would another male complete the relationship of that being we call man? Homosexuality as a whole, tears down the idea of bringing male and female together, which is the catalyst of why this gender war is even happening. Therefore, as the parent, whom supports homosexuality, you must explain in great detail, just what a man does with his penis in regards to another man, and the purpose for it because that is what being a fag is all about. For it is their *identity.* If you are not telling them the whole story, then you are abridging key aspects of the so-called; *identity,* which would prevent your child from making an informed decision about the rest of their life. Is that what you; the parent whom supports male-on-male anal copulation, wants for your child? It could be quite a blow when a man is lying on top of them, penetrating their body in a most unnatural fashion, but that is what it takes to have a homosexual identity; *right?* In layman's terms, this author believes, that it was once called; *initiation.* Note; this author does not recall the black community going through any form of initiation to receive their pigmentation in order to justify their identity, but as a woman would say; *that's different.*

Then again, you discover that your son has gone to the other side or has come right out and told you about his gender orientation. Whatever the case, they make the excuse that God made them that way or you feel as though you were not there for him when he was growing up. As a Christian, you have to make a choice because your child has given you one by saying; *either, accept me for who I am, or you do not accept me at all.* They have phrased that deal in such a way as to compel you to make a choice. Accept their behavior and reject God or reject them and accept the fact that you are a lousy parent. In effect, denying you; the parent, your right of free will. Your son, is using his free will to condition your free will. A gross violation of your natural rights. Consider the analogy of an alcoholic who is a friend or family whom says; *God made me this way, accept it or you do not accept me.* What would you say?

As a Christian myself, this author has a duty to remind other Judeo-Christians, that you cannot support homosexuality, gay, fag, like-gender praxis, whatever socially descriptive language we may utilize. You can love your child, but that is as-far-as it goes. If you do not notify your child that they are committing an offense against God or what we call a sin, then you may be held accountable for your lack of action.

In order to walk away from a sin, you must first acknowledge its existence. Your duty as a man of God is to refuse the sin, as-well-as all those whom embrace it. No matter how much they say, they believe in God. By acknowledging their homosexual behavior as a legitimate practice, they are in direct violation of God. If you are aware of another Christian committing a sin then you are required to notify them of their infraction, in the event that they may be unaware that they are committing a sin. Under Judeo-Christian rules of faith, you cannot side with God and view any sin as an acceptable practice. Yes; a choice is necessary, and realistically, it should not be a difficult one. You must recognize the sin for what it is in order to better serve God. There can be no exceptions.

The biggest mistake a parent, friend or family member can make is going down with the ship when there is no need to do, so. The idea of; *If you are going to hell, then I am going with you,* is not an option. What you are doing is committing spiritual suicide. Spiritual suicide is any blatant act of surrendering your spiritual being based on your unwillingness to make a definitive effort to acknowledge sinful acts for what they are. In other words, you are revealing that you do not truly believe in God. That you are simply going through the motions.

CHAPTER 10

Should your man-child exhibit a little too much bohemian, he still has a right to know what is expected of him as an adult. He has every right, every opportunity to grow up as a healthy *normal* human male. Yes; this author is saying what no one else wants to admit to anymore, and that is male-on-male copulation is *neither* a normal psychological or biological function of the human body. Their actions and activity provide absolutely no beneficial result to the species of man. They are mentally unstable; *period.* Just because a certain kind of person can interact with the community has absolutely no bearing on the facts. The reality is, the human brain is like the bottom of the ocean or deep space. Our scientific-arrogance presumes that it knows what it is, and that we can even control it, but this is in fact a lie. If we had an absolute understanding and control over our brains then we would not lose control; and do not delude yourself into believing that we do not lose control. We all lose control. Sometimes passively, sometimes actively. The best-known loss of control is our sexual desires. For others, it's alcoholism, and for a great many of us, it's anger, and yet most of us are capable of interacting in society with our varied emotional states, respectively. The irony is that for most people, it does not take much to send them over the edge; especially in cases involving currency.

CHAPTER 11

Anyone with a logical mind will tell you that heterosexuality is not an identity, but a behavior we exhibit in order to attract the attention of the opposite gender as a means of human procreation. So, are we reclassifying homosexuality to a point of making it a whole new living being? Are we redefining what creation is? Are we saying that men whom anally copulate with one another are, so, different that they require their own scientific classification? Probably not because we know that a homosexual male can still copulate with a female and procreate and/or infect her with disease. No, we need to look at this from a rational point of view instead of being injudicious and completely rewrite a million years of the evolutionary process.

If heterosexual copulation is a natural state of being of the human condition, then logic dictates that homosexual copulation must be an unnatural state of being of which, like-gender marriage would be a government sanctioning of an unnatural act of the human condition. Was this viewpoint considered by those serving on the Supreme Court of the United States of America, when formulating an opinion that we have all been conditioned to abide by?

How do those whom conduct and/or support immoral behavior, administer cultural conditioning? You must find a way to make immoral behavior socially acceptable. That way, terms such as homosexual, dandy and faggot would not be effective; however, they are good words for drawing sympathy from the concerned. A word is required to get the ball rolling. Gay, is already in use for those exhibiting unusual behavior. Traditionally, gay was a word with a singular meaning; happiness, cheerfulness, running upon green mountain meadows with, so, much energy that you felt immortal. It is a word with a very broad meaning that could be used by people in all walks of life. So, why not apply it to a certain form of physical pleasure. The use of language is key, by subtly altering its meaning, so, that it becomes an exclusive title, making the practice of sodomy sound benign, almost innocent. That way, applying the term homosexual would seem as though it was demonizing and demoralizing the very behavior it is meant to define. A word without a broad meaning.

No longer is the word gay, utilized by the general populous to define other feelings or passions. Consider that when you feel really good about yourself, and life is going just great, and you are at the peak of happiness, do you say you are feeling gay? Why not? The word has become tainted. Cast aside, from average use, for it has been; *homosexualized,* much as an innocent child in the hands of an adult male seeking hot physical passion.

264

Homosexualizing; is a circumstance in which, the initial use of something becomes corrupted. Guys who are best friends were once defined as partners. In certain communal circles when a person was happy, they were gay. Civil Rights was based on racial grounds. The Rainbow Coalition was about bringing peoples of different backgrounds; races, beliefs and cultures together in peaceful harmony. All of these things were intended for a specific purpose, and then perversely hijacked for the intent of making an immoral act socially acceptable.

Infiltrating journalism is a huge necessity. People involved with mass media as a whole, say; that males whom behave as females on every level are acknowledging who they are. They are not harming anyone. They are simply getting in touch with themselves. When is it getting in touch with ourselves just a simple matter of self-control? We often forget that one unusual behavior has a domino effect across the entire psychological spectrum, resulting in a cafeteria handling of logic and reason in our legal system. If our logic and reason are shaken up, then will our perceptions of law become distorted?

Fagging or what we now, term as gay, is about what a person does, not who they are. A behavior that has been redefined as an identity; for it is not self-awareness that makes us human, but our ability to practice self-control that separates us from the animal kingdom. The ability to control our behavior is key to making us a higher intellect. Animals do not have a soul, they have instinct. They are not self-aware. They simply propagate themselves.

The next step in conditioning a culture is to focus on the errors of what could be deemed as your greatest opponent; the Catholic Church or simply, the Church. An institution that has always been a leader in reminding the people that a man whom lays with a man as they would a woman is a perverse activity. Alas, like any large organization, perfection is not a realistic expectation. Police departments, public schools, many institutions including the Federal Government as a whole, even families are also imperfect; and yet, so, much emphasis is placed on the fallacies of those involved with the Church. Many Catholics forget that those whom make up her very structure are imperfect to begin with. Anyone who has read the Bible should be aware that Christianity is a deliberate arrangement to help the sinful cast off their improper behavior; and that all institutions have individuals whom fall short of expectations. If that is the case in regards to the Church, then what gives her the right to critique any person's imperfections? The answer is, that when striving for a goal you must have a set of guidelines to follow. Without guidelines, how do you determine a path? Remember, that she; the Church is perfect, made up of imperfection due to the idea that bind the imperfections together to generate perfection in the whole. Look at the Empire State Building, and it is perfect. You look at one of its bricks, and you may find a few cracks, and yet the building stands strong, as a symbol of success, beauty and strength. It is a sign of ingenuity courage and faith in ourselves.

The next step would be to bring the scientific community in on the matter, so, that they can add their voice to the conditioning process. A doctor is always required to properly institute the conditioning of the mind. They know what words to say to make a convincing case. Do not take this author's word for it. Research your history: When the tobacco companies employed doctors to inform the public that smoking was healthy, what happened? In the same manner; the doctor of psychology says that a behavior is an identity, and does it, so, smoothly that homosexuality actually gains exclusive rights over other behaviors. To do this, you must further strip away similar behavioral traits; disassociate yourself from transvestites, men whom behave like women, even rapists and pedophiles. Create your own little existence within the overall substructure of the idea in order to fit into the mold of the very people whom you are conditioning.

Next; find a popular movement that can be easily infiltrated without conviction to quickly perpetuate these ideas upon society. A celebration designed to represent people of different races, religions and creeds, complete with its own flag.

Then you convince those involved with the judiciary to create a relationship with existing laws that are designed to protect those

266

whom cannot conceal themselves and/or deny who they are. You even go as-far-as as to buy the loyalty of those groups whom are unable to conceal who they are, not with only money, but with fear and misgivings.

Finally, you tell a lie. You say that you have been denied your rights under the eyes of the Constitution of the United States of America; but what rights have been truly denied?

Do any of you reading this, see an eerie parallel to Hitler's rise to power?

The oddity of the whole affair is the haunting quiet of the medical community on the subject. We humans do all kinds of things to ourselves that make no sense, and medical professionals seem to have an opinion about it, except in cases of the anal penetration of a man by another man, or is there something else going on? Could journalism be blocking our need to know? Why would they do that? There are certain people in our society who are attempting to rewrite the dictionary to suit those whom have unnatural tendencies. This is a process once called whitewashing. What is going on is the separation of the act from the person, while at the same time, redefining a behavior into an identity. We need to guard ourselves from this kind of reprogramming on the basis that it will have an adverse effect on who we are as a species.

As previously mentioned, we are all born heterosexual regardless of how you spin the language. That is not an identity, but a necessity for procreation. That is who we are, nothing more, nothing less. Anything else is an act of will power, for we all have free will. It is how we evolve as individuals. Without it, we become an abomination to the very meaning of life. In laymen terms, we are conducting modifications to suit our needs. Some of those modifications catch on, while we disregard others. Some people like to smell the flowers, while other like to pick the flowers, and then smell them. Soon, the people whom just smell the flowers realize that picking them, will result in nothing left to smell. Therefore, rules are created to protect the flowers, compelling the pickers of the flowers to modify their behavior.

We think of the idea of the United States of America as being a place of freedom, but the reality is a person cannot have true freedom without restrictions. Everything cannot be free. If that were the case, then we could not call ourselves a civilized people; however, what we are all born to do is to become more civilized in our way of life. To achieve this state, people must have an equal understanding of disputed matters. Therefore, one side should not dominate a topic, and thus, those of like-gender praxis should not be allowed in areas involving media, politics and legal formalities on the grounds that they would represent an absolute in human conditioning. Now, you are wondering about the use of the word; praxis in regards to those whom live an unnatural lifestyle. That is because homosexuality is a relationship unto itself. We all have relationships with one another. There are those whom support homosexuals, but are not practitioners of such; parents, family and friends, are in fact homosexual in nature. You cannot say; *I accept homosexuality,* but then disagree with sodomy. No; you accept the homosexual, but in reality, you do not accept homosexuality. Unfortunately, people of the like-gender praxis do not want, what they practice, taken as a negative connotation. Those whom practice homosexuality believe that if you cannot accept the act, then you cannot accept the person. Is there a darker familiarity taking place in our existence? Let us attribute that same byline to a pedophile. Even to our children. If you found out your adult son pursued relationships with children and he told you; *this is who I am.* What action would you take? Do you accept their behavior or reject it? Do you accept him or reject him? In his mind, if you cannot accept the behavior, then you cannot accept him. Is he still a pedophile if he has a relationship with a single man-child, and calls it love; deep romance, or some other form of emotional bliss? If, so, then the homosexual community may be inclined to get involved. Let it be known to those of you reading this, that we; in this country allow broad discretionary powers to our children in making personal decisions about themselves. All it takes is for one child to walk into a courtroom and state; *"I have a right to choose who I want as a partner. Someone who makes me happy based on the U.S. Supreme Court's interpretation of the Fourteenth Amendment,"* and as usual, a sympathetic judge agrees, and let this author further remind you; the reader, that there is always a sympathetic judge because even a person whom wears the robes of the judiciary can fail to see the big picture. Examine the history of the Supreme Court of the United States of America, and you will notice a stark reality to culture. It is a body that is more concerned about the appeasement of those seeking to bypass the political process in regards to the application of questionable behavior in order to bend the will of others, rather than getting at the truth. In other words, they; whom are responsible from preventing the twisting of law are in fact, practitioners of that very action.

CHAPTER 12

Those whom practice fagging want people to focus on who they are, instead of what they do, to deflect attention away from their unnatural activities. They want some form of perverse tolerance. Absolution of their behavior. Someone to finalize the process of normalcy. The problem with perverse tolerance is that it is, so, broad and seclusive. Not to mention that those perversions can also influence the mind to such a degree, that it becomes impractical to allow any perversion to be even slightly tolerated. We cannot simply say, that we will allow this group's ways, but then deny all others. No form of physical intercourse other than that, which is a communal necessity, should be legitimized by any community.

What those in the homosexual community want more than anything is for God to accept their practice as a normal biological function of the human body, and they will go as-far-as to compel the *state* to make unto itself a religious entity in order to force God to accept what they do as a legitimate practice. By acknowledging their legitimacy, the *state,* in effect, defies God? No. The *state* literally offends God to the utmost. Any government body that, so, much as accepts male-on-male copulation becomes an offense against God and is subject to His wrath. As a representative of the *state,* you cannot truly separate church and state. This is a lie told to us by those wishing to ease their conscious in regards to their questionable behavior. That religion and nothing else is actually the catalyst for social violence. Those whom are Christian were given a choice by Christ, and that choice is; you cannot serve two masters. You cannot simply say; *I'm turning off Christ* when moral law conflicts with desire. That is why there is no language in the Constitution of the United States of America denoting the separation of church and *state*. To do, so, would result in a paradox of law. That the *state* would have power over God. Resulting in a total atheist/deist existence, of which we conveniently define as secular. Meaning, any person with the power to create, interpret, influence or enforce law would be required to recuse themselves from the celebration of the Christ. Yes; a harsh reality; however, to ease the burden of worry, consider that the creation of laws for those outside of Christianity is not a complicated process. Moral laws must be adhered to by the people first and foremost before any other forms of law, or none of it makes sense.

CHAPTER 13

Look at the United States of America, and what do you; the reader see? A country under corrupt, paranoia. Fearing, not the world, but more of the truth of what it has become, and how it is affecting each of us. Let us look at the trail of events leading up to our current state of affairs. The Barbary Wars; setting the stage for a global presence. The Civil War; break the hold of the states, over the Central Government. The Spanish-American War; establishing a colonial presence on a global stage. National Income Tax; feed more money into the Central Government to strengthen its overall global presence. World War I; solidifying a European position at the global table. The Great Depression; breaking the family level of government in order to establish a subtle form of legalized feudalism on an unsuspecting populous. World War II; cementing a global economic presence for a voice on the global stage. Events of the 1960s; secularism solidifies, breaking national unity in order to keep feudalism in play. Fuel shortage of the 1970s; restrict leisure movement of the average citizen throughout the country. Professional sports; distract the populous from global affairs. The subsequent
270

drug explosion; subdue the general populous into a mindless state of dissolution. The technology boom; break public socializing in order to create a populous of depraved indifference. Post Y2K journalistic media; seeding ambiguously sourced noise to the populous. What of the future? A populous, voluntarily allowing tracking chips based on the idea of child safety? Then keeping the chips in play as a means of preventing identity theft? Of course, those internal chips will make it easy for you to obtain what you need to be a social component in what would become; *The Big Lie.* For once you accept that form of existence you must wear the sign of the beast.

CHAPTER 14

Therefore, once the *state* associates homosexual activity on the same plain of existence as with the practices of such, regarding the natural understanding of the idea of marriage, and how it not only relates to the whole, but benefits the whole. Then it is clearly acknowledging what is deemed an unnatural physical process as a natural state of existence with no beneficial result to the whole. Associating an immoral act with a moral charter corrupts the very meaning and understanding of what should be a positive existence. Of course, once legitimizing a behavior as an identity, all that comes with it, must be accepted as a public practice; due to the fact that law cannot restrict a persona in any way. You cannot simply make exceptions to render it more suitable, and acceptable because doing, so, would be a reversion to a state of Jim Crowism; separate, but equal. When people are similar in some way, and choose to be different, they make a declaration. When people are visibly different and want to be treated equally, they require clarification. People of African blood and/or descent were already granted rights under the law prior to the Civil Rights Act of 1964, but were simply denied those rights by the opinions of others whom based their views on prejudicial grounds of skin color. On the other hand, fags and lesbians have those same rights, but want modifications based on their *personal* perceptions and wants.

271

Let us clarify the Jim Crow paradigm. *I am a homosexual, and I can come and go as I please, but I cannot anally copulate with my partner in a restaurant? I am a black man, and I can come and go as I please, but I cannot sit in the white section of a restaurant?* Civil Rights made it possible for people of African blood and/or descent to sit anywhere he or she wanted; either on a bus, in a restaurant or a theater. What will acknowledgement of like-gender marriage do for; *them,* in a public setting?

Again; homosexuality is about what you do, not who you are. Yes; people whom have been incarcerated have been dealt a serious blow by our legal system. Now, that the Supreme Court of the United States of America has declared homosexual marriage a pursuit of happiness. Therefore, why aren't all behaviors a pursuit of happiness? Those of you whose behavior has been excluded from the list may now, have lawsuits pending.

Oh, and while on the subject of the use of language that is surely offensive to a great many of you. Fag or fagot is a word deemed derogatory by those whom partake in an immoral act. That is unless you happen to be British. Nigger is a word that defines a social demographic, but made derogatory by cultural ignorance and insensitivity. Their meanings represent two different states of existence, and even of mind.

CHAPTER 15

Does the homosexual community accept the idea of imposing restrictions upon themselves? Demanding the right to be publicly accepted, but then deny themselves the right to fully express themselves openly? At first, they will; however, self-imposed restrictions on a person's identity is a travesty in any case; a complete contradiction of the XIV Amendment, of which, was the basis for allowing same sex marriage in the first place. Realistically, homosexual behavior as a whole would have to be a publicly acceptable practice due to the spirit of the XIV Amendment. If not, then our culture is a lie. Interesting how law is interpreted to grant an unnatural union that can be publicly acknowledged under the XIV Amendment, but the actual practice of such behavior; now, affirmed as an identity by the Supreme Court of the United States of America, does not have the same privilege? So, in a sense, they would be homosexual in name only. They would be denied the right to actually be homosexual in a public setting whenever, and wherever the need arose. Does that mean a person of African blood and/or descent is publicly acknowledged under the XIV Amendment, but cannot practice their identity publicly? That is; after all, was the purpose for the Jim Crowe Laws, of which, this author will remind you; the reader, was an idea initially supported by the Supreme Court of the United States of America, of which now, homosexuals are imposing upon themselves. A practice that the people of African blood and/or descent fought, so, hard to get rid of in the first place. Naturally, that makes absolutely no sense to this author. Color of skin is an identity. The word identity comes from identification: To see what it is, and know. Certain factors that are built into the method to avoid social uncertainty, so, that the unforeseen does not manifest into unexpected hostility. We are creatures guided by our senses to determine perceptive interaction. Clearly revealing why homosexuality does not belong in the ranks of an identity or perhaps people of African blood and/or descent should cover their skin, so, that it cannot be seen publicly. Perhaps there is an ulterior motive taking place. Deliberately placing themselves in a second-class citizenship status to; perhaps, further their social agenda. *One thing at a time; no?* Oh, and for those of you preparing to use this author's prior notion of applying common sense to law, consider the following. Our common sense is a process that we utilize in the understanding of a practical, useful purpose of social interaction. For that person whom would say, that homosexuality is both an identity and a behavior; please, stop twisting our social perceptions of logic and reason. Only woman has that exclusive privilege by means of a completely natural process ordained by God Himself.

CHAPTER 16

Let us take a look at perhaps the greatest ally of like-gender praxis in our social forum, and that is journalistic media. They have absolutely no concern of the homosexual community's impact on a child's perceptions on life; interfering with direction and even purpose. Speaking their opinion without any form of retribution. Observe the social environment in not just the United States of America, but in most capital rich countries of the world, and that is how the media spreads misinformation upon the populous. The LGBTQ+'s control over the general public is considerable. A liking to the Nazi Party. A few controlling the majority through use of erroneous language leading to the abridgment of details and the manipulation of the truth. Perhaps we should classify this organization as Homo-Nazism.

If journalists are unbiased, then why have they taken a one-sided approach on certain topics such as the homosexual movement? What about those in the homosexual community whom exhibit violent tendencies against those whom disagree with their choice of how they live? Do those in journalistic community truly believe that people who are homosexual are completely benevolent? In a nutshell, journalist and those in the celebrity arena imply that homosexuals are a subjugated people whom can do no wrong. Case in point: When members of the Church make poor choices, journalists are all over them like frosting on cake, and the same can be said of politicians and police officers; however, homosexuals apparently never commit heinous acts in our culture? Notice how journalists cover stories regarding murder and rape of women on a regular basis, but seem to be just a little weak in regards to stories of fathers, uncles and cousins raping their male family members. Why is that? Family sex crimes are some of the biggest, if not the biggest domestic atrocities in this country, and it receives no attention from journalists. Why? The truth of our culture is why. You cover it too much, and you start to see the truth of homosexuality. Nazis, and the communists employed varied types of propaganda tools to win the hearts of the populous; however, when a group does no apparent wrong, what is that? Covert propaganda? We always do good, never bad, and it is designed to make a group appear as a necessity for the betterment of the community. To be one of us, you must agree with us or our secret police will make your life very difficult, and let this author be clear of the facts; that any entertainment medium and journalistic organization that supports homosexual behavior are, in effect, the gestapo of the LGBTQ+.

Why is there no oversight on those whom represent journalistic media? Has journalism become a safe haven for expressing unnatural points of view without reproach? What about those whom would speak out against homosexuality? Why are they not represented in journalistic media? Could it be due to a lack of oversight in journalism itself? Though many journalists may disagree, the reality is, the media can behave much like a political machine, which begs the overall question; shouldn't both sides of an argument have representation in journalism? Has journalism become an exclusive voice for a people whom practice questionable activity without an understanding that they are doing nothing wrong? Is the journalistic community conducting a practice that violates the very sanctity of its profession? Are those seeking journalism degrees being compelled to stifle their views. In effect, applying a one-sided approach towards reporting the news? What happens to those in the public-light whom express opposing views? Dissected for every little mistake they have ever made? Treated like the worst criminal in American history? Why; because they disagree with a thing? Anyone whom tries to express their opinion are immediately put away; *why?* Not why are they being put away, but why are homosexuals being treated most favorably in our society? Not even the most persecuted peoples in the history of the United States of America have been given such latitude in these matters, so, why is a behavior given such latitude? Why do journalists and even some celebrities ostracize those, whom do not agree or support the homosexual idea? Why are we not allowed to disagree? Even voice our concerns? Since a person disagrees with certain views, they cannot have a job in media? Why?

Should the journalistic community in the U.S.A. be allowed to continue to bask in Constitutional privilege? Journalism should behave more as a moderator or umpire not a conditioning agent of human will. Both sides should be allowed to present evidence to the facts, in order to get at the truth; so, that the human-will can work properly on the facts, and not on speculation and opinion.

If practicing homosexuals, and their supporters are allowed to work in mass media, voice their concerns without reproach or are in any position that allows them to stifle a person's right of an opinion without retribution, then perhaps those people should be removed from their position. Any practicing homosexual must accept the fact that there are those whom do not accept their lifestyle. To deny the opposition their rights and/or pick them apart based on their choices and failings due to having an opinion is not fair. I can voice an opinion about anyone, except homosexuals? For we all must remember that shortcomings are a given. It is; after all, what makes us human. Journalist have been known to make personal opinions from time-to-time about the shortcomings of others, and there are few agencies and organizations whom could reveal the imperfections of journalists. In a matter of speaking, the difficulty in any such setting is deciding, which imperfections are manageable in such a way that does not interfere with the progress of what it means to be a reasonably logical person.

CHAPTER 17

Marriage should not be allowed between like-gender couples on the basis that it establishes a rule that works for a specific group of individuals with a behavior that compels others whom are opposed to such behavior to accept it. Also consider that though a brother and a sister love each other just as much as homosexual couples, they are denied the right of government-imposed marriage; *why?* They do not copulate in the bedroom in some way? What about fathers and sons, mothers and daughters. Interestingly enough; should brothers, mothers, daughters, sisters or fathers decide to have an incestuous relationship, then it is viewed as; let this author see if he understands this clearly; *immoral?* Now, two heterosexuals whom care about each other and establish a mutual agreement in order to take advantages of certain laws are allowed to marry? This clearly denotes a glorified partnership because all-n-all, that's what all of this is about; *right?* Take advantage of certain tax laws. The natural law of family planning is as follows; man meets woman, marries her and generates offspring. In turn, her man supports the idea of the family structure, with some form of job. Family is not just about obtaining a child. Family is an experience that begins with the miracle of conception. The togetherness of maturating life within a wife. Holding her in your arms for nine months. The torment, worry, and fear. The trials and tribulations of your child growing in her womb. The happiness, thrill, and the hardships of a woman whom resents the living hell out of you for making her that way. Then thinking; *What shall I name this new addition.* Experiencing the difficulties of childbirth through a wife's touch. All of the things we as a modern American culture take for granted when determining what a family is; however, we have a tendency of cutting corners on all aspects of life. Especially in regards to the human experience. Even human existence. We are a result of secularism, and it is tearing us apart.

CHAPTER 18

For those people whom are not practitioners of homosexuality, but support homosexuality; this author has a challenge for you. Ask the person whom practices male-on-male copulation if they have ever given oral pleasure to their partner after engaging in unprotected anal copulation. Should they answer yes; then follow up with the question of: Did they anally discharge within you beforehand? Oh, and if you should find those questions revolting then perhaps you should rethink your position on what is identity, and what is behavior based on the understanding that many of the answers we are seeking are overlooked due to the focus of trying to create a standard of living that is impractical in regards to daily living just to benefit the very idea of making that, which is unnatural in fact natural. Notice our laws following the same pattern. We think that by being accepting of an unnatural act makes humanity a more advanced life form; however, what most of us do not understand is that we are actually craving the simplicities of living. To be as children, and not worry about the complexities of social interaction.

Ever wonder how children can simply come together and play a simple game of tag or kick the can? That is the key to why homosexuality is not an identity. Our children are our immortality. They continue the understanding of who we are, and since homosexuals cannot reproduce, how do they continue their immortality? How do they pass on the physical traits of who they are? They cannot. All they can do is corrupt in order to continue the behavioral aspects of who they are, and that can only be achieved through means of an eventual physical process. Which is why homosexuals should not be allowed to foster children. It is only natural that at some point in its evolution, homosexual behavior will encourage those whom are living a heterosexual existence to cross the line. First; by words, then by example, and what they will never be able to explain to the child is the overall purpose of doing what they are doing. What is the end result? Death. Whether it be death by disease or death due to a lack of immortality, it is still death. Perhaps that is the goal of those whom desire pleasure with those of their gender.

Now, should they answer; *no,* to the first question, then ask the following: Did you feel they were undeserving of the pleasure they bestowed upon your body or was it something else? The reality is that most homosexual men provide pre-oral pleasure; therefore, if they are not providing post oral pleasure then perhaps they too realize the truth behind anal penetration. Should they refuse to answer your question by saying; *that is none of your business,* then consider that when you are being supportive of who they are, then why are they not open about what they do? Funny, that they made it their business to notify all of their private affairs. Let us be realistic. A person asks you to invest in a project, and you say okay without knowing the details? A person cannot make a public declaration of something, and then demand privacy over the issue. You make a public declaration in order to voice a concern. A person has to publicly declare that they are homosexual, and once doing so, they become subject to public scrutiny. Heterosexuality is a natural state of being, therefore making an open declaration is not required, and since people do not declare that they are heterosexual, they are not subject to scrutiny. Once you make a declaration of anything, you become a target of scrutiny; this is what makes a free-state work. Take that away, and we become something else. Therefore, a person whom says; *I am gay,* cannot in turn bar a person or group from making an opinion on the subject. Every person has a right to challenge any form of declaration made by another. It is the responsibility of the one whom makes the declaration to convince opponents of the social legitimacy of their proposal. Simply forcing a group to accept someone else's behavior through the judiciary process by means of modification of set behavior is not the democratic way. It is the grossest violation of our natural human instincts and rights.

Oh, and one last thing: Should you say, it is no one's business to ask such a question, then you are truly in denial of the truth. Especially if you happen to be a woman. Do you truly know what has been in his mouth before you kissed him or where his penis has been before you provided him with oral pleasure, let alone copulating with him?

CHAPTER 19

Perhaps we should examine this from a different perspective. This author shall assist another community in achieving identity status. Pedophiles require a less derogatory word and should take a page from the homosexual rulebook. First; find a universal word that will make your practice more sociably acceptable. How about joy? That way when everybody tries to express themselves in that fashion, they will have to contend with being associated with a certain kind of behavior. Next, you must find a way to make yourself the victim in society. Get the populous to accept your ways as being no different than say; the Black Experience, Civil Rights movement-type stuff. Next, keep your activities a secret until you have established official organizations and a legal network to fight cases for you across the country. Finally, you get a major court case that is sure to draw national attention, involving a child seeking his sexual rights. Voila, you have now, laid the groundwork for gaining your behavioral rights also, or should we say; behavior made an identity, but beware, you may find your biggest opponent will be from the homosexual community. They may even side with their biggest opponent, the Church to persecute you. In other words, they, whom would practice the fine art of hypocrisy, may take offense to some others seeking rights along similar lines. Then again, if you are an adult male whom prefers the company of boys, they may be sympathetic to your desires; *who knows?* Good luck.

CHAPTER 20

So, what is broken? The answer to that question is our very perception of life itself. Consider this; male-on-male copulation is a threat against womanhood. A threat against the woman herself, and yet; again, as in the garden, we the man are standing by and doing absolutely nothing to deal with it. Of course, when we do take action, it is she; herself, whom comes down on us; the man, whom is trying to protect her from the insidious activity that has brought HIV/AIDS into *her* existence. She is guarding the very sanctity of immorality by means of the motherly mechanism incorporated into her very being. She is conducting an improper act by supporting the very thing that is, in fact, killing her, and we are supposed to correct her. Deal with the threat of her coming under the charms of the serpent.

Therefore, we must ask the most important question of our modern age, in regards to an activity that is having a profound effect on our way of life as a whole. Quaking the very foundation of our religious freedoms. Plaguing the very moral understanding of our social sanctity and sanity. Should capital punishment be considered for males whom fag one another? Should we be allowed to kill men, whom lay with men as they would a woman? The answer to that question must be approached, very carefully on the basis that it is, so, easy for complete social mania to get hold, leading to eventual insanity; however, there is an interesting point this author will make, that has been completely missed by all of the intellectual minds of our modern age, including those with religious affiliation. Killing someone whom is a threat to the very fabric of human
280

existence is a part of our natural instincts in the preservation of our species. Look at what we allow in our modern culture. The murder of children in the process of creation. Sexual intercourse without the intent of procreation. Preemptive breeding practices. No logic or reason behind any of it. Can we truly call ourselves human? We have seen time and again what happens when you interfere with nature. Damming rivers seems like a great idea at first. Nuclear energy was all the rage. Sending people to Mars is the answer to a better future for all; however, we discover that by interfering with nature creates more problems. Oh, and this author is betting that you are asking how sending people to Mars interferes with nature. We think that taking water off the Earth is insignificant, but our planet is an extremely delicate eco system. Science has said it. So, if we pay close attention to the history of going into space, and the drinking water problems, could there be a relationship? Could the little bit of water that we take into space have an effect on our eco system? Who knows, but we do know that over time the smallest crack can bring down the biggest dam, and we have been going into space for quite some time.

As we have discussed in this segment, homosexual *behavior* or identity; however, you want to dress it up, has absolutely no benefit to the continued existence of the human machine. Going unchecked will result in the failure of the machine. Male-on-male copulation is a cancer; nothing more, nothing less, and what is the best way to deal with cancer?

In regards to the lesbian? Females simply react to the natural environment and deal with it as best as possible. They follow the pattern of man, and if man is wrong, they are wrong. If man is correct, then they will be correct. They are not bad, they simply play off the instincts of the male of the species because in all likely-hood, when a male sees a female he wants, he will possess her, regardless of the feelings she may have for her own gender. Woman knows her duty when it comes to sustaining human life. Though she may be ignorant of her actions in regards to murder.

LIKE-GENDER PRAXIS

CHAPTER 1

Why does the Church, and other certain religious institutions place, so, much emphasis on such an apparently harmless topic as homosexuality? The answer is as follows: It is necessary for those affiliated with religion to inform those, whether or not they are religiously orientated, that they are committing an abominable act under the eyes of God. To remain quiet is an offense against the Lord. Remaining quiet or lack of action in regards to the topic is also perceived as accepting the abominable act. Over time, their actions become acceptable, and though we do not see the harm of homosexuality on a community; religion is all too aware of what it does not do for a community. Telling someone they are engaged in deplorable actions is not a precursor towards conditioning them towards a more religious minded view. If they show disinterest, you simply move on. Should they spout off about their rights, then you make clear your rights because as we whom are religiously orientated are not allowed to push our beliefs on others. Then they too, should not be allowed to force their ways; their behaviors on others, either. You; whom believes in God, have every right to defend your religious principles regardless of your political affiliation or government orientation. There is a difference between defending religious beliefs, and imposing religious practices. Since the founding of the country, the national government has never imposed religion on the people, and yet, the Federal Courts have forced the immoral will of others on those of us whom are religiously minded via a secular framework.

No person whom is religiously orientated should ever be forced to act or behave in such a way that violates their moral conscience, whether in the private or public sector. Forcing a person to accept another person or group's wants is not only unconstitutional, but quite simply undemocratic. We need not even take a religious

282

philosophical point of view to make that clear. There is no need. The religious card applies to those whose life revolves around religion. Besides those whom claim to be religiously orientated have it set in their minds that they cannot impose their beliefs on others with an understanding that it must come from a supernatural source. Guess what? You are that source. Nonetheless, since most of you have it in your heads that you are not righteous enough to speak up against immoral behavior or even represent your religion in situations of immoral conduct, then we shall approach it from a natural state of being, applying logic and reason to our analysis.

A behavior should never be given identity status, and thus never be given prominence over an idea designed to promote social order on the basis that law is designed to govern behavior not an identity. We lose sight of who and what we are, then we lose track of our purpose, and direction, leading to an eventual cease in social progress. Consider this; we now, live in the computer age, but have we truly done anything with ourselves as a species since its incorporation into our daily lives? As a whole, we still depend upon fossil fuels. Allow the color of skin to determine direction. Alcohol and other drugs are still a means to an end. Sex runs rampant through our civilization. We are gearing our way towards computers because we have lost the wind in our sails. When something no longer serves a purpose, it becomes obsolete, and must be expunged from existence. We neglect the Bible, and yet, it points out the obvious. Pre-flood of Noah's time, Sodom and Gomorrah were moments when people served no useful purpose. We of the Church cannot accept the idea of just getting along when looking after the flock. If wolves, coyotes and lions approach your flock, do you simply invite them in and say; *we can all just get along?* You buy a house and cultivate a beautiful green lawn, a flower or vegetable garden, and a weed starts to grow; *we can all just get along*; *right?* No, we cannot because we know there are things that are harmful to the flock, the lawn or the garden, and many of them are unseen. No one wants a lawn full of crabgrass and dandelions because it takes away from the grandeur of what is trying to be accomplished.

Predators will slaughter relentlessly. Weeds will choke off the useful component leaving something that serves no useful purpose. Things that have a negative impact on goals are kept out. Sure; being a fag seems benign, until you have a clear perception of the goings on in a private setting. This author has trouble with the understanding of why, so, many in our society find it acceptable for a male to embed his penis into another male's anal cavity and ejaculate his reproductive fluid. One part of the body dispels life-giving ingredients, and the other part discharges hard bodily waste, and many people have no qualms with the mixture of the two. Explaining why we, in the religious community view any judge whom makes a ruling supporting same-sex marriage as the wolf, coyote, or lion. In fact, we view any supporter of like-gender relations as such; a danger to those whom are unaware of the truth. They are a threat to the flock.

CHAPTER 2

Now, for the big million-dollar question; what is the harm of homosexuality? What is the harm of being homosexual? Why do individuals whom deal in like-gender praxis come across as being harmless? Good people whom are being shunned in some way?

A subconscious algorithm tells us that reproduction is necessary to keep life in play; and that algorithm will drive us to do what is necessary to keep human life in play. Now, consider the two parties that interfere with that algorithm; feminists and fags.

Next, it is the duty of this author to remind the public, that HIV-AIDS is a fag's disease that spread to the female population due to the popular notion of either blood transfusions, a drug addict's used syringes, prostitution, or this author's preferred explanation of transference through means of bisexualism. In any event, whether or not the latter occurred deliberately or accidentally is inconsequential. What is interesting is that we; the man, have failed at our number one task assigned to us by God, and that is to protect the woman from harm. We say that homosexuality in regards to a male is not harmful, but ask a woman who has been diagnosed with HIV-AIDS due to her husband being on the down-low, and she will say

284

otherwise. Lesbians who have never been involved with men do not contract HIV-AIDS. Heterosexuals do not contract HIV-AIDS from virgins; therefore, let us be realistic; if HIV-AIDS was spontaneous in the heterosexual population, we would seriously be a short-lived species. Of course, bisexualism was never a topic of discussion by journalists of the 1970s and 80s. More than likely it was kept hush-hush under the pretense of corrupted men deliberately contaminating women due to jealously. Interesting how we never considered the possibility of corrupted men deliberately infecting our most precious asset. Be realistic; people will go to any lengths to make a point. Men are notorious for being serial killers of women, so, why would it be far-fetched to consider that a fag would not do what it takes to ensure that women become infected? Once our most prized asset became susceptible to HIV/AIDS, an all too familiar phrase was applied; *"It's not just a gay disease anymore."* We have been greatly conditioned to ignore the facts, by those whom practice fagging, and those whom support that practice, and yet, we know that it occurs, and we do nothing about it. So, for all of you; conspiracy theorists, who are busy with topics such as super-secret societies, the Kennedy assassination, existence of extraterrestrials, or whether or not NASA actually landed a man on the moon. There is a bigger topic for you. Newborns and sexually active women whom contract HIV-AIDS withstanding; examine the change of our history by certain groups whom allow unnatural activities to be socially acceptable, and the truth will reveal itself; and that is, HIV-AIDS is in fact a male disease resulting from anal copulation.

The interesting aspect of HIV-AIDS is its abrupt emergence on the scene. Yes; scientists and even philosophers tell us that it has more than likely existed from the beginning of time, but the question no one is asking is why the sudden explosion in the 1970s? The opinion of this author is that up until that time, those who exhibited male-on-male copulative behavior were greatly restricted by the establishment; however, the free love movement changed all of that. So, much happened all at once, that our social network completely broke down. An event that was easily on par with the stock market crash of 1929. With the advent of mass communications; radio, television, and the telephone; let us make a general examination of events taking place up until that time. What were the people going through? Segregation, the Bay of Pigs, Missiles of October, President Kennedy's Assassination, Vietnam, Civil Rights, capitalism-vs-communism, the threat of nuclear war, sexual revolution, Malcolm X, breaking movie censorship, the attack on organized religion, Vatican II, out with the old, in with the new, UT Austin Sniper, new ideas, old ideas, British Invasion, Black Panther Movement, nuclear/biological dumpsites, Dr. King's assassination, another Kennedy assassination, Kent State, Jackson State, the movers and the shakers, U.F.O.s, the enemy makers, protests, riots, protests and even more protests, drugs and rock-n-roll, Arab-Israeli conflicts, landing on the moon, pollution, Mexico City Olympics, Zodiac, Woodstock, Helter-Skelter, airline hijackings, gas shortage, Munich Olympics, disco, Watergate, and of course; the fall of Saigon. Easily, this author has not covered everything; however, it was a period when the country as a whole was naïve. As if our culture was being stripped of its virginity. There was a complete breakdown of the understanding of our very nature that kept us socially aligned, due to the contradictory behavior of our forefathers. The country had been built on sand instead of rock, and that sand completely eroded away by the 1970s. The dragon in the Book of Revelation suddenly loosed upon the world to break the Church's hold on society. The seeds of anti-Christian thinking were planted, and today they have influenced an entire generation into believing that Jesus Christ is a sham, scam, plot to rob the human race of its existence. Do not take this author's word for it. Look at it for yourselves. What is going on? The NFL owns Sunday. In the past, the previous generation would step aside for the younger generation. We called it passing the torch, but the older generation spoiled the new. The new generation does not want to grow up, and the old does not want to die, and in the middle of it all, are those who relish male-on-male copulation. They; whom

286

prefer the company of the same gender in the bedroom sprouted dead center of all the muck, and confusion, and now, they hail themselves as the saviors of society, while in the meantime our children lose their identity.

In the 1970s, male-on-male copulation was no longer being policed. In fact, quite the opposite. They were being cultivated; nurtured, allowed to expand their views accordingly into every aspect of life; yes, including our temples of worship. Psychiatry said that male on male copulation was not an abnormal condition that prevents a person from interacting with society. Of course, neither does sadomasochism, rape or any other form of sexual assault. Even murder does not prevent a person from interacting in society. There are many behaviors not meant for a general setting; certain behaviors that must be contained; again, in order to maintain an orderly, productive, civilized environment. Terrorism is a behavior; if it were not, then the World Trade Center tragedy could have possibly been averted. These malicious parties interacted with the general public as anyone else would, and then without any consideration, conducted a brutal act that devastated an entire world. These people did not announce who or what they were. They remained quiet; however, if they had announced to the world that they were terrorist, would we have treated them differently? You bet your ass we would have. Nobody cares until someone opens their mouth or a certain action takes place. Out of sight, out of mind; *oh, how ignorance is bliss.* Perhaps what people of the like-gender praxis want, is nothing more than attention after the fact. What this author finds interesting, is that in the past when individuals played out their homosexual tendencies they believed that it was an act of privacy. Today's homosexuals have different ideas. They want everyone to know who they are. Why is that? Do they want the community to be proud of what they are or again, is there a greater agenda?

Now, you; the reader, consider that in ancient times when a person had leprosy, they were isolated, even killed. What would have happened if leprosy advocates won an argument to allow those who were contaminated to exist in the general population? Yes;

leprosy is not a great comparison tool to HIV-AIDS on the basis that not many had it, but do we truly know its origins? Consider, that in less than a generation of this modern age, we associate HIV-AIDS to all genders, though we know that it affected only fags originally. Could leprosy have started in the same way? No way to prove or disprove, but one thing is for sure about human existence, and that is, history truly repeats itself.

We have allowed the psychiatric and legal communities to conveniently shave off specific aspects of homosexual behavior, such as the sexual assault of male children. Adult males whom prey on little boys is clearly homosexuality; however, we have been, so, conditioned by those, whom have neatly wrapped up adult males whom pursue little girls and little boys, into one convenient package called child predators, for the benefit of those who want to practice their urges on one another. Interesting how we have placed individual rights over those of the family. Sacrificed our children's individual rights to benefit those of the adult community whom are seeking a physical and psychological satisfaction with one another. A girl is raped; *period.* A boy is raped; *period;* nothing more, nothing less. Do we hate our children to the point that we are willing to sacrifice their rights; their well-being; their very will just, so, several men can partake in anal copulation? An adult male who has a certain fervor for a man-child is forcing his homosexual addiction, his homosexual beliefs onto the innocent; the ignorant of mind. We say that he is a sick individual, but he knows exactly what he is doing, and it is the same psychiatric community who says homosexuality; fagging is not an abnormal condition; and yet conditions the public into believing that a person who sexually; no, anally assaults a boy is not of right mind? Let us consider that we have proven that these people can interact with the population just as easily as anyone else. If they were unable to interact in society, then how do they gain access to our children to begin with?

Let us examine this thing we call social interaction. Jack the Ripper apparently interacted in everyday society; he had to eat, drink and pay his bills somehow, and yet he was a butcher of women.

288

This person did not climb into a casket after murdering these women. This person did not lock himself in a room after murdering these women. He and people like him had to eat and sleep and socialize in some way. Even more recent; NBC's; *"To Catch A Predator"* revealed people interacting in the daily social routine who preyed upon children, and their family, friends and coworkers had no clue. Many people partake in sadomasochism and swinging. Should their behavior be openly accepted? And yet, these people are also interacting in normal everyday society. Picture the Supreme Court of the United States of America making a ruling requiring everyone to partake in *swinging* as a normal part of life or even sadomasochism. As despicable as it may seem, some pre-Christian cultures of the ancient world viewed this kind of behavior as nothing more than routine. Therefore, just because a person can interact on a meaningful social level does not mean their atypical behavior should be deemed as an acceptable practice by the public; especially if those whom are not practitioners of a behavior, have made it clear that it should not be accepted.

A man seduces a woman who says; *no,* and he is a predator? That kind of behavior is a fact of life. Though many women will not admit it, most relationships begin in this fashion. A man seduces a child who says; *no,* and he is a predator. A man seduces another man who says; *no,* and he is a predator? What we are sure of is the man being seduced reacts by killing his seducer, and he is a murderer? Forget the fact that he is reacting to a demeaning activity that is offensive to his very being, and yet, he is still a murderer, and not only is he tried as such, but what he did is viewed as a hate crime? You bet your ass it's hate, for God hates men who lay with men as they would a woman! Then again, the big question that is swimming around in the back of your head is; *how does a homosexual male seduce a normal male?* A teenager sees a beautiful woman, and does what men do when they see beautiful women. They are the perfect match, and it does not take long for the saliva exchange to take place. The touching, the groping, dates, invested time, exchanging of well-thought out words of passion.

The both of them hit it off, and then one night on an intimate date, the passion is extra hot, and she actually forgets that she is in fact not female. Now, how should the straight guy react? The one thing we never take under consideration is just how fragile the human heart truly is, whether male or female. When a woman is hurt, she is emotionally devasted and lashes out with tears, but a man? He gets emotional, and he has to stop being a man? He more than likely lashes out with rage, and when he does, it's a hate crime? Sure, the male whom feels like a woman has genuine affection for the straight man, but not enough affection for disclosure at the moment of first contact? In any case, males impersonating females are not hurting anyone, they are simply being who they are; *right?* Yes; but, at the expense of our social perceptions of familiarity.

CHAPTER 3

For all intents and purposes, homosexuals cannot hold public office on the basis that they represent a form of existence that is contradictory to nature, of what it means to be united in regards to sentient existence; and the safeguards of rational thinking in regards to the benefit of the whole. In fact, they are a process that is disassembling the very idea of rational thinking at its core. Case in point: We the people of the United States of America are a nation built upon teamwork, and most importantly; sacrifice. Homosexual-living isn't about sacrifice, but more of personal and individual wants and needs. How does a man experience the sacrifice of physical comfort during pregnancy, and giving birth? How does he experience the nagging, antagonism of another man whom cannot go through the process of motherly metamorphosis? Feeling the strain, and difficulty when holding hands with a mother giving birth? The feeling of knowing that he is a part of bringing a new addition into the world? Their need is for a satisfaction that has absolutely no result, beneficial to the concept of what it means to be a community. *I see a man who is like me, and I want to spend my life with him because it pleases me. That woman is like me, and we have chemistry, and I want to be with her.* Homosexuality is a case of personal need, and nothing more, and they use legislature to further their agenda,
290

which is nothing more than a conditioning of immoral guidelines. Yes, the traditional family is having great difficulty in these modern times, but the reasoning behind the difficulties is, so, simplistic in its foundation that we are completely missing it. They; whom have absolutely no problem representing a person's behavior have done nothing more than twist our perceptions of what is natural, and what is unnatural; of what is gender responsibility and what is gender abnormality. What it means to be a team player without being a part of the team. What it means to be a United States of America without being united in truth.

Hitler, Mao, Stalin, Mussolini; none of them tolerated male-on-male copulation. We often forget another fact of history, and that is those whom opposed them did not accept the practice of male-on-male copulation either, but tolerated it to a certain extent. Historically speaking, no one favored male-on-male copulation at all, more than likely on the basis that it destroys that, which defines what is male, and what is female. This is perhaps the most dangerous thing in our very existence that we must not allow to happen, and yet we as a society overlook it as nothing more than a flower blooming in a meadow. The problem is, that flower is a dandelion and if we continue to let it fester, it would mean the very failure of not only our humanity, but society; our very civilization as well.

Oh, and when people say; we're not ready for homosexuality, especially in regards to fagging, what are they talking about? What do they mean by not being ready? What they are saying is a basic generalization of acceptance with no clear perception of why. Basically, a latent form of subversion, and they have been doing it for years. This idea works especially with people whom are highly credible. That they can say anything, and their supporters will accept it, regardless of their intuition. The truth of the matter is; we will never be ready for it because fags are not a persecuted people, they are a people living a perverse lifestyle. Not to mention that they offend God.

Homosexuals should not be given mainstream jobs on the basis that they do not contribute to the natural law of family planning because from their point of view it is not a viable idea. They have pulled apart the very fabric of our culture with their vast financial resources from which, they have accumulated under the guise of being harmless; to further their agenda of convincing the greater majority of the people that homosexuality is not a bad way of life, but is, in fact, a normal way of life. Convincing society that it is perfectly okay, and even normal for a man to install his penis into another man's anal cavity and ejaculating, with hopes that the sperm will somehow bond them to a long-term commitment. They have convinced modern society that male-on-male copulation is perfectly harmless, through means of pitting your children against you; using your own sexual deviance against you; turning women against men; and convincing women to view men as a socially combative entity. Now, why would men whom seek males for romance want a woman to go against a man? Once gaining rights to openly express their behavior, they used their vast financial resources to convince those whom believe in God to step on God. In other words, they convinced you; the God-fearing person, that God is wrong; that God is imperfect, and that male-on-male copulation is right and even good. That man being with a woman is actually bad, and that a man should explore options because in reality, it is not a behavior, but an identity.

DECLARING WHO I AM

We the people of the earth have all that we need in the ways of perpetuating into a superior state of intellect without infringing on our rights as human beings. We would like to take this moment to give thanks to God for providing us with the initial moral imprint for which, to build a civilized state of mind, but that we can now, take it from here. Therefore, let no being whether of Heaven or of earth refuse us the pleasures that we seek; whether it be vaginally, orally or anally, to our social evolution for as we see fit. We will insure that all levels of human development will be accepting of it. For it is the driving force behind our social progress, and whether agreed upon by the masses or not, suspension of civil liberties may be necessary to propagate its growth in the community. Any man who is unable to adapt to these ideas will be either ostracized or incarcerated accordingly until such time as it is deemed necessary to be released as a properly conditioned citizen who is morally and ideologically pure in their understanding of what is proper and improper. Therefore, we declare unto ourselves, and dare to say that we the people of this modern civilized culture of the early Twenty-first Century are severing our ties with the Lord; Jesus Christ, and are no longer in need of His services.

Unfortunately, certain ideas have twisted our perception of what should be, and what is. Physical pleasure is perhaps the most powerful force in our existence. It even has the power to divert our attention away from God. What we have forgotten is that you begin as a man, she; as a woman. Then you; the man, evolves into a husband and she; a wife, and then you become a father and she; a mother, finishing out the evolutionary process and becoming a new being that we call man; however, you; the man, have failed the woman. You have forgotten that the process of sexual intercourse is the beginning of changing who you are as a human being. You are no longer a man, but a father. She is no longer a woman, but a mother. Whether or not children exist has no bearing on the facts. Its very intent is about responsibility. Yes; there is a certain level of pleasure involved in the process; however, responsibility must supersede pleasure. You as the father must tend to the mother's needs at all costs; save, but one; and that is your duty to God.

The difference between a man and man is a matter of perception from any of us. When you are a man, you are just the run of the mill male. It takes a wife to make a male whole, and the reason for the need of faith in God, so, that the process can be bound together to form the being that we call man. Only a representative whom is in alignment with God can make this happen. No government can do this. No institution outside of the realm of God can do this, for there is nothing alive to bond the man and the woman together. A document or digital equivalent cannot breathe, cannot speak, cannot hear, feel, touch or express emotion. It is the modern equivalent to idol worship. Thus, the only thing accomplished by said document is nothing more than an agreement between two separate bodies; a contract; partnership; business arrangement between two people, and nothing more, and if need be, can be dissolved; torn up, broken. Yes; men and women divorce, but this author has news for you; the reader. The bond is still there. Secularism destroys the sanctity of marriage by distracting men and wives to look at the institution of marriage from a financial standpoint instead of a spiritual point of view. Now, if a contract can be broken, then why call it marriage? Remember, marriage is about the intent of two becoming one, not sexual proclivity. A shorter way of saying; a man leaves his mother and father to cleave with a woman. Yes; we've attached the term marriage to other instances. Using it figuratively or metaphorically: *That person is married to his work. That person and his dog are inseparable, practically married. Those guys are, so, close they are married.* Today, we've taken the figurative notion out of context, and are simply applying it to any bond; *Why can't we be married for real? Why can't I marry?* We as a culture have a bad habit of altering the true meaning of a word, perverting its intended use to the point of corrupting its intended meaning and over all understanding of life. When you do not maintain a high sense of philosophy and rhetoric then the basic understanding of why a thing is what it is, becomes lost in the noise. Marriage was viewed as a religious word, a holy word, a positive word. Now, it has been made into a negative word, a cuss word, a dirty word. Interesting how our evolved social stupidity goes hand-n-hand with our perceptions of what is and what should be. Withal said; if your intent of marriage is anything other than building a family, then it is nothing more than a business venture. This very idea has driven like-gender couples to seek, and even gain marriage rights; equality to the basic idea of an ancient religious tradition. Again, a worship word meaning making two people one through an extraordinary process, and that it should not be used out of context. Its meaning is clear under the eyes of the religious. Therefore, if two people want to announce to the world that they are of a certain kind, then, so, be it with their little contractual arrangements, but please, do not attempt to establish some form of relationship under the pretense of a sacred ceremonial process. It not only distorts the very fabric of religion, but insults and warps the very truth of the I Amendment to the Bill of Rights, and most importantly God Himself. Oh, and let this author make it clear that this to be true of any marriage outside of the traditional sense.

Again, man and God are a relationship, and since God finds fagging an offensive *behavior,* then, so, too should man; and yes, that includes even those whom are practitioners of such behavior. Also, a man should consider that if he is a firm believer of God and violates Leviticus 20:22, then he should cease his unnatural activity due to his relationship with God.

Ironically, homosexuals declaring discrimination, actually creates an atmosphere of discrimination for others. Basically saying; their behavior has exclusivity. No other behavior has been given such latitude. No other behavior, not even heterosexuality has identity rights respectively speaking. Therefore, a homosexual has the right to practice their behavior at any time, and in any place on the basis that like-gender marriage has been deemed legal under the opinion of the Supreme Court of the United States of America. Therefore, governments that conduct and recognize marriage between like-genders are basically saying the following: *By law, we recognize certain rights that comes about by your behavior, and that in order to fully take advantage of those rights you can now, conduct your behavior, now, elevated to an identity, anywhere you, so, please, whether it be in a restaurant, a school or even in a park. It is now, legal for two men to strip off their clothes in a public setting and copulate. Any laws that would hamper their ability to conduct their identity are currently null and void.* Of course, if the Supreme Court of the United States of America decides to interpret law in such a way as to affirm all behaviors as an identity to avoid the controversy…

REMEDY

Arrest control of your behaviors and separate them from your reasoning and logic centers; from your decision making, but not from your religious beliefs. Your religious beliefs are engrained into the very fiber of your being; of who you are. Note: This concept only applies to people whom are seeking a life with God. When a person is brought up on a certain value system that works, you do not simply shut it out; or as some politicians have said; *keep them separate from my political agendas or responsibilities.* If you; the politician, are in a desert with a dozen people discussing how to survive, and your religious beliefs tell you there is water nearby, would you be compelled to keep that information to yourself, under the notion of separating your religious beliefs from your political affiliation? If your religious values have an answer to a political problem you wouldn't use it? Look, if a politician of like-gender praxis is allowed to declare to the world who they are, and defend his kind in the legislature, then why are you not declaring to the world who you are, and defending Christianity? Oh, and, so, that we are clear on one thing; Christians declare who they are by following the rules set down by the Christ. That is because they are two different ideologies that will clash in every sector of the human condition. One represents disorder, the other, order. One places a restriction on what a person can or cannot do, and the other says; do absolutely anything you want. Only one has a relationship with order. Everything else is a travesty.

296

A person cannot embrace their behavioral flaws and the Christ. They must embrace one or the other; however, embracing Christ; though a person may be behaviorally flawed, does not mean they should look upon themselves with distain. You acknowledge the behavioral flaw for what it is; an obstacle of the flesh, and fight it as you would cancer. You hate the behavioral flaw for what it is, not yourself. For you are a victim of the flaw. Never accept a behavioral flaw as who you are, you must find clever ways of not, so, much, controlling your behavioral flaw(s), but more of fooling your behavioral flaw to feed upon itself. This is how you overcome it, and most importantly you keep your flaw(s) contained. You do not acknowledge a behavioral flaw as a normal state of being. You do not elevate a behavioral flaw to the ranks of an identity. No person should be forced to accept another's improper behavior whether it be a flaw or not. On the basis that a behavior can be concealed. An identity cannot. Furthermore, be aware of passing on behavioral flaws to your kith, kin and strangers alike. You are committing a serious offense on many levels of existence that may be deemed as punishable by forces we categorize as supernatural.

The remedy to the dilemma of like-gender praxis is as follows; first: We must push for the identification of what is and is not, a behavior under the eyes of the law. This author believes that this course of action is actually a travesty, and tramples on the very notion of a democracy. The very understanding or idea of common sense; of which was the basis for establishing this country in the first place. Unfortunately, it is necessary to establish, under law a precedent that preserves the sanctity of the very laws we live by on the basis that it is law that regulates a person's behavior, *not* their identity. Once allowing one behavior to cross that line, then all behaviors must be allowed to cross that line or it becomes a social contradiction. Of course, once all behaviors become an identity, then law is no longer necessary, thus, it nullifies itself. Then we would be unable to govern anything. Now, once the law defining identity from a behavior is in place, it will nullify any rulings by the Supreme Court of the United States of America based on like-gender relationships.

Second, we should not be making law that reads like a 1990's credit card terms of agreement. Law should be based on simplicity, not complexity, so, that even a child can understand it because we tend to forget that our children are protected by those same rights or are we saying they have no rights? People break the law because it has been made too complex for anyone to understand, let alone remember. There should not be any legal tricks or loopholes to prevent the layman from representing himself because we tend to forget that our court system is not supposed to get a person off, but get at the truth.

BUILDING A GOVERNMENT

CHAPTER 1

After establishing an understanding of where a government begins, let us take a crack at building a new government from scratch. Let us see what a man can do, to begin the construction method. First things first: When dealing with this subject, we need to be absolutely clear that choosing female companionship is a greater prospect than buying even a house, and do not let anyone tell you otherwise. Relationships are fragile things requiring lots of attention and a tad of prudence.

As the male of the species, your first duty as a potential husband would be to prepare a fine nest for that future wife for whom you haven't found yet. Achieving this at the age of eighteen or younger is possible for some, but not practical, and that includes the receiving of wealth and/or inheritances. There is more to building a great house then just having a large bank account and a familiarity of daily living. A man must have fidelity, humility, patience and temperance; to say the least. Experience life beyond the confines of home, in new and interesting places. Those little unforeseen intricacies that makes a male into a responsible man.

Interact with those whom you do not know. Gathering information, forming allies, committing to heroic deeds, and perilous journeys that would benefit a stranger in order for you to propagate into something of real substance, so, that you can smoothly transition over to fatherhood when the time comes. This leads to a path of wisdom, responsibility and a greater appreciation of life in general; beginning, of course; with the Bible. That is; by the way, your first instruction guide in regards to evolving into an excellent husband, a great father and eventually even a trusted community leader.

Now, you; the eligible bachelor, have amassed a small fortune, made connections, have gained a rudimentary understanding of life, molded yourself into someone of real substance, capable of being a significant contribution to the community. What you have done is made yourself into that person whom people want to be friends with. Little do you know; the girls are paying attention, for you have that fire they are looking for; that go getter attitude. That apparent bad boy nature without the rebellious ignorance that comes with it. They know that with you they will go places, and see new and interesting things.

Contrary to popular belief, girls are not attracted to bad boys. They are attracted to the bad boy's energy. If there is anything a girl desires in all the world, it is energy. She wants excitement and effervescence. Bad boys like to go against the grain, break the rules, torment those whom play by the rules; and that takes lots of energy. You need not be a risk taker to garnish the attention of a fine, young prospect. Simply lead an active lifestyle, and if her face is not in her phone when you are around, then you have won her heart. The nice thing about girls is that you do not need to know where the action is; the drugs, the drinking and revelry, to keep their interest. Just seeing the world is enough. That is why you live life first, and then pursue a relationship. God created Adam first, so, that he could show woman the world. Naturally, many girls go against this concept. Such as when she makes the first move. What she is doing is crossing that delicate line between male behavior, and proper feminine protocol, on the basis of whether or not that special guy, may or may not be interested in her. One thing is for sure, and that is the woman whom makes the first move is clearly sending a message that will be misread, putting her through a difficult dilemma or even a trap. After all is said and done, what she does not realize is that she has been caught up in a little feminist trick. Her impatience has made her unbalanced in regards to understanding male behavior. The feminists do not say; *discard patience,* but they do encourage females to act upon their passions forthwith. Woman should not choose the man. Choosing is part of a man's rite. He builds the bridge, and accepting a man's offer to cross that bridge is a woman's rite. What most women do not understand is that it is easier for her to fall in love with he, whom loves her, then getting he, whom has no interest in her, to fall for her. The latter knows he's got her because she is building the bridge, and when she crosses it, he will be gone. Should even her stubbornness persist; in the end, she will miss the attention given to her by the one whom she had no interest for, and come to regret it. Wasting the rest of her life tearing down the bridge she built without realizing that all she need do is cross back to her side and it would simply disappear. Another point that women do not realize is that our attraction for one another is always out of sync with the moment. Ever notice the domino effect of the guy whom likes the girl, whom likes the other guy, whom likes the other girl. As if the fallen one is applying reluctance in the hearts of men and women; and who knows, perhaps that is the case. Then again, it could be a simple case of eugenics. Two guys are attracted to a girl; however, one has a little more flair then the other and wins her heart. The other guy leaves. The winner dumps her based on the notion of; *she can do better, but she is not good enough for me.* Keeping girls from true love, and of course there is the female equivalent. In any event, we must be honest, and accept the fact that there is never a moment when a girl is truly not in the mood to meet a guy, but there are moments when she is not prepared to meet that special guy.

CHAPTER 2

Lay an immortal foundation. A long-term goal for who you are; from birth to the end of time, unless your father has established some form of meaningful groundwork. Then it would be your duty to make adjustments. Sharpen those goals to make them more concise and functional to the needs of the whole. Invest your money wisely. Live as frugal as possible because you will not give up the night-life or the ballgames unless someone says, so. In any case, just be smart about it because pursuing the pleasures of life; the dance-spots and pool parties are a dead end. They pay you nothing. Basic television, basic car; basic everything. At least 75% of what is left of your income after you pay your religious institution, needs to be set aside for your future family. For your whole purpose as a future husband/father is to establish a solid platform for your immortality. Yes, this author understands that you can afford the Ferrari, but choose instead, the Ford and divert the excess money into some form of interest-bearing account for your future family, specifically your children, because technology like woman-hood, will continue to evolve, and all you are going to do is become pissy mad when something better comes along anyhow. Besides; this author has heard that private schools and colleges are very expensive, and you want the best for your four-plus children because they are what makes your immortality real.

Naturally, you are entitled to a high standard of female, even perhaps a trophy; however, for you; the man, to obtain a trophy wife, you must acquire a trophy career. You must be flawless in matters of faith. Interweave your religious virtues, and values into your daily living. This is not an option, but a requirement. To have a strong house, you must have a strong faith in God and His Church, that is; should you happen to be Jewish or Catholic, or non-Catholic Christian. Doing all of these things takes time; however, you are impatient and you obsess over a fine prospect. You date her, marry her and when she does not behave properly you get angry at her? You pursue unfinished, unpolished young ladies, whom are street. They are feral females. Independent thinkers with chaotic minds, whom are unwilling to be a part of your game plan. Naturally, should they be polished and not feral, then they look at you with distain. You are the one who is street, unpolished. Lacking a game plan. So, guess what? Both; boys and girls must polish themselves if they want prime stock. This goes without saying, for the world can only be, what we make of it.

Do not rush your development. For humans, even females, do not develop at the same rate, physically and mentally. Whereas the female is practically born sexy, and attractive in the eyes of a male, for most of us, as the male of the species; obtaining perfection in the eyes of a female does not occur overnight. Though there are just some males whom seem to develop quicker than others on all levels. Some males have photographic memories, while others require repetitive instruction. There are males whom get it, while others need to be taught it. This is not a flaw in who we are, but simply how our species works; to better challenge our very being, our basic instincts, our very existence. Imagine a world where everybody developed mentally and physically at the same rate. Where is the challenge in that? Ever look at the trees in a forest. No two are alike. Some are straight, while others are not. Some have more branches than others. Some look a little more colorful, while others are completely different in color. Therefore, ask yourself this question. Is it the existence of the forest that makes it beautiful or the differences of the forest that makes it beautiful? The same can be said of *man* as well. Is it our existence that makes us beautiful or our differences that we enjoy? The different sizes and shapes, are a necessity, because we like variety due to the excitement that it brings into our lives. Those differences guide us, invigorates us to be much more than what we are. Without unattractive, there can be no attractive, and yet we are all attractive. It makes, making a choice of courtship and/or friendship palatable. What one person perceives as a flaw, another may perceive as an advantage. It is those differences that make us such a top-notch adaptive species. Without them, we stagnate and die. This is why we should not judge each other based on physical appearance; attributes and/or mental abilities, for everyone's abilities serve a purpose in the grand scheme of things. Yes; and that includes homosexuality, for to have a correct, you must also have an incorrect because without it, free-will could not exist.

The reality is our attractiveness, and even sexiness in the eyes of a female maturates quickly, but it takes years for a male to *properly* develop both physically and mentally. Oh, and just, so, we are clear on the subject; what females view as sexy is not the same as what males view as sexy. What females find *most* attractive in males is the ability to take charge without appearing overly aggressive. They like a man whom can fight with words, without the expletive insults, and fists. They like a man whom knows what to say, and when to say it, so, that embarrassment does not overshadow the relationship. This is not to say that she is unattracted to the physical stature; just that she prefers to experience the body in private. That is because others may influence her opinion, and tastes of what is physically appealing. No one likes a critique of what makes them feel good because realistically, in our case, it is not the size of a woman's breasts that we truly like, but the reaction we generate when we touch them in a sequestered romantic setting. The same goes for us; the male, in regards to a female, except in her case, she is further stimulated by the act of knowing that she is pleasing us, and in many cases, that pleasure is not through a physical attraction as it is more of a visual appeasement. That is why woman places, so, much emphasis on cosmetics, attire and accessories because looks are everything to her. She wants to know that she is not camouflaged by the competitive environment. She does not want to be just another face in the crowd.

CHAPTER 3

The impatience of you; the teenage boy, can lead to unnecessary extremes such as steroid use and other chemical derivatives and even overzealous desires. You want to be a giant ahead of schedule; lead others without learning how to follow, of which destroys the natural process for proper male maturity. Then in the long-run, you suffer from both physical and mental burnout.

Allow nature to take its course. Do not worry, for even when you are in your forties you will still have a great life ahead of you. Play your cards well, and you will have greater virtuosity with just a touch of teenaged veracity when your wisdom comes to fruition. You will have an even greater life with greater vitality, and virility in your wisest years. Just remember, a woman is much like any creature of the wild; cute and cuddly when young, but a tossup when reaching her later years. When searching for a trophy, consider a twenty-year difference, because by the time you hit your sixties, you will be thankful for the companionship. Trust this author, the girls are not going anywhere, and you will see that when you are in your mid-thirties and early forties, you will be prime stock in the eyes of a seriously minded female; a super beauty. At that point, give her *man;* maturity, direction, and you will have a topnotch wife by your side during social gathering, and in the toughest of moments; and there are always tough moments no matter how well you have prepared. Oh, and by the way, if you have not wasted your seed in your youth; sixty years old is going to be fabulous. Stepping back to when you hit your thirties; you will feel like a million, no matter the time of day, and you will start to see girls differently. By the time you're forty, you will be exploding like a kid out of the house after a day-long rainstorm. When you are fifty, you will feel as though you are ready to lead the country out of its greatest turmoil. In your seventies and eighties, you stop thinking about aging because you have become immortal, and your wife will be a goddess. Just beware of the arrogance, impatience, and selfishness of a trophy.

As you mature, gather the clues and the facts of the finer qualities of woman. Your school years are your practice arenas to familiarize yourself with what to expect in the many varieties of feminine behavior, in order to determine the kind of woman you will be spending the rest of her life with. Over all, there are two choices: The selfish, uncaring haughty with the nasty disposition whom will spend your wealth irresponsibly, or the reserved, selfless, virtuous, potentialist, whom will have great faith in you, and follow you to the ends of the earth.

If she is a glory seeker, then she is not a potential companion, but a competitor. Remember, men are fools and women are stupid. As harsh as that may sound, makes you wonder why we even allow homosexuals relationships to exist in our culture. A good wife makes her man wise and righteous, and a good man makes his wife infallible. Both cancel out each other's flaws. A good wife compliments her man. Holds her own in conversation, but not at the expense of her man's pride and dignity. A wife makes her man look good, but she can only do this if he is 100% faithful. Cheat on her, and she loses that grandeur that makes a wife delightful to that, which is man. She loses credibility, for infidelity never remains a secret for very long. The man that never cheats is admired, and even envied by his peers. Over time, he becomes incorruptible, and she becomes the star of the community.

CHAPTER 4

Why can't a woman dominate your setting? She is not bringing her ideas to your setting. She is bringing another man's ideas to your setting. Whether that other man be her father or a relative or a man she dated; the potential of trying to mold you into something of her previous experience is always there. She had a great time with her previous boyfriend, and, so, she tries to mold you into what he was. Make you into a carbon copy of that other guy whom rocked her world in the bedroom. Some guys try to adapt, but the reality is, you can only be who you are. Nevertheless, she will distance herself from you, until one day she is gone; and due to you being, so, obliging, you do not realize that your ability to be yourself is also gone. Though she is gone, you continue to make yourself into something that you cannot hope to maintain. Got news for you. No man can sustain being the other guy. Now, withal said, factor in the premarital sexual intercourse, and you have yet another understanding of why a female is a slut and a man is not.

You must learn to make your own decisions, and avoid undue influence because everyone has an opinion, and those opinions may conflict with your ideas, and beliefs of a good woman. Do not allow Hollywood to influence your decision on your choice of direction in life or your choice of what you perceive to be an ideal woman. It is an institution of illusion; nothing is real, not even the people whom work for it. Everything about it is a lie. Hollywood's goal is to put into your mind that, which is an abomination to the Lord, and justify its practice as legitimate. Gone are the days of creativity and obedience to the finer points of life. It is, perhaps, even the very source of secularism. Examine American History. Hollywood and secularism have grown hand-n-hand since the early Twentieth. Religious creativity withstanding, the Hollywood machine is countering moral values in this day and age of the early Twenty-first, and the country is growing sicker for it.

CHAPTER 5

For you; the man whom feels that his stature would be less than appreciable in the eyes of a woman whom he views as a goddess, do not despair. Your first impression must be confidence. In a woman's eyes in regards to us; the male of the species, she is superficial; quite trivial in regards to our being. There are just two sides to a male; attractive and unattractive, and in truth, women treat different sized men differently. Now, be mindful that unattractive does not mean you are ugly, but simply someone whom does not meet her physical standards. On the other hand, let us examine ourselves as males. Yes; we behave the exact same way as she. When we; the male, have a choice between the exotic, erotic female, and the plain looking female, we will pursue the former without consideration that she is simply bolder than the other, revealing a tell about herself from the onset. That is because; as previously mentioned, a woman does not have to work hard to make herself attractive. She is born as such, but she does work hard to make herself sexy because she is what makes sexual interaction work. There are also those whom are athletic, making themselves into Amazonians, of which, they will more than likely decline the offer of a relationship. To include even if you; the male, whom possess an excellent stature. In any event, her figure may play a factor, but the reality is we want a woman whom has; not necessarily a big booty and breasts, but pep in her step, and the long flowing hair is a plus.

306

The same has to be said of the opposite end of the spectrum. No matter her height, she wants a go-getter, she wants energy; she wants a man whom pursues life. Express negative emotions and you greatly cut your odds at gaining her favor. Your introduction must reflect confidence because she is viewing you as unsubstantial. No pickup lines. No gimmicks, and especially no lies. Just flat out, block-to-block confidence is all that you need. Now, if she rejects you right out, that's okay; however, beware that she is more than likely prejudice. Yes; stature prejudice is a very real thing in the case of a male, and there is a serious danger to this kind of female. Should you happen to land a trophy, she, whom initially rejected you will run interference, spread rumors. She will do everything in her power to turn your prospect against you. That's the prejudice at work. You are an inferior male, and not entitled to prime stock. Especially if your beauty queen's looks are comparable to hers. This works on your behalf on the basis that if your love interest is not suspicious of the other, then she is not worth your time; however, she does have a right to be cautious of you. Additionally; she whom had rejected you initially, is living with the thought of having made a mistake. Remember, this author mentioning females not wanting to be alone in their mistakes? If she can convince subsequent females to reject you, then she feels better about her choice due to her refusal to accept the fact that she makes poor choices when trying to live up to the feminist hype.

CHAPTER 6

Do not affix your eyes on any specific female or limit yourself strictly by race or physique. Do not allow yourself to be deceived by a fine figure. Just because a woman has an hourglass figure does not mean you want an hourglass mind. Stay away from *street* for after she opens her mouth for the first time in front of others you will find yourself without an invitation to social gatherings that are a necessary resource towards the success of your house. Watch out for, *mouth!* There is nothing worse than a woman whom just never shuts up; constantly interrupts a conversation, changes the topic of discussions, bitches constantly, and loudly. These are women whom want it all their own way. They can never be satisfied because they spend their entire life searching for something to complain about instead of relishing what they already have. Avoid them like the plague for they are selfish, vain and indignant, and they will make you wish that you were a soldier fighting on a nuclear/biological battlefield.

Look for the attentive female whom cautiously eases herself into the relationship. Do not rush it because this is her comfort level, and she must feel as though she is making a proper decision in regards to a man. A female whom will not agree with everything you say, but at the same time, will not make you feel like the enemy of the world. There is a fine line between saying the right things to ease your burdens, raise your spirits, and leaving you in a state of despair. Amity requires a certain level of skill that cannot be taught to a woman, but must be nurtured. All females are born with this quality. Pay close attention to her mannerisms; the type and level of cosmetics she wears. Lots of makeup denotes something to hide. All women are sexy, and many of them just don't know it. Amazing the effect of cosmetics on a naïve, homely looking girl. Over time, she will experience a boost in confidence, and come to see her beauty in all its fruition, and learn to use it, to arrest power for herself. For there is nothing wrong with a female having power, but she must earn it, not demand it. That old adage of; it must be given, not taken, applies more, so, in the case of gender interaction; and yes, you do want her to control you, but in a passionate way. She is taking control of you by means of doing those little things that mothers do; straightening your collar before you leave for the day. Gently blowing out whatever is in your eye. Saying the right words when no words are needed. Have dinner hot and ready when you step through the door after a hard day's work. Kiss away the tension. Be there for you when all of your family and friends have abandoned you. Talks to you about nothing when you are bored. Wants to hang out with you on those hot summer days of boredom, and make snow angels with you during the cold winter storm. Drapes that long flowing hair across your bear chest on those hot steamy nights, and says; *I love you* when you are not in the mood for that mushy stuff.

Play the wild little nymph when your mind is elsewhere. Do those mundane things that you would normally take for granted. Make you feel tingly inside when you are trying to be serious. Nurse you when you feel rundown in years. Give you purpose to live. All in regards to your overall mental aptitude.

There is absolutely no restrictions to her nature if she, so, chooses. She may apply it to animals, people, even a chair. To whatever means necessary to draw out happiness from herself and others. She will do anything to see this through; however, she may have established a threshold for herself. So, you must be aware of the female whom has not established a threshold. She does not have a clear perception of the people she is dealing with around her or she may run interference or cause delays in the agendas you have set forth. She is simply naïve. Be prepared for this when looking for that special female. She; whom has no pleasing threshold, can be personally beneficial, but you must guard her with your life. For there is absolutely nothing better than a woman whom can make you feel as though your body has been loaded with pain killers, and stimulants, while sitting in a warm whirlpool bath. She can be the greatest drug if properly handled, and not abused. Sound familiar? Consider the following; drugs have a shelf life, and some are inert right out of the bottle. So, make sure you shop carefully for the right girl.

A key characteristic that you are searching for in a female is a craving to feel needed. Someone whom is searching for purpose. A female to your heart's desire. What is the purpose that she is searching for? A willingness to follow along the guidelines you set down when determining direction for yourself. A prospect must adapt to your needs, not the other way around. For a relationship to work, she must be prepared to make you the center of attention, not second guess your every move. Young females have absolutely no problem adapting to your needs based on the reality of realizing their purpose. A good girl wants to be submissive to you; adhere to you; adapt to your wants and needs. She wants to please you. Be a part of your life. It is a female's nature to please, comfort, and to be caring. To be with you. To share life with you. To do for you; the apparent suitor seeking marriage. To guard your immortality. For that is extremely important to you. What is your immortality? Your children. Specifically, your male children. For it is they whom pass on the breath of life. You continue to exist in this world through your children. Therefore, you want breeding stock because your goal is to become a patriarch. You want to be able to say: *Those are my five sons, and I am proud of them.* That's why it is, so, important that your children, especially your boys be raised accordingly; and to do that, a trust worthy mother is necessary. Your children, whether they be boys, girls or a mixture of both, reflect yourself; not the teen babysitter, daycare service provider or the occasional family member or the available friend to assist you with childcare. Your way of doing things are imprinted onto your children, and are the very basic ingredients of government. Naturally she; whom you have chosen to be wife, will superimpose details from her own ancestral experiences upon your immortality in order to enhance your legacy. Your family's ingredients combined with her family's ingredients to improve upon the original formula and structure. Resulting in an improvement on the previous generation. Something new.

Another feature to look for in a female; is if she knows when to be a child, and when to be an adult. Not for your children's sake, but for yours. When to be a harlot, and when to be a lover, in order to diversify the intimacy, and further stimulate your senses. This is not a bad thing. It is simply those little idiosyncrasies of the flesh that keeps life interesting. She needs to know when to be cruel, and when to be kind. For this author does not know a man whom does not need a good slap on the face to wake him up to reality. For we men, can be easily caught up in unrealistic expectations. Finally; and most important of all, she must know how to apply your religious beliefs without sounding like a minister, and to never diverge from it, no matter the case.

Once you find that submissive female you must clientele to her needs because it is those needs that make her submissive to begin with. Furthermore; love is not something to be toyed with like some pornographic skit. It is a fine art form that is delightful; pleasurable to the senses. A respectful medium to the feminine being, resulting in maximizing the masculine complex. In other words; her ability to bestow pleasure thrills you to the point of freely surrendering your independence in order to propagate the species; guaranteeing your immortality. A thing that is never to be rushed; always slow going because she; the female of the species is such a complex creature. You; the male, must take the lead in pleasing her. Like taking her on a nature trail; you must show her all of the fine points of the unknown. The art of love must be like the witnessing of the sun rising over the ocean or the moon going through a lunar eclipse over the desert. Watching the flow of water in a brook or stormy weather from your porch. To the female of the species, love is like watching the clouds over the ocean on a warm breezy day or the city lights during the still of the night. It can be as subtle as Christmas or Easter or a walk in the park on Sunday or as lively as New Year's Eve, Halloween or a Friday night at an amusement park. With her it is always a matter of beauty in response to daily living. The actual copulation will bring joy, but it is the event before and after that will have the overwhelming effect on her thoughts. So, remember this when the clothes come off; and you will be a master of love, and the dominating force in her life. Everything she does from that point on will be for you, and no one else.

Do not be concerned over her level of education in regards to going beyond a high school degree. Nor should you apply any undue pressure should she be unwilling to pursue a degree in higher learning or seek a specific skillset. Realistically, you do like someone to ask questions, no matter how mundane those questions may be because deep down it makes you feel useful; *needed.*

Yes; this author understands that the previous sounds crazy. Makes no sense, but consider, that not all people are college material. This is not an irresponsible thing. Nor is it a shameful or bad decision. There are just people whom feel that college is not for them, and a lot of these people have incredible talent. Truth be said, we have all been conditioned into believing that you must obtain a college degree in order to succeed in life, but the reality is, that many colleges have geared themselves as nothing more than a vehicle for social fratricide with a whole lot of moral ambiguity, instead of intellectual growth. More inclined to a business venture whose intent is to motivate students into figuring out ways of finding money for them. An assembly line of sorts, not an instructional guide for making anyone an all-around better person, but altering potentials to be more of a mechanical component in the greater machine of cold needless waste. A system of placing the human organism in a discouraging loop of discontent resulting in a self-deprecating condition of hopelessness with no chance of evolving beyond the state of a muzzled ox.

Our purpose is to live life in such a way as to delight in bringing joy to others; however, there are those whom find it exhilarating to bring about misery and suffering to others. Many people are placed under a terrible financial burden just to satisfy an education system bent on greed, instead of the advancement of mankind. Yes; colleges and universities are employment sectors that require profits more than prepping a person for the truth. They need your hard-earned cash in order to stay in business. Take a good look at your life after you have a college degree. Did they really teach you anything that could not have been learned under an apprenticeship? It is about the money and perhaps even the comradely and nothing else. It has gotten, so, bad over the past thirty years or so, that a layman cannot even get a meaningful job after serving in the armed services. An institution of real hands on experience, and still many businesses require a college degree. That is what companies wanted in the old days, hands on experience and a patriotic spirit. Now, it's a matter of; *what college did you attend?* This author is just wondering how long before McDonalds requires a college degree to flip burgers?

CHAPTER 7

If you are seeking a destiny for yourself, avoid the harlot at all costs. Nature drives wives to become mothers, and when she gives you daughters, she will drive them through the same fate as hers. Your sons will waste their time and seed on frivolous pursuits retarding their minds and bodies from reaching their full potential.

Making them less of what you are. Is that the plan for your immortality? To become a social, even a communal weakling?

Avoid a miserable female. It is a sign of bad parenting, and the potential for her being a bad parent to your immortality. That is unless you feel you are capable of removing the sadness in her life.

Pay very close attention to her mother's behavior, activity and even her build. Almost always, daughters imitate their mothers in nearly every way. So, if her mother has a rotten attitude or is overweight, then you have no one to blame, but yourself when your wife behaves a certain way and/or turns into a disgusting fat-body later in life. Of course, some of you reading this, may prefer the company of a robust female, and that is okay too.

In regards to the assertive woman: Chances are, if she petitions, you will almost always accept, depending upon the woman, that is. Then again, a man whom accepts the petition of a woman is either a fool or desperate. Be mindful of the woman whom petitions you. She may be out for something more than a romantic relationship. There are lots of shady women out there, not to mention the out-and-out crazies. Do not assume for a moment that you are in control when you get involved with one, for she has her game, well-planned out. Sure, you may think that you are smarter than a woman. Society may even say, that you are smarter than a woman, but it just ain't, so. A truly intelligent woman simply lets you think, so.

- Be leery of she, whom is all party and no business. She will run your well dry.
- Look out for she, whom is trying to make herself respectable, not acceptable.
- Search for the long flowing dress. Everything else is harlotry.
- Honor, humility, and fidelity are the marks of a superior woman, not her ability to apply cosmetics.

Beware of she with a degree in higher learning. She quickly adopts rebellious attitudes. Becomes self-interested, abandoning sacrifice, and develops the one-two philosophy of not being a baby-making machine. Books dictate her behavior instead of her natural instincts. People outside of the home whom are not family will garnish her attention more than yourself in situations when you just want to do it yourself. When you step on her tail she will seek blood, and never let go.

CHAPTER 8

Never tell a woman you love her. It's your trump card for when you really screw up; and you will screw up. Besides, telling her you love her too early in a relationship is just a lie anyhow. If men truly meant it, then why do relationships end? No one falls out of love because there is no true understanding of what love is to begin with. It is a childish use of the word. Children say things they really know nothing about. They say; *give me that,* or; *let me have that.* Then once they possess it, they discard it because it wasn't what they thought it would be. There is love, and then there is lust. They are commonly confused. Most modern relationships occur through lust, and that is why they fail.

There is a tiny detail of which males tend to overlook, which could strain a bourgeoning relationship with a fine prospect if not promptly dealt with in a proper manner. Females, especially the super beauties, have a propensity for seeking excess activity. This author is not speaking of your average extrovert. No, this author is speaking of she; whom you must make an appointment with to go out on a date, and then places you on some form of time allowance. Sure, she may be very beautiful, but trust this author, you do not want to maintain a relationship by appointment. To feel as though you are being sorted in with all of the other daily routines is a recipe for emotional fallout. On the other hand, there is something about her demeanor that prevents you from acting accordingly. Then; when you finally get a little time with her, she may be a bit irritable for no expected reason; abruptly gets angry. No worries, for you have done nothing wrong; however, you may have made a

314

slight error when honing yourself into that ideal male. There is a little nuisance that plagues females on a seemingly unconscious level due to her adaptation to such a harsh and abstruse world. When her feet hurt, it is subtle, resulting in an auto reflex action to rub them. Master the art of foot massaging. In fact, learn all forms of massaging. After you have driven the stress from her feet, she will love you for an eternity because most men do not think of such things. She will not love you for relaxing her. She will love you for doing it without her having to ask. Then she more than likely will date you without an appointment.

Naturally, there are those of you whom will display yourselves in order to gain the attention of a female, and that is reasonable and completely acceptable. You are revealing to her that you possess the stamina necessary for a strong relationship. Consider also, that a strong body requires a strong mind because realistically, females do not like a mentally challenged man, though they are blind to the prospect of an unstable mind with a great physical build. It leads to violence on your part that eventually involves her or worst-case scenario; direct brutalization of her; both physically and mentally. If she is fearful of you, then you are failing at your duties at being a man. She should be comfortable around you. Once her comfort-level is met then a trust-construct can manifest itself. That trust then solidifies into a meaningful relationship, and from that point on, the sky is the limit.

CHAPTER 9

For an item heavy on the minds of the average male, and that is; do not be concerned about your sexual attributes when interacting with a woman, for some men just have it better than others. If you meet a woman who is concerned over certain physical attributes, never speak to her again. A sensible woman is unconcerned over such things. Besides, as previously mentioned a female searching for an appendage of maximum depth is preoccupied with a notion that will essentially have no meaningful social contribution. Contrary to what certain psychologists, and some doctors and even those in the entertainment industry may have you believe, copulation in a relationship is not important. What a woman wants more than anything from a man is presence; for her husband to be there to comfort her when the pain of life becomes too much. Life always becomes too much for a woman because she wants to fix the world. It is not a flaw, but in her nature to fix the hurt. When a woman loses her desire to help and to heal, she becomes more dangerous than the most hardened of criminals. There are lots of treacherous women out there, so, be extremely cautious when you date them. They will exhibit signs of kindness or something else when you date them. The tell in this case is her level of patience; avoid the *highly* impatient woman at all costs. If on your first date she is running late, that is a good sign. She more than likely is a perfectionist, and wants you to see her at her best.

CHAPTER 10

Let us take a step back to examine this thing we call submissive. In our modern sexually corrupted culture, submissive has been associated with sex. Not in, so, much a bad way, but to the feminist it would be viewed with distain in regards to the female of the species. The truth behind being submissive is nothing more than wanting to be a part of someone's life. Young minds want to go out into the world, and experience new and interesting things. Girls and young women have it programmed within them to be with a man because there is something about seeing his strength; your strength at work, that excites them. Something about being held in a man's arms that touches a certain part of them; that sends a tingling sensation throughout their bodies. What we tend to forget as men, is that loneliness impacts a woman differently than it does us. That is because we are better equipped at dealing with that, which could be perceived as a living creature. A creature that exists out of the corner of her eye. Its touch brings a cold chill over her entire body. Not the cold of a winter storm, but that of death, and for some unusual reason, only a man seems to have the ability to keep that creature at bay. That is why it is extremely important that you; the male of the species, do not take advantage of a submissive female. It is that submission that has been taken for granted; used as a means

316

of protective services rendered. When you find a female that makes you feel comfortable, you may want to consider marriage for there is nothing more pleasing then having someone whom will be there for you. For loneliness cannot be killed. It can only be kept at bay.

Oh, and let us be honest with one another; *man-to-man:* What you want as a man is a girl, not a woman, but a girl. To have pure children, you; the suitor, must have a pure wife. Again; a wife is an investment. If you are going to surrender the breath of life to a female, wouldn't you want her to be fresh and new? Female companionship should represent how you feel, not your age. All people age differently, both mentally and physically. Marriage should be based on her level of mental maturity, and the application of wisdom, not her age. Therefore; being attracted to a female whom is under twenty is not a dirty thing for a man over thirty. You possess the vitality of a boy; without; this author reminds you; the need for pharmaceutical assistance. You did a great job at taking care of yourself throughout the years, so, why not entitle yourself to certain eccentricities.

Woman; on the other hand, denotes used, harlotry, experience, over-voluptuous attributes that may or may not be artificial, and then there is the attitude. She may not be a bad person, but she shall truly put you through hell when you make a mistake. Besides, all women were children at one point in their lives. Even the vivacious ones. Should you decide to pursue a female who is in your age bracket, having never bore children, and perhaps never married; then be very careful; for an unstable sleeper will implode all that you have built. Your predecessors obviously saw something in her that you are missing. A good prospect for wife must be someone whom will not put you through the wringer over trivial matters. It is easier to fix a house that is putting you through hell than a touched-woman. For they can be your absolute worst nightmare. Besides; marry a woman whom is your age, and she will grow old right before your eyes, and when you look at that sexy teen goddess passing you on the street, what will go through your mind? Better to play it safe; marry a girl. You want to be able to say to yourself at the wedding reception; *I cannot believe she is mine* for the alternative is waking up next to a woman who reminds you of just how old you truly are.

Now, the previous statement does not presuppose that all women are harlots, and that all girls are innocent. The term girl is a state of being, to one whom feels youthful, and new to the world. It does not hold the same meaning in American culture as it does in other parts of the world; however, due in part to a confused state of mind in our twisted cultural perceptions of life and of course the influx of immigration, its understanding has resulted in a cross between what is girl and what is juvenile. Whereas the term boy is viewed with distain by a man; denoting inexperience, small-mindedness; someone whom is not to be taken seriously. Girl is more compliment than insult in regards to her, due to the reality that there are lots of women whom behave as juveniles in our society, and we refuse to acknowledge that someone's age means absolutely nothing in regards to behavior. Note: This author suspects that the reason behind, so, many juvenile adult females in our modern culture is due to the social malfunction. Simply put, birth control prevents females from experiencing motherhood at a more reasonable period in their lives, and without the institution of motherhood, these women simply remain juvenile for the better part of their lives. Even in marriage, the result is the same, leading to impatience on the side of the man and eventual divorce. Even if a female becomes a mother, she restricts herself, resulting in juvenile behavior. A female is meant to give birth to many children in order for this juvenile behavior to make sense, but instead she gives birth to one or two children. The children grow up, and the mother within is expecting more children, but there are none.

Now, the reason for the *application of wisdom* opposed to just wisdom is because we all absorb knowledge at different rates; however, the one thing that a person does not seem to grasp very well is the ability to express wisdom in such a way as to not infer some form of offense. This is perhaps why a child prodigy is not allowed to become an active part of adult social affairs. Applying wisdom properly is crucial to maintaining a trusting environment.

318

Arrogance, impudence and impatience is the biggest killer of a thriving culture, and is perhaps the first, and foremost sign of a person whom is not ready to engage in an active social environment. To say that a person who is eighteen or twenty-one years of age, whom is behaving immaturely, is ready to interact in a typical social setting is simply illogical. This author believes that we as a society place too much emphases on cold hard numbers instead of good ol' fashioned intuition and logic. We should learn to embrace our human side again, and be accepting of those whom show good qualities and proper conduct. A well-mannered child should be permitted to sit in on adult conversations. How else does someone acquire proper social skills? On the other hand, a juvenile-adult should be cast aside until they are able to arrest control of certain offensive attitudes. This adult immaturity complex may explain why we have, so, many difficulties in bureaucracy. Why greed is, so, prevalent in our modern culture of the early Twenty-first. Just because a child can pass their exams in high school, does not mean we should simply set them loose on society. Perhaps what we need is a detailed social examination to determine a child's level of maturity before handing out any form of diploma.

Yes; a mature thinking female, whom is loving and strong is what you want, not a female whom is mature in years. There are some females regarded as minors by our current social standards, whom are quite capable of handling themselves in mature social settings. The best way to determine how she handles herself in a mature social setting is how she behaves around her own family. How do they treat her; react to her; behave around her. Quiet, cheerful girls are the best because they are attempting to gather information to better integrate themselves into a more sophisticated social setting. Therefore, pay close attention to their behavior not their figure.

Yes; this author realizes that the age-difference will perhaps be of serious concern to her, but consider; is she basing your age on simply a number or your lifestyle? Interesting how an apparent apathetic female teenager will say; *you are too old for me,* of which, in all reality you are simply someone whom is; as-far-as she is concerned, of an inferior stock. Whereas, avoiding the topic of age all together in regards to he who is of a superior standing. This is the immaturity of a female. She does not understand that there is more to a relationship than physical build, and thus wields the power given to her under a secular dominated state. *I have a body built for sin, of which, gives me empowerment to seduce. The law gives me the power to be the innocent fool when suspicion about my infidelity comes into question.* Her lack of understanding the difference between what is proper and improper social conduct is telling. Resulting in dating one wrong guy after another, of which, all of whom, have scrambled brains themselves. There are the fits of rage for no apparent reason. Searching for comfort from uncertainty, and she is ignored. Being abandoned unexpectedly has a profound effect on her overall aspect of life. Her parents did not teach her what to expect of the world, and she is being caught up in a bad situation every time because the bad boys know that a little marijuana will go a long way after treating her like trash or just being a plain little whore.

In any event, an older man speaking with a younger woman is not a dirty thing. The older the male, the more appreciative the interaction. The younger the female; the more pleasurable the experience. Dialogue with one another is how people determine a state of mind. She makes great conversation. She's fun, and you enjoy her company, and what? You discover she's sixteen, and all bets are off? Look; you have chemistry, and that's what's important. I mean, come on; are you going to say, that you can identify a minor in today's sex crazed culture by looks alone? Sure; if she is ten years old or riding in a baby carriage. The reality is, girls can start to fill out at a very young age. Between thirteen and thirty it's a toss-up, and that is not speculation. The innocence of long flowing dresses, bobby-socks and saddle shoes are gone. Hence, you cannot set an exact number to physical maturity; however, our modern generation of tender morsels denote the same innocence and freshness of their contemporaries, with the gorgeousness and shapeliness of a goddess. They are a newness refusing to surrender their youthful looks well into their thirties and forties, with a fire that cannot be quenched.

Dying for some real excitement, fun, and a willingness to follow a man to the ends of the earth. Consequently, when she becomes physically attractive and her parents allow her access to fashions that extenuates her burgeoning figure, then it is only natural for all males; not just boys, but men alike to see her coming of age, and these young girls have absolutely no qualms about displaying their figure to all comers. She is in search of someone to bring a fulcrum of purpose; some meaning into her life after high school graduation. Sure; she is at the dawn of her life, but she will have an attraction for you; the older man. The time of the independent woman is waning. The old ways were not, so, bad after all, and if she plays her cards right...?

CHAPTER 11

When engaging a prospect, treat her as an adult, not as a child because she is more than likely already being treated like a child by her family, though she is trying to behave otherwise. Where you are attempting to stabilize a lifestyle, she is looking for a stable lifestyle. Your words will have a powerful effect on how she behaves. Encourage her to shed senseless, childish attitudes. At times, a person just needs someone to say; *do this instead of that;* or, *try it this way,* and they will correct themselves. Especially if that someone has taken a serious interest in them. On the same note; do not, under any circumstance apply demands, harsh attitudes or the word; *no,* during the shedding process. You do not want to lose that connection with her? So, do not sound like her peers or her parents, and regardless of the topic of discussion, do not go against her in debates of which she is clearly in error. You must learn to formulate discussion in such a way that eases her out of a subject without her realizing it.

Using psychology on a woman should be a pleasurable activity to her without the intent of bringing about personal gain through a physical means. The psychology you apply should result in happiness and cheer, not remembrances of bad moments of her past. She should never be reminded of the pain in the world. She should be delighted to be around you, not obligated. You are her protector from such things not her cultivator. You are the one whom gets wounded by the pains of life, and she mends you; sometimes on a daily basis. Of course, if she is a career woman, the mending process may take some time before it can occur on the off chance that she has been wounded and requires healing herself. You bear the brunt of the cruelty of the world, so, that she does not have too, and she mends your wounds in return. That way you have no fear to be with her when you both go out into the world.

Now, marrying a much younger female is quite logical when considering that most females do not pick up on feminist ideas until they have been mentally abused, and physically used, due to females going through their changes before reaching their teens. Some of those girls peak quickly, depending upon their lifestyle, and child rearing. Less attentive parents allow a girl's sexuality to manifest itself even in their preteen years. Usually due to a bad role-model or some form of social media dogma. Celebrities grab her attention before all else. They wear the provocative, behave immorally, and the child emulates it all, and the wild lifestyle will stay with them for a very long time. Why parents allow this to happen is because they have been focused on their careers and/or themselves more than their children. Consider; most women give birth to children out of wedlock, and those that do have children after wedlock are divorced within a few years. In any case, there is not a full-time father present to pass on the other half of the human traits. Visual entertainment media, becomes the other half of the traits, and, so, guess what?

Another point to consider is that her parents are grooming her behavior at a very young age. She is still a child, striving to be an adult. We are not looking at the juvenile. We are identifying the girl striving to prove herself as a willing participant in social affairs. The interesting point this author will make about the overall notion of maturity, is that we see parents prepping their girls all throughout society; beauty pageants, finishing schools, ballet and other art-forms and even sports. Why do parents put their girls through such rigor, if not to garnish the attention of a well-put together male? Therefore, make sure she is a well-put-together girl who is being groomed or finished. If all went well, then the only hint of her age is the awareness of the years she has been alive. Other than that, if she is polished in social conduct then her age should have no bearing in any social engagement; and in regards to alcoholic beverages; she should have an appreciation for its effects on her mind, and avoid its consumption, that is, with exception to ceremonial purposes; *of course*. Oh, and by the way; her mental hygiene is a must on the basis that you are literally placing your entire house in her hands; and to say that would be a colossal undertaking, even for an experienced woman, would be a huge understatement. So, when she is of a more mature state of mind, you want to make sure she is ready to take on the challenge of running a government; your government; your house. Naturally, possessing the capabilities of being a socialite is a big plus in regards to community affairs because a man wants to do more than retire in old age. There is more to life than just living. Success is achieved through a fine woman; that's the ticket.

Next; premarital sexual intercourse is completely off the table. This author cannot stress that enough. Yes; she stimulates you sexually, this author gets it. That's what she is supposed to do. It is built into her overall mechanism; however, fight the compulsion, for contrary to what you may think, it is not she, who is stimulating you, but the feminine culture as a whole that is stimulating. Do not tempt her, or threaten her with the idea of a break up if she persists on keeping her virginity. She is not some used automobile that you can take out for a test drive. She is a living breathing creature possessing warmth and compassion. Encourage her. Even refuse her should she want to surrender herself in the bedroom. Do not make her feel uncomfortable about her sexuality. Steer completely clear of the subject as is practicable, and yet, flatter her regularly. If you notice the topic of sex coming up often, then start preparing for marriage. Just consider that marriage before eighteen years of age is an incredible risk in our time, but not impossible. In fact, it was commonplace in our country at one time; still is, for many places. You go down that path, you had better damn-well make sure that she can handle herself in a crowd or you will surely be the ridicule of your kith and kin, let alone the friendly stranger. In second thought, just compel her to be patient and continue to develop her intellect. Another point to make is to not be critical of her physical appearance. You cannot recarve a finished sculpture or you will lose all the initial understanding of the unique beauty that is being projected, amid the cold cruel world.

What kind of clothes does she wear, and how does she wear them? This is crucial because in the case of identifying a prospect, you want to judge a book by its cover. Most females adorn the provocative outside of athletic venues. This may not necessarily be a sign of sexual availability, but more of an unwillingness to be fertilized. Prostitutes act in this way, except they do it for financial gain. Some prospects may be testing the waters. Date them. See how they carry themselves. Is she willing to open her legs for you prior to marriage? What's the point? Is she selling herself to you? Allowing a test drive before you buy? Consider what made the teenage-female, so, attractive in high school. It was not just the clothes she wore or her shapeliness, the cosmetics or the hair. Females are not unlike the elk, the deer or the antelope. The thrill of the chase is what made her attractive. The obstacles placed before you, and near misses; pursuing the girl in high school was fun because you liked the interference she threw at you; that her parents threw at you; however, once she allowed you intercourse with her, the thrill was suddenly gone. You can only get, so, many bites out of the apple before the good parts are gone. Even worse is when you can just ask for sex or hint of it, and get it. No challenge at all; basically prostitution. Men like the thrill of the hunt, not strolling through the supermarket for a piece of meat that is trust up and ready. Why would a girl want to copulate with a guy prior to marriage anyhow? Let us get complicated: There are smart females, intelligent females and flat-out stupid. Now, we men always seek the path of least resistance. Especially in regards to women. Examine our culture closely in regards to our gathering of knowledge. There was a time when men valued a smart woman for a relationship even ahead of intelligence. What is the difference, you ask? A smart woman knows that she is not highly intelligent, but that she is valuable, and not to be treated as a child. The interesting thing about intelligent women is that they lack the ability in regards to the application of smarts, of which is why, they have a tendency of falling into the realm of the mundanely stupid. Explaining why there is a certain threshold of understanding in regards to why the male must dominate, but to do, so, he must possess a certain IQ.

Another question to ask yourself is what else does she offer you? What is it that makes her unique amongst females? Note: If her only selling point is her body, she basically becomes a live-in prostitute, and since she has nothing else to offer you, then she eventually becomes a nuisance; lounging around, allowing the house to fall apart, and perhaps gaining lots of weight. Eventually as a man, you get tired of doing nothing, but spitting out your seed without a result because sticking your phallus in her body does not keep loneliness at bay. The same can be said, if all you can do is imagine her on her back or in dirty little sexual positions; then at what point will the relationship evolve? There are literally a million things you and a woman can do in the world, and all you can do is engage her in sexual intercourse? So, much sexual intercourse; in fact, that you suffer from low energy. Then you try to counter the low energy with certain substances that place you in an unnatural state of being. Remember; though your life is in your blood, your energy is in your seed. Females whom draw your seed with no beneficial result are nothing more than vampiresses, and depending upon their level of seductiveness determines how long the relationship will last, and trust this author, it will not be lasting. Therefore, avoid the non-virgin whom does not practice abstinence. For obtaining an apple that is already bitten into, makes no sense to this author.

Now, her eagerness; for example, will determine her level of maturity because sex is such a childish behavior adopted by adults. Therefore, you do not want her dressing in the nude in a casual setting; skinny jeans, yoga pants, short-shorts, etcetera. Her figure will attract the attention of other potential suitors whose words might be more pleasurable to her ears than your own. Oh, and please, do not, for one moment think you are that good; there is always someone who is better at seducing females. Remember, she is vulnerable whenever you or a guardian are not around. Tell her that she needs not show off her gluteus maximus, minimus and breasts to impress you, but reveal her intellectual abilities. In either case, if you want her to dress appropriately then you must be involved financially because her focus will be on school, and there is no bigger influence on a girl then her peers. As a suggestion; establish a small line of credit for her. That way you can examine her spending habits first hand. You will simply have to use your best judgment in this area because you may want her to dress sophisticated or simplistic. Should she possess a good disposition, then guide her eyes to more appropriate styles. The ideal woman is the one whom wears appropriate clothing regardless of the season. Minimal formfitting attire that may reveal a certain attractiveness for the intentions of family life. In any case, she will feel good about herself when she has the means to dress modestly, maturely; more responsibly. Respect is gained by how we project ourselves. When you look a certain way then you behave a certain way. She keeps herself well-groomed because being woman takes a lot of effort, and that's before she prepares herself for a day of activity. Any female is a woman, but it takes a special woman to be a refined lady. An amazing aspect of females is that they are always willing to adjust, and as an eligible bachelor, you must also be prepared to yield in some areas.

Closely examine her immediate pedigree. Though bad parents can lead to bad parenting, this does not mean she will be a bad mother. You will just have to be prepared to put in a little extra effort with helping her understand key concerns in regards to your immortality. Ideally, you want a certain refinement, a debutante, but do not assume that all debutantes are the right kind of girl. There are many choices out there, so, do not bond immediately with any specific prospect. A little awareness and common sense goes a long way. Do not put yourself in an uncompromising position or ambiguous situation. Do not lead any female on. That would be cruel and unusual punishment should your true destiny unexpectedly cross your path, and you suddenly feel a need to break it off with she whom was first to experience your desires. Your intentions, though innocent, would result in an unnecessary heartbreak for her. Simply keep your interactions to a friendly medium until you are sure, she is the one.

CHAPTER 12

Restrict your religious affiliation. This is perhaps the most vital characteristic of them all. Especially for Catholics. All Christians as a whole; *in fact.* Including females whom say they are Catholic, and yet do not practice their faith to the letter, on the basis that not all Catholics believe the same way. Not all Christians believe the same way; however, you meet a woman who is willing to convert to your understanding of the Christian celebration, then you may have a shot at a great relationship. Who knows, she may be able to teach you a thing or two about your beliefs after she finishes an RCIA class. In any event, if you happen to be Catholic, make sure that she; whom you are considering, is a *practicing* Catholic. Yes; there is a difference between a Catholic and a *practicing* Catholic. A Catholic simply goes through the motions. Whereas a practicing Catholic actually devotes themselves to the betterment of the community. If you are not Catholic yourself, but have an attraction for she who is Catholic, then take an RCIA class. You may find something that you may have been missing all of your life.

Remember, your choice will depend upon the prayer you made; that is unless you made no prayer for the perfect woman. There is nothing worse than tempting fate; *no?* You want the perfect woman, and, so, you ask God to provide you with one. Think that superstition? Consider this, you know someone who is in a rotten marriage; ask them if they asked God for the perfect woman. Think of it this way; can't hurt to try, and no one will be the wiser. Oh, and just for the record, ask Him like a poor man playing the lottery because when you receive her, it will be like winning the jackpot, and you are not looking for anything less than six numbers.

At this point, you are asking the question of why shouldn't I marry outside of my religious affiliation? The Church calls this practice of marrying outside of your religious affiliation; mixed marriage. When you marry a woman, whose beliefs are different from your own, there will be a conflict of religious philosophies resulting in

327

the surrendering of your prodigy to a different course of religious understanding than what was intended by your forefathers. Or you hold fast to your religious convictions and compel your prodigy to make a choice later in life, which will more than likely be your wife's religious practices. Quite a few Catholics have faded away due to this choice. They became lost because they did not receive the necessary religious training to maintain a tight hold of their side of the mountain. A term known as cradle Catholic. Only the Church has a tried and true method for properly traversing the mountain. You would deny this to your prodigy on the basis of a fine figure and a beautiful face? Think about your children before you allow yourself to be seduced by the hot bodied non-Catholic girl. Part of your duty as a potential Catholic father is to maintain Catholic tradition. You owe that to your fathers, not to your wife. Furthermore, she will be looking for answers to certain questions in matters of faith and life, and you had better have those answers because she will be putting herself in your hands. She will want to know that should she fall, will you be there to catch her. Faith is what a relationship is built upon, not sex. Besides; with you in her life there is a chance she will not be used and abused, for someone else may not be respectable with her as you would. Just remember one thing; do not abuse the privilege. You may find yourself without power and stamina at any time.

CHAPTER 13

Naturally there are people whom will view the notion of pursuing a much younger female as obscene, and strenuously object to such a venture. Why is that? The answer is because we live in such a highly provocative environment. We assume that the attraction must be solely sexual in nature resulting in eventual copulation, and depending upon how she behaves, and her choice of attire, that may be true. Keeping the relationship secret is an option; however, making it known to her parents that you have established some form of liaison would be in your best interest; besides, there is no law that would prevent you; the suitor, from making arrangements of guarantee with the parents of a minor. Hence, make one with her and her family. Yes; sounds completely absurd, but making marital arrangements was common place in the days of antiquity and all, but forgotten in the United States of America. That is until money comes into play. Knowing that she will not be caught in the vacuum of a twisted culture is a refreshing notion for any parent. Also consider that many of you reading this trust your daughters to make many adult decisions, and choosing to accept a proposal is not an invitation to allow him copulation. Therefore, when you; the suitor identifies an ideal companion your intent should _not_ be sexual in nature, but compatibility. It is not, so, much a woman with brains that you want, but good dialogue. You want a woman who can make good conversation, and girls make great listeners too. You want a woman who can seduce you with words then sooth you with touch. Again, do not pursue her for sexual intercourse. This author cannot emphasize that enough because the first thing that will attract you is her figure, of which she will be displaying like a new car on the showroom floor. This is not her fault, but simply our current social standard. Again, a female is your greatest investment, so, you must be extremely careful. You want someone who is capable of keeping you company, not keeping your erection. Your goal is a lifelong caring companion, not a sexual triviality; a temporary mating ritual like the beasts of the wild. Marriage, divorce and marriage again like some high school thing. This is incorrect thinking. Marriage, especially for Catholics is huge. That is why, so, much emphasis is placed on the actually ceremony itself. The Church wants the couple to understand that marriage in its true nature and usage is a serious affair in regards to a logical relationship, and is not meant to be trivialized. Therefore, make sure that your choice is compatible with your ideas and goals in life. That way your children; presumably more than two, will have a fiery young ma and a wise ol' pa as a source of proper mental nourishment. One parent of youth and one parent of wisdom and experience is how the team works in order to cultivate productive law-abiding citizens.

Should the parents be accepting of you, be prepared for certain rules and conditions during the courtship. They have that right to implement such things until the wedding day. Oh, and just as a side note: Since your future wife will likely be much younger than yourself, her parents will want to know that she is safe and secure. Do not shelter her from them. Remember your scripture; it is you whom will cleave to a wife. Ergo, you more than likely will be in her family's domain. This will work to your benefit in the long run. Next, she will make mistakes. Her focus will be on your children, so, do not expect perfection, and make sure you bestow that same sense of empathy on her. She needs only be caring and mindful of her setting. Make sure you pay attention to the little things. This is very important to her. She likes to know that you are paying attention to her because as previously mentioned, females see the details in life, and from her point of view, the little things she does, appear as giant high-rises in Manhattan. Treat every moment as though it was your first time with her, especially in moments of love-play. Ideally, you want every attempt at conception to be a honeymoon. Take her to a distinct destination to impregnate her. Her psychological well-being is your responsibility. If she is not straight in the head, then your children; especially your daughters will be unstable in the mind. Nothing worse than a house full of crazy women. They will turn your man-child into one of them, and you may find his behavior just a little too feminine for your tastes in regards to your immortality. Most importantly; get off the smart-phone craze. It will interfere with *natural* social development of your house. Not a suggestion by this author, but a necessity.

CHAPTER 14

Now; this author is willing to bet, that you; the reader, are asking; *why marry a female, so, young?* Why not? Realistically, you can go younger. Twelve or thirteen years of age is the best period for reproduction; however, there is more to the reproductive process than pregnancy. Females must have a high mental state of being and a clear perception of life itself. This has nothing to do with academics, but more of communal harmony. Raging hormones, may result in mood swings, emotional dilemmas and an influx of over-eagerness and rebelliousness. All of which, may send the wrong signal. By the age of 18 you will be dealing with a hardened foundation of ideas that may conflict with your needs, but interestingly enough, she will still be manageable because all girls look for some form of social stability. Usually, after their first year of college, feminist ideas have taken root, and the potential for defiance against you becomes a serious risk. Of course, this author could simply say; girls are losing their virginity at an astoundingly early age for various reasons. The reality is, lack of proper supervision or concern by a sex-crazed culture bent on the idea that has become the dominate sexual shoal of idealism: *Girls will eventually allow sexual intercourse, so, just accept it.* Building brain matter was the key to the allowance of such a young girl to be a mother. She maybe precocious or she is simply ready to take on motherly responsibilities, and should she meet the right man...?

On the other hand, when a girl knows she has someone waiting in the wings, she will behave differently. She will have a greater sense of pride, develop good social conduct, and strengthen her moral objectivity. She will make it a point of avoiding the sexual charlatans. Staving off her *sexual rite* of passage will give her a greater sense of responsibility and expectation. Treat her as an adult, and she will behave as an adult. Do not think; for one moment, that you can go out, and play at your leisure. You must assume that she has eyes in the least likely of places. Continue with the construction of your house, for you will need a sturdy income to support her ego, and among other things, her beauty-needs. For what she does to capture your attention and keep your interest is an illusion. The illusion of extreme youth and beauty; however, beauty is superficial. Again; do not focus on a prospect's physical appearance. Though she may not look like Miss Universe, the question you have to ask yourself; does Miss Universe truly look like Miss Universe when she is not made over? A female's words; what she says, and how she says them are what truly makes her beautiful. If you happen to meet a girl who is plain looking and still eye-catching, consider yourself lucky, for you will not wake up surprised on the day after your wedding night, contemplating, gnawing your arm off at the shoulder, while she is still asleep.

Now, considering all sides; you want that illusion she provides. It is what motivates you. Gives you; the male, purpose in life. Your job may be the worst sort of job out there, but when you marry the right kind of woman. The kind of woman that provides you with the illusion, then there is no hardship you cannot endure, but there is a catch. If you want the illusion to continue, you must pay for it. For when she was under daddy's roof, he assumed her debt of illusion. Now, you are her daddy, and you must provide her with the necessary implements and resources to maintain that illusion. Oh, and making her go out and get a job to pay for the illusion is not an option, because one; she is exposed to others, and she may prefer their attention over yours. Two; it takes time to prepare the illusion, and she must have that time in order to give you what you want. A rush job is what harlots do. Your wife is not a harlot, so, do not shorthand her. Three; she deserves it. This is why you wait until you pursue a relationship, in order to learn to understand a woman's needs, and that she is a significant investment. Besides, by that time in your life, you should have enough money to support three wives and at least ten children. If you do not, then you have failed at achieving your financial goal in life. Usually the result of a habit. The number one habit is of course sexual pursuits, the second is drugs, and alcohol of which for all intents and purposes are the same. Third, are toys; the sweet car, or some other form of gadget. Again, do not rush to financial success, or you will lose in the long run, and when you are searching for that special girl, make sure she is willing to adapt to your needs and that she is mentally and physically intact. That way, if you do not have a million dollars in your pocket, she will make you feel like you do. For it is the woman whom makes the man, not the other way around.

CHAPTER 15

Do not completely forsake the female older than the suggested age. There are chances of conflicting notions. For these females have been used to the extent of having a twisted perception on life, and relationships; however, there are ripe tender apples in their ranks also, including those in college as well. Oh, and by the way; older woman in this case denotes a female who is in her twenties. More than likely, they unwittingly submitted to a worthless male, and are going through psychological changes. Amid all of the junk and noise, they are trying to come to grips with themselves; why they did it to begin with. Why they did it with that particular guy. What are the feelings within, that makes handling themselves, so, difficult. In other words, there are just some females whom have a big heart, and do not understand the world around them; human behavior in general. Most importantly, the meaning of the word; *no,* or perhaps they are simply ignorant to the kind of men whom roam the world. Note: This is a result of naïve mothers whom lead by example, but do not have a clear perception on how to finish detailing certain aspects of human behavior. This is what happens when independent ideas set into women whom are meant to be a part of a group. Whom look out for one another in the herd. Not fool proof, but nonetheless safer than being alone. A regretful woman can be a very valuable asset to your house. If you sense a good quality about her, then go for it. A woman who has been taken advantage of, can be beneficial to your future daughter. Not to mention that she will have a strong constitution against those men whom prefer the company of married women. Just remember, they are a higher risk factor. Also, most college girls usually limit their birthing skills to two children. To have an effective first level government, four or more would be ideal.

CHAPTER 16

Okay, more than likely, most of you are asking; *why am I going to wait until I am in my mid to late thirties to seek a female? Why would any man or boy for that matter want to avoid the hot passionate breath of a beautiful female for, so, long?* The answer is quite simple, really. Though you think that you are at the peak of life when you are hitting your early teens; in fact, you are furthest from it. Forget that your entire body is still developing. The reason for waiting until your later years to become sexually involved is due to your mental outlook. You are still going through crucial social adaptations. Making key

333

improvements to your interactive skills. We; men, will discover certain truths not taught to us during childhood development. Such as patience because crucial opportunities are extremely brief. A greater sense of time management, and most notably, furthering insight into the fine art of basic communication. When coming to grips with the first three, you discover that she begins adapting to you, growing, learning, changing; however, her adaptation is finite. In your early years, you make changes to what life throws at you; constantly changing your mind; usually in the most mundane of circumstances, and more than likely due to frustration. Establishing a relationship during this point in your life is burdensome to her, and as the two of you grow older, she becomes frustrated with your constant changes. In time you make excuses, which eventually leads to divorce because part of your later years involves learning a greater perception of human perseverance. Your wife adapted as best she could, but she was geared to what you were; rather than you became. Like going back to college for a completely different career, but with one huge difference. She is no longer your ideal woman, both physically and mentally. You broke her with your constant changing and shifting of your perceptions of life when trying to find yourself. Then you either seek out the other woman or another woman usually, much younger than yourself, whom can adapt to your newfound stable lifestyle. Of which, in any case, you; the man, requires what is termed as a trophy-wife. Funny how in most cases it was that first wife or what we now, term as; *starter-wife,* whom helped you find yourself. Of course, no human being can learn everything during their growing years; however, there are certain details that must be discovered through life's experiences to avoid the complications in a bourgeoning awareness to life. A lot of this has to do with interaction with others; different ethnic backgrounds, beliefs, ideas, and in due time, an appreciation for woman. Let us be realistic; from adolescence to your early twenties are your years of religious education. History, culture, philosophy, *classical* music and literature all piggyback on this understanding, in order to develop a greater sense of patriotism that will help maintain what it means to be, not just an American, but to be alive.

CHAPTER 17

A note for those in the military; life can be lonely at times. Do not subject a woman to that loneliness. Roles are reversed in the military. You; the man, are clambered together in a crowd, and she; who is to be communal, is alone. It is unnatural for a woman to be alone; without the company of close, familiar, compassionate relationships. She is meant to be in a group setting. It is nerve racking, and it may lead to mental instability, unnecessary pain, especially if you are the kind of man whom loves the company of females. Until she starts bearing children, she will be on the brink of disaster. So, remain single in your military years. Remember, 20 years is the length of time for the average military career. That places you at the prime marrying age for a young spirited female. You should have foundation, a good investment portfolio, logic and skill to handle a squad of troops; and with your experience, a good job in the civilian sector. Trust this author; there are lots of mid-to-late teenage, and even girls in their early twenties waiting for a guy like you. You will have a new insight and appreciation for them. They will be far more beautiful than those from your preretirement years. Many of these girls will reject you, and that is okay, for it is their right. They are simply not ready for true romance. Do not restrict yourself either. On that rare occasion where the girl is a bit young, again, work a deal with her parents. If they tell you to beat it, then leave and continue your search. Again, it is illegal for you to copulate with a minor, not conduct a conversation. If she does not act or look like a child then make your intentions clear. It is her naïveté that places her in the ranks of the minor because we all know that even an adult female can be naïve, and in some cases very immature. Again-and-again, we live in a lazy society that determines maturity by a number, not conduct. Many young girls striving to be adults hate to be locked into an immature situation. Young girls learn fast at what it means to be an adult, and many of them have an overabundance of patience, so, why let that go to waste on an ignorant society. When you find

335

a young girl, who wants you, she will be of a mature state of mind capable of balancing you out. Her parents may hate you with every fiber of their being, don't worry, they will become your biggest allies on either your tenth wedding anniversary or when they see their daughter is happy, safe and secure.

Again, life does not end at high school graduation. It does not end on your 21st birthday. It does not end when you turn 30. Wait; and you just get better and smoother in your approach to life. Girls like guys whom have their *life* together, and can bring about a diversified joyful experience and pleasure. Therefore, get a grasp on your patience, and an RSV and CCC and avoid constant heavy drink and the promiscuous women. Keep yourself fit and trim, and focus your money towards the children you do not have, and you will be amazed at how long you will keep your youth. You will be the greatest ruler this nation has ever known, even though it may not know of your existence. You won't be decrepit for many years, which means a woman your age will not cut it. Get a teenager. Lots of them are looking for a Ward Cleaver, trust this author. These young women are ready to be matriarchs, and want to share in that youth you are still experiencing.

CHAPTER 18

Okay; we've covered the ideal female. You have identified her, and you are sure she is the one for you. Then obviously your next question is how does a man over 30 approach a child; a minor; a little girl without appearing like some weak pathetic fool? Note: You more than likely will run into a prospect at some form of social gathering or event, and it will be a chance meeting because chance meetings anywhere else will be dubious; suspect, but not necessarily impossible. You are an adult male, and there are few venues where adults and young teens actually cross paths in such a way as to notice one another, other than some form of social gathering, whether formal or informal, but you are also an eligible bachelor, and she is seeking her heart's desire.

Now, to answer the question of approaching she; who is not considered an adult. The answer is simple; you don't. It is she whom decides to enact some form of meet and greet. Okay, so, how do you gain the favor of a prospect? First, you need a lure; make yourself attractive in her eyes. Note: Even if you happen to be that guy born to attract females; in fact, especially for you: Wait, so, that you will be that more appealing. This is selling power; star appeal; star power, the thing that makes you exciting in the eyes of a girl. You must have it or you will be nothing more than another average guy. Oh, sure, you have the occasional female who says that having star power is unimportant, but consider this as a man. That same female will never place her full confidence in you. For you do not display the qualities of competence in complicated matters. She will be expecting you to fail, so, that she can pick up the pieces, and take control of your life. Therefore, yes; your star power is your lure, and you must have a lure in order to prevent yourself from appearing desperate; placing yourself in a desperate uncompromising situation.

If things are going according to plan, then place yourself in a tandem orbit with her. How does that orbital process begin? An interested female will use some form of body-language; a smile, constant glances, twirling of the hair. Whatever the case, she will signal you in some way to say something to her. Express the usual introduction. No need for a pickup line. Clever words are for those females whom have no interest. Oh, and by the way, while making conversation, pay close attention to her tone of voice. It must flow smoothly to your ears in a seductive manner. Regardless of how high or low, she must know how to use her voice effectively in order to enact a stimulating response. Possessing you without dominating you is the name of the game.

If all is working out, then your orbit will begin to slowly decay, by means of her consistent conversation with you, but on a somewhat discreet level. Just as you have lured her, she wants to hook you, for other girls are interested too and the competition is stiff. Ideally, she will make her intentions clear through her parents; however, good parents will already know she has an interest. They will be extremely cautious of you, clearly on the basis that they may be your age or near it to say the least. Even more difficult is if they already know you. Which means, if there is ever a moment when you do not want to rush things, and that is when solidifying your relationship with her parents. Considering that her parents will be a part of the relationship equation, if she is unable to communicate with them, then that would be a serious deficiency, and make for a difficult courting ritual. Do not rush getting to know her. For you are the popular bachelor that everyone wants to be friends with, and you come off as being the next great American icon since JFK. People are saying; there is something about you that is different. Therefore, after building a bridge with her father, allow her to instigate your relationship with him. Though being cautious, a good father will want to know that you are honorable; however, be mindful of the mother. For she too is observing. Preparing to hit you with an unexpected broadside should you, misstep, and she will hit you hard, should you be less than appealing in her eyes. Win the mother, and success is assured, but do not grow overconfident. Keep your ego under control because deep down they are hoping she will come to her senses. If you are feeling uneasy about the situation, then you may want to make yourself scarce, but beware that your sudden departure may have an adverse effect on her because her confidence is high when expressing her attraction for you. Parents should allow her to get her feet wet. That way she is able to build consensus between males whom are fully developed mentally, and those whom are still under psychological construction. The interesting thing about that process is that if the adult male is behaving like a teenager, then she knows he is bad news. Should her parents prevent her from developing good social skills, she will become sheltered and afraid or the worst-case scenario; desperate for appreciation. The one thing parents do not want is a daughter lacking confidence, for there will be moments when she will have to deal with the; *yes;* social assholes. *Pardon the expletive.*

As time passes, you; the suitor, will become her logic and reason. Her source for what is moral and proper. Thus, you must be pure of heart, or reasonably speaking, better than average, and strive to be without sin as humanly attainable. Get serious, and say to her; *I*

338

would like you to share in my life experiences, or something along those lines. Should you have something better, and your intentions are honorable, then use it. After that, simply be yourself. Do something interesting with her, that you know a lot about, and go from there, but remember, she is female, and, so, you must approach her from a point of beauty and happiness because that is what she wants. To simply be happy. Even if she falls into a mud puddle, she will be happy, and that is all she really craves, and that is all that should matter to you.

CHAPTER 19

Should the decaying process not occur, then allow the orbits to simply spiral away from one another. That way, if things do not work out, then there is no loss of pride, dignity or respect to either of you. Remember, you are searching for submissive. You want to know if she is truly interested in adapting to your lifestyle without committing yourself to something more serious at the onset of the meeting. There is no happy medium. It's your way or no way at all. Although, friendships are always a great alternative. Especially if you should ever need a little feminine advice. By the way; there is another aspect of first contact situations that you must be aware of; and that is kind rejection. Move on because obsession can lead to disaster. Her inner mother maybe trying to protect you from what you cannot see. Besides, beautiful females are as numerous as the lines on every roadway in America; however, finding the line that will suit your needs is next to impossible, for you have a habit of riding the fast lane more often than not, limiting your sight distance.

Another point to consider is that not all females are marrying material, though they believe they are. It is up to you to choose wisely. Many females are mindless whores bent on displaying their physical attributes with no intent at being a passionate caring helper. You meet the proper woman, but pass her up for the wild obstate girl with the oversized breasts and glutes that may not have been a part of her natural development. We men like the bad girl because we prefer the lie over the truth. Everything about her is a contradiction to logic and reason. She comes at you with a cool and calm, erotic

339

and exotic tone of voice. Eyes like a hungry leopard. Bad girls do things to you that makes you feel good. Those are your selfish desires in action. It is you whom should be satisfying the woman. You want the submissive woman, not the bossy bitch. You already have enough to contend with when you go to work. Why do you want to compound your burdens when you're at home? Marry a witch and you will beg for death. Find a submissive female and serve her well, and you will conquer the world in the end. For there is no greater feeling than a woman who believes in you.

CHAPTER 20

There is an interesting point to make about relationships that we take for granted. An oddity to the whole scenario of dating, and that is; attracting a prospect, and keeping her interest. Once attracting her, you must hold her attention. Now, it is easy to attract, but difficult to keep interest, and like all things in life as with a relationship with a female, there is a grace period. The proper woman requires much. How do you keep your prospect interested? Go, go, go is the secret. You are a mature adult, and you have seen and done many things; the Amazon Rainforest, India, Arctic glaciers, Rome. Withal that you have done, there is absolutely no way you can mess this up. A keen sense of awareness is key. She more than likely has done the teen things, and the adult venues are limited; however, you must consider mature locations when dating her.

Naturally, the biggest concern on a woman's mind is devotion. That is perhaps the most difficult thing for a man; even in regards to God. You are a creature with animal instincts; one male for the herd. Now, unfortunately, most men behave as animals; make children with multiple females, and then move on. Can a man whom behaves as such, be called human? Just because someone looks human does not mean they are human. Should these human-looking animals be entitled to the same rights as a person whom behaves like a human? If a monster movie trailer portrays you as the monster then why spend the money to go see it? Something to keep in the back of your mind when examining our social welfare. That is why religion is male orientated with a male deity. To stave off those animal instincts in

340

order to evolve into a more civilized creature in such a primitive environment. Woman is dependent upon that civilized environment to prevent her from being harmed by the unforeseeable. For it is difficult being a civilized woman, and concerning herself with the wilds of nature can interfere with that process.

Once you get past that grace period, then it is simply a matter of being faithful; that is all she truly desires from you; however, if you should choose to be a philanderer, then you have pretty much screwed it up. Should you remain faithful, and you are having fun with her, then you have gotten past that grace period, and you can look forward to a life-long relationship with her.

CHAPTER 21

Let us briefly touch on the subject of what it means to be human. A lot of you are more than likely taking offense to this author's previous scribing in regard to people not being human. Believe it or not, the rules for being human have already been established. We are creatures that move about, never staying in one place for very long. Never taking in the same smells, the same sights, the same sounds, tastes and touches. Always, changing, adapting, moving. Doubt this author? Lock yourself in a small room and wait for the result. Not just on a psychological level, but on a physical level as well. The human body does not like to be confined in a repetitive lifestyle. Something to think about in regards to a caged animal. Life needs room to exist. Needs change. Something new to look at. Contrast between us and the beasts of the wild is that they like to be familiar with their territory, even during periods of migration. We; humans, like to experience the unfamiliar. Again; part of the evolutionary process of growing and adapting to an everchanging world. Of which explains why we have not died out. We thrive off change, and if nature does not change then we will more than likely become extinct. An interesting hypothesis would be; could cancer be a result of the body not changing things up?

Whatever you do; no, nightspots, unless it is a place that is simply out of this world. If you want to do the nightlife with her from time-to-time, then go to places far from home, where you can carouse with new and interesting people. Such as France or Istanbul. Whatever, you decide to do, just don't bore her. After you see a movie with her, ask her what she thought of it. Do not let her off with a; *it was good,* routine. Get her in an out-n-out discussion of the details. Keep the movie exciting after the fact. This author's personal favorite for a regular attraction is the symphony orchestra. Why? You know the musicians are doing more than generating a sound, but feeling the natural emotion of being alive. Think about what you get for your money when you attend a modern musical performance by your favorite celebrity. Lip-synced burlesque? Guess a lot of people like to be distracted by the half-nude dancers on stage. Personally, for this author; if he is going to shell out his hard-earned money for entertainment, then the music had better be live because strippers do pretty much the same thing to music, and they are not singing either. On the other hand, her parents may have already taken her to see a symphony orchestra; however, attending one with someone intimate is a different experience for her. It lets her know that she will do the familiar with you.

CHAPTER 22

So, your relationship has reached its peak. She is eighteen and the time has come for you to take it to the next level. You propose, she accepts, and you are on your way to a new life.

True marriage is more than puppy love. Both of you are saying that you are ready to make a meaningful contribution to the community. That is why marriage is more than a contract, but a binding oath. An oath only carries meaning when enforced by that, which is supernatural. When you lack religious principles, then marriage has no meaning, and neither does testifying in a court of law. Something you would have to do when ending the marriage.

Now, you are just going to love this next suggestion. You; the man, should not partake in a bachelor party. Bachelor parties are a joke. Whoever the jerk was that invented the bachelor party had to be in league with the fallen one; if not the fallen one himself. It makes absolutely no sense whatsoever to go out and frolic with harlots, wenches, hoes; women, whose whole purpose in life is to get a guy

342

or guys to make the wrong choice. Oh, and please do not make the excuse that it is a way to determine if the groom is ready to settle down with just one woman. Consider for a moment, that most; if not all adult women in the United States of America are promiscuous in some way. Infrequent or blatant withstanding; they have been with multiple men. You yourself have also engaged in premarital sexual intercourse on occasion. You relish the thought of engaging in multiple relationships; therefore, what is it that makes the woman you chose to be your fiancée, different? *Love?* So, the reality is, your marriage will be based on sex in any case, and thus is your bachelor party. You have more than likely copulated with your fiancée, so, what is the point? Sexual intercourse is a universal experience between two people. If sexual intercourse is what brought you two together, then your relationship is nothing. The relationship has to be built on a foundation of bedrock. Sexual intercourse is not a principle foundation. The result of the intercourse is the binding factor, but it is not part of the building of the relationship. So, you have copulated with multiple women prior to asking your current prospect to marry you, so, what makes her stand out? Timing! Nothing more, nothing less. Chances are, you are going through a downturn in your life for some reason, and you are trying to reason things out. Something is going wrong; whether it be financial, or the girls are simply ignoring you. Whatever the case maybe, something is wrong. Lack of religious conviction is more than likely the true cause, but you ignore that possibility, and simply say; *maybe it's time for me to settle down;* and some unfortunate girl will become the unwitting starter wife because the girls will suddenly notice you again after you are married. This is due to either; one; your wife has gotten you back on your feet; cleaned you up; made you attractive because she was more than likely the girl whom always wanted you, but that you ignored. Two; the fallen one is setting you up for failure because the girls are no longer blinded by sexual proclivity. Three; girls have it in their mind to always test a man's faith. Something that is greatly ignored in our society. Fail the test and divorce court is almost always assured. Funny how wives never consider that the test of marital faith in this modern era of the United States of America to be nothing more than a no-win scenario. When the candy is free, you feel compelled to fill your pockets. That is the kid in us; the man. So, perhaps candy should no longer be free.

Instead of a bachelor party, you should prepare yourself for a lifetime obligation. Regardless of your religious belief, make prayer on the eve of your wedding; for your entire life is changing and you must be pure for the ceremony. You have been found acceptable in the eyes of a gift from God; Himself. Besides; for a man in today's world to go out of his way to convince a woman to surrender the one true thing of worth in her world, is everything. For an unspoiled womb is meant for the reception of the breath of life, not for the mere pleasure of copulation. Her vagina is a shrine. The centerpiece of the house you will be building. If the support column of your house is infested with termites then what's the point? There is no future for rotten immortality.

For you; the Catholic male, you need to make confession as-well-as prayer, the day before your wedding. Contrary to popular belief, as a man, you will be bonding closer to Christ, and you will have a greater understanding and responsibility that is essentially unfathomable by the average human-being in regards to marriage. You are responsible for keeping the Church intact. Keeping the faith alive. Insure that there is a surplus of children for future parishioners, and that seminaries are kept replenished, and that our daughters; whom do not marry, do not choose a path of the sexual hedonist or the prostitute.

Let us dabble in the wedding ceremony itself. This is her time to shine. An event far greater than prom or the Academy Awards. Everything about her will come into fruition. Why is that? She is losing her individuality, virginity or celibacy, her womanhood, independence, and yes, in time, perhaps even her mind-blowing shapely figure. Interesting thing about the traditional wedding ceremony is that it is an opportunity for the family, not the bride, to reveal their maximum beauty potential to the groom.

Let us examine the contradiction to modern marriage. You are involved with a career woman, and you have obviously taken her or you were taken to places of high fashion and glamor; therefore, she is revealing her full beauty potential prematurely. The wedding night actually takes place on date night, and you go back to her place and copulate. Then on her wedding day, she actually has the audacity to wear the purity of white? What makes her pure? Does this mean a female cannot wear white? Purity is not about the physical distinction, but more of a frame of mind. She may have unwittingly surrendered her virginity, and practices a high sense of abstinence until she is married. A huge undertaking in our modern culture, and upon success, traditional convention demands that she wears white from head to toe. She has earned it, but as-far-as the promiscuous female is concerned, she is not making herself special in any way. She is simply masking herself from the truth. The next point is why would an independent woman seek marriage to begin with? She exhibits independent behavior; actions; thinking, and it sticks out like a sore thumb, so, again, ask yourself; *why does she want to get married?* That is the feminine cultural contradiction at work. She loves the grandeur of the past, but wants to incorporate modern feminist ideas to the process. Hence, it's more about her want of power, control and dominance over you; the male. She wants a financial beast of burden. Which means, she has no intent on following your game plan. Again; no matter how glamorous and shapely she is; ask yourself; *why does she need to put on her wedding-best prior to the ceremony?*

CHAPTER 23

Under certain religious guidelines, such as Catholicism, a female whom exchanges vows with you; the man, becomes a part of you. She is no longer an individual, but literally merges with you. She is no longer an, I, and contrary to popular belief, she does not become an us. In fact, there are three words that should never be used by a man and wife; and that is; we, us, and ours. She is you; *period.* Nothing more, nothing else, nothing less. Skeptics will naturally disagree, and that a wife still has individuality; however,

345

when you consider human interaction as mentioned earlier, an interested female makes subtle alterations to herself, so, that she can make a more concise psychological connection. Over time, she devotes, so, much brain-matter to who you are, that she literally becomes you. Sensing when you want food, even before you get hungry. Knowing that you're in pain before you even admit to being hurt. Aware of your worries, and yes, even being keen of an affair with another. Her love for you becomes, so, strong that she knows you better than your mother because your mother is geared for your father; your mother does not allow you intercourse with her. That is the overall cleaving process with a female. A process that does not work the same way between like-gender couples. It also does not work with the woman seeking a career outside of the home, for she is devoting most of her brain matter towards her career. Therefore, there is not enough to devote towards the marriage. She is nothing more than a girlfriend wearing a wedding ring. When you look at the use of brain matter in regards to a relationship, how much do you think a divorced woman will devote to a subsequent marriage(s)? Unfortunately, in the past, men had gotten it in their minds that she is not a part of him. This was more or less a result of an aberration due to a secular diet in the process of interactive creativity. The absence of a harmonious interaction, and a lack of religious education, principles and values resulting in the rotting of the very foundation necessary for a healthy marriage. Again, religion is not for the woman, she is born to obey. No; it is for you, the man, so, that you can develop obedience to God. To understand what it means to be humble. To drive the God-complex from your heart in order to better understand what it means to be God. Yes, you are God, and for generations you have abused and corrupted the privilege. You are meant to keep yourself pure of heart, focusing on what it means to be God, but what do you do? Corrupt yourself with arcane thoughts and ways. You lust instead of love. Covet instead of abjure. Lie instead of speaking the truth. Practice gluttony instead of fasting. You are impatient, quick to judge, and unforgiving. Greed dominates your life, and the sheer thought of

346

thinking that you can do anything you want without retribution has become the status quo, literally an obsession. That is until you get old, and your mortality hits you like a fastball without a helmet. You know what happens next? Your Father in heaven, whom you are supposed to imitate is upset because you have wasted that precious gift that He has given you. What is that gift? Your very life.

Back on the ceremony. As the star of the show, let the cameras flash. This is her red-carpet moment. In regards to ceremonies, none are bigger than marriage, and she should be smiling to the point of suffering from lock jaw at the end of festivities. So, make sure that you remain by her side at all times, for she will want every moment to be a sign of things to come. Giving her confidence in knowing that the relationship will be forever. Most importantly, there are no restrictions on her behavior. She; whom is now, your wife can giggle, laugh-out-loud, cry, shout, throw cake, dance crazy. She is living the happiest moment of her life. So, let her be happy. Just make sure you share the same flute of Champaign. For alcohol does crazy things to a woman, especially the young ones. For they may come to like it too much, and reality dictates that women and alcohol just don't mix.

As the man, you must show compassion towards your new wife. Your first responsibility is setting up a comfortable environment for her before children start to come. Note: This is not the same as preparing a nest. Therefore, the best and easiest way of achieving that task is by remaining in her family's sphere of influence, unless she feels a need to get away from them. Females sometimes get caught up in a whole lot of stressful events, and just need to be around someone familiar to help them settle-in and take stock. The stress is a result of your lack of presence in her life. Believe it or not, being away from her is demanding on her psyche; her emotional state of mind. The other option is to indoctrinate her into your family. This works if your family matriarch is accepting of her; however, if she is beautiful, well-mannered, and of the same religion, this should not be a problem. Even if she is of another race. Be mindful; though, of family members whom are out of touch or are a bit touched. They have a tendency of adding needless tension, and becoming a burden with exaggerated insinuation and irrelevant details of past family experiences. A third option, which is the most difficult of all, is integrating her into your religious community. Why is this the most difficult? You more than likely do not have a religious community to begin with.

Before we continue, this author will tell you a secret that will garnish jeers, sneers and laughs from the scientific community, and exacerbation, and ridicule from everyone else. You want a man-child? Then you; the seeker of immortality, should avoid sexual intercourse for about 30 days. Sugar is the key to why, so, many girls are born. Cutout sugar from the diet for at least the same amount of time, and avoid stimulating experiences. Workout extremely hard, either at the gym, in a pool or on a run, and do not hold back either; for you must bring out your inner masculinity from within. Bring out man. Thirdly; and this will be the toughest thing of all: You must completely dominate your wife. This means, you must be on top during the lovemaking process. If she is dominating you, then she is retarding your testosterone. Preventing you from reaching peak masculine efficiency. As a note: Do not hold back your aggression, she may be upset with you afterwards, but only for a short time. That is part of male behavior. Be rough and tough, she will adapt, and love you even more because women like it rough. Oh, and just as a side note; give her patient, fervent sexual intercourse on those hot summer nights, whispering dirty flattery in her ear. Females live for spontaneity, especially in regards to the physical experience. The most important aspect of offspring, is to beckon the Lord vigorously for child-specifics, for He is the true science behind the physics of life. Getting a man-child is only half of the battle. You want a healthy child overall without defects as well, whether boy or girl. Again, constant prayer and proper behavior is the key.

During intercourse, you must have pure thoughts, even righteous thoughts. Though it may sound odd, your sperm cells are complex reproductive tools containing within you, everything about you; who you are. What you are. How you think, and how you've thought. Your sperm can be based upon positive thought or negative emotion or left to the very will of nature. Realistically, you do not want your offspring left to the will of nature, and you surely do not want them being anti-harmonic. You want a child that is going to make the world work. Make those around them feel delight for life, and want to make the world into something of worth. Doubt this author? Then ask yourself; what of this world of the early Twenty-first? Delight and wonder or stuck in a hole? You decide.

Once your children start to come into play, they become your greatest responsibility. They represent who you are. Your son is your immortality. Your daughter is your strength and wisdom. Note: Smart and wisdom may share a common ancestor, but they truly grow on different trees today.

A child should not be wasting brain matter trying to find their way in life. The groundwork should already be laid for them, specifically the male children. Devoted brain matter towards an established course of action. Ideally, that course of action should come from the parent, primarily you; the father. Does not matter how many boys your wife gives birth to, all of them should be an extension of yourself. All of them should have a collaborative effort in the construction of your immortality. Not a state of branching off, but making your immortality much stronger, remaining familiar to you. Building a connection with Heaven.

Human nature makes it hard for people to follow a preestablished guideline to life; however, it is also difficult for people not to have goals; to know not their purpose. When a child is left to their own devices, they will decide what is important to them and almost 99% of the time it is something that strictly benefits themselves. Self-institute their brain matter to needless activities and ideas that have no beneficial result to the whole. What do children of this modern period of the early Twenty-first devout themselves to? For females, it is their phones; more than likely social media. To boys, it is gaming. Neither of which has no beneficial result to the whole.

Give your man-child direction in order to establish a baseline for which to make consensus; beginning a state of comparative decision making to help guide him on a proper productive and exultant way of life. Should your children engage in mischievousness, then you are a mischievous person as well. You are all well-aware that smart children are more than capable of being a party to shameful activity. When a parent; specifically, a father is not involved in a child's developmental process, that child will begin to work on self-destructive vices designed to keep the mind in a negative state of being. Brain matter will be devoted to ways of sabotaging instead of supporting those around them. When instituting a greater positive, there are those whose whole life is about countering the positive with an even greater sense of negative or perhaps more familiar to us is bitterness to a situation. Why does that happen? A person begins a vindictive lifestyle designed to encourage conflict and hostility due to neglect by their fathers. Growing up and all they wanted was for their father to institute a positive interactive medium, but they got nothing and it hurt very much because they felt alone. Even in the presence of others. As they get older, they want the world to share in their pain and suffering of abandonment. On the other hand, you enter the fray boasting about how good you feel, instead of utilizing that feel good to help others. Help those whom are simply going through a downturn in life and would like to know that they are not alone, but you just look at yourself when you are in an upturn. You leave those in pain behind to build upon your feel-good moment. You are selfish in your ways. When you devote brain matter to positive thinking, you reinforce that positive with doing for others who are down in their luck by helping them to look at the positive side because people have a predisposition of always focusing on the negative of a situation instead of the positive, and the reality is; there is always a positive to any situation. A person loses their job, then that person was meant for something greater. The car breaks down. Then perhaps walking is meant to encourage a healthy way of living. That person keeps bugging me about his problems. They are using you as a tool to keep their sanity in check. Every person impacts the world, and can drive the social system in the right direction, unless their brain matter is

350

devoted to one's self. Then everything gets flipped upside down, and living a secular way of life dominates; and secularism only leads to failure every time. Especially when your upturn turns to a downturn, and everyone experiences a downturn.

Your children reflect your teachings; so, teach them well. Not science and mathematics, but kindness and respect. Even if you had a tough life, or you were engaged in some form of questionable activities, those traits can be filtered out when you train your child. The things you did made you tough, but now, you have a chance to make your own destiny. Guide your legacy in a different direction. Teach those traits that made you strong without the things that wrecked your character. You want your child to be tough, but not cruel. To know when to fight, and when to walk away. Most importantly; to understand the importance of law enforcement. Though you may have had run-ins with the law, you know that it is better to side with authority then to go against it. A police officer has a job to do, and that job always comes with emotion. Though it may not seem, so; police officers are always the first and last defense to our perceptions of civilization. Lose them, and nothing else matters.

THE WOMAN'S SEGMENT

Now, this author would have to be a complete fool to think that those of the opposite persuasion would not read the material in this book. Therefore, let's make an examination of the difficulties that you are facing as a modern female, in the early Twenty-first. Ask the questions and face the fears directly, so, that you will no longer crawl along the base boards of darkness and fear.

Should women be at the forefront of the conflict or should they be in the background? Should a woman be equal to a man or subservient? Should a woman have a voice in society or kept quiet? Should a woman be more mindful of the impact she is having on the overall social structure or should she continue along the current

351

status quo, and hope for the best? Perhaps the most important question we will have to examine is should a man have the right to dictate policy over a woman?

We live in difficult times, and as a species in this world we have to make an examination of whether or not we can fix that, which is broken, and let us be realistic; it is broken. At best, we should at least try to fix it before we reach a point of an unrecoverable event. Therefore, let us begin with...

CHAPMAN'S LETTER TO THE TEENAGE GIRL

Why are you; the teenage female rebellious to your parents, especially your mothers? You have reached a natural point in your development; the age of motherhood, and though you consciously love your mother; your parents in general, the need to attract a mate is overwhelming. Your parents fed you, clothed you, provided you with the necessities to be beautiful; creature comforts, a cover over your head; and yet subconsciously, you hate your parents, your mother. Why is that? Your body is peaking, saying that you are ready to produce offspring. You are ready to be a matriarch, and you are thinking; *I will be there for my children; my daughter, when the really tough questions pop up.* Guess what, your mother said the same thing when she was your age. The problem is, things never workout as they should. Your mother failed to program you for what your body is going through. Failed to explain, how to cope with the changes. That is due to feminine impatience. She; like you, was in a rush, and she psyched herself into believing the first guy in her life was the one for her. The problem is, you follow in her footsteps and, so, he is your age or near it, as your father was to your mother, and he has not established himself. You; like your mother, end up in the workforce and guess what? Before you know it, you are looking in the mirror wondering; *where did the time go?* You think you have plenty of time to be a mother, but realistically, you make a choice, and that is keeping food on the table, clothes on the back and a roof over the head in lieu of proper rearing of she; whom you call daughter. Think about it, you are supposed to be the mother, but she looks at you as she does her school teacher, police officer, even the politician whom she has never met. In other words, you are simply foreground noise, while everything else is background noise. Queen bee rules the hive, but if another queen should be born, what happens? There will be conflict. Certain insects; however, produce princesses to go out into the world to perpetuate the species, but we are not ants or termites. So, what's going on? Oh, and if your mother is calling this author crazy, consider that she preps you hard to be a scientist, mathematician, and all other aspects of life at a young age. She tells you that you can be a doctor, a lawyer, even an astronaut, of which is all well and good when you are a child, but your first responsibility is to be a wife, and then a mother. That is not something you can simply run away from or pop a few pills to stave off. Like with the urging to experience sexual intercourse, so, too is the need to start a family, and yet mothers teach nothing to their daughters of what they have already been through in regards to the process. A very huge oversight, and as a teenage female in this modern era of the early Twenty-first, certain actions have occurred in your life that are affecting your psychological makeup, and perhaps even your physical maturity. Throwing you into complete turmoil, fear and anxiety. Bad parenting is usually a result of this, and it is this author's duty to get you back on track of what it means to be a proper, well-mannered teen.

Now, you need to understand that bad parenting does not equate to bad parents on the basis that your parents are more than likely ignorant of their actions or lack thereof or made an error in judgement during a premarital relationship or are simply caught up in the idea of having financial security. Look closely at what has happened. Like a baby squid, your mother is gone and, so, you wander the ocean unsure of what will happen to you. Your fate will be determined by the direction of the currents because you have no parents. You are searching for something; a purpose in life. *What is my purpose?* you ask. That is the question, and since no one can or will tell you, then you go Goth, retro, seductive attire, imitate celebrities or you just go plumb crazy.

As the daughter, or perhaps more accurately; princess, you represent a significant investment to your family on the basis that you are more than a potential wife, but a potential ambassador. Your parents wanted to bring out the best in you. To show others that your family had their stuff together. The braces, dance and piano lessons, athletics, the clothes, the shoes, and everything else to make you an excellent prospect in the eyes of an eligible bachelor were not for your benefit, but for your family's benefit. Ever come across a girl whom was defiant? Moody? Bitchy? Just a plain loud mouth? Got news for you; that's the story of her family. She is part of a family whose father had no game plan. Built his house off speculation and hope. What father's want are innocent, virgin princesses, whom are well-mannered and behaved; not clandestine harlots whom use their bedrooms as pleasure alcoves for less than desirable suitors. As a young woman, you must see the world through your father's eyes. When you were born, he held you in his arms, and loved you even more-so, than your mother because contrary to popular feminine belief, you are his child not hers. Your virginity is everything to him, and it is your obligation to keep it intact.

For some reason, some of you have gotten it in your heads that ceding your virginity is the most important thing in the world, and that it is the only path to popularity. What you do not consider after copulating with a dozen or, so, guys, is how you feel when you meet that one special guy you have been waiting for all of your life? You are special in his eyes, but you have lived a reprehensible lifestyle, and, so, you deny yourself true love? Admit it; after you meet Mister Right, you almost always say; *if I had just waited.* In fact, you are, so, pathetic, that when you become a mother, you don't even teach your daughters the kind of world that is out there.

Women get into rape situations because they degrade themselves in the face of men. Do things that make absolutely no sense. Consider a proper female, or what we call a lady. She is treated differently in the presence of ill-mannered males because she behaves differently; and the wild female, whom drinks and behaves unladylike? Clearly a miss cue; therefore, how are ill-mannered males supposed to behave in

354

their presence? The one absolute fact of reality is that females and alcohol simply do not mix. It is a drug of opportunity. Whether beer, wine or spirits, it is a drug of choice for date rapes, and yet, females continue to freely ingest them in large quantities in the presence of wild males. Why? Then men backpedal as a means of rationalizing what is irrational. Placing blame everywhere else, but on her.

Females want to live an independent lifestyle, but without the hardships that come with it. What does a woman lose when living an independent lifestyle? Everything that says; *I'm a good girl.* What does a man lose? Sometimes the farm; however, we men will, more often than not, warn each other of the risks, but women do not warn each other; particularly in cases concerning dubious circumstances, and doubt of a rational mind. What is deplorable in our culture is that women of power are now, telling foolish women they are not wrong for putting themselves in perilous situations. That getting drunk with a bunch of ardent males is perfectly okay, but is it? Who is truly at fault? Predators are a fact of life, and yet women continue to make themselves vulnerable?

The reason why girls continue to make themselves vulnerable to rape is due to their mothers getting into avoidable circumstances when they were the rebellious teen daughter. Look; the reality is, women keep secrets, and when the time comes for her daughter to go out into the world without a husband, how does she explain the predatory perils? She doesn't; because she believes that she will sound like a hypocrite when telling her daughter not to do something she did; and that is, rebel. Tarnishing her reputation in her daughter's eyes because she knows that her daughter sees her as the confident feminine leader whom never makes mistakes. One thing a mother fears above all else is losing her daughter's trust and confidence, and, so, she simply does not tell her daughter what to look out for, in the cold cruel world. Why would a daughter's confidence in her mother be shaken? Though her mother played a part in her daughter's life, she did not grow up with her. That true bond of confidence when mothers passively explain life's dark details for innocence sake without needless distress to the clueless naïve daughter, of which the details of dos-and-don'ts would be interwoven into her psychological growth, so, that she will not be disappointed by her mother's careless decisions.

CHAPMAN'S SECOND LETTER TO THE TEENAGE GIRL

Let us closely examine the aspect of being a teenage-female here in the early Twenty-first. You are not a physically ugly person, and yet you have an obsessive need to be like the next girl. You think that since you are not popular no one is paying attention to you because you are doing something wrong, or that you are behaving incorrectly or it is your wardrobe. You naturally rush to judgment, and almost always, you rush to judgment on yourself. You observe the popular girl who is receiving praises and attention, and, so, you adopt her ways, but what you do not realize is that the very thing that makes her popular is the same thing that attracts men to prostitutes, and the minute you mimic her, she turns on you because you become the competition. Ask yourself, do you drink alcohol because it is good or do you drink alcohol because someone told you it was good? If the latter, then you have been conditioned into doing something you do not want to do in order to fit in. Are you wearing skinny jeans because you like to show off your glutes, or do you wear the skinny jeans because other girls are showing off their glutes? Yes; you say it's a fashion craze, because everyone is hyping-up skinny jeans. Then again, if you wear a long dress then you must be part of some religious sect. Again, those mysterious others dictating how you should live and behave. Oh, and those same popular girls sometimes grow up to be celebrities, even journalists and psychiatrists, and they carry with them that stint of harlotry. Be mindful of what a person says, it may not jibe with your perceptions of proper and improper social conduct, and should they be a celebrity, then deprived them of your attention, and of course, your money.

Ugliness is not a physical trait, but a psychological conundrum of wits. A subconscious lie programmed into you by those in the glamor industry or perhaps society in general. Placing into your mind a false sense of expectation of what a woman should be, what she should be doing, and even whom she should be doing it with. Coercing you to go against the very fundamentals of social workmanship. Yes; as woman, you want to portray a difference about yourself, but at the same time you have a moral duty and responsibility to the whole mechanism that we call; *man.* To understand a thing, you must be aware of a thing, but you follow those people whom have made themselves demigods, forgetting that they are nothing without you. You and thousands like you; made them what they are, and, so, you listen and follow without considering that someone is pulling their strings, and at least they are getting paid to have their strings pulled, and believe it or not, the person paying them is in fact, you.

This author is going to scribe to you something that you really do not want to read, but it needs to be scribed, and that is, you possess the worst habit in the entire universe. You completely devalue yourselves in regards to just being human. If you were of no value then why do boys work, so, hard to obtain your most prized possession? Some of you would even dare to contemplate suicide. Let us examine suicide in general, even from a sense of feeling socially inferior, awkward, lost. That you lack the personality; the finesse of popular attraction. To make matters worse, whatever you do or touch falls apart. As if you are jinxed. As if there is a hole in your perception of how life should unfold, and that frustration is your only friend. You figure that your only solution is a bottle of pills, a sharp blade, or a swan dive off a high-rise or whatever your imagination can conjure up. Well, if you are contemplating it, don't because if you do, the result is a paradox. Sure, you do not see it as such, but how do you know what part you play until you are given a script. Even a bit part can have a major impact on how the story unfolds. Consider that this whole dilemma of hatred and violence in our modern culture may have been averted by the one girl whom committed suicide. Do not be that girl. Wait, and see how the performance plays out, then you will see the difference without seeing yourself in character because life is not about you or that girl whom garnishes the attention of the boys. She is the prostitute.

She attracts everything instead of those whom are specialized in the fine art of humility. She plays on guesswork and speculation on who is the best man to take her into the bedroom instead of the best man whom could show her warmth and compassion. Life is about what you can do for others. You are the can of soup on the shelf in the supermarket, or the bag of chips or the box of laundry detergent. Just because it is there does not mean no one wants it. Your time to be needed has not yet come, and if you are not there, then what happens to the need? You are someone's moral compass, and neither you or them may not realize it, but truth be told that without you, life is meaningless. Therefore, always maintain a cheerful disposition. A cheerful disposition keeps a person beautiful for a very long time; usually until death. You will not get old after high school graduation, but you will wear out when copulating with multiple individuals; this author promises you that. A brick of gold is still valuable even when it sits in the vault.

Be carefree in what has been given to you by God. You need not flaunt your shapeliness, for true beauty comes from a cheerful disposition. Trust this author on this issue, he is a man. Not that we men do not like watching the harlots in their running-tights, yoga-pants and skinny-jeans, trotting about the parks and supermarkets, but that deep down we would rather meet a woman on a more intellectual level. We guys want someone around who actually cares, and sex does not care about anything, but herself. You set the standard, no one else does. So, do not do a thing just because others are doing that thing, for you are more than likely meant to travel a different path.

In the case of you; whom has inadvertently surrendered her virginity. Heed these author's words. It is not the end of the world, but it does become a much harder one for you to live in. It does not mean take up a career of being a pornographic performer. No, no, no, no; performer of porn. No; how about sexual hedonist. That is a more appropriate description for that kind of activity. You simply made an error in judgment. Allowing someone to copulate with you once is a mistake. All after is harlotry. You become a slut; whore;

easy-woman. Remember, once you lose your virginity to the first guy, he is going to boast about it. Announce it to the world because it gives him a sense of conquest; empowerment; however, his conquest over you is in fact a lie. All he has done is announce to everyone that he is nothing more than trash, leaving himself wide open to your scrutiny; and any girl who climbs into bed with him after the fact is truly a slut. Do not even look at him. Most importantly do not speak of him when asked by your girlfriends what he was like in the bedroom. Regardless of your answer, it will only make you look worse, and should your girlfriends distance themselves due to your choice of being silent about the matter; better to be the lonely chaste outcast than the popular slut, and you can bet the farm on that.

Your goal; after the fact as woman is to heal the wound that he made, not perpetuate a careless situation. Acknowledge the mistake and begin practicing the fine art of being a chaste woman. Attiring yourself in such a way that is not revealing of your figure, and this is very hard considering that we live in a culture that perpetuates the exploitation of the feminine physique; however, if you dress like a slut, then you are a slut. Again, a woman can be naked, even with her clothes on. Also remember that it is human nature to crowd around the bargains, and there is no greater bargain than free. So, make sure you raise your prices beyond that, which anyone can pay, and do not allow rumors to discourage you. It is unimportant for others to know that you are a chaste woman, only important that you and God know. Avoid the male whom wants to copulate with you, he is bad news. Even those whom are considered cool by your peers. Avoid those kinds with great prejudice because the first guy you allowed inside of you has put the word out that you are an easy mark, and all of the hormone raging boys will line up to have you relieve them of their physical stresses.

You have purpose. All girls have purpose, and contrary to popular belief, no girl's purpose is to party, drink and participate in sexual activities. As a teenage female, you do not understand your purpose. Your purpose will materialize slowly, and if your thoughts of self-interest does not cloud your judgment, you will flow into your purpose as easily as the tributaries of the Niagara, and the result will be just as memorable. Then when you do meet that special guy, you can better prepare yourself for him.

Being a sexual hedonist is not on the list of purposes either, for even a sexual hedonist is still innocent. Virginity has nothing to do with innocence. The sexual hedonist is just misguided. She knows not her options or her purpose. Consider this, if you are a young woman contemplating going in front of the pornographic camera. Make a self-examination of your life first. Your parents invested heavily in you; shelled out money for braces, for music and/or dance lessons. The softball, cheerleading, or whatever form of athletics you showed an interest for. All of the nice clothes; things that made you attractive in the eyes of the public. Shelled out their hard-earned money on the medical bills for when you got hurt or sick because they believed in you. Believed that you would become something of great value. Your parents did all of that because they wanted you to represent your family. Instead, you plan on repaying them by disgracing yourself before the public eye; before the world. Honestly; this author asks the question; are you being fair in the whole process of a caring loving parent/child relationship? They busted their ass to make you look good, and you are planning to devalue yourself because you made one simple error in judgement in regards to your body? Or someone took advantage of your naïvety? There are options when considering how powerful you truly are. Look at yourself in the mirror. You are not ugly, so, there has to be a more dignified beneficial means of surviving life. There are many organizations out there geared towards helping you on a more legitimate level, whom will bend over backwards for you, instead of you bending over backwards for sick-minded perverts whom will greatly profit off your energy, when perpetuating social perversion. You got what it takes to succeed at something real. You make it work, no matter how long it takes because you are going to look good for a very long time, and there are a lot of lonely men whom will take notice of you and care little about the man whom has abandoned his child that you are raising alone. Fatherhood is not based on the passing of genes, but the traits of a relationship. Go to a homeless shelter and find a man whom is down on his luck. Tell him to get a job, and that you will date him. This author would be surprised if that man told you to beat it. It's a sure bet that he would beat feet to the nearest unemployment center and get a job. Then clean himself up, just, so, he can spend a moment with you. That is the kind of power you possess; and the interesting thing is, you will not even have opened your legs to wield that power. Your words; how you say them, is your true power. That soft voice can bring about a sense of self-esteem or uncertainty. It is up to you to decide which path to take. Forget the parties, drinking and drugs, because none of it is truly worth it when you get down to the truth of life. Give up your need for independence; it is not worth your body to do, so, because it is better to be under the thumb of a husband or father than under the thumb of those greasy fat slobs who may pay you a few thousand dollars for all of your hard work, while they pocket millions off your loss of dignity and self-respect because reality dictates that you are not performing. They even dare call it an art form. In the vernacular, it is nothing more than sanctioned panderism; you are being used. Oh; and that big Las Vegas porn awards ceremony you attend? Guess what? You paid for it. Your pimps are using the money gained from your exploits in front of the camera to lead you into a false sense of achievement. Conditioning you into believing that by inserting a man's penis into your mouth and allowing him to cast his semen across your face is somehow rewarding, or that you are some form of a sex educator or a hot sexual goddess. Sure; being humiliated is something worth celebrating. Personally, if this author were a woman, he would rather clean toilets at a truck stop, then to be humiliated in front of millions because again, contrary to what you are being told or what you believe, you are not acting, you are simply a face to justify the mad, humiliating gray area of the legalities of what is nothing short of rape. Oh, and by the way. Let this author be clear about the darkest side of the adult film industry that is being ignored by the bureaucrats. They do not hire girls, they harvest them. Doubt this author? Then consider what happens to girls whom lose that certain pizzazz that perverts desire.

For those of you whom are already involved with the adult film industry. For you; the sexual hedonist, whom feels there is no redemption for your actions. Your mother failed you. While you were searching for answers to life, she was out trying to prove something, or trying to retain a hold of her youth, or find another mate; whatever the case, you were set up from birth to be a failure. Well, get this; what you have done makes you uniquely qualified to be Christian. You feel that the Church would not be accepting of you. This author is here to tell you, that there are no gates on heaven, but there are gates on hell. Not to keep something in, but to keep something out, and right now, you are in hell trying to keep something out of your lives. When you erred, we erred, but we know that when we have erred we have erred, and we know to get back on the path; however, there are those whom are unwilling or unknowingly aware that they are off the path or reluctant to get back on the path. You have fallen down, but you are unaware that you have fallen down, and, so, you are not even trying to pick yourself back up. Ever walk up a flight of stairs; misstep, and for a brief instant, you lose feeling in your feet just before you hit the step with your foreleg or even a knee? It is those whom have fallen whom He is seeking. You are the lost sheep for whom the Shepherd is in search of. You are the prostitute mentioned in the Bible. Yes; your errors are what make you most qualified to come before the Lord. You have met the lie. Now, acknowledge it for what it is, so, that you can embrace the truth and make yourself into something unheard of; a rescuer of the dispossessed. Abandon your current lifestyle, and speak out against the very industry that would exploit your hardship. Not necessarily for yourself, but for those whom could benefit from your knowledge and understanding of a lie. You deserve better, and, so, too are those searching for the truth whom are waiting for your guidance. So, what is the lie? Your actions are not the violation, but simply improper conduct. No; your belief that your actions are okay is the actual violation because then you guide others to commit the same violation. Adopt proper conduct, and you will see the violation clear as day, and let us be honest; you do have a huge impact on the little girl, and guess what you do when you find out she is imitating you? Thus, the lie. For little girls imitate the popularity. There is also a secret that you are unaware of, and that is, there is a man for every woman in this world. The problem is, when you became a sexual hedonist, you denied your true love his right to love you. Some men become priests and ideally, their would-be helpers are meant to become nuns, but they do not. Choosing instead to become something else. Another fact to consider is that those men whom pursue other men for some form of sexual orientation that would otherwise be meant for you; the woman. Well, you can probably look at it as killing two birds with one stone, quite literally. Then you as the woman can have a clearer perception of why the Lord hates those whom would fag one another, or perhaps a more appreciable term would be gaiety for the company of his gender.

Interesting, how the psychiatric community is quiet about the adult film industry as a whole, when considering how much we; as a society invest in their opinion. It makes this author wonder; what is truly going on? Could this be the overall weakness of psychiatry as a viable source of social assistance? Otherwise; when you really think about it, a person is basically paying someone to listen to them anyway, and provide rudimentary guidance in moments of anxiety, and; of course, keep it all a secret. This author wonders if there are others whom would be willing to listen, and apply helpful direction, and keep it all a secret without charging a fee.

The other mistake that many of us make; both men and women alike, is assuming that the exploiter of women is always a man. The man is nothing more than a tool to be used. The true enemy is more than likely that woman whom gives you the impression that you can only trust a woman. Girl Power and ladies unite, and yet, she is leading you astray? Yes; previously mentioned: She knows that she made mistakes, but refuses to accept the notion that she is capable of making mistakes. Coaxing young women to copulate increases the satisfaction of knowing that her mistake was no mistake at all. They will even go as-far-as making you feel like an outcast or recruit others to do their dirty work.

While we are on the subject of exploitation; be mindful of your girlfriends for they will say; *let's get dressed up, and go to the party;* or perhaps the more familiar; *frat party.* Naturally, there is absolutely nothing worse than getting blindsided by those whom you call friend; and when you do listen, the feeling of guilt sweeps over your body like an ominous specter waiting for the lights to go out. Say: *No.* Sure; all of the girls talk about the wild parties, going out and having fun, and, so, you sneak out of the house, and get mixed up with the bad boy, without realizing that today's bad boys are truly bad. They have absolutely no scruples in regards to what it means to be responsible. The prior ten or so, girls in their lineup are just like you; another pregnant statistic in the wild herd; nothing more, nothing else. Looking at the slinky tight-fitting attire when you go out shopping? Say: *No.* You do not have to dress sleazy to be breezy, and most of your fashions are sleazy; on a subliminal level. You are woman, which by definition, you are sex. You are sexy; you are hot; you are glamorous; you are gorgeous; you are who you are. Trust this author; guys notice you whether you are wearing the running tights, leggings, skinny jeans, form-fitting T's or crop-tops or not. Before you cross the line of sexual deviance, consider that perhaps that kind of life is not meant for you. Keep your clothes on, unless you are seeking a profession in some form of athletics. This author cannot stress that enough. Be clever in your self-expression. Learn to give boys what they need, not what they want because we like the pretty long dress too, and like the theater curtain, the anticipation for what is behind the shroud, powers the imagination. Pretty face and shimmering hair withstanding, we will simply attach our ideal body to you. Do not be concerned over your figure. Attention to body language first and foremost. Feminine mannerisms, not your body, gets our attention because though you may not be the top of your class, you will be that person whom we call; *hope,* in this dark, treacherous cold world.

364

Does a change in your attire mean that a man's mind will not be about sex? No; but it establishes a rudimentary understanding between the two of you that places the power with you. He cannot say, *you* mislead him or that *he* received mixed signals. You dress a certain way, he behaves a certain way. Plain and simple.

CHAPMAN'S THIRD LETTER TO THE TEENAGE GIRL

Let us examine that thing called premarital sexual intercourse more closely. What is it? The result of uncertainty? Curiosity? Quenching the thirst for physical need? Perhaps even to satisfy the desires for motherhood? Let us just say that it is simply a *being* of temptation that torments the soul to the breaking point of the manufacture's recommended specifications. In other words, the greater the ambient population, the harder it is to deal with the thought of who you are.

For you; the woman, premarital sexual intercourse involves a whole slew of factors. It is a force to be reckoned with; and we all reach a point of sexual volatility due to it being a something that is required, but incorrectly implemented. It is what drives you to be a liar, a cheat, even a thief and admit it, you will lie, cheat and steal to protect your integrity. You will drive down; crush your naïvety. Think of it as losing your phone. *That little life line to nothing.* How would you–did you feel? Well, that's how you will feel when you lose your virginity, accept that it can never be recovered or replaced, and there is no excuse for losing it because it is physically attached to your body. Sure, you will get over it, but that little annoying feeling of *what-if* will always haunt you.

Being naïve is not a bad thing, but appears as such, due to our current environment. Naïvety and independence are incompatible, and yet many of you are attempting to make that semblance a reality. As a female, you are never truly sure if you should engage in anything, due to the caution-mechanism built into your design. That anxiety; that subtle fear of venturing into the unknown is not a flaw, but a necessity for the male/female construct. Which explains why you become attached to those whom lead you into the unexpected. You are grasping a psychological hand as a means of social safety, of which why some males insouciantly input a little twisted-psychology and/or quaintly administer a bit of inebriating substance to the social exchange. Once you are relaxed, your caution-mechanism simply goes into standby. Naïvety requires trust in someone, in order to allow your full compassion to flow throughout your very persona. To express yourself in the open. That feeling of when all-woman comes out, and flows freely into the world, so, that the children will be happy, and be loved. That feeling we call, vulnerability is not a weakness as some may have you believe, but is a part of feminine nature, feminine architecture, feminine being. It is a part of your senses; a seventh sense if you will, that is saying; *you are in need of male presence;* however, you cannot do this if you are engaging in premarital sexual intercourse, and do not misinterpret this author's words as anything sexual in nature. Again, we live in such a sex crazed culture that it is only natural for you; the reader, to mistake male presence as a need to provide some form of sexual gratuity. It is natural for a man to assume that you are seeking sexual intercourse when in fact you are simply trying to be a helper. To simply be there for him. Now, we are not speaking of friendship either because a friend would not necessarily denote care and love; *no.* Presence, is knowing that if something goes wrong he will be Johnny on the spot. Prevent you from walking into traffic when your nose is in your smart-phone. Wipes away the tears when none exists. Tells you that you are beautiful without a sexual agenda. He is the guy who is not searching for any form of gratification, but knows that when he is on a quest you will live easier. Of course, you do run the risk of making yourself vulnerable should your relationship with that special guy evolve. When you allow your feelings to flow freely on the basis that, should he die or commit to an affair, then you feel the emptiness; the pain; the loss; the hurt within: Knowing that you have been betrayed. There is, but one thing worse than betrayal by someone who is to protect you, and that is being lied to by your protector.

Furthermore, your mistakes are not a bad thing. A good guy will see the mistakes you make, and help you overcome your anxieties because as a good guy he knows that you need his help, and that he needs your companionship to keep him healthy. Though you may strive for perfection, do not allow it to overwhelm you. You will only break your mind like an egg shell. Let the guy worry about perfection. All you need do is be yourself. He is not looking for your imperfections, he has other things to contend with in life, such as wondering if he is attractive to you. Remember, you are not like him. Superficial things do not bother him like they bother you. That whole seeing the details in life thing. Guys instinctively like to help, we like to rescue the damsel in distress. It fuels our existence.

The downside to the overall male/female construct is that some of you want it, while others do not. Fact of the matter is, you; the female, always say the opposite of what you mean. A highly dangerous state of mind to be in when considering that you are never sure if whether or not he will use and abuse you like some prostitute. In fact, ask yourself; when a man is finagling you out of your panties, is that what makes you happy or is that what is expected of you? Let us be honest; when you do copulate before marriage, what are you doing? Selling yourself, and you don't even get paid? Yes; free sex. Why would you want to be a gratis prostitute? The man loses nothing; well, actually he does, but he does not realize it because he is stupid, and, so, begs the question. Who is the more stupid, being the slut or losing the seed. You are losing your self-respect, your dignity. Imagine if the public could see what you are really doing in your bedroom when your parents are away? How would they view you? What would you be in their eyes? You say you wouldn't care, but that is a lie. It is important for you to maintain discretion for the benefit of your integrity, to maintain the properness of ladyship. That is what all women strive to become; prim and proper; however, when they achieve that prim and proper status, it is nothing more than an illusion; a lie. Must be the drugs you were introduced to by the in-crowd or your parent's marijuana that ensnared you before you inhaled it yourself.

Okay, so, you are feeling reluctant about committing yourself to any form of intimate activity. Then you should go with it on the basis that something in the back of your mind is warning you about the unforeseeable. This author's proposed sixth sense is at work, and you are choosing to ignore it? Yes; what this author finds disturbing is that you; the virgin teen female, having worked, so, hard at making yourself into hottest item since the invention of the microchip; the beautiful clothes to identify your refinement; the braces to define your perfection; the sports, to hone your physique; the dance and piano lessons to show off your talents. All that has been invested, and what does daddy's little princess do with herself when she decides to rebel due to her lack of perception? Throw it all away for some cheap thrill whom has absolutely no intentions, other than to serve himself? Someone, whom has no game plan, no substance, whatsoever. No integrity, fortitude or motivation; however, he is capable of obtaining marijuana? Something little girls seem to find quite intriguing, though this author does not understand why. Other than his need to break your resolve. A date rape drug by any other name is still a date rape drug, and thus the feminine double standard. You say: *Sure; I did some marijuana. He said it was okay, and he was right. I felt, so, enlightened, and, so, I decided to show my appreciation by sleeping with him.* Then again, who would ever, in their right mind, even dare call marijuana a date rape drug? Sure; covertly administering a drug is criminal; however, using some form of backward psychology to get her to self-administer a drug is... criminal? In any event, you are in complete denial about yourself as you materialize into a slut-bomb, and whom do you blame? Everyone, but yourself. You are, so, willing to surrender your most cherished asset at a whim that you do not even realize that you are socially immature. Not ready for the complexities of social interaction. Which explains why street lingo makes you vulnerable, and why mothers belong in the home, and not in the workforce.

You have a trifecta, wild turkey, royal flush; and you are folding your cards? For what? He's the popular star athlete, the musical genius, Mr. Cool, or is he your... *school or university instructor?* Your contemporaries viewed the long-haired hippies in very much the same way. Look, the whole world is out there waiting for you, and he has nothing! He doesn't even have a pair, and you're folding?

368

If stupid is not the perfect description for who you are; the female with everything, whom gives it up; then this author does not know what is. Did you forget that the popular guy cannot be popular without you? Therefore, your virginity alone is worth more than all of the gold in 1849-California. Guys will kill for the girl who says; *no,* and you are saying; *yes?* Look; guys whom pursue you for your most cherished asset are nothing more than door-to-door vacuum cleaner salesman. They are trying to sell you something that you do not need. You are seeking a lifelong relationship, not a break-in-boy.

Let us further shed the lies; shall we? If a girl or a young woman is giving into what is perceived as a natural biological function, then why is an adult male prosecuted for helping her to ease those raging hormones? If the man is over eighteen then it is rape? While in the same instance we as a society encourage the young female that losing her virginity is perfectly okay? Now, this author is just a little confused by the double standard. Sure; the older male is more than likely seducing her; however, she is also being misled into believing that giving into her raging hormones is also okay, and let us also acknowledge the fact that what we define as a minor under the legalities of law is antiquated. We cannot simply place a number on feminine maturity, and say; *that is that.* Mind-struct should be what determines a minor from an adult, not a number. The human mind is simply a matter of social perceptions based on the environment for which it exists, of which science thinks it has a basic grasp of its workings; however, the reality is, the human mind is the substance of earth, and like all things of earth it must be tamed before it is understood. Let us quickly examine this controversy. You; the teenage female, have the presence of mind to surrender your virginity if you, so, choose; however, you do not have the presence of mind for whom to surrender your virginity to? So, if you; the young female, happens to fall in love with an adult male, and you have no interest in being with another man; and that older man wants you to be a part of his life, then you fight the compulsion to have intercourse until you are of age. Then what is the point of engaging in premarital sexual intercourse? You are obviously aware that your hormones are raging; so, guess what? You can fight the hormones, can you not? Then if you wait the few years until you are of legal age then you might as well get married. Let's be honest. When someone makes you mad and you want to kick their head off their body, you control yourself; *right?* The boring classroom instructor; what prevents you from simply walking out of class? Run a red light in front of a police officer; *why not?* There are other things that you would like to do, but you stop yourself from doing it; however, when it comes to sex, you simply say; *oh what the hell.*

Okay, your girlfriends know you are dating a guy; he's older, and they ask; *are you sleeping with him?* You simply reply with a smile. No one needs know the truth. Better to play it safe, for no one needs know of your sexual disposition either, and that includes the most cherished and trusting of your friends. Wait; so, you can focus on fine-tuning yourself into being an even greater person because the need to satisfy does not exist as of yet. Then when the time comes, you discover an interesting fact; the Church's initial assessment is feasible. Perhaps you; the teenage girl, are listening to the wrong institutions.

Part of the blame for all of the confusion comes from that thing we call the age of consent. Reformers had it in their minds that you are under the age of 18, and not yet an adult, and with good intentions; however, nature does not recognize the legal authority in regards to perceived ideal conditions. Whom said 18 is the age of adulthood? The answer to that question is quite simple, actually: Men whom abused naïvety; however, in this modern age of blatant sexual innuendo the problem still exists. A result of living in a secularized infrastructure, which is contradictory to our understanding of reason and logic in regards to determining what is proper and improper conduct. Let's throw in a little hypothetical, shall we. To begin, 18 is no more than a baseline of averages, in order to satisfy the status quo, and we have been following that standard for a very long time. When familiar with history, you come to realize that for many children, childhood was nothing more than a pipedream. There was a time when child labor was a fact of life, and children were forced to work long and hard in the factories. Ironically, when children are categorized as laborers or workforce, they are arbitrarily inducted into the sex-force. She is old enough to bleed, she is old enough to breed, and the result was sheer mania. When reforms came into play, numbers were required as a baseline for the needs of employers and society as a whole. Unfortunately, the United States of America is an incredibly lazy culture. As with skin color to determine who would be a slave, 18 was chosen to determine adult-hood; however, human beings do not develop at the same rate; along the same lines. Therefore, those urges of rebelliousness that you; the young teenage female, are experiencing is a result of a natural randomization of human development. You are viewed as immature based strictly on a number without consideration that even those whom are perceived as adults under the law behave immaturely. That those who are viewed as adults make poor choices as any child would, but are punished without consideration that perhaps they are actually still children who should be under parental control; however, again they have been programmed by the culture that 18 is the magic number, and whether ready for life or not or better yet, whether the rest of us are ready for them or not, they enter the fray because the status quo is 18; and then the truth of why 18 was decided upon comes to fruition. It is a decision based on the unacknowledged premise of declining parental responsibility because the truth of the matter is, consent in the early days of the United States of America was under the age of 16, when mothers were more inclined to apprentice children in regards to proper social conduct. Reasonably speaking, that number should be set higher today, due to a further decline of parental responsibility.

Sure; parents view you as immature. That you are not ready for such things, but that is a lie. Your mother insists that you obtain a career first in order to stay true to what women fought for in the past; liberation, and that you will figure out; eventually, that you are empowered to experience sexual intercourse on your terms, so, that man will not have exclusivity in the relationship. The problem with that notion is that you are more than likely sexually active. Over time you go crazy because you are engaging in one process; copulation, but then popping pills to stave off another process; motherhood. Those are unnatural stress factors being imposed upon the human body. The body is saying; *okay, you've been with a man. Where the hell is the baby?* Believe it or not, your body is an extremely complex machine of which again, science thinks it understands; however, that is not the case. Your body thinks there is a malfunction, and it is trying to correct itself. A self-calibration and repair system is active, and you are fighting it; sending your body into shock. Think of your computers. There is always something working in the background, so, that things run right; however, something goes terribly wrong, and you go nuts trying to figure out the problem. Sound familiar? So, basically, you discover that something has gotten in there that does not belong. Again; sound familiar? Of course, you want to keep that little thing that got in there, and you simply deal with the turmoil. The downside is, your system will fail, and we are not speaking of your computer at this point, but your mental state of mind; of which, for all intents and purposes is a computer. An extremely powerful computer and you are grossly mismanaging it. *Interesting.* Everything about you is geared towards the 3-Ms; man, mother, matriarch. You want a man in your life. You want to be a mother, and to have a house of your own. A woman's true power is not liberation from a man. That idea goes against human nature. Do you; the female, ever wonder why every time you seek greater liberation, the greater your need becomes for a man? Your responsibility as a woman is to be a helper to a man. Not another woman, a dog or cat or some other type of animal. Your extensive compassion is meant for a man. Yes; that is singular. So, what happened to the idea of being with one man for the rest of your life? This author has one idea in mind. Yes; you have the big college degree, and with it came the big job. Then the spending spree, and no man told you what you could or could not have or even do. Still; though; something is missing in your life. Oh, sure, you have a guy or two courting you, but something is still missing. That is because you are fighting the compulsion to take the leap of faith in regards to cutting the strings of feminist ideas. A tough prospect when considering that today's male is not trust worthy. Now, consider trust worthiness on a social scale, and yes, this author has already mentioned this; how does *he* resist a woman in its truest sense of the word? Remember, it is not about whether or not you are sexier than the next woman, but your willingness to be submissive. When in the presence of the female populous you will always lose on the basis that it is not the more beautiful woman or the more submissive, or the woman whom has more in common with the man in your life. No, what you are up against is the primordial instinct of *him* wanting a herd. That he is subconsciously entitled to multiple female relationships. This is just one of the reasons for the existence of Judeo-Christian values. To suppress those animal instincts within us; the male of the species; however, when a culture rejects Judeo-Christian values; those instincts become prominent. Now, before you go ballistic about this author's previous statement, consider the following. There are some men whom take a bath without the intent of using soap, and there are some men whom will wear down a fresh bar of soap to a sliver to get clean. Telling them apart can be just as difficult as finding a four-leaf clover in a field of clovers the size of the Great Plains. Naturally, modern feminists have a simple solution to the overall equation, that is; of course, contradictory to feminine intuition as with everything else they teach, and that is treat all men the same. Interestingly enough; what you; the woman, fail to realize is that a man whom cheats on his wife commits other moral offenses as well. Simply divorcing him does not solve the problem because you have devoted, so, much of yourself to him, and though you are angry and resentful, you are also hurt by not, so, much the betrayal, but more of the lie that accompanies the betrayal. No; the only solution is the Church because earthly ideas do not have the answer that is reasonable or objectionable. As he gets further away from proper moral values, the greater the witch's control becomes. Most men don't even become warlocks, but zombies; a thing to be used, and then cast aside. As woman, you draw his seed, and you have many ways of doing, so. You being the same as a man is the thinking of the witch. A woman does the opposite of what a man does because men have a tendency of becoming set in their ways. If women did not change things up, then man would rot and die. That is why a female's primary responsibility is to be companion and not competitor, but we men got set in our ways and allowed the modern witch to propagate through means of a potion that we created. Our immortality was the key, and we tampered with it. Look at our culture today. What are we doing? Yes, you got it: Nothing, but violence, hatred and selfishness.

Contraception is an ingredient that was never meant to be incorporated into the human existence. It does not cure, it does not heal, and as its terminology would suggest, it simply retards a natural process, and when you retard a thing, you start to have problems. For example; we dam rivers, and though these barriers appear to be useful, realistically, they do more harm to the environment than good. Atomic energy was a big game changer, and, so, was the harnessing of fossil fuels. Well, the same goes for contraception. Messing with the body in such a way always leads to serious complications that we are taking for granted, and most of those problems fall on the psychological side of life. Do not take this author's word for it. Consider what we do know about treating ourselves. When our body hurts, we take pills to retard the pain, and yet if the body is hurting isn't it trying to tell us something? What about steroids? What about all of the celebrities whom passed away due to drugs that pushed their bodies into an unnatural process, and we haven't even touched on the illegal stuff. On the other hand, birth control is not about pushing the body to its limits, but more of forcing the psychological beyond its limits. What about all of the psychological expressions that have been formulated over the past half century by the psychiatric community. Birth control is telling you that you can be with as many men as you want, and think about that; you are trying to adapt to the needs of each of those men. Trying to understand each of those men. Keeping a mental record of each of those men. Your brain is storing all of that information, along with all of your other daily routines. No matter who you are. In time, something's got to give. The brain was not designed to take in that much sensory input. Something just doesn't jibe with our perceptions of human development, and we ignore it because we just assume it is a part of nature. Even when you see a parent having a good time with their teen child, it does not hit you that something is different about yourself when you are distant from your family. Simply put, birth control is a drug that the body does not want or need.

Regardless, as a teen-female, you do not understand why you surrendered your virginity to begin with; however, this author will explain the reasoning behind your actions. Remember the details about a woman being a companion? As you become more engaged with a male, the closer you become emotionally. No surprise there, but due to social corruption, you have been conditioned to interpret the closeness as a precursor to a fornicating event. Consider that you have emotional ties to your family and friends, so, what makes a particular guy different? Why do you have an attraction for this person at all or why does he have an attraction for you? The Bible, not science explains why. We are all related. We are all family. That means we are all tied in; linked together by means of a process begun by God. To ensure that we do not come out the same way; or alike, He incorporated free will into each of us. When you think about it, the whole process is not unlike some form of complex cell division. With free will, the choices we make alter our genetic programming just enough to say, we are not closely related. All the while, there will be certain subtleties that will affect all of us in some way, and that includes our perceptions of one another. Think of it along the lines of a pareidolia. You see something that you think is a something, but it is something else entirely or you see something out of the corner of your eye that isn't there or was it? That is how we perceive existence as a whole, including the people around us. You simply pareidolia people; guys especially, and you perceive the obscurity as something distinct. More than likely working through means of this author's proposed sixth sense of empathy. Who says that pareidolia is limited to what you can see? Which would explain a lot in regards to why we do some of the things that we do. The obscurity makes you curious, and you must investigate further. If you are familiar with the "Face on Mars" phenomena, think about the effect it had on the people when it was first discovered. People wanted to investigate; they wanted to believe, and if there had been a means for people to travel to Mars, they would have gone to satisfy their curiosity.

In the case of us, all of our senses can pareidolia, especially in regards to girls to guys and visa-versa. There is interaction; perceived chemistry. *If only these walls could speak.* Well, in the case of the guy, he is a wall that speaks, and he will remove the obscurity one way or another. Just a hypothesis. Now, with your freewill, you will determine how to interact with his game of chance. Certain gestures and words guide the relationship, and, so, when the topic of sex takes the stage, you are the very embodiment of the subject. This makes you the mistress of the whole discussion. Between the genders, you have a better understanding of what you are, which explains why, when you surrender your virginity, you are held responsible; however, if he takes it, then it is rape, and there are many ways open to him for taking it. That is why you remain on guard. Think of yourself along the lines of a house or car or cyber security. If you do not guard yourself from thieves, they will get in and take what is yours, then what becomes of you? And that is how you get into trouble. Of course, the best way to make up for an error in judgement is by making sure his daughters, whom you have not given birth to as of yet, do not make the same error.

Look; it seems like everyone is encouraging premarital sexual intercourse; however, what if someone says; *Do not allow anyone to engage in premarital sexual intercourse with you?* Okay, this author will tell you; *Do not allow anyone to engage in premarital sexual intercourse with you.* Listen to no one whom tells you that premarital sexual intercourse is perfectly okay. Then again, of course, it is. That's why murder and other forms of crime such as rape are at an all-time high. That is why psychologists and therapists are thriving off the growing demand of those lost in the cultural noise. The entertainment industry as a whole thrives off the dysfunctional and general gossip. Worst of all, it is next to impossible to discern the prostitute from; well; the average girl in these turbulent times of the early Twenty-first. Truth be told, you have been lied to by your peers. Another dirty little secret that no psychologist, therapist or even your friends or family will admit to; and though you may even disagree with the Church's logic on the matter of premarital sexual intercourse, and that is, losing your virginity is a traumatizing event. When a person; whether male or female loses their virginity, they go mentally ballistic. This author believes that for a female it is far worse than for a male; devastating to a young woman because she is taking something into herself, which is sending her into sexual shock. Every time you allow someone to engage in sexual intercourse with you, results in you actually losing a part of yourself, mentally. It's easy to bond to a man through sexual intercourse, and when that happens other hormonal actions come into play. You adapt to his level of aggression and appendage type, accordingly. You are the passion and he is the aggression. Seeking that gentle balance between yourself and a man is a fine art of tender patience. Anything else results in a stimulating feeling of physical interaction that is not a healthy prospect, but a trap. Signifying that all forms of premarital sexual intercourse is rape; plain and simple. Being of a consensual nature is of no relevance. Think about a rape situation for a moment. Your hormones are raging, interfering with your reasoning. A guy catches your attention, and you are just flipping out inside, maybe outside too. Physical contact of any kind is a prelude to rape. Doubt this author? When you hold hands, how do you feel? Heart racing out of control? Nervous? Sweaty? Perhaps a little apprehensive? You kiss for the first time, and what happens? How do you feel? Then there is the intimate moment when you can really take stock of the situation. As a culture we create opportunity to make physical contact, usually through dancing at some rhythmic ceremonial ritual, and yet you; the woman, fail to understand the point of first physical contact. You are actually tempting rape. Touch is physical intimacy. A signal to the brain of what to expect of who and what he is, and if you are careful, then it can be beneficial; however, you disrupt your sensory input with some form of inebriating substance, making clear to him your intentions. We've been over this; skimpy outfit and booze, then add to that the body movements and what is he to expect? You are basically telling him that you meet the criteria of a physically attractive woman. Now, ask yourself; *what more do I have to offer?* You have; in effect, placed the cart before the horse. You show him your hot body first, basically setting the stage for what direction the relationship will go. You have put him in a certain state of mind that will eventually lead to copulation. In his mind, the relationship will always be about your fine figure because that is what you presented to him first. Then there is more than kissing, he is touching your arms, breasts even your vagina, and you are popping like soap bubbles in a tub. He is making you feel good; turning you on, and your brain is, so, far gone that you just let him take off your clothes; *no;* you help him take off your clothes. He gooses you, and the next day, you are on top of the world; *right?* Guess what? You've been raped. You are thirteen to thirty, unmarried. Consider the following; did you truly understand what was going on? Did you have all of the information necessary to make a real informed decision? Did you make a decision? If yes; then how did you know? Your thoughts were a shambles. You were weak, and he took advantage of your vulnerability. Eve of Genesis was vulnerable too; however, the guy that takes your virginity is not Adam, but the serpent. So, yes; premarital sexual intercourse is really great if you are a person without eyes, nose, mouth and ears or any sense of compassion.

Continuing down the path of personal-satisfaction blinds you to the truth. What is the truth? That when you become, so, addicted to sexual satisfaction that you are unable to identify he whom has absolutely no concern over a woman's well-being, and he whom has true concern for her, and you will hurt those whom would care about you and your feelings. You; the sexually active female, will keep a mental record of appendage and level of aggression from your previous relationships. Make comparisons of each successive male accordingly, with hopes of somehow obtaining a respectable, and yet, sexually satisfying male. The interesting point is, that by avoiding copulation all together allows you to focus on key aspects of overall male behavior to determine if he is made of the right stuff. Trust this author; when your mind has been stirred up by sexual intercourse, you miss the subtleties of what would be a poor choice of a male. You fail to listen to that little voice that we Catholics call our guardian angel, while others call it, intuition. Whatever the case, you sense something is wrong, and you are unsure of yourself. No matter how much your friends, or so-called friends tell you it's okay to do something, there is actually no better guide to the do's and don'ts of life, than simply listening to yourself. Even if you think he is right for you, being cautious for the long term is a must. So, this author says that it is better not to do a thing, knowing that you will forget about it tomorrow; then to do a thing, and come to regret it later because deep down you know that it will dog your subconscious for the rest of your life. Besides, ask any sexually active mature female; and they will tell you that losing your virginity is almost always with the wrong guy; and even if he is the right guy, you ruin the potentiality for something greater than the current standards of living. You also set a sexual precedence that may be untenable; especially if you are a serious-minded female; and if you are viewing yourself as anything less, then you are setting yourself up for failure. To be nothing more than a vampiress. A lifeless entity.

Your boyfriend, perhaps even future betrothed will be expecting kinkier bedroom adventures of which, over time, may lead to unnatural acts. Bedroom interaction should be a continuation of the wedding ceremony. A harmonious interaction between the two of you. Not exploratory sexual surgery on the basis that like all drugs you will seek a higher-high with each engagement. That is why the Church says; wait until your wedding night before ceding your virginity, so, that the regulation does not become perverted, and that your actions will have meaning.

Realistically, no man, short of your husband deserves your most precious asset. There are just some things in this world; in this very existence that are only one shot; virginity, marriage, the very words you say, and of course, life itself. There are no second chances in any of those cases. Even for Catholics, an annulment only works if the person tells the absolute truth and/or is on a truly righteous path in life. Lying to the Church will not set well for them in final judgment. The Christ does not like people whom lie to His bride. It is the worst kind of betrayal imaginable, and many of you know what that feels like. Therefore, when accepting a proposal, be mindful, because saying *I will;* and saying; *I do*, are two different things entirely.

Guard your virginity with your very life. Do not treat it like a football; handing it off to some hormone raging running back. Take all of the necessary precautions to keep from losing it prior to your wedding night. That includes fighting the urges of the flesh with every fiber of your being because no matter how great he may be. No matter how popular the guy. No matter how strong, tall, good looking, or his sexual pedigree. No matter how much you idolize him; no matter what you may have heard about him, do not, under any circumstances copulate with him. Do not even allow him to French kiss you. The absolute worst thing on the face of the earth for you; the female teenager, is a sexually active male. Avoid them like the plague for they are all about themselves. Seeking girls to relieve them of the pressures of life, and we are not speaking of the testicles. Fail to do, so, and they will view you as nothing more than a slut. Is that what you want? 1-800-DMUFALF (dial me up for a little fun). Of course, installing a harsh expletive in place of *fun* is your prerogative; however, the point is still the same. Deal with the thought of sex because the physical aspects are practically impossible to overcome once crossing that line, and that is something you do not want to contend with in these trying times of the early Twenty-first.

Then there are those whom have had their sexuality inadvertently switched on, either by means of a physical act or visual interaction

380

or suggestion. All of which, is rape. From that point on the body becomes used and abused and sex becomes misunderstood. A sexually active child is perhaps the worst human condition, and yet, is the most ignored. An adult immaturity complex has been thrust upon the child without understanding, and, so, they run with it as best that their undeveloped minds can reason. It is pleasurable, and feels good. Like eating sweets for the first time; however, they do not understand that they are not ready for such advanced sensory input. No one can ever have just one cookie, and they will continue to feed the frenzy until it rots them. Just as with the story of Genesis, we assume that Eve was an adult when she ate of the tree of the knowledge of what is good and evil, but the reality is, she was, but a child, not ready for life's lessons. Her innocence was stolen by the serpent. She did not understand what was happening to her body and she tried to cope with it as best as possible. The sad part of the story is that Adam failed to protect her; and that is the whole tragedy of man. Note: This author is not hinting of Eve copulating with the serpent, but that all of our sensory input is a fragile enigmatical that is subject to shock.

Your father is Adam, and he failed to prepare you for the truth. What is the truth? You are new to the world and like smelling flowers for the first time, tasting chocolate for the first time or playing in fresh fallen snow for the first time, a male whom is attracted to you is a refreshing experience; however, his position is highly dubious from the start. Therefore, if your father, any man for that matter, becomes aware of you or any woman-child on the verge of being seduced, he is required by God to intervene without any form of gratuity. He is your; her protector. She requires his fortitude. At the point of the seduction, she believes that what is being done to her is proper, for she is trusting and unaware of the alternatives. All it takes is someone to intervene with an alternative, or perhaps more commonly; *the truth*. Then she can better rationalize the situation and turn away from the potential of, or, what is being done to her. A man or father must learn from Adam's mistake and take prompt action, and if necessary, apply deadly force. Though the Church frowns upon such behavior, sometimes it becomes necessary for the shepherd to putdown the threat in order to protect the flock. Therefore, males should be of rational mind; aware of their duties, for dangers lurk in the shadows of our existence, and men represent the only barrier between ignorance and innocence. You, as the woman, must insure that we; the man, remain steadfast in our duty.

Right; this author did say that a woman cannot partake in the calibration of man; however, there are times when she must wake him up because if you give into his lust then you bring him down. By resisting him, avails him the opportunity to get back on track of being more responsible to you the woman, and if not, then you know to avoid him in any future engagements. Just make sure that you warn those whom may not be, so, keen on his guile and deceit, that he is to be avoided.

Naturally, there are people whom will disagree, but who are those people? Why would they not want you to hold fast to your virginity until your wedding night? They are people whom thrive in the chaos, and many of them are your most trusted confidant; family, friends and when they say; *that it is not true,* consider that the serpent told Eve that eating of the tree of knowledge of what is good and evil was not true also, and when she did not listen, things got tough. Lose your virginity and this author promises you, that things will get tough. Remember; you get better advice from a righteous man than a wise woman because a righteous man passes on information from God, and a wise woman goes by what she feels, and woman feels the world in many strange ways.

You have the potential to become a great matriarch. Marry a proper guy, and you will never experience a loss of mental aptitude. That is because he is soothing you both physically and emotionally during copulation. Telling you how beautiful you are or how good you are, is enough to keep your emotional state of mind intact because the wedding ceremony is not only the bonding of a male to a female, but a preparation to hand off your virginity to your

382

betrothed. You give your virginity to your husband, and his first child opens your womb. That is the order of man.

Okay, so, by this time you are asking; why are women whores, sluts and harlots and men are not? Remember your basic human biology and physical structure. The vagina induces the penis to surrender semen into the womb. When a female collects semen from multiple sources what is she doing? Being a slut? That is a very incomplete chauvinistic perception of the complexity of human nature ever perceived. We do that; you know. Take a long drawn out explanation and attempt to sum it up in just a few words. That cannot be done for us as a species. That is if we want to continue to count ourselves as being at the top of the food chain.

The overall understanding of what is whore, slut and harlot has been greatly twisted beyond all recognition. It is a perception taken from the laziness and ignorance of human culture. The unabridged explanation is that you, the woman, are the most irresistible drug ever created. Understand this; you are a living component that gives birth to an addict. Whether male or female, for nine months a human being becomes addicted to you; the woman. Which proves two things. One: Your overall need to be with a male through thick and thin verifies the Old Testament claim of woman coming from man. Two: Men whom desire males as they would females are mentally unstable. You; the woman, are a drug with no natural resistance, and thus a man has to have an attraction for you. That is unless he has placed himself in a supernatural state of existence. Interesting that both one and two together explains the legalities of lesbianism, for she too is addicted; however, built into her design is that overall need to be reconnected to man. Which explains why lesbianism can be broken, and the other must be...?

That is why Judeo-Christian teachings explain that your womb is designed to contain one semen. Anything else is a travesty. Only your husband or a medical necessity to preserve human life should be entering a woman. So, what is the big deal, you ask? The womb is the big deal. Not some trivial part of the body such as your ear or finger. Under religious guidelines and understanding; explicitly, Judeo-Christian, it is a sacred chamber where life begins for the human race; which makes you; the woman, sacred to the species of man. A pure woman results in pure offspring. Which means that like your heart, it is a fragile place that is easily broken when not properly cultivated and maintained; and if you do not like your heart broken, then do not allow a man to break your virtuousness. It is only when you treat yourself less than sacred, does he; the male, treat you as something else. Therefore, as man, we see the importance of the womb, of which we define ourselves as different from animals. To clarify the evidence, we make unto us certain rules to reinforce our perceptions of being closer to that, which is supernatural because there is a supernatural entity telling us that we are something more than an animal. Christianity is more than a worship, but a preparation of the body and the mind on both a conscious and unconscious level, both male and female for an existence of free will. Examine the animal kingdom: Do animals make any form of preparation with the understanding of being supernatural? If we do not prepare our bodies and our minds on both a conscious and unconscious level, then we are as any other animal on earth; and it is why you; the woman, are the whore, the slut, the harlot. You must prepare your body and your mind. Once doing, so, then sexual intercourse with numerous males becomes unreasonable, unfathomable, illogical. With that; feminine wisdom returns, and the clothed nudity dissolves. So, by all means, keep yourself pure.

CHAPMAN'S FOURTH LETTER TO THE TEENEAGE GIRL

By this time, you are perhaps asking; *how is premarital sexual intercourse, rape?* There is nothing identifying the intentions of a long-term relationship. Yes; some of you are saying; *that's not true,* or *that's crazy; completely ridiculous,* or more accurately; *B.S.* From your point of view, you've had boyfriends for years; even married; however, you did not grow old and die together. There is no time frame on anything. Time is an illusion that we perceive as significant. When losing your virginity, the intent is a one-time action because like the seal on a bottle of whiskey or wine, it is broken, and unlike whiskey or wine, it is not meant to be shared. The point being, the male will eventually move on. He has no intent of remaining with you; the female, for the rest of your life, and what does a rapist do? Depending upon the situation; engage in sexual intercourse, and then move on. Like everything else in our greatly fragmented culture, we have lost our perception of what is rape due to premarital sexual intercourse being, so, prevalent in our culture. Thanks to certain groups previously mentioned in this book, and varied opinions of intellectuals, we as a society can no longer discern between the subtleties of rape and sexual addiction. We are second guessing, contradicting, going by sheer speculation on what it is, instead of reinstating the values of human dignity that would clearly reveal the truth behind rape in order to punish those whom are truly unstable in the mind. In fact, most females do not even realize that being seduced when not in the mood is a prelude to rape. Do you recall this author previously scribing the boyfriend whom touches you inappropriately when you were not in the mood, and you find yourself suddenly copulating with him, and enjoying it? There are males whom are quite capable of seducing a female on the spot; convincing them to not only engage in sexual intercourse, but other illicit activities as well, and again, since premarital sexual intercourse is such a common thing in our modern culture, the subtleties of rape are completely missed due to addiction, denial, ignorance and fear. Consider also that girls are extremely vulnerable throughout their attractive years, and predators exist on many levels, and they are not the ugly trolls lurking in the darkest corners of some foreboding alley. They are the boy next door, whom everybody says is a good kid. He can be the high school all-star, cousin or some other relative; a school instructor, police officer or fireman. Sexual predators can even be disguised as your priest or some other form of religious orientated person. All beings of this realm are subject to the *will* of the fallen one. We are all vulnerable to *he* who is bent on destroying reason and purpose, law and order, obedience and fortitude. For a teen female being broadsided by a sexual shyster is a very real thing. So, what is a female to do in today's society? The shocking aspect overall is that since most females are promiscuous when they are forced into that kind of situation, they simply surrender because there is nothing to truly fight for. Virginity has long since been cast off, and the rape occurs; forcing this author to ask the question: Can we define rape in our modern sex crazed culture? Thanks to those possessing degrees of higher learning whom say that sex needs to be taken maturely, lots of females; young females; especially, are duped into keeping quiet about rape, due to those whom profess being intellectual, and yet express an abridgment of the facts based on a point of view that; *you should be mature about your sexuality.* Resulting in you trying to reason out a circumstance based on a vague sense of reality; *you're an adult, so, deal with it!* That is a result of the intellectual not having a viable explanation, while at the same time trying to keep their credibility intact. Much like a politician who is asked a question that they do not have an answer for, and so, you get what was once known as double-talk. Now, this author; whom is not a Ph.D., will approach sex as an immature activity. Like all immaturity, practicing self-control is an absolute necessity, but not taken seriously. What happens when a boy behaves immaturely with you? Yes; you tell on him. As a teen female, you are never truly ready for sexual intercourse, even after the marriage ceremony, which is strange when considering that you are the very definition of sex.

Sure; it's hard accepting the word of a man in cases such as this, but this author will tell you that the crisis we are currently facing is due to the idiocy of those whom think the Mary Tyler Moore scenario is viable. The reality is, no woman wants to be alone, and no woman wants to deal with the trials and tribulations that are best suited for a man; and yet women, place themselves through it anyway; why? Stubbornness and impatience; *period.* You have got to have it right now; *damn it!* You are bossy, presumptuous and arrogant beyond all imaginings. You refuse to humble yourself because it is your responsibility to uphold Girl Power and Women Lead!

What is Girl Power? It is a contradiction to the very notion of what it means to be woman. Its evolution takes you; the woman, into the realm of feminine domination, not equality. You want to be empowered. You want control, and in that realm of thinking there can be no equality. There can only be one star of the show. You want to live in a world where you do not need a man. Think of that for a moment. A man's existence would be strictly for reproductive purposes. Now, if there was only a way to reproduce without him. Then you; the woman, could see Girl Power in its fruition. You would be totally free of us, forever. Of course, every pregnancy with a male fetus would have to be terminated. No problem there; *right?* What is not being considered is the effect that Girl Power is having on little boys. Male children imitate the hero, and girls desire the hero; however, should the hero be a heroin, what happens to the boy? What will be the girl's desires?

The reality is; you want to be controlled. You want a man to tell you what to do. You want him to dominate the very aspect of your being. Think this author crazy? When you are vulnerable, he will do what is necessary to help you, protect you, even die for you; however, when your attitude is; *I don't need your help; thank you very much,* then you get pissed when you are hit by a train, and the first words out of your mouth before you die are; *why didn't you warn me?* Again, always the complete opposite of your wants and needs. Always the contradiction.

What you do not like is the manipulative man. A man who has a total disregard for who you are. A man who has absolutely no other purpose in life, other than to provide you with pleasure, along with a half dozen other girls in your community. You don't want the man who listens without hearing. The man who speaks fire that has no warmth. The man that looks at you, but does not see. The man that touches you, but does not feel. The great kisser who does not taste your heart's desire; and by the way, you are stupid beyond all recognition to let another woman dominate you; with exception of your mother, of course. The idea of the lesbian is the result of feminine stupidity to its utmost. Lesbianism is nothing more than an opinionated approach to a relationship, resulting in a one-sided collaborative effort. Just as a man cannot fill the role of woman. Neither can woman fill the role of a man, not in the least. Without a male point of view, a relationship has absolutely no substance. This author attributes that kind of thinking to all people having no left hands or everyone being born without thumbs. A man regulates feminine emotion. No woman can do that, no matter how hard they try. A pair of pliers cannot tighten its own nut to the bolt.

Okay; so, why would a woman want a man to dominate her? The answer is quite simple. It has been engrained into the very fiber of her existence; your existence. You are meant to be physically and mentally attached to man because somewhere in our distant past males and females were actually one being. Perhaps even hermaphrodite; for there are some bible translations that say man was created both male and female, and later woman was separated from man. The act of marriage or what was originally known as cleaving, returns man to that original state. You; the woman become his third arm, his third foot. That additional brain power he needs to keep him from the threshold of foolishness. Oh; and by the way; males who become Catholic priests align themselves with the Christ; in a sense, becoming the Groom. So, do not bother with that argument. Without you; the woman, males have no purpose, no reason to be an orderly productive citizen. You become his force of will. By allowing your man to dominate you, he is; in effect; serving you. That is what love is all about. The ruler serves those, whom he is to rule, but that notion has been twisted like everything else in this world. There is a fine line between attentive and abusive.

You are meant to be a healer, a helper of people, and, so, before you choose to go out and lose your virginity; whether by rape, or by freewill, of which in any case your goal is to lose your virginity; consider a life as a nun. Yes; why would you want to keep your virginity, and give up the cosmetics. The sexy little wardrobe, and your wild little social network? Yes; why would you want to give up the parties, and the bad boys? Why would you want to give up your life? The answer being; there are better things in life, and you know it, though you deny it. Better to become a nun and maintain a hold of your dignity and respect, then teeter on the edge of what it means to be a sexual hedonist. Again, lose all respect and meaning of being a human. As a sexual hedonist, you can give a person something they want. As a nun, you can give a person something they need. This author will let you figure out which is better.

To get right; deny yourself, by whatever means necessary, the need to copulate. A chaste woman can easily retrieve the qualities of a virgin. Take back control of who you are. Take back your identity, for all you have done is bonded yourself prematurely with a man without conducting the proper procedure for the bonding of two people. Robbing yourself of a more meaningful experience. How do you take back control? Completely clear your palate of guys for one year. Do not mingle with any guy, and ignore new ones. That means you may have to live like a nun in a cloister. Wouldn't hurt to say a few prayers while you wait, and if you do not know any; then learn. Your mind has been filled with noise, and you need solitude, so, that you can see the truth. Oh; and get rid of the smartphone. That little nuisance is most of your problem. Once your head is clear, you will make a more informed decision on being a part of a suitor's life. Oh; and bear in mind the one thing that got you in trouble the first time. Usually a case of trying to make yourself popular; trying to please others. Once regaining control of who you are, keep control, and consider, the right guy will be supportive of your needs, and willing to help you keep control. Oh, and to survive without a smartphone, make your parents install a hardline phone because your goal is to get out of the fast lane before you get into another wreck because when your parents bought you the smartphone, they did not consider how dangerous a drug it truly was, and you need to institute an electronic device withdrawal, in order to see the beauty of the real world for yourself.

What is independence in regards to a woman; *honestly?* Well, this author will tell you that independence for you is not the same as being independent as a man. Why is that? From a scientific standpoint this author is clueless; however, from a religious standpoint the answer is quite simple. Man came first, and thus has known the world without human companionship. Though dealing with loneliness comes easier for us; the male. In reality, it is not practical. Once woman came into being, someone was here to greet her. She has never known what it means to live in a lonely world. Therefore, loneliness is not a natural state for you; the woman. You must be in the presence of someone to keep your sanity in check. That is more or less why female-on-female zeal is not frowned upon in scripture as is male-on-male copulation because with woman, it is about presence. For men, it is about perversion, self-satisfaction and dominance. A completely unnatural state for him, but not for you; the woman.

Let this author explain a little oddity in regards to an independent female that she is in denial about, and that is, she is unwilling to be obedient. She is feral, and being feral may or may not be of her choosing; and though she may be part of a close-knit group, that group may not be of a kind possessing true warm feelings.

What you; the obedient female are in search of in regards to a relationship, is a man's complete obedience to God. With all of the boasting made by an independent female about not needing a man to take care of them; the reality is, if she is not involved with another female, then she will have no qualms about pursuing another female's man. Consider that the independent female is behaving as a male, and what does a male do when they are not obedient to God? When another woman's man seeks them out, they will engage them, whether they themselves are married or not. Therefore; as you can see, the problem with our culture are those whom are disobedient. Male disobedience to God, and female disobedience to man.

Closely examine the Feminist Movement for what it is; gender subversion. In the past, women knew they were the key in keeping males in line, and, so, women policed each other accordingly. Being independent is actually a contradiction. Today, the feminists dominate, and they are doing everything in their power to destroy obedient females. They are a major component to the secular machine, and many of them are involved with the Church. They are a contradiction to God's idea of a woman's purpose, and many Christian and Jewish worshippers have allowed them to conduct religious ceremony. Yes, these women are not obedient to man, and yet they are allowed to conduct religious ceremony. For some reason, this author finds something morally indignant about such an allowance. Woman serves man, and man serves God. That is the order of life. Feminist mothers; however, are not pushing their male children in the direction of a greater religious stance, while propagating their daughters in the ways of Christianity. Sounds a lot like the beginnings of the transformation of Judeo-Christianity to the worship of Asherah.

There is a secret that women are unaware of in regards to the Feminist Movement, and that it has a defect built into its overall architecture. The basic notion of the movement is empowerment; however, for that idea to work, then she; the woman, must exploit herself; and yet, the quintessential feminist abhors that very notion. How is that empowerment ascertained without exploitation? If empowerment is gained without exploitation then is there feminine success? Which means that in order for empowerment to work, women must exploit women. If exploitation is allowed to thrive then the idea of empowerment is a sham, and if that is the case, then what would be the point of the Feminist Movement? Of course, when one side of womanhood realizes the truth of the matter, what will it do? Start a new movement? God is the answer; and the truth of the matter is, you; the woman, came from man; revealing that being a helper to a male is your movement. Therefore, you must stick to it until the end or we may all find ourselves falling into the abyss.

The interesting point that feminist do not acknowledge is that even before a woman leaves the gate, she must contend with a whole lot of issues. Simply put, and as previously mentioned, it is hard just being a woman. You forget that life has the potential for spinning out of control, and when you think you have regained that control, the only thing you have accomplished is prioritizing your natural routines. Feminists tell you to be sexy. To express yourself. The idea behind expressing yourself, is to keep you from falling into a depressive state of mind. The problem with the overall notion of expressing yourself, is its goal. When doing anything, there should always be a goal in mind. Interesting that you are being told to express yourself, but without a clear and definite goal. In situations regarding your psychological construction there is only one goal, and part of feminist thinking is to empower yourself. Pursue a career outside of the home. Focus on everything except being an affectionate, thoughtful human being. Empowerment is a word that is quickly falling under the category of being overly used and abused. As woman, you are always missing something in your life, and that something is a *stable* relationship with a male. Expressing yourself from a state of being sexy does nothing for you in regards to life in general on the basis that as woman you are the very definition of sex. Therefore, why does sex have to be sexy? Perhaps it falls under the pretense of a sportscar needing to be fast, but you are not a car, you are woman. So, what is the overall goal? There is none; plain and simple. You get your goal from man, not a woman. You want him who will give you a sense of being needed. Think about it; does a celebrity feel needed by their fans? No, because their fans do not see them as a person, but as product. The wrong guy has an agenda and your Cairn Terrier is not going to hold you when you need true warmth and compassion. When your anxieties get the best of you.

Without you even realizing it, you are being conditioned to go against the very nature of who you are, and that conditioning has resulted in you being selfish, uncaring, hateful, spiteful and vindictive. There are those who will tell you that being as such is your God-given right. Well, this author is here to tell you that it is also your God-given right to be responsible for who you are. Yes; this man will tell you what a woman is supposed to be: Kind, insightful, caring, generous and unselfish. What this author finds even more interesting is that you are working, so, hard to be independent, that you no longer see yourself; know who and what you are. In the not, so, distant past, a woman groomed herself into being something of real substance. Today, it's the fake hair, nails, heavy cosmetics, the garment accessories. No time to do it right because you refuse to accept the fact that being woman and being independent is simply untenable. In, so, many words, it is hard being a man too. With you; the woman, always a cheat; shortcut to prove a point that you can still be a woman and do what a man does; but this author is unfair; *right?* Our entire social disfunction is a result of you; the woman, trying to prove that you can do it all, and your stubbornness will prevent you from seeing the truth. That you; the woman, do not work as a whole, and yet you are more comfortable in a herd. We men, prefer an independent lifestyle, and yet we work as a whole to preserve a proper social functioning. You are an intricate mechanism, living life should not be complex, but simple. As to why you do not belong in the running of daily affairs of the community, the question is now, answered.

You; the women of the United States of America must return to a state of submissiveness. Cast off the feminist ideas because there are lots of submissive women in the world whom are more than willing to be the woman we men desire.

Now, being submissive does not mean letting yourself be run over. To be submissive means to manipulate. You want to be told what to do and you have to manipulate him into telling you what to do, through your ability to be submissive.

The idea of the feminist is the very epitome of stupidity; a farce to the very meaning of what it means to be a viable species. Feminist is a word with a root meaning of feminine; of which, unto itself is associated with submissiveness, and yet it defines an idea that is contrast to its actual meaning. Contrary to popular feminist opinion, a woman being submissive is not a weakness. She; who is woman can be submissive on, so, many levels, and all of them are strengths. It's what makes her strong.

Now, for that big question that is on your mind; and that is, why is it acceptable for men to bare their chest in a public setting and not women? Woman cannot go without a shirt in public due to behavioral reaction to her surroundings. The world touches the genders differently, whether it be the wind, the water or the earth. The sun, the moon and the stars. Even darkness and light. Especially the darkness and the light. What the world does to the genders is generate a different reaction to its very meaning. Again, with all things there is no guarantee, but simply a general notion. So, ask yourself, as a woman, how would you feel if a man touched your chest? Even with your clothes on, you would take offense. A man loves to be touched on the chest by a woman. A woman only loves for a man to touch her chest when she allows it. Again, you want to commit to a risqué act, and expect men to simply behave. When baring skin, you want different rules for the same situation. Look at how life works; a man just out-and-out bares his body to the world; however, a woman simply teases the world. She is applying the old adage of; *I am not a bad girl, I am just built that way.* In any event, for you the woman whom desires to expose herself when strolling down the street like some aboriginal villager, this author has absolutely no problem with this concept, provided we dispense with all forms of technology first.

What you do not understand is that for the comfort of civilization to remain intact, the male must venture into an uncivilized zone due to the understanding that civil environments are always hewn out of the wilderness, and require shoring up from time-to-time.

Besides, it is not males whom insist that females cover their breasts, but fathers whom insist that their daughters cover their breasts in order to make unto us a civilization. This is the act of concern for the well-being of what we males deem as precious to our existence.

Observe the behavior of our daughters. They have a certain affinity for the wild side. They see us; the man, as the wild stallion, and desire to place a bridal upon us; to control us in some way, or at least that is the idea. The problem we are having to contend with; both as males and females alike, are feminist ideas. Feminists break the rules of etiquette for their personal desires, and take the idea of control beyond the bounds of reasonable expectation; disrupting the harmony between what is male and what is female. Feminists want everything, and are unyielding to the truth of reality. They are a contradiction to our very perceptions of nature, lacking an appreciation for the order of man, and are blind to the social mechanics that make civilization work. They want perfection in a world where imperfection is the motivation for progress. We are a stagnate culture due to the feminist stuck on trying to make the wheel more circular, instead of repairing the road for which it rolls upon.

The wheel is our conscious thought. Wanting more from one part of the species, while doing less for the other. The road is our perception and understanding of life. There are certain natural rules that must be obeyed that are formed around reason and logic. If the logical is not recognized, then the illogic will be the force that binds us, leading us to nowhere.

What this author finds interesting is that when a person has a full belly, and wet lips, how all reason and logic seems to go right out the door; however, when a civilized person has an empty stomach and parched lips how quickly reason and logic also goes right out the door. Being civil is an extremely fine and delicate line in daily living. To have civilization, you must be prepared to go without the pleasures of life in order to maintain the necessities of life.

The question you; the woman should be asking is; *why do I have to display my body to the world? I have to do all of the hard work in the relationship; why must I prove that I meet male expectations of a physically enticing female?* You; the woman, never realized that the world works on a psychological level, due to your parents having forgotten that little detail or were simply too busy to teach it, or just plain lazy; whatever the case, you are feeling the natural process of life. The male of the species of this world must live up to feminine standards, not the other way around. Males should be buffing themselves up from a young age. Making themselves strong, and then displaying themselves as ballerinos before the crowd. Strutting about the avenue, revealing their breasts to denote their strength, as with the golden age of empire, in form-fitting clothes, makeup and lavish hairstyles, as if the world were a stage. Performing for an audience with hopes of gaining the attention of a fair maiden; *perhaps.*

Around the late nineteenth, early twentieth, feminine clothing styles gradually reversed, due to perhaps the Suffrage Movement, and the advent of contraception. Now, the following will be odd to some of you, and that is, with contraception came an increase in female births. In the past, there was always a surplus of males, and when you factor in the devastating effects of modern weapons going back as far as say; the American Civil War, there was just no give when it came to the carnage. Another possibility is that we consume far too much sugar in this modern age, and it too is affecting the natural reproductive method. In any event, lots of masculinity is wasted in what would be a male's ideal years of reproduction. Male seed is not put to proper use. He spends years building himself up to perfection, and when it comes time to put all of that man to work in creating new life, it simply gets spit out of the vagina. Constant sexual intercourse without a result, and our force of will and seed gets weaker because it is not being properly utilized. Something feminists relish greatly, and yet, it was men whom developed an effective drug to fight the great pregnancy pandemic. Guess we thought we were pretty smart; *huh?*

Wait; what does the increase in female births have to do with feminine fashion? Whatever side has a surplus, naturally results in a competitive lifestyle. More men to women, and we men show ourselves off, scooping up whatever females are available. When there are not enough females, we men make an excuse to go to war. More women than men, and what happens? We are seeing it today. Remember, you women are sex. With you, it is about sexuality, and you are inadvertently sharing men, whether you want to or not. This author is not speaking of the male population in general, but the wholesome males you desire. The Daniel Boones and the Davy Crocketts. You want the bull, lion and the bear. The stag with the great crown of antlers. The rest of us, simply hope to get lucky.

Another point is that people did not bother with the tiny details of history. Again, it is human nature to cut corners when passing on information; proven fact. The feminists pushed for women to be like men forgetting why men did what they did. Showing off his body. Taking off his shirt to impress a certain kind of woman. What happens when both sides behave the same way? The wrong message is sent. Notice that when feminine fashions adopted trousers, they began as loose-fitting, and today, what is the popular cut for pants? Again, a certain kind of woman was what a man was looking for; and that kind of beauty existed in the face; however, where did the average woman get a springboard for attracting a prominent male? Usually in some form of medium that required a woman to display her legs and bottom, such as ballet or being a chorus girl, and yes, there is the all too familiar burlesque show.

Still, this author has not sufficiently explained why things were reversed. You; the woman, are so, superficial in deciding on what an ideal male is that you more often than not hit the ground running without even realizing that you have fallen over. You see the great build, and you know that he is a man. Not just a man, but someone who is attentive about who he is. Seeing a strong man sets off a primordial reaction within you; the woman. Like the horns of a rhinoceros, tusks of an elephant or the mane of a lion; a man bares his body; broad shoulders, robust chest, and flat stomach, that is a raised relief map of delight. A subconscious communication that he is in good shape, that he is real.

Yes, holding his hand is okay. Again, gauging the hands is another form of determining choice, but for moments of intimacy, you like to lean against his chest, for a strong chest speaks volumes in regards to his lifestyle. That he has worked hard to make himself into something of worth. He is telling you; the woman that he is fit for reproductive purposes. Naturally, there are those of you who will resent this author's words, but due to the reality of our modern age, the social noise clouds perception and reason. No matter what you may think or say, your primitive side is still in there, and deep down you want the bull, even though that is what you more often get, without the physical conformities. For even a big boy can have a certain unattractiveness in regards to his behavior.

Interesting that there was a time when the robust female was the ideal mate, and in parts of the world, that is still the case; however, something happened in Europe. This author suspects that it was the constant wars that led to food shortages, and the acuity of robust simply thinned. Women were still shapely; however, they were weaning the bulk due to necessity. The male; of course, had to adapt accordingly. Do not allow the Hollywood stereotype to blur the truth in regards to period films. They often apply modern convention to the past. A common mistake in their profession. When certain kinds of people get control, they impose their views on the audience. That is where the modern feminist should be focusing their attentions, not worried about equality. Controlling the standard of what a woman should be, not what she could be, is the name of the game.

Oh, and just an offhand tidbit of curiosity. In case you did not know; women are always chosen to be first in most situations due to being first to experience the unexpected, but not the unknown. There is a difference between the unexpected and the unknown. What is that difference? Based on our religious perspective, Eve experienced the unexpected when she ate of the tree of the knowledge of good and evil. Note, that the tree was known to her. The result of the unexpected is unknown. Man would experience the unknown because it is he whom crossed the line of what is obedience and disobedience, not she.

SNARE A BACHELOR

CHAPTER 1

You have made certain choices in your life, and nature is now, whispering sweet nothings in your ear. Sure, you are resistant, but with, so, many gorgeous hunks wandering about, how can you say no? That is the problem; is it not? So, many possibilities? You say to yourself; *if only there was some form of technology capable of highlighting that one special guy for me.* Fortunately, there is no such technology because human interaction in general is meant to be a slow process. Think of it as going from the bottom of the ocean to the surface. Passing through the atmospheric pressure too quickly results in complications. An interesting little oversight in regards to human interaction is that we focus, so, much of our attention on failed marriages that we do not consider the amount of failed friendships that occur in our culture. Again, too much pressure leads to problems.

What is interesting about your contribution to the government construction effort is that you are right in the middle of all of the action without even realizing it. At least that is the idea. As if you are hustled into holding the first support beam for which the rest of the structure will be placed upon. When you look at it from that perspective, then it becomes clear why a career outside of the home would not be tenable. Allow yourself to be distracted for just an instant, and the structure comes tumbling down. The nice thing about the whole process is that the greater the construction the lighter your burdens. Not because you are getting help, but that you are getting stronger. Once you become a matriarch, you become the home, but until then, you will need a great builder.

Unfortunately, you are the teenager whom has fallen for multiple guys. You make a choice, and allow one of them to engage in premarital sexual intercourse with you. Things do not workout with him, so, you date the other guy, and you allow him premarital sexual intercourse with you as well. What are you doing with yourself? What would you call that? Be warned that once you are sexually involved with one guy, any subsequent males may simply view you as worthless. Some guys do not like being second, especially if they know the previous guy or guys.

Another scenario, is that you are dating a guy and a new guy enters your life, and you feel that he is a better fit. You do not know how, you just know; you just feel it. That is female intuition working, perhaps even your guardian angel. Neither guy is really bad, it's just that the guy you are involved with seems to have reached an interactive dead end. Got news for you; premarital sexual intercourse always leads to an interactive dead end because he has been milked of his seed, drained of his energy; drained of his man-hood; drained of his motivation to do anything other than go through the motions, of which to you are boring, and, so, he is not in the mood to really do exciting things with you anymore because he is dating a prostitute. Another point to consider is that he no longer has to be creative in persuading you to provide him pleasure. Sexual intercourse is the climax to romance. There is nothing beyond it, but your wits, or perhaps more accurately, his wits. It is his responsibility to keep the excitement in your life going, not the other way around. Teenage boys cannot do this, for they have no practical experience. Have never been anywhere. Have never done anything, other than engage in mischievous activity. Oh, and for you; the female whom thinks she will bar him from copulating with her on a regular basis; got news for you. You've already copulated with him. He's got what he wanted, and he's got other girls to tidy him over, while you play your game. He will sexually besiege you, and after a while, you will decide that he has been a good boy and give in, won't you?

One last, but most important scenario is that it hurts a man whom is dumped by a woman that he likes. Not the idea of being dumped, but more of the idea that you will not come back after being used and abused by the other guy. Thrown away like a piece of trash. From his perspective you are perceived to be pure, special, but once going down the road of infidelity, you destroy the dream, and that is what hurts him. The one whom cared the most about you.

CHAPTER 2

As an understanding of how relationships work is quite simple, very confusing and just a bit outlandish, but first, this author will explain that how we conduct the business of gender interaction makes no sense, and is completely unfair in regards to yourself; the woman. Truth be told, that the greatest mistake you make in regards to compatibility is, so, elementary that you completely miss it. Regardless of how you spin it, when you choose the male, you lose nearly 100% of the time. You are becoming a part of his life, and it is he who is searching for that special someone whom will work for him. Not the other way around. As crazy as this may sound, you; the female, are designed to adapt. Arranged marriages were all well in good to a certain extent, but usually failed due to male pride and arrogance. Not on the groom's part, but usually the father. In ancient times, when fathers wanted to end an alliance with a rival, they would simply take back their daughters, ending the marriage. Now, isn't that a trip?

In this modern age of the early Twenty-first, there is a crucial aspect to social interaction that is beneficial to the health of our species, and that is how to express yourself without words in such a way as to get subconscious attention. Perhaps the most difficult part of first contact is proper translation. Guys have a tendency of being *thick* and missing all of the subtle cues. Key facial gestures, certain body movements; overall body language in general. How you twist, turn, bend and stretch. All of it is sexual to us; the male of the species. Perhaps it is safe to say that many of you are clueless to the effect you have when you reach for a book on the top shelf in a library or for product at a grocery store. Leaning over the professor's desk to review an exam or bending over to pick up something off the floor. Even the casual brushing back of the hair speaks volumes. The little things that you; the female of the species take for granted when focusing your attention on the menial labors, drives us men crazy. You communicate on, so, many levels without realizing it, which is why you must place great thought in *everything* you do. In fact, there was a time when women placed great thought in their overall public conduct; however, due to the need to modify their place in society, that conduct has been greatly neglected, due to a lack of education and easily, an end result of the Feminist Movement.

The reason why you are bad at communicating without speaking is due to a lack of proper social conduct. You do not practice proper social conduct because you pollute your thoughts with modern feminist ideas; career, school for career, study for examine for school, car to get to school, makeup to look good for school, clothes to feel good for school. *What are they saying about me? What's going on with my parents? Big concert coming up.* Social media, texting. The latest trends. The latest fads; music, television, and fashion crazes. Cheerleading, track-and-field, softball, and volleyball. *Damn; my butt looks good in these jeans. Guess I shouldn't have bent over the teacher's desk when seeking help for a difficult assignment. Damn it, now, the* (expletive) *pervs and nerds are looking at me. Sexual harassment! Sexual Harassment! Sexual Harassment!* Just more noise to the overall distraction.

You; the female of the species, must rediscover proper conduct; so, that your mannerisms, will not lead to misunderstandings and misdirection. One misplaced word can mean the difference between life-long joy or anger, sadism, torment and despair. Your actions must be expressed with a certain emotional content. As when you are angry; you raise your voice, the same can be done with body-language. When you are sad, you soften your voice, and again the same effect can be achieved with body-language. Being able to make love without making love is the technique; the art form, that you must master in your daily lives. Remember, a car or bike says nothing to get the attention of the man. Pets say nothing to get a man's attention, and just the same, your very presence is enough to get our attention; not your physical shape, but simply who you are as a living being. After getting our attention, your mental shape becomes key, and this is the thing that keeps that special guy to you; keeps him in your life. If that special guy is not picking up on the subtleties of your bodily communication, then perhaps his heart is not in the right place. If his heart is not in the right place, then perhaps it is due to other desires.

CHAPTER 3

Keep a top eye for the subtleties of a good guy, but be mindful as to not completely forsake the other guy, for he may be ignorant of his actions, and in much need of kindness. Note: Do not mistake kindness for sexual deviance. Big difference. *Big difference!* Simply, do not be harsh or cruel. Be nice no matter what because he is possessed, and his purpose is to torment you until you break.

402

Why be kind no matter what? It is the wish of the Lord that we do, so. You see, we; as a culture, have perpetuated into a state of being, so, damned critical of each other; and for the smallest of things. So, critical in fact, that we miss the subtleties of what could be paradise on earth, but instead, we have rotted the very fabric of our existence. Now, there is absolutely nothing wrong with being critical of someone, but we simply lack the skill to properly express that critique in a meaningful productive fashion that is beneficial to the whole. This is due to our lack of appreciation of how the world impacts everyone differently. You have no idea of what a person has gone through, the experiences, the hardships, abuse, bad manners of others before you ran into them, and the reality is, you probably do not care. How do you know that you do not care? When you criticize or mouth off to someone, but then discover that they have been through a traumatic situation in their lives, you do not apologize for your conduct after the fact. No; that would denote fault on your part, and, so, you simply say; *I didn't know,* in order to exonerate yourself from any wrong doing.

Be leery of the first guy whom approaches you, he may be a player; charlatan. A man whom is all about himself is not ideal for a relationship. Always observe, and never give up your virginity for any reason. Especially in cases of sympathy. He is taking advantage of your generosity; your need to be selfless. Be mindful of the apparent patient man, he may have a side dish or two. Cast aside the liar for there is nothing worse than a person whom has no qualms about speaking an untruth. They are a murderer of reason and logic. Make sure he is not divorced, and avoid a man whom is a multiple widower. You may find yourself in a real-life slasher movie. Stay away from the guy whom sweeps you off your feet. Yes; this author understands that the last statement makes no sense because if you are swept off your feet, then how can you avoid him? Nevertheless, recover your senses as best you can for that guy is more than likely a professional woman hustler; philanderer. In the black community, they are what is known as players or macks; short for mack-daddy. A term, which means pimp or exploiter of women. They will destroy you in, so, many ways that you will wish you were never born, and some of you may even find yourself working the streets for them or being used to make the men at a party happy. Oh, and that guy whom has a child; you have to play it by ear because like you, he made an error, but he is still a father, and must behave as such. No need to express the importance of that; however, that does not mean keeping his previous relationship active.

Naturally, some of the guys you date will lie to you. This is good. They reveal the kind of person they are from the onset. Thus, disqualifying themselves accordingly. You do not want to commit yourself to someone whom conducts perjury. Even though you are a part of his life, the relationship always swings in your direction, for it is you, whom are giving up everything in a marriage, not he.

Naturally, your need to know does not mean play 20 questions. When you speak to him, make sure you do not sound as though you are conducting an interview. Your voice must do more than convey words. You must be expressive, using certain vocal inflections to touch him in ways that your hands could never do. Intonation and pitch to evoke sexual emotion to stimulate key parts of the brain, without the generalities of sexual pleasure. You see, when God separated the woman from the man, the male portion retained a piece of woman, so, that the communication between the two of you could occur. You; the woman, are the key to the interaction, in order for the relationship to begin. In other words, you need to speak to him in such a way that places him in a state of inebriation, so, that the brainwash will be more effective. Yes; a dirty concept, but it is how our species works. Oh, and by the way, you may want to bone up on your Judeo-Christian writings on the basis that bad people either avoid the topic, or show their cards making it clear that a serious relationship is not their intent. Then again, the fallen one tends to know scripture better than the layman, and like he; a bad suitor will attempt to use your knowledge against you. Twist your perceptions of scripture to benefit himself. That is the tell of a charlatan. The details of communication is an ancient artform that

404

we have chosen to cast aside in this modern culture of lust. Both sides must redevelop the skills necessary to make gender interaction work.

If a suitor says; *I love you,* then it is more than likely a lie. No matter what people may say; love at first sight is a farce, so, don't you believe it. Should you feel stimulated by the suitor, fight the urges with every fiber of your being. There are unknown forces in the universe and one of those forces is called magnetic attraction. Some guys have it, while others do not. The biggest mistake you; the prospect makes in first contact situations, is trying to determine what kind of a man that he is at the spur of the moment, and why you have an attraction for him. No matter what universe you are from, no person can make an on the spot evaluation about someone without error. Oh, sure, some people think they can; however, there are those whom have that certain ability to mesmerize like a predator, right before applying a deathblow. Something to consider when that certain someone captivates you. There are even some of you whom take psychology and philosophical classes in college in order to try and understand male/female interaction. Complete foolishness. Look, your job is simple. Once he passes the preliminaries of being *Mr. Right,* then you must learn to adapt to his needs. He's already got a game plan, whether he's a stargazer or police officer; he is doing something with his life. From there, you guide his development along lines that are beneficial to you, for your job as mother is the hardest job of all. Never; out of any circumstance, do you try to dominate him; and most importantly if you are not a virgin, but chaste, do not assume for one instant that you can; as the street lingo would go; *pussy-whip him.* Trust this author, he will recover or you will dislike his weakness. In any case, the relationship will eventually sour.

As-far-as the whole love-trip goes; your feelings are, but a mustard seed. There is absolutely no difference between love and Christianity because the Christ created love. Notice that love goes hand-n-hand with the growth of the Church. It seemed in question at first, but over time, it became something great. So, just as a man will tell you; *I love you,* when meeting you, so, too are there individuals whom will say; *the Church does not run on prayers alone.*

They are the biggest fools on the face of the earth. Beware of them and keep your distance. That is perhaps the true reason why you wait for the hand of an older, more experienced suitor. Boys just don't have a full grasp of the Church, that is if you are even Christian. There is no such animal as love at first site. A baby does not start out loving the mother. The child's love maturates over time. On the other hand, a mother develops a strong loving bond over the nine months of child growth in her womb. At first, a mother is unsure of her feelings for the child developing in her womb. That is why there is no specific stage of human progress in regards to the act of sexual intercourse. The actual intent of sexual intercourse begins the process of life, whether a pregnancy occurs or not. Woman is designed to give birth, and a man is designed to make birth possible.

Also consider that there are two types of love. You have natural love; for example, you go into the wilderness and see the trees and all of the beauty, and say to yourself; *how beautiful they are,* and how you love the view, and that you can enjoy the scenery forever. Then you have unnatural love, and the example of that is, you look at the trees. Look at the beauty of the wilderness, so, delightful. *I cannot wait to cut it all down and destroy it.* Most of you prefer the unnatural love. The love of the man whose only purpose is to destroy the very sanctity of beauty; your beauty. Not your physical beauty, but the beauty of thought and mind. You girls have rational minds; however, bad men mess with it, and in time you become a mass of conflicting emotions, and when you look in the mirror, you see those emotions, and pile on the makeup and the tattoos, thinking that it will solve your problems. The problem is your want of a something, opposed to your need of a something. You would rather live a lie than allow truth to be your happiness.

To get a better grasp of your perceptions of social necessity, then you need a baseline for what you are truly looking for in regards to a meaningful interaction. Know your Shakespeare. The play; "Cyrano de Bergerac" is a great example for the arranged thoughts of an ideal, caring man. His words must be constant poetry. Sure; what guy knows poetry? If you read the first half of this book, you will remember a little something about viewing the genders as a whole. You; the woman must force the man to adopt a more complex social accord. Oh, and just, so, we are clear on the matter; rap and hip-hop are not cultured mediums for a pleasurable amorous interaction. It does not hold the same degree for what you are looking for as a cultured woman, unless you view yourself as substandard. He must earn your trust and confidence. Not force his will upon you. For if you are not comfortable with him, then what is the point of a relationship?

CHAPTER 4

Now, this author has brought up seemingly impossible topics in regards to meeting that special someone. As the world currently stands in this age of the early Twenty-first, meeting a cultured adult male whom has never been married and with no children, may be just a little unrealistic, but not entirely impossible. In any event, you; the teenage female, are living in the here and the now, and are more than likely dating guys. Therefore, let us cover the current situation as it stands. He is present in your life, physically/virtually; holding you in his arms, speaking your language. Saying things that you want to hear; however, interlaced into the frames of the message are certain liaison encoding practices that lead you into a state of trust. A pattern that you must follow because you are female because we live in the cold cruel world of secularism, which is no different than being hunter-gatherers. Eventually, you will be facing your vulnerability when you get a sense of him walking out of your life. Without saying a word, he has made it clear that he wants to copulate with you. You have bonded to him prematurely, which explains why males and females should be segregated during their education years. Premature bonding is a result of integrating boys and girls in the classroom. You feel obligated. What do you do? He is leaving you for someone who is more receptive, or, so, it would seem. Remember that schools are the boy's practice arenas, and, so, guess what? They are your practice arenas as well. Except that you are not dealing with a respectable boy. He is a child with little or no parentage. Therefore, not only is he impatient, but you are a cheap little thrill; nothing to him. Oddly, his motives are not what you think they are. He simply has nothing else to offer based on never having lived life. Being an athlete is simply the potential for living life, not the actual finished product. He believes that with sexual intercourse, you will have committed to his sexual prowess in lieu of any real substance. Look; he knows that you are his: *What?* He needs to seal the relationship with sexual pleasure? You feel obligated to copulate with him? *Really? Why?* Physical pleasure is not a guarantee to a life-long relationship, and that is a proven fact. He wants sexual intercourse for self-satisfaction. Key word; *self,* of which is found in the word selfish. Coercing you into a foolish state of desire gives him power, not over you, but your life, and yes, even womanhood itself. If he impregnates you, the longevity for a meaningful, productive relationship is not there. Which means that his immortality means nothing to him, for he has not geared himself for fatherhood; no game plan; *remember?* Violating the law a few times proves that he is capable of what? Going against the grain based on his perceptions of life? The problem with that notion is the conflict that will arise when children arrive. Offspring get hungry, hurt or sick, and require an education, and you like the ease at which, civilization affords you such necessities. Especially when you need diapers for the baby. Attacking the establishment simply means he has an unregulated opinion built from chaotic sources bent on the destabilization of civilization. Over time he will make opinions on you in regards to what he does not like, which is nothing more than an excuse to be with someone else. To run away from his obligations. Then what will you do? Should you make a mistake; and what will he do? No; you want something more real. Not conning yourself into believing he is right for you.

Realistically, you should not come around to his way of thinking. You are a cultured female, and his force of will lacks compassion. Do not try to be his friend, for friendship with a woman is clearly not on his list of social ambitions. On the other hand, do not insult him. Simply phrase an excuse to end the relationship in such a way as not to intrude upon his pride and masculinity. Even if you have to place blame on yourself; do, so, for you will lose nothing in the end. You have no pride to lose, just your vanity, and virginity legitimizes vanity. It is the foundation for vanity. Your dignity is a pillar to the community. Of course, should he be stubborn, and be completely obsessed with you, then he may badger you constantly on both a conscious and subconscious level, using guile, treachery and deceit if need be to obtain your most prized possession. Revealing to you that he has absolutely no divested interest in your well-being or having a future with you. In fact, he is, so, focused on the need for sexual pleasure that a useful game plan for life is not even an option. Self-interest is his game plan. If he is insulting you, then that further reveals the potential for a bad relationship. He insults you when he wants something, and then loves you when he gets what he wants? Like a pouting child. How do *you* feel after the fact? Your feelings mean absolutely nothing to him. All of it, is the sign of an addiction or worse. In any event, he is clearly revealing that he is not the man for you, and yet, you throw yourself upon his mercy? Then he will use his last line of resort: *You are a stuck-up self-righteous little bitch who just thinks she is too good for me. I didn't really like you anyway;* or something along those lines interlaced with strong expletives because for him, failure is not an option. No man wants to be a failure; however, failures have to start somewhere in life. He uses the *stuck-up* routine to place you in a condition of second guessing your state of mind, and even your will-power. Do not give in. Just tell him he is right. That you are stuck-up, and that he shouldn't be talking to you until you clean up your attitude and end the conversation with a cold, but simple; *goodbye.* He will get mad. He will go away mad, and of course, he will get his other conquests to bring you down. He will be able to do this because he will make it seem like you have made them look weak for giving into him. You gain their favor by simply saying: *He controls you based on a lie. Break his hold by telling him; no, when he wants you to do something for him.* The one time you must use *that* word that brings anger, reluctance and fear from a person seeking malicious intent. Then you watch him unravel. Once you resist him there is a good chance that the next girl will also resist him and you would have started something wonderful. Comfort your sisters whom have lost their virginity to him, for they need of compassion not judgement. Show them that life is not about indifference and discontent, but self-control. Help them to understand that chastity is the better part of valor and they will be the best BFFs you could ever have.

CHAPTER 5

Okay; so, some of you are probably thinking to yourself that literature is not the same as a real time case scenario; such as being with someone who is intimidating. You are trying to admit to yourself that you are audacious; however, you know that all of the Hollywood hype about girl power and being strong does not jibe with the reality of the situation. Even your self-defense training is nullified by the motherly intuition of not wanting to hurt him or worse, that he may come back at you in complete rage; and this author does not care what Hollywood is portraying on the big screen. A fully enraged male is something no female is ever ready to face, for he catches you, when you least expect it. Fear is the source of why you keep the relationship going. Like some form of covert social Stockholm Syndrome or public duress. You want to run, but where can you go? He knows how to find you. Whenever you are alone with him, a sudden chill runs down your spine. With your fear complete; he either undresses you or you know to undress for him, because a willing rape is far more dignifying than being forced. At least that is how your subconscious has worked it out, in order to be accepting of it. Once viewing it from that angle, you can see why all forms of premarital sexual intercourse is rape. A lot of you whom are reading this, do remember your first time. Deep down, you really did not want to engage in sexual intercourse, but, again the situation was secluded with no means of escape. Though you dreamed of having the school superstar, or whoever it was you wanted; once you were alone with him, things were not what you expected. Guess what? Those feelings you felt as he was seeking to break your resolve was your intuition; your guardian angel, telling you that you were in a bad situation. Another; guess what? Those little last-minute trepidations you felt before the date, were not due to anxieties of finally being with someone that you were crazy about. No; they were initial warning signs, and you ignored them due to a sense of commitment. That is why in antiquity, a chaperone was necessary because there are men whom have a certain need to seduce, to intimidate and in some cases apply direct force.

Though he may not have practiced abstinence or even be a virgin, by refusing him, you make him think twice about who he is, for he is obsessed with the very thing that gives you an edge over him, and that is self-control; and be honest with yourself; one of you has to possess some form of self-control in the relationship, for the benefit of truth of life. Therefore, until you are married, your obligation is to your father, not your boyfriends, and the best way to make your father happy is by keeping your virginity intact.

There is a particular guy you like? Then evoke him into a state of processing a complex equation, of which will; hopefully, place him in some form of mental anxiety. All males have to overcome the intelligence factor before seeking something on a more physical plain, and, so, what is the equation? Well, consider that you chose to involve yourself with a guy who is, or at least near your age. That is part of the conditioning of childhood culture, and, so, you take a stern position. You are mother by sheer instinct, not, so, much to the children that you will give birth to, but to the adult whom does not know better. Look him straight in the eyes as a mother would, and do not flinch, not in the slightest and simply ask him; *define a meaningful relationship. What is your game plan for life? For me? What makes me valuable in your eyes, or will I simply be just another one of your playthings?* Then you closely examine his eyes, and the truth will materialize. Do not ignore his petrified reaction for it is crucial to your future. Ignore it, and you will know hell on earth.

On the other hand, do not shun him if he wants to discuss sexual intercourse with you. He may simply be seeking answers to tough questions to help him better understand what he is feeling. A woman's insight is always beneficial to the psychological needs of a man. Again, you are sex. Whom better to answer his questions; and

411

if you do not know them, then learn because like drugs; sex can be highly addictive, and that those whom say otherwise are the biggest fools on the face of the earth.

Drug addicts want a more potent high. From a female perspective, she is not seeking love, but a more powerful thrust; however, if sex, like drugs are instituted properly, they can be controlled and even beneficial to not only the human condition, but to the community as a whole. What are the proper means for controlling sexual urges? It must be intertwined with Judeo-Christian beliefs. Yes, right now, you are saying that's crazy, but consider this; sex is a natural part of the biological function of what it means to be man, and yet, it is an addictive substance. You see; sex, unlike homosexuality, is both a behavior and an identity due to you; the female being the very embodiment of that behavior, and when you see it as such, you are simply intertwining who and what you are with your Judeo-Christian beliefs and values. In fact, it is necessary that you do it on the basis that you have one unique quality, as a drug, that no other drug is capable of exerting; and that is, you are self-addicting. Do opioids, marijuana, methamphetamine feel reluctance before being used? Are they self-stimulating? Are they ready to be consumed? Sure; *that's different,* and yet, like a woman, they are used, and abused. Those kinds of drugs are not alive; however, you are a living drug, and in many cases, unlike inanimate drugs, you possess concern. You are self-perpetuating the ingredients to your own addiction, resulting in a recipe of sexual neglect if not properly managed. For sexual intercourse is a huge undertaking, that is taken for granted. Not by the male, but by you; the female. What science is aware of, but fails to explain is that sex is the very basic of human ingredients in regards to perpetuating the species. Animals basically eat and reproduce. Look at the human species in this modern age of the Twenty-first, and what do you see? We are eating and reproducing. Many of us, are simply going through the motions of reproduction. Are we advancing? Moving ahead on an intellectual level? Sure, some people are, but as a whole, what are we? Of course, without the addiction, life in general ceases to exist. Which is why males must be guided along a healthy path of respect for the reproductive process that results from the pleasurable byproduct because his benefit can easily overshadow your need as woman.

Another point to make is that you do not want him pursuing other men, for then you lose your purpose in life. No; not to conceive, but as helper. Yes; we've already been down this road, so, moving on: Since the rise of the Feminist Movement, you; the woman, have moved in the direction of displaying your physique more illicitly without considering the impact you are having on society as a whole. Again, the feminist contradiction of the female taking on the role of being the attention grabber, without the consideration that you are the very force of nature that makes human existence possible. Essentially, requiring social modifications with the assumption that our children; particularly males and adult males will adapt accordingly, but truly, this author says to you, the female reader, we; the male are not adapting. We are being retarded, and it is driving us down a path of extreme violence. When this author scribes that all women are whores, sluts, and harlots; he wants you; the female reader to consider the effect you are having on the overall social dynamic. Not just your clothing, but everything. You are presenting before the public eye; before a man's eyes, an illusion. Do not deny it, and do not dare justify it with a lie. The hair-weave, the body-shaping apparel, implants, makeup, even tattoos are all designed to make you; the woman into something you are not. To conceal, and in some cases even perhaps reveal either the physical or psychological or both. You are, so, easily influenced by opinion that you forget that it is only your opinion that matters. Women of the night have been exhibiting this exact kind of behavior from the beginning of civilization. You are fishing for a specific kind of man to satisfy your sense of accomplishment, and when you fail to land that fish, you get the impression that you do not measure up. So, you pile on more illusion until you reach a point to where you appear as nothing more than bad graffiti. News for you; a serious man does not want a *lie*. You as the female of the species are here on earth for a purpose, and that purpose is not meant to be a sexual edifice, but the happiness of life.

Before we continue, this author has a question for you; the modern female, that you may find a bit eccentric. You change your hair, finger and toenail color, your cosmetics, jewelry, hell; even your eyes, denoting your propensity, for difference. Hence, why the permanent tattoos? Logic dictates that since you would never behave as a cartoon character in regards to your wardrobe, why do you get something permanent when you change everything else? Wouldn't temporary tattoos be more of a woman's fashion MO?

CHAPTER 6

The following may make you feel just a little uneasy; however, it is the absolute truth; and that is, God sends you a guy and, so, does the fallen one. In this realm of existence, there are always choices. Here is the rub; the guy you are least likely to be attracted to, is more than likely the guy for you. Life is never fair for you; the romantically lonely female, but reality dictates that there are simply forces in the universe that you are unaware of. Things that you do not see from your perspective. He; whom dwells in heaven needs you to follow a certain path; therefore, whether short, fat and stubby is of no consequence. The apparent nobody is probably the one for you. Yes; you are a goddess in your own right; the pageant queen. The hottest babe since Farrah, and common sense tells you; tells your family and friends, that you should be with the tall, good looking, athletic type. He; whom looks as though, he can wrestle a bull to the ground. Ever conduct a comprehensive study on how long a relationship with a superman lasts? Neither has this author; however, what he does know is that a lot of apparent perfect couples almost always fail due to *his* wandering eye. Again, do not allow yourself to be blinded by his physique or his facial beauty because a beautiful mind must be searched for, and is almost always ignored when found. Not to mention that this author has heard it said that the fallen one is quite a handsome devil.

Again, not fair, but no worries for you must consider the rules of engagement: No premarital sexual intercourse. Attention to strict conduct. Dress modestly, and the most important; patience. This all comes from your Judeo-Christian values. Once you adhere to the rules, realistically speaking, it is permissible for you to date as many suitors as you, so, choose in order to cultivate your options. Suitors, whom find that notion unacceptable are automatically crossed off the list; *right?* You want God to be fair? Then you must pray for your dream guy, not play the secularistic game of chance. Prayer works. You simply do not see the effects due to the fallen one running interference. With prayer comes a moral path devoid of hindrance. Always remember the hardest rule to abide by, and that is, life is not about you, but about those around you. Treat them like trash and that is what you become.

Again, the male chooses the female, not the other way around; however, once he makes an intimate declaration you must run him through the wringer. He must possess strong religious convictions; there can be no exceptions. Again, patience is a must, and most importantly, his ability to communicate on many levels must be high and devoid of expletives. Sure, he may have a wandering eye. That's okay. Look at the world from his perspective. He is a male bison trying to be involved with one female bison in a herd of female bison. The rules of engagement in the animal kingdom; one male to the herd. In the civilized world; one male to a female in the herd. Until the day comes that feminine fashions revert to a less than stimulating allure, this area of social interaction will always be a catalyst for difficulties. If he is spending the bulk of his time with you, take it and be satisfied because it is also hard to look at just one purse in the department store, that is if any are left.

Do not even consider those dating sites and services. Part of the challenge of meeting someone is the adaptation. Compatibility is not necessarily guaranteed. The right guy is not a matter of what you want, but more of what you need. Your ability to adapt to his game plan, while seducing him to your requirements is the challenge of any relationship.

Do not attribute failure of gaining a good man's attention due to a lack of physical beauty. A little-known secret is that when you dress for a specific kind of male, you are in fact making a futile gesture. You fail to realize that your ideal male can have any woman he sets his sights on. Contrary to what your girlfriends or classmates or family may tell you, or hint of, it is not your responsibility to get a man's attention. Therefore, there is really no need for you to display yourself in a provocative manner. In fact, he will not make a move on a woman until certain urges compel him to do, so; therefore, do not force the issue. Believe it or not, when the time comes, you will be caught completely off guard, and, so, will he. That is why your ideal male always bumps into you when you are least prepared. He; like most of the guys gawking over you, do not care about you on the basis that you have projected yourself in such a way that is contradictory to his needs. That is unless your needs are strictly of a physical nature. More than likely; of course, that is not the case. You want a meaningful life-long relationship? Then clothed nudity is not the direction you want to go. Placing males into sexual shock over what they cannot see is the game plan because there is a dirty little secret about most men. We are child predators, in accordance to modern convention, though many would deny it. Some are simply better at self-control than others in regards to their desires. Now, this author is not speaking of the little girl playing hopscotch or jump-rope on the playground, but that gray area between what is physically enticing and mentally ripening. Present to him the high school demeanor without the high school attitude. In other words, be the naïve little girl. Give the impression of vulnerability to test his candor, and most importantly, do not try to be someone that you are not.

For you; the female, whom thinks you are not, attractive; this author will tell you a secret that others in your gender do not want you to know. The little nuances for attracting a man; brushing back your hair, that subtle glance, the slight touching of the lips with your fingertip is something that comes natural to all females, and that men find stimulating. Your problem is, you rush the moment. As the man must be patient, so, must you; be patient in your actions. Brush the hair back slowly, pretending you do not notice.

416

Casually glance at him, but not, so, often. Touching your fingers to your lower lip, should seem like a subconscious act, even smiling, but not at him. All of it gets his attention, so, do not worry. He is looking, though you may think otherwise. Just remember, your beauty is not given to you, but groomed to perfection. Believe it or not, you can guide your physical attributes, even the intricate details of your face. Yes; the human brain is that powerful. The problem is, you must constantly stare at yourself in the mirror, and that can lead to overwhelming self-consciousness and serious vanity issues; which may not be a bad thing if you learn to control the attitude. Your smile makes all of the difference, and is the true power of feminine superiority.

Beware of the dirty old man, for he is a cunning and experienced manipulator and a liar, and his kind exists in droves and on all levels of social familiarity; however, they stick out like a sore thumb when you have been properly prepared for them, for the apparent smart guy, is in fact as stupid as a john, who is petitioning a mannequin for sex.

There is absolutely nothing wrong with flirting. As a single female, you have a right to flirt with those in your sphere of influence as a means of furthering your lure. Note: Flirting is not an expression of body melding attire or a point of extenuating your figure. You are flirting, not petitioning. Some of you are asking; what is the difference? Flirting is a woman's way of discreetly communicating that she is open to dialogue. Petitioning denotes intent. Just remember, there is a fine line between flirting and petitioning. You may even go as-far-as hinting of intercourse. That is perhaps the best way to test his resolve; however, a very tricky maneuver that can easily backfire should he be the kind of guy whom frowns on fast women. Yes; those kinds of men do exist. On the other hand, he is a fool to accept, not to mention the opportunity for you to break it off. Now, remember this; though you have more to lose in a relationship, he can only handle, so, much sexuality. So, do not attempt to break him because he may become incensed. Too much flirting is equivalent to too many spankings, so, be considerate when trying to determine if the guy pursuing you is a charlatan or a legitimate potential suitor.

Once he petitions you, do not allow the general criteria of what this author has set down in this book blind you to the obvious. Avoiding the wrong kind of guy is not difficult. Believe it or not, a part of you already knows a bad guy when one comes across your path, listen to yourself. Be mindful before opening your gate to him. Honor, courage, strength, and fidelity are the marks of a good man. Search for these instead of the kind of shoes he is wearing.

CHAPTER 7

Okay, a guy takes notice of you in some outlandish way. As previously scribed, meet and greets are very difficult; therefore, unless he is just flat out insulting to what it means to be a woman, then cut him a break. There is no rule that says you have to commit to an intimate moment. You know the game; keep your distance, but do not burn the bridge because if he turns out to be respectful of who you are, isn't that more important than knowing where to go to have a little fun?

Reply with a simple; *"Hello"* and a brilliant smile. That is all you need. Again, communication is key. In fact, communication is everything. Believe it or not, guys will not look at your pedigree if your ability to communicate is excellent. No matter your race in regards to any first contact situations, the old adage; *your first impression must be your best impression,* never gets old; and guess what your first impression is? Your mannerisms can either make you or break you. You come off being sleazy, and you will be viewed as a harlot. Appear loathsome, and you become a social misfit. Yes; there is a sweet spot, and you must discover it. Do not worry, it's not rocket science. Do not be concerned over skin blemishes or acne. A good conversation always blinds a man to those kinds of things. We know that in our society acne is a given. If you believe he is concerned about a spot on your face than you are a fool. The most important thing a man wants out of a girl is health, fitness and conversation. The most important thing that he needs, but does not realize is an understanding of God. So, if you have

418

trouble finding that sweet spot, then better to be the social misfit because being sexy is a given to your gender, of which can lead to problems you cannot handle. Just as a rule; avoid drinking and other forms of drugs; yes; that includes marijuana, and be attentive to bodily hygiene. This, you already know, for it too sends a message; though, some men can be a bit strange from time-to-time.

Keep the conversation on him. You need to know what he is all about. You need to know what his game plan for life will be; career goals. Does he plan to settle down, and where? Would he like a family? If, so, then you must pay close attention to his behavior because a man cannot just walk into fatherhood. He must be prepared for such an endeavor much as a woman has to be geared for motherhood. Sure, they will know you are young; however, your appearance will speak volumes over the hot and sexy they look at on a daily basis, setting the mood for first contact. This is when you charm him with words of your choosing, giving the conversation a direction of your choosing. All females have vaginas, and many of them use them very well, but not all females have charisma or are capable of generating a good conversation. In the long-run, that is what wins the day. Oh; and just as a reminder, there is such a thing as wasting your words. Quoted in the Bible by the Christ as; *pearls to swine.* It is perhaps the best way to determine if that guy is right for you. Therefore, he will have no choice, but to take you seriously, and since you hold the high ground, you will be prepared for any approach he makes that is less than appealing.

Remember that you hold one crucial card, which means that you control the deck. He will view you as innocent, and all his. End the socializing at its peak. Tell him that you have to leave. Make up an excuse that is truthful in nature for a lie, even a simple one, sets you on the path of what is improper. This is for your benefit because sometimes even your own words can be overwhelming. Do not worry, your fishing line is long, he will always come back to your boat, no matter where you are situated on the lake or sea.

When he does come back to you, the most important thing to remember is that life is about mental conditioning. Do not be direct in your approach for a more appealing relationship. Place the obligation on him, and begin the process of gaining his devotion, but it must be voluntary. Do not rush into the relationship. We live in an age of instant gratification; light-speed; like, right now, stuff. Isolate your prospects of a relationship from that kind of behavior; ensuring that you have met the right man does not mean you rush into it. Make him work for every inch of who you are. Why not? He has waited over thirty years to meet you, so, he can wait a little longer. If he was not sure that you were the one, he would not be talking to you. He sees his destiny in you, so, be the proper girl that he wants you to be, and torment him a bit. Make sure that he has the patience and temperament you are seeking in a successful relationship because contrary to popular belief, there are not 21 dimensions of compatibility to a successful relationship. There is just patience, kindness and adaptability. You are losing your identity. Make sure he is the right man to get a new one from.

CHAPTER 8

When dating begins, ask yourself this one simple question. No; better yet; ask him this one simple question; *what do you bring to the relationship?* If you decided to accept the petitioning of a much older man, and he does not have an established plan of action, ease yourself away from him. Even a wealthy man has no worth without a game plan for life because there is nothing worse than having a million dollars and being unhappy. Sure, he dresses very well, but if he is dumbfounded by the question, behaves irate, goes into a tirade or speaks gibberish, then he brings nothing, but his penis. On the other hand, he may even come right out and tell you that he is good in bed. That ol' reverse psychology bit. Is that what you want? Is that all that you want? If, so, then why do you get upset when he philanders after your relationship with him begins? His life is all about providing sexual intercourse, and that will be the basis of your relationship. So, does it matter that he is keeping his skills in tune with other women for you? After all, it is what makes him good in the bedroom; *right?* Explains why men pursue the prostitute and the pornographer. She is well-practiced in what she
420

does. So, consider that when you decide to copulate, for any man whom has a rudimentary understanding of love can be physically gratifying. It is only an illusion that a man is bad in the act of sexual intercourse. He is either selfish or he is generous. From your earliest childhood, you had thoughts of having a man hold you in his arms whether in the bed or outside of it. He must know when you want to be held, and you must be receptive of his protective arms because in the long run you become his greatest prize.

The biggest subject that you need to avoid at all costs are feminist ideas. He wants to be a man for you, do not step on his endeavor with ideas of; *I can do it on my own.* He wants to do things for you. Feel as though he is being a gentleman.

Do not attempt to conquer your interest by the queen bee method. As woman, you have seduced him, why attack his masculinity? You have made him happier then he has ever been in his life.

If you are a woman of another race being pursued by a man of European descent, then you must avoid subjects of a racial nature to a certain extent. If he attacks your gender and/or race, you must analyze the reasoning behind his actions and behavior. Was it his friends? Then you must compel him to spurn them or lose you. Remember, you are woman, the female, sex, emotion, passion and compassion. Bring all of that to bear on him when he is wrong. His reaction will determine your next course of action.

The next mistake women make in a relationship is condemning a man for looking at another woman or other women. Especially if the other women are looking at him. Got news for you. They are not looking at him. They are trying to figure out what he has that has attracted you to him.

Unfortunately, the potential for a man to be a philanderer is always there, and, so, you must be extremely observant. Most importantly; never let your guard down for any reason. Be mindful of the fallen one, for he is extremely clever.

Another point to consider, and that is something you are already aware of, is that the other woman is saying; *I can take your man,* or; *your man is weak, you should dump him.* Whatever the case, her power over men is overwhelming. Ignore the whole affair, and casually make yourself unavailable to him. If his attention wanes from you for more than a second or he keeps looking at the females as they go strolling by, then either make him walk on his knees or dump him. Of course, if you should invite him to a location full of attractive females then you should be forgiving; for even a recovering alcoholic cannot resist looking at the top-shelf every once in a while, and there is always someone out there whom is more attractive. Not that you are not beautiful, but that he has gotten used to your beauty, which is nothing more than relationship-evolution. Like being with his sister. A little love, a little anger and a whole lot of presence is sign of the evolution.

The sad thing that you will never consider is that the modern career woman is still a prostitute. Their employer allows them to do their second job gratis, thus making available a source of desire that would otherwise be out of sight, out of mind. Keep in mind that a man does not cheat until he is spending quality time with the other woman, not copulating with her. Yes; difficult to determine; however, he should not be taking her out on dates or letting her cook for him. They are the other woman after all, not a girlfriend.

In fact, let us dabble in the arcane. Divorce is a very unusual substance in regards to human existence, but what is it really? A farce. A means for male and female to play in the fields of sin. Ask yourself as woman; when you discover that your man is carrying on with another woman or women, what is truly going on? No; let us simplify the matter, and say; he slips up. He is not a bad man; however, the events could not have been in better alignment then the moment he engaged in a hot erotic moment with another woman. Even he does not understand why it happened; however, you discover the infidelity, and thus rush to judgement instead of investigating. Was the infidelity accompanied by a lie? Did he provide you with ample presence? Was the home-front properly maintained? Did he maintain appearances? The only real loose-end is the other woman, and that is the truth behind the divorce. She wants your man, and this author's got words for you; the wife. He is a clueless little boy, and that is the Lilith effect. The other woman is nothing more than a marriage breaker. She will not pursue a marriage that is nothing. She wants the trifecta; wealth, property, and most importantly, happiness. It makes her feel good to break a happy home, and let there be no doubt, you are living in a happy home. You are the epitome of that happiness. Your man has simply taken your ability for granted. Remember, the warm house? That is part of it. The other woman cannot do that because she is a Bedouin. Her goal is not to settle down. She is an unstable woman having no clue to the details and complexities of life. In reality, she is going out of her way to get your man. What she wears, the cosmetics, her mannerisms are all geared to catch an unsuspecting insect. She is a nothing, making him into a nothing, and that is why religion is key to a relationship and not sex. With religion you see the truth of the infidelity. With sex, you see only competition. Not with her, but with him. You are competing against his trust and faith, which is not there, and perhaps it never was, but something about you makes the preconceived notion of our cultural existence in regards to why is woman different, and that is the true competition.

Oh, and by the way; the reason that females and water go, so, well together is that at first glance they are a commodity that may seem abundant, but in fact are rare, greatly abused, misused, wasted and fought over, and when unavailable; greatly desired. Other than that, you will do okay; and when you look at yourself in the mirror, and see fat and ugly, then you simply need to recalibrate your mind, for you are perfect, and it is the world that is imperfect, but do not tell anyone else that.

WHAT IS A MOTHER

CHAPTER 1

Now, unless you are in pursuit of helping others to find the path to God; every fiber of your being is geared towards being a wife

423

and eventually a mother; *to a male*. There are people whom would have you believe that your instincts are all that you need to be a mother and wife, but like anything else, motherhood requires preparation. Learning motherhood is just as demanding a process as the act of doing, so. A woman waits until she is pregnant and gives birth to a child, to learn how to be a mother? One of the most important aspects of woman-hood that is being grossly neglected is the proper training to be a mother. You do not wait until you are pregnant to learn what it means to be a mother. You do not wait until you give birth to learn what it means to be a mother. Let us apply that same methodology to piloting an aircraft. No need to study and train to be a pilot, just wait until the aircraft is loaded to bear and fully fueled. You can figure things out when you climb into the cockpit. Then we ask the silly question of; *what is wrong with our children?* Motherhood is not something that you can simply apply at the last minute, cut corners on, or simply wing it. You attend a university to gain a skill at something. How long does it take? Motherhood is not supposed to be guesswork. The reason why your mother and your mother's-mother said that you will just figure things out, is due to laziness of culture. Motherhood has apparently followed along the same path as food preparation. Food is fast and guess what?

You must execute the entire process at key moments in your life, and in its entirety or there will be problems with the children, and even the marriage itself. Doubt this author's hypothesis? When a doctor prescribes fifteen antibiotics and you take only nine because you feel better, what happens to the virus lurking in your system? You; the mother cut corners, and, so, when your daughters become mothers, they too will cut corners, and with each subsequent generation, a little more is shaved off, until you have nothing, but the fat. Today, we take the entire process completely for granted. Today's children are out of control, and until we admit that, then it cannot be fixed. Again; do you doubt this author? Every crime committed in our society is by someone's child. This is a result of mothers going out into the world to prove that they can do anything a man can do, when in fact they should have been preparing sons and daughters for parenthood, and especially teaching their sons to be respectful of women.

It is your responsibility to ensure that his children whom you have given birth to, are socially aligned to the traditions and culture of the community in order to avoid serious degradation to the very necessity of what it means to be human. You do this by whatever means necessary; however, be aware that too harsh a method will have an adverse effect on the child in the long run and essentially society as a whole. Nevertheless, tough love always has the desired effect, more, so, then timeout. Remember, that mother's spankings draw tears. Father's spankings draw anger.

Oh, and to you mothers whom are having a bit of difficulty with your preteen or teenage son: He does not take you seriously because you do not dress seriously. How can he take you seriously when you attire yourself in the same fashions as the girls that arouse him at school, on the street, at the mall? You do not fashion yourself differently; professionally, as a mother should dress. So, when you go about bestowing discipline to your defiant son, you cannot because in his mind you are as the hot bodied, mouthy high school girls he has a crush on in his class, whom bitch at him constantly for being a nuisance. They wear the clothed nudity, and he knows they are promiscuous. Therefore, what does that say about you, his mother?

Interesting, how the fashion industry went into strict competitive mode in regards to feminine attire. Going from modest to risqué seemingly overnight. Eventually the disease went from daughters to mothers or perhaps more realistically; when children became unexpected mothers. Without downhome experience, those child-mothers refused to shed the teenage mentality due to the influence of an education system lacking the understanding of what it means to be responsible. In other words, waning maturity gave us the term; babies having babies. That is who you are. Not physically, but mentally. Not learning what it means to be a mother. So, if you did not learn, then your daughter did not learn because now, it is all about girl power and women lead. A career outside of the home is the name of the game now, and thus, we have irresponsible overshadowing responsible, of which is having an effect on the whole marriage process, which explains the high divorce rate. Women are thinking the high school reset button works in the real world. Oh, and since domestic professionalism is a dead practice, then why would mothers wear anything other than leggings and skinny jeans in all walks of life? How did the professional housewife dress in the heyday of proper domestic practices? How did Barbara Billingsley, Donna Reed and Jane Wyatt dress? Oh, and for those of you whom are thinking that was just Hollywood hype, there are archival reels showing what life was like back then, and this author is pretty sure that women were not strutting down the street in dense pantyhose. Sure, maxi-skirts and flare dresses are not commonplace; however, neither are they out of fashion. They are clothing styles that make a statement. That you are about business, not BS, and your children will look at you differently. To be treated a certain way, you must dress a certain way. When you dress a certain way, then others will behave a certain way.

What about the idea of a professional wife? When your man comes home from work, he sees you like all of the other women; his coworkers, those walking down the street. You are just another woman to him. Dressing as a professional mother also has an effect on him because as previously scribed, he too, is, but a child.

This author will enlighten you on a long-lost fact of social etiquette. When men dominated daily living; how did he attire himself? There was something about uniformity that gave him a sense of social unity. Dress shirt and tie was the name of the game to include a dress jacket. That idea lasted for a very long time. That uniformed identity allowed men to connect with an understanding of being part of a team. Whether it be the private sector, daily living or the government, men uniformed themselves in the dress-shirt and tie mentality. Especially athletes. Women loosely followed the program except with you, there was a sense of individuality. You love to be different. Part of that attraction thing. You are making yourself special for us; the man, but

426

at the same time, you are maintaining an understanding of cultural similarity. Consider the old days? Boys mimicked their fathers, and girls behaved more as adults. You see, what you; the modern female of the early Twenty-first, have forgotten, is that motherhood is a profession, and like a policeman, fireman or soldier, you dress according to your profession. When you left the home; however, that professionalism waned, and reporting to work in just any old thing became the norm because just being woman is hard. It took time to prepare yourself and by the 1980s you were in the workforce in full force, but time management principles are different in a male orientated world. You women were built around the understanding of Kairos time, which means; *it gets done, when it gets done.* We men invented Chronos time to maintain order and schedules. Therefore, time management principles were not something you were and are not accustomed to, except in regards to the rest of the world. Your employer coerced you into making a subconscious choice. Either keep the cosmetics or keep the fashion. You cannot have both because there was a little secret that we men had in order to dress properly and still be on time for life. That secret was you; the woman; however, you bailed from your domestic responsibilities, and now, like you; we men dress in any old thing. Especially in regards to Catholics when attending mass. Oh; and you kept the cosmetics, but not the clothing and whom do you most closely emulate in this modern age of the early Twenty-first?

Yes, you are running away from the truth of time. That the beauty queen/mother and employee is not only untenable, but impractical. Hollywood, celebrities in general, and of course the wealthy, have always portrayed that little illusion to the contrary; however, how many wealthy women succeed at a lasting marriage with one man? Have well-behaved children and never appear overwhelmed and frustrated in public? Having your pie and eating it too may be possible for some, but at what cost?

Now, as a mother, you have to be beautiful and energetic. Not your teenaged son's high school delight. Also, there are your man's other children whom you gave birth to, and you must adjust your behavioral traits for each age category accordingly. Remember, this author's earlier scribing of reverting to a child-like state? Each successive child requires a tailored approach. The four-year-old will become an eight year old and you must adjust for that. Adolescence will eventually evolve into a teenager, and again, you must become a teen again. Wait; this author made it sound like being a teenager was a bad thing; however, you must revert yourself to a teen state of mind for the benefit of the teenaged child, but it does not mean adopting the current teen standards of living, including the clothing. Your responsibility is to lower yourself to a teen state to elevate the teen to a higher state of existence. You do not live in a teenager's world, you are simply visiting long enough to get your teenager's hand, so, that you can uplift them to a state of adulthood. Of course, if you are at work outside of the home, then how can you do this? Naturally, you may get stuck, and that is the purpose of the man whom has cleaved to you. He brings you back to a proper state of mind. Now, imagine having a toddler, an adolescent and a teen. You must adjust for each category accordingly, and at a moment's notice, and you must do it in such a way as not to lose your connection with either child. Now, when looking at mother-hood from this point of view; the complexity of mind, the details of heart, not to mention the biggest little boy whom married you, and the maintenance of the house, how does a woman with a career outside of the home accomplish the task of mother-hood? She doesn't; however, when you focus everything that you've got onto being a mother, then your motherhood comes to fruition. You get a clearer perception on why the boys you grew up with were such babies. Behaved, so, immaturely. You understand and are forgiving of their behavior and are more patient with them. At that point you have reached true motherhood. You are a true adult. At that point you understand proper rearing of a man-child, leading them into a more beneficial state of maturity. Of course, with career outside of the home then something has got to give, and that something is usually the children.

What mothers with careers outside of the home do, is force his child to meet them at the adult level. They want the child to evolve up to their level. Those mothers do not tell children outright that they need to grow up, though; more than likely, you do have those with the propensity to be direct. *No;* harsh actions are the preferred methods. Unreasonable psychological application and criticism to force the child into adulthood. As if you are up in a tree, telling a child to figure out for themselves how to join you. No demonstration, no example. Just do it! The child tries, and falls. Whose fault is it? The child's? Now, apply that example to our current social circumstances.

CHAPTER 2

A mother teaches her daughter what it means to be a woman, not trying to be her friend. A mother should not be teaching her daughter about contraception, but how to dress appropriately, so, that she does not send the wrong message. A girl whom dresses like a harlot is perceived as such. No matter what she says to the boy, he just sees the booty. He will push, and she will grow even more angry until a wall of animosity develops. The only result from the encounter is anger and violence between the both of them. There should never be anger between the genders. Does rain hate the ground? Do clouds hate the sky? Does the night hate the stars?

You as the mother, must teach his children, whom you gave birth to, about the faith, so, that they can cultivate their options in order to make an informed rational productive decision about their choices in life. This is perhaps why, so, many men fall to the ranks of the dispossessed or become homosexuals. They did not receive proper guidance in their growing years, but instead the short-end of the stick from an ignorant society cultivated by the Flower Power Movement.

A person's duty, especially a woman's, is to heal, not to harm. To propagate the species not snuff it out. To help, not to hinder. To encourage, not discourage. To properly guide everyone, especially the young, along moral choices of reason and logic, without compromising the natural order of man.

CHAPTER 3

Naturally, this author is not proposing that premarital sexual intercourse did not exist in the past. What we are dealing with is a change in our perception and even ideologies. Teaching and encouraging self-control is apparently no longer practiced. Premarital sexual intercourse is all the rage. The Flower Power Movement talked of peace, but at the expense of responsibility and tradition. So, when your mother's-mother became pregnant, she had a rudimentary understanding of what it meant to be a mother because it was handed down to her by her mother, whom was teaching her at a young age on how to be a mother. Unfortunately, she did not pass that little trait along to her daughter; your mother because she did not want to give up the parties and drinking or she simply did not understand how to explain it in such a way as to keep your mother interested. That whole rebellion thing during the Flower Power Movement. Yes; rebelling against the system; the *state;* the *man;* that was the thing, and dysfunctional families propagated quickly due to the Drug Age of which is still going on, by the way. Oh sure, marijuana is really great. Get high, get pregnant and eventually stupid little girl is no longer stupid, but stuck with a child because Mr. Cool has moved onto his next victim. She got too old and smart, and realized he was brainless. He cannot function with an adult female, and, so, he finds another unwitting mental minor. Now, take note that it is a female's need to be a helper to a man, but what happens when male intelligence declines? This author hopes you are seeing the pattern. *Hell;* maybe her mother did not pass the trait of motherhood onto her in the first place. Who knows the truth in this crazy misguided world? The one thing that this author has noticed, is that dolls do not have the same meaning as they once did. Now, the norm went from being a responsible mother passing on the traits of motherhood to instead, just keep partying and drinking. Laziness quickly set in like wild pigs in a garden of fruits and vegetables, and the new motto became; *you will figure it out.* Do not take this author's word for it. You the reader, reason it out for yourself. You; the female say that you think you are not born a mother, but you cannot deny that you are designed to be one, and therefore you require explanation, guidance and understanding of what it means to be a mother, and that takes time; however, what are mothers doing with their daughters in today's culture? They teach their daughters to be lawyers, doctors, engineers, but nothing to prepare them for being a mother; as though motherhood is an accidental in today's social arena, or that females are somehow born knowing; resulting in treating pregnancy as nothing more than a disease. Placing more emphasis on preventing the disease, or if catching it; methods of curing it. A child's development begins at conception, but we as a society like to play God, so, that women can feel better about themselves after making a regrettable decision? The reality is, to avoid the debate; avoid the temptation; ignore the ridicule, and avoid those whom say; *there is absolutely nothing wrong with sexual intercourse before you are married.* Again, as previously scribed, they want you to make the same choices they made because they don't want to be alone in their mistake, or is more insidious: *Oh, just go ahead and do it; who cares if you get pregnant. Your body, your choice. It's not murder, it's empowerment.*

The truth is that human development begins with conception and ends, not at physical death, but at Judgment. Regrettably, we have allowed ourselves to be led into the idea that contraception is a necessity, and that true life does not begin until there is some form of person outside of the body. There are even some people whom say that life does not occur until the child takes their first breath. These people are the foolish of society whom speak very loudly, and say absolutely nothing, but they do manage to get attention; *why?* Sexual intercourse, whether premarital or post-marital is a huge undertaking. Making the possibility of conception a responsibility, and yet we treat sexual intercourse as though it was nothing more than using a smart-phone? The big debate is; what determines a child? This author says that we, as a species are truly not qualified to make that assessment; however, if the substance within a woman is not a person, then a redefinition by the medical community is in order. How would science define the human substance within the woman? Alive? Not alive? Growth? Mitosis? Life? The substance is not viral, not cancerous or a bacterium. Nor is it a parasite, and yet we have been conditioned into believing that the substance is harmful. Again; the question to the medical community: What are we dealing with? Apparently, a question that has never been truly asked because in all reality, you only remove that, which is harmful to the body; right? The judiciary; however, has made it clear that due to their apparent medical expertise; the substance within the female is not human because if the organism is human, then they would have to act accordingly. If Biblical language is insufficient, then follow the science and the philosophy. Science says life. Philosophy says human. Thus, the XIV Amendment applies to the unborn child, not *she,* whom is seeking empowerment.

Look; if you; the woman, want to play rough, then be tough. Life is beginning, not ending, and will be something wonderful. For us; the male, who happens to be reading this; he is the continuation of your legacy. You make the child a stable legacy, for he is not her problem, but your responsibility. Do not run from fatherhood, for you did not run from her open legs. Oh; and for the question of a child being alive when taking their first breath. The breath is the fertilization, not the inhalation thereafter.

Withal said, you; the woman, should be preparing yourself to be a mother from the onset of awareness. Of course, this cannot be done without *your* mother. So, in a sense, what this author is saying is for you; the mother, whom already has a daughter or daughters. You begin their training by providing her/them with a training medium: Baby doll. Which is why little girls are given dolls, to help develop their caring side. Their sympathetic side. Their loving side. That way, when they do give birth to their man's child, they will not experience feelings of wanting to kill the child. They will not have an urge to abandon the child in a separate room. Again, a child senses loneliness more, so, than you; the careless mother, realizes, and it is a scary prospect. Loneliness feels like the siphoning of the very aspirational energy necessary to feel alive. Placed in a dark closet without a means of escape, a person dies without dying. The child has been attached to you for nine months, and then you suddenly leave the child alone? During the night, you place the infant far from you in another room? For nine months, the child was close to a beating heart, a living presence, and you; the parent, suddenly leave the child alone? Notice how hospital care givers are in the company of newborns at all times. This is not exclusively a liability issue, in regards to an outside threat, but one of logic and reason. A newborn needs the presence of an adult because the child feels vulnerable. Just because the child cannot speak or put into words what they are feeling does not mean they do not feel. Again, you must remain in the presence of his child on the basis that they are helpless, and that they do not know any other way because they have not learned any other way yet. Just like you wean his child from nursing, you must wean his child from the fear of your lack of presence, but until then, that child is vulnerable. Sometimes, when a child does not sense that presence, they will simply shut down because the presence of another is, so, vital to their health. As vital as the nutrients that is fed through the mouth. The body absorbs presence in pretty much the same way, and if it is not continued after birth, what happens? Remember, this author's suggestion of a sixth sense? That's not something that comes into being with puberty. Another aspect of your motherly training and development that is taken for granted is to learn never to lose track of the child. That is another reason why little girls are given dolls. It only takes a millisecond of indecision, forgetfulness to bring about disaster. Of course, you can offset this by bonding yourself to God with prayer. Believe it or not, the angel of the Lord does exist, but to make use of this powerful piece of heavenly-power, you must have faith. Funny how some mothers will place their newborn in a room away from them, but keep their pets close at hand.

Now, the method of teaching motherhood works better if you; the mother, are giving birth to more than just one or two children. That is because children, whether boy or girl, are imitative. His daughter will follow your lead with her doll when you are taking care of the next child. As the mother/teacher, make sure she does not allow herself to be distracted by mundane things; like wanting to play with the puppy or kitten or wanting to leave with daddy. Most importantly, no smart-phone, television or gaming console. She should be taught to keep an eye on her doll at all times, even when helping you in the kitchen or doing something else. From time-to-time, allow her real-time training with her younger siblings, this will help immensely in the future.

Let us examine two or more daughters growing up together. This presents a real challenge to you; the mother because you are attempting to accomplish the seemingly impossible. You must teach each daughter to be vain and beautiful, and yet kind, caring, respectful and humble to one another, and those around them. Though it sounds hard, it really is not. Your instruction guide is the Bible. What mothers forget, when raising children; whether boys and/or girls is to interweave scripture into their daily lives. Everything you need to know is found in the Catholic Bible. Sorry; the King James version; though an excellent translation, is missing key elements to the proper rearing of children. Not that this is a bad thing, but that you need these crucial elements to prevent your children from getting out of control. To continue; daughters require guidelines to beauty, without the use of cosmetics. There are certain products not meant to extenuate beauty, but to simply maintain what she already has. As a man, this author is guessing that the most difficult part of a woman's beauty is maintaining her hair. This is a status symbol, representing who she is. A woman's hair tells a lot about her, and though guys do not openly admit it, they do like the long hair. Especially when it is caught in the wind. Perhaps another helpful hint, in case you do not know, is that you; the mother, have to ease his daughter, whom you gave birth to, into her beauty very slowly because what you want is her natural beauty to maturate, not a false pretense. Besides, his daughter may want to be an extravert, and therefore she will require her natural beauty to show through the grime and the grit of the great outdoors. Yes; girls are extremely competitive. Even more, so, than boys. You must get his daughters to always praise one another, and to never allow them to be disparaging of one another. Do not allow any of his daughters to fall into a psychological dilemma. Though one of them may feel as though she does not measure up, you; the mother, had better not tell her that! She is an equal among her gender.

So, if her siblings are beautiful you must push her that much harder to see the beauty within herself. The only thing that makes a sister lesser than her siblings is her age, everything else is equal. Especially her training to understand the Church, for her beauty must come from within; cliché, this author knows; but still effective. Do not allow her to become affixed on her feminine anatomical parts. This will lead her to a lack of confidence. If guys are attracted to nice breasts and a booty, then they lack the ability to foster other possibilities in a relationship. A female should not be getting any form of physical augmentation to get the attention of, or hold the attention of a male unless she has gone through some form of disfiguring event that is beyond her control. Anything else is an unnecessary subconscious sexual solicitation. Now, should this be the case with a prospect, then she should distance herself from him immediately. His mind-set on the truth of what a relationship should be, is tainted. He should not be considered for anything serious.

One other point to make; and this is the hardest of all aspects of mother-hood, and that is avoid choosing a favorite. Nothing worse in human culture than a parent having a favorite child; however, there is an old saying about which child a mother loves the most, and that is the child who is sick or in need of attention.

At this point, you; the mother, should be getting the gist of it, so, let us move onto the man-child in your life. There is only one way to describe the boys, and that is; they are a handful. For you mothers who have them, you already know this. They are such babies; always wanting all of the attention from you, and yes; we are speaking of the adult boys as well. So, what do you do with the boys? As the mother, you have to lay fire into them fast and hard. Lay down the law quick, and that does not include timeout. What is timeout; exactly? A pointless means of dispelling punishment that has absolutely no long-term effects on masculine behavior. The belt is what they remember and as the mother you want to lay fear into them not for what they do when you are around, but for what they would do when you are not around. That way, when your boy is a scrapping 6'6" 290 lbs. of linebacker, beast or more, he will cry when you jump down his throat for misbehaving. Not that he fears you, but that he knows that you care for him that much, and in time, he will have to care for you as you once did for him. The two crucial things you must teach him are the ways of the Church, and to be respectful of the female; however, a woman-child should not be physically abusive of your son, and that includes his sisters. He has every right to defend himself against unladylike behavior, and most importantly, do not allow any females, whether kith or kin to treat him as a female. The rest has already been covered.

Another forgotten aspect of motherhood is that your man is your first and biggest child. Yes, previously mentioned; however, it is important to remember because like all of your children, he needs encouragement. He is facing a warzone out there. The rage, madness, twisted logic, noise, cold, heat, rain, snow, sleet and hail, is hitting him from all sides. He is a good man facing the hardships of the world to keep you; the woman safe. Those hardships wear him down, and can discourage, even depress him. You, as woman, are designed to drive depression out of his life, and encourage him, so, that he does not lose his motivation to work. If you do not know. The employment sector has no compunction in regards to driving workers to the breaking point. That is why you maintain a little teenager; a little girl within you, so, that it will recharge him. You are the magic potion in his life. You are the joy and gaiety of the earth. So, get out the pompoms, tie your hair into a high ponytail, and put on the cheerleader uniform. You do whatever you can to bring pleasure into his life because you give him purpose; a reason to live.

ENDING

All throughout this book, this author has touched on some very sensitive topics, clearly offending a lot of people, which will make him the subject of public scrutiny; and that is to be expected. His intent was not meant to be presumptuous or sound arrogant in any way, and you; the reader may say; *whatever,* but that is a word unto itself denoting ignorance, and an unwillingness to get at the truth. There are just too many coincidences for our current circumstances to be anything, short of a deliberate act of social sabotage. Deep down we all know, or to say the least, sense what the problem is, and, yet, we pander around the obvious, while our entire social infrastructure crumbles around us? We continue to remain quiet and hope that certain issues will resolve themselves? Sure; there is nothing truly new in what this author has proposed, but simply putting into words certain aspects of our culture that have existed for quite some time. He also realizes that some of the things mentioned in this book are completely outlandish; and that there will be those whom will challenge this author's notions of what may or may not be the problems plaguing this country that we call the United States of America. Oh, and this author has news for you; the reader. Problems never resolve themselves without tragedy, and someone must speak up to get the ball rolling. Therefore, the question: *Why are we standing by and doing nothing about it? Why are we not reacting? What is wrong with us? Do unforeseen forces have that much control?* Perhaps, we are those unforeseen forces, making the excuse that there are secret organizations at work in order to justify our own shortcomings.

Many people will also object to this author's proposals based on a lack of statistical data or higher-learning credentials, and that is reasonable; however, when someone with an accredit degree says that those whom lack a degree as not being a credible source for expressing some form of social critique, what would we call that? Though the findings may be rational, even logical in some way, their proposal is invalid? What? We must wait until someone with an accredited degree comes up with similar, but slightly altered conclusions in order for the rest of us to accept the outcome?

Sometimes people need clarification of human behavior to get a perception of life, and that perception can be from any source, but apparently, secularism has such a tight grip on our overall perceptions of life that we have forgotten how to even challenge what is proper, and what is improper social behavior from a perspective of just being an average citizen. Remaining quiet on the matter is not an option on the basis that the coming generation has a right to the truth, regardless of its source. If you see a dam leaking water, you do not standby to determine if you are qualified to warn those in immediate danger downstream.

There is no denying the obvious that what is seemingly harmless is in fact harmful to us; however, what is fueling the confusion? Sure, we are a violent, selfish, frightened species, unwilling to let go of our primordial instincts, but why do we seem to behave along the lines of the scientific notion that we are descended from fearful primates that once lived in trees? Unfortunately, we cannot see the big picture from where we are sitting. It is difficult for a goldfish to perceive itself in the cloudy fishbowl, and perhaps we refuse to even look at the big picture because we do not want to give up those little idiosyncrasies that we enjoy, so, much. The old days were about setting an example. What kind of example are we setting today? Do what you like, and forget all of the rest? To be accommodating to the unlawful? We can all just get along; *right?* Feminists, fagging, form-fitting fashions, and prochoice represent dirt in the great engine of life, and eventually, that engine will break. When that happens, it will be too late, for there are no spare parts, and it will simply be game over.

Now, this author suspects that one person could have prevented all of this immoral dominating conduct. That one person failed to initiate the proper combination of actions at their proper moment, that would have resulted in a butterfly effect. This author has also concluded that he is the source of the butterfly effect that is now, plaguing this world. Yes, a bold and even outlandish statement; however, hindsight about this author's life brings to the realization that certain actions in the past could have been avoided or at best, treated differently. Yes; this author knows what you are going to say. *How could he know that?* A reasonable understanding of direction exists in all of us, and quite simply, requires a nudge to do what is proper. We always suspect what the proper course of action should be, and yet we seem to always make the improper choice. Do we crave the sins of life, so, much that we are afraid to make the moral choices necessary to avert catastrophe? Do we crave the risk of knowing that we are tinkering on the brink of self-destruction? We know what is wrong, and all we need do is take that one necessary step to fix it all. What will we do?

In any case, the whole point of this book is to point out one crucial aspect of this existence, and that is, you cannot define a thing without a thing to define it. You cannot have a positive without a negative. You cannot identify what is red unless you have a blue. Without the poor, there can be no rich. There is no wet, without a dry. No cold without a hot. What is high if there is no low. To put that into a logical perspective; look at the night sky, and what do you see? A veil of stars against a palette of black. What is it that gives it, its beauty? The brightness of the stars or the deepest of black? You cannot have one without the other. The light and the dark play in the overall grand scheme of things. They make the overall palette of beauty possible. Again, without the black you cannot define the beauty, and without the stars you cannot define beauty. Which begs the question: is black the source of beauty or is beauty the source of black? Which also brings to fruition the truth about human culture, and that is, without a shadow of a doubt, the existence of God. For only God can create two diametrically different understandings of existence in order for them to work together. Only a supreme intelligence can create the opposite of one another in order to get a better understanding of what one is from the other, and if that is the case, then at some point that superior intelligence would like to interact with those whom can view the creation. How is that accomplished, while maintaining the initial rules established by that superior intellect? You cannot establish a law or a rule, and then go against that rule. Doing so, violates the very notion, and purpose of the rule. Generating chaos, which explains the existence of a devil. That means something has to be correct, and something has to be incorrect. Christ; the King, has to be God, and not just a profit because a profit does not bring that superior intellect to invigorate evolution. A profit brings just a warning, but not change; however, Christ brought a warning, brought change, brought us opportunity. The end, for now.

Resources

In regards to this book, this author must acknowledge certain sources that motivated him to create it. Most notably, basic observation of society, and of course the Lord Himself. Everything is out there at our fingertips. We need only open our eyes to the truth.

A comparative understanding of the Holy Bible and the Constitution of the United States of America and how they relate to all of us.

Various journalistic sources, and all forms of media in general.

Personal social interaction

Catechism of the Catholic Church

"Humanae Vitae" by Pope Paul VI

The works of Dr. Janet Smith, Dr. Scott Hahn, David Barton were all crucial to the completion of this book.

Most importantly, divine intervention in the form of the Holy Spirit must be mentioned to make clear that life is not just about the human component, but those forces we are all familiar with, but know little about.

To voice your concerns, send your correspondence to: iamnotaphd@gmail.com

www.ingramcontent.com/pod-product-compliance
Lightning Source LLC
Chambersburg PA
CBHW062150270326
41930CB00009B/1492